Geographies of Identity
in Nineteenth-Century Japan

Geographies of Identity
in Nineteenth-Century Japan

David L. Howell

UNIVERSITY OF CALIFORNIA PRESS
Berkeley · Los Angeles · London

University of California Press
Berkeley and Los Angeles, California

University of California Press, Ltd.
London, England

© 2005 by the Regents of the University of California

Library of Congress Cataloging-in-Publication Data

Howell, David L.
    Geographies of identity in nineteenth-century Japan /
David L. Howell.
        p.   cm.
    Includes bibliographical references and index.
    ISBN 0-520-24085-5 (cloth : alk. paper)
    1. Japan—Civilization—19th century.   2. Japan—
Social conditions—19th century.   3. Ainu—Ethnic
identity.   I. Title.

DS822.25.H68   2005
306'.0952'09034—dc22   2004009387

Manufactured in the United States of America
14   13   12   11   10   09   08   07   06   05
10   9   8   7   6   5   4   3   2   1

Contents

Maps

Acknowledgments

In the long course of writing this book I accumulated sizable intellectual debts to numerous institutions and individuals. I received funding for my initial research from the National Endowment for the Humanities; the University Research Institute of the University of Texas at Austin; the Joint Committee for Japanese Studies of the Social Science Research Council and the American Council of Learned Societies with funds provided by the Ford Foundation and the National Endowment for the Humanities; and the Japan Foundation. The Northeast Asia Council of the Association for Asian Studies and the Princeton University Committee on Research in the Humanities and Social Sciences underwrote additional trips to Japan. I did supplemental research and wrote much of a preliminary draft during a year at Keiō University on a Fulbright Senior Scholar Research Award from the Japan-U.S. Education Commission. I made final revisions to the manuscript while in Kyoto at the International Research Center for Japanese Studies. I would not have been able to write the book without the support of these institutions, and I am pleased to be able at last to acknowledge their generosity.

In Japan, a number of universities and archives facilitated my research. I owe special thanks to Hokkaido University, Keiō University, and the International Research Center for Japanese Studies for hosting me during my research visits. I did research at those institutions, as well as at the Chiba Prefectural Archives, Hakodate Municipal Library, Historical Museum of the Tsuyama Region, Hokkaido Prefectural Library,

Muroran Institute of Technology Library, and Okayama Prefectural Archives. Back in Princeton, I benefited greatly from the expertise of Martin Heijdra, Yasuko Makino, and other staff members at the Gest East Asian Library.

Over the course of writing and revising the manuscript I had the opportunity to present my ideas at conferences and colloquia held at the Australian National University, Brown University, Columbia University, Harvard University, City College of New York, Historical Museum of Hokkaido, Institute for Advanced Study, International Christian University, International Research Center for Japanese Studies, Jōetsu University of Education, Kansai University, Montana State University–Bozeman, New York University, Princeton University, Stanford University, Swedish Academy for Advanced Studies in the Social Sciences, University of California at Los Angeles, University of Chicago, University of Illinois at Urbana-Champaign, University of Kentucky, University of Texas at Austin, and Yale University. My heartfelt thanks go to the colleagues who so kindly invited me to speak, and to the many people who attended my presentations and whose insights and comments have enriched my work.

I should like to thank a few colleagues by name for their help and advice. Tessa Morris-Suzuki, Brett Walker, Anne Walthall, and Kären Wigen all read the manuscript in its entirety at one stage or another, as did anonymous readers for the press. Their comments were invariably thoughtful and thought provoking; I am sorry I have been too stubborn to follow more of their good advice. Carol Gluck read and commented on various parts of the manuscript in various incarnations; she has, moreover, been a great source of support throughout my career. Ronald Toby has likewise been an inspiring mentor over the years. Mary Elizabeth Berry gave an early draft an especially thorough and characteristically incisive reading that forced me to think more clearly about my goals for the project as a whole. Many other colleagues have offered counsel on the project over the years. I am particularly grateful to David Ambaras, Daniel Botsman, Susan Burns, Albert Craig, S. N. Eisenstadt, Gerald Figal, Takashi Fujitani, Andrew Gordon, Marta Hanson, Harry Harootunian, Christine Marran, Hirota Masaki, Kawanishi Hidemichi, James Ketelaar, Kikuchi Isao, Mitani Hiroshi, Herman Ooms, Gregory Pflugfelder, Henry Smith, Tomiyama Ichirō, and Tsukada Takashi. Tashiro Kazui was my gracious and generous host during a year at Keiō University; more recently, Komatsu Kazuhiko and James Baxter created a collegial intellectual environment for me at the International Research Center for Japanese Studies.

I started work on the book while I was with the History department at the University of Texas at Austin and finished it after moving to Princeton University, where I am a member of the East Asian Studies and History departments. My colleagues at both schools and all three departments have always been extremely supportive of my work. At Princeton I have profited particularly from the insights of Stephen Kotkin, Susan Naquin, Willard Peterson, and Ruth Rogaski. I have, in addition, had the privilege of working with an extraordinarily talented group of graduate students at Princeton; their comments have forced me to sharpen my thinking about this project and about history more generally. Finally, I owe a special debt of gratitude to my colleagues in Japanese history at Princeton, Martin Collcutt and Sheldon Garon. For two decades I have enjoyed their friendship and mentoring; it has been a great privilege to work with them.

Matthew Stavros drew the maps and helped me to think about the most effective ways to represent spatial information.

At the University of California Press, Laura Driussi and Sheila Levine offered encouragement and patience during the project's long gestation. My editor, Reed Malcolm, was especially supportive at a time when the whole project seemed to be in jeopardy.

I would like to acknowledge with gratitude the permission I have received to include in the book revised (sometimes heavily revised) versions of work published previously. Material from my article "Territoriality and Collective Identity in Tokugawa Japan" is reprinted by permission of *Dædalus,* Journal of the American Academy of Arts and Sciences, from the Summer 1998 issue (vol. 127, no. 3, pp. 105–32) entitled "Early Modernities." Parts of my "Ainu Ethnicity and the Boundaries of the Early Modern Japanese State," *Past and Present,* no. 142 (Feb. 1994), pp. 69–93, appear with the permission of the Past and Present Society. My article "The Meiji State and the Logic of Ainu 'Protection,'" pp. 612–34 in *New Directions in the Study of Meiji Japan* (1997), edited by Helen Hardacre with Adam Kern, appears with the permission of E. J. Brill. Finally, parts of my "Civilization and Enlightenment: Markers of Identity in Nineteenth-Century Japan," in *"Japan" and "China": The Teleology of the Modern Nation-State,* edited by Joshua A. Fogel (forthcoming), appear with the permission of the University of Pennsylvania Press.

I first began work on this book more than a decade ago. I wish I had been able to finish it in time to show it to two men who influenced my personal and professional growth profoundly. My father, Richard W.

Howell, and my mentor, Marius B. Jansen, passed away within two months of each other in 2000, and I feel the loss keenly. Fortunately, two others precious to me entered my life during the course of research and writing: my son, Isaac, was born just as I was getting started with the project, and my daughter, Momoko, was born well after I had expected to be finished with it. Much as I love my work, I have enjoyed the time spent in Isaac's and Momoko's company much more than my solitary hours in front of the computer screen. And speaking of love, I send it out to Kōko, who has meant so much to me over the years.

CHAPTER I

Introduction

The history of the world in the nineteenth century is an anthology of radical change. The period from the French Revolution to World War I saw the impact of republicanism and socialism, industrialization and proletarianization, imperialism and colonialism, and all the other hallmarks of modernity. Among the many stories of metamorphosis, perhaps none is as striking as Japan's. At the beginning of the century the country was relatively isolated from the rest of the world, prosperous and stable to be sure, but governed by political, economic, and social institutions poorly suited to cope with the challenges presented by an increasingly expansive and self-confident West. By the time of the Meiji emperor's death in 1912, Japan, alone in the non-Western world, had joined the ranks of the advanced military and industrial powers and had enthusiastically embraced the institutions and ideals of Western-style modernity. Most important, it underwent this transformation without succumbing to Western colonialism.

Japan's transition to modernity has long been one of the big issues facing historians of the country, both within Japan and abroad. This book is a contribution to this important investigation, though writing such a book was not my original intent. When I began to work on this book I planned to write about how contemporary Japan became ethnically and culturally homogeneous—or, more properly, about how the idea of ethnic and cultural homogeneity came to be a defining feature of Japanese national identity even in the face of manifest heterogeneity. Questions of

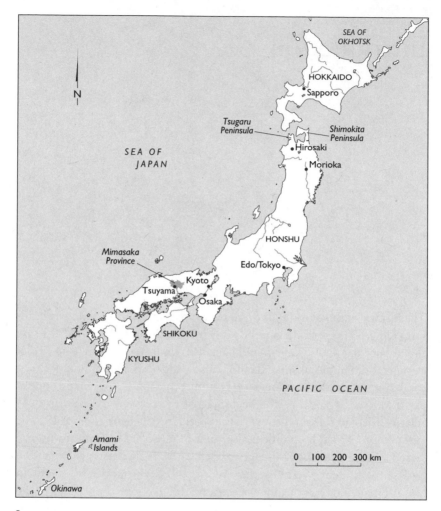

Japan

identity remain central to the work I ended up writing, but, rather than
tracing the origins of contemporary notions of homogeneity, this book
examines the ways social groups were constituted and reconstituted over
the course of the nineteenth century.

At the core of the study is the question of how the institutions that
made early modern Japan work connected through their dissolution to
the emergence of new institutions that made modern Japan work. This
book thus follows institutions across the divide of the Meiji Restoration
of 1868 and finds important continuities in the context of revolutionary

disjunction. Although about half the text deals with the period after 1868, I write as an early modernist looking across the transom into the modern world. For the most part, the institutions I examine are not the sort of surface-level structures that previous scholars have studied, such as the Tokugawa bureaucracy or the making of the Meiji imperial order, but rather the substrata that supported them and held them together as a coherent system. I aim to demonstrate both how Tokugawa Japan could not be "modern" and how the same institutions that made the Tokugawa state decisively "premodern" nonetheless prepared the way for the adoption of the structures and technologies of the modern nation-state. Continuity and disjunction were one and the same, and it is because of this sameness that Japan changed rapidly and with relatively little disruption.

Like other recent contributions to the literature on Japanese identity, this book starts with the now commonsensical premise that ethnic and national identities are historical constructs.[1] Its organizing idea is that three "geographies of identity" situated individuals within social groups and social groups within the political structure of nineteenth-century Japan. The first is the geography of polity, which in the Tokugawa period (1603–1868) delimited a core of shogunal territory and daimyo domains surrounded by clearly subordinate but nominally autonomous peripheries. The second is the geography of status, which placed social groups in Tokugawa Japan in specific relations of power and obligation vis-à-vis the state and, by extension, other groups. The third is the geography of civilization, which distinguished civilized subjects of the shogun from barbarians, both on the peripheries of the state and within the core polity itself.

I use the phrase *geographies of identity* to highlight my premise that Japanese ethnic and national identity is the product of a long process of border drawing. The delineation of the Tokugawa state's political boundaries in the seventeenth century led to the formation of civilizational boundaries between the Japanese and the peoples on Japan's peripheries. Although the physical contours of the early modern polity were clearly bounded, the distinction between the state's subjects and the peoples on the state's peripheries was marked not by an identification with the nation but rather by a conception of civilization borrowed from China and adapted to fit Japanese circumstances. Outward symbols of civilization, including clothing, hairstyles, and language, distinguished the subjects of the Japanese state from the peoples of the peripheries. However, standards of civilized appearance obtained within the core polity as well, with the result that territoriality was fluid even within the state's boundaries, despite a growing identification of the state with the realm of civilization.

Complicating this story of border drawing is the nature of identity within the core polity, which changed considerably during the transition from the early modern to the modern period. Rather than subscribe to a monolithic conception of Japaneseness, the early modern Japanese perceived their identities in terms of social status; they considered themselves samurai warriors, peasants, outcastes, and so on. Identity in early modern Japan was rooted in the code of status *(mibun),* and so the early modern roots of modern Japanese identity lay in the workings of the status system *(mibunsei).* The emergence of a modern nation-state in the latter half of the nineteenth century forced a redrawing of Japan's political boundaries and a reconception of both its internal social structure (including the status system) and the content of civilization. At the heart of this entire process lay Japan's transition from a feudal to a capitalist regime.

The geographies of my analysis are not solely spaces of the mind. The geography of polity was clearly spatial insofar as physical borders separated the shogun's realm from its peripheries to the north and south. Civilization and barbarism had important spatial dimensions as well, despite barbarism's presence both within the core polity and beyond its borders, for Japanese-style civilization had meaning only through its association with the bounded core polity. Social status, too, affected the way people understood territoriality, with the result that members of different status groups sometimes subscribed to different actual maps of the same physical space, maps that illuminated boundaries, rights, and mechanisms of authority invisible to people of other statuses. Moreover, connecting identity to physical space with the term *geography* fits my broader aim of highlighting the power of political authority and economic relations as shapers of identity. I am less concerned with the language with which people talked themselves into thinking they were "Japanese" than with the institutional forces that got them thinking about that subject in the first place. The tangibility suggested by a word like *geography* suits my purposes well.

The Tokugawa shogunate was the first regime in Japanese history to define the political boundaries of the state clearly, although it did not mark them unambiguously. Inner boundaries separated the core polity from the dependent yet autonomous peripheries of Japan, while less well defined outer boundaries set the peripheries apart from the non-Japanese world. Together, these boundaries situated Japan within the East Asian geopolitical order. The inner boundaries were physical borders, the outer ones amorphous zones defined by trade, diplomacy, and ritual, subject to Japanese territorial claims only in response to the Western challenge of the nineteenth century. Discussions of the early modern Japanese state refer to the area enclosed within the inner boundaries, for it was only there that the authority of the shogun and his proxies applied unambiguously to all.[2]

To be sure, the idea of a central state was nothing new in early modern Japan: the imperial house had claimed authority over all of Japan since at least the mid-seventh century, and throughout the ensuing millennium the idea of a unitary state in the Japanese archipelago retained currency among political leaders and thinkers. But although the imperial house and its warrior proxies had long asserted their authority over the Japanese islands, they had never set clear boundaries for the country; and, in any case, no regime before the Tokugawa was sufficiently powerful to enforce such boundaries. In short, although earlier regimes had claimed authority over all of "Japan," none had ever defined exactly what "Japan" was, at least not in even remotely precise geographical terms.[3]

Early modern Japan's borders were not the unambiguous lines on a map that separate modern nation-states from one another.[4] Even within the inner boundaries of the core polity there existed zones that were autonomous yet subject to the authority of the shogunate. These internal autonomies included the daimyo domains (whose physical borders were usually but not always clearly defined), territories under the authority of Buddhist temples and Shinto shrines, and the more amorphous realm of the outcastes. The internal autonomies of the early modern polity were situationally defined according to the rules of the status system, so that different social groups understood the political geography of Japan differently.[5] However, the complex internal geography of the core polity had a coherence that derived from the fixity of the polity's borders: daimyo domains, outcaste territories, and other spatial units were part of the political order of the Tokugawa state and had no meaning outside the context of the state. The core polity's inner boundaries linked the overlapping internal geographies of shogunate, domains, temple grounds, and outcaste territories into a coherent institutional whole.

In considering the early modern roots of modern Japanese identity, I do not intend to argue for smooth continuity across the divide of the Meiji Restoration. On the contrary, one of my aims is to demonstrate how profoundly things changed during the transition from early modernity to modernity. In any case, to understand what is "Japanese" about

Japanese ethnic and national identity, clearly we must consider how the project of building a modern nation was informed by earlier structures. Only then can we do justice to the particularities of Japan's historical experience even while resisting the temptation to argue for Japanese exceptionalism.

In fact, each of the early modern geographies of identity was transformed after the fall of the Tokugawa regime. Japan acquired a single set of unambiguous national frontiers, lines on a map recognized as valid by the imperialist powers with which it now interacted. Shortly after it came to power in 1868, the Meiji regime repudiated the institutions of the Tokugawa status order and replaced them with imperial subjecthood. And although the Meiji state continued to recognize realms of civilization and barbarism, the attributes of these realms were reinterpreted to fit Japanese understandings of Western-style modernity.

The key word missing from the chapters that focus on the Tokugawa period is *ethnicity*.[6] I avoid the term because it misrepresents the way difference between the Japanese and the peoples on the immediate peripheries of the Tokugawa state, including the Ainu people of Hokkaido, was understood. Early modern Japanese did not see essential cultural or racial differences between themselves and the Ainu, but rather perceived Ainu identity as an expression of the Ainu's customs *(fūzoku)*, specifically visible features like hairstyle and clothing. Customs were fluid and pliable. So too were the identities and allegiances marked by them.

The Ainu's customs marked them as barbarians *(iteki)* who lived beyond the realm of civilized *(kyōka)* humans *(ningen)*. When Tokugawa officials sought in the nineteenth century to civilize the Ainu, they did so by encouraging them to adopt Japanese customs. Changing the outward emblems of Ainu identity—by shaving the men's pates, assigning them Japanese names, and registering them as residents of Japanese-style villages—was sufficient to mark them as subjects of the shogun and hence as Japanese. The officials involved in this civilizing project realized that their policies would have little immediate effect on individuals' sense of themselves as Ainu, as expressed through social, religious, and economic activities. But private beliefs and even communal practices were not immediately relevant to the creation of civilized subjects, and at any rate were matters largely beyond the officials' ability to address systematically.

If customs had been relevant only as markers of civilization and barbarism—if they had served only to indicate a dichotomy between barbarian Ainu and civilized Japanese—ethnicity would indeed be a useful way to conceive of difference in early modern Japan. In their formation and function, civilizational boundaries were akin to what Fredrik Barth calls ethnic boundaries.[7] As Barth argues, there is no universal litmus test of ethnicity, be it language, race, or culture: ethnic boundaries are marked by essentially arbitrary (if hardly random) attributes, including the features of physical appearance covered by the notion of customs. However, customs in early modern Japan marked not only the difference between civilization and barbarism, but distinctions in social status within the core polity as well. Civilizing the Ainu meant assigning them a place within the status order. As a result, attempts to intervene in "ethnic" relations necessarily implicated the status system and its dual role in demarcating differences among social groups while at the same time binding them as the constituent entities of the core polity.

In my discussion of the Ainu, and indeed throughout the book, I emphasize status as the central institution of the early modern political order. Although the status differences that separated the samurai from commoners are frequently mentioned in the literature on Tokugawa Japan, few scholars have considered the tremendous—indeed, defining—impact of the status system on the political, social, and economic structure of Japan in the early modern period; fewer still have investigated the implications of the dismantling of the status system by the modern state. Moreover, no study in any language has ever attempted systematically to elucidate the connections between status and nation building in Japanese history.

After the collapse of the Tokugawa regime in 1868 status ceased to be the principal criterion of membership in the polity, and eventually it was replaced by a notion of imperial subjecthood. Thus the outcastes became known widely if unofficially as "new commoners" *(shinheimin)* in 1871, and the samurai lost their status privileges by 1876; both groups formally joined commoners and members of other status groups as more or less homogeneous imperial subjects. At the same time, the idea of Japanese national identity emerged, a notion that had previously existed only latently as a subset of status and civilization. Concomitantly, the identities of minorities had to be reframed explicitly in terms of membership within the core Japanese polity, which entailed assigning to them a Japaneseness equivalent to that of other subjects. Denial of politically significant difference and assimilation replaced affirmation of civilizational difference and separation in the state's dealings with its minorities.

The creation of a modern nation-state in the latter half of the nineteenth century entailed a redrawing of Japan's political boundaries to incorporate into the core polity its autonomous yet subordinate peripheries. In the north the Ainu homeland, known to the Japanese as the Ezochi, was renamed Hokkaido in 1868; in the south, the Ryukyu kingdom became Okinawa prefecture in 1879. It is important to note that the Meiji state asserted sovereignty over the core polity and the old Tokugawa peripheries but not over other areas, with the sole exception of the Ogasawara Islands. The people of the peripheries—the Ainu and Ryukyuans—became imperial subjects and were thereby subsumed politically and institutionally within a broader, homogeneous Japanese identity. This was accomplished through a systematic process of ethnic negation: the state denied the validity of minorities' non-Japanese identities and promoted their acculturation (and eventual assimilation) as the ultimate goal, though it did not immediately require it.

At the same time that the political boundaries of Japan were extended to include Hokkaido and the Ryukyus, the realm of civilization was reinterpreted to include the inhabitants of the peripheries. One element of this process was a reorientation of the concept of civilization itself away from the naturalized version of an originally sinocentric worldview that had prevailed in the early modern period to one expressed in terms of the West. As a result, the composition of civilization changed: civilization was linked not only to outward emblems of civilized appearance, but also to modernity, and as such it encompassed livelihood and an explicit connection between the individual and the state in a way that it had not before.

The reorientation of civilization therefore operated on two planes simultaneously. On the one hand, the realm of civilization was extended outward to incorporate peripheral peoples. On the other hand, new standards for civilization were applied throughout Japanese society, with the result that practices once considered unremarkable, such as mixed bathing and public urination, were marked as uncivilized and hence targeted for eradication. Creating a modern regime meant, moreover, that civilization had to be internalized to an extent unthinkable (and unnecessary) in the early modern period: encouraging people to think civilized thoughts and believe civilized ideas was as important as getting them to adhere to civilized standards of physical appearance. Whereas Tokugawa officials intent on spreading civilization had needed little more than a razor (to shave Ainu men's pates and Japanese women's eyebrows) to accomplish their mission, their Meiji counterparts deployed a full Foucauldian arsenal of technologies of modernity—schools, the military, prisons, pageantry—yet they were never satisfied they had achieved their goal.

Universal processes like the formation of ethnic and national identities are embedded in the particularities of national histories. To do justice to those particularities, a significant portion of this book focuses on relations between the Japanese and the Ainu, and in so doing reveals how even a group apparently external to the Japanese nation was transformed by the same processes that transformed the Japanese themselves. (At the time of the Meiji Restoration in 1868 there were about fifteen thousand Ainu in Hokkaido, two thousand in Sakhalin, and perhaps a hundred in the northern Kuril Islands; until at least the eighteenth century and perhaps later a small number of Ainu lived in northeastern Honshu as well.)[8] Tracing the formation of Japanese identity by examining relations with peoples on the peripheries of the archipelago is a common enough strategy in works like this one, but in fact most of this book focuses on the core of the Japanese polity and on the internal boundaries of identity that placed and re-placed subjects in the social and political space of early modern and modern Japan. This book is thus not a history of the Ainu, nor a history of Japanese policy toward the Ainu, nor, for that matter, a history of the discourse of Japanese ethnic and cultural identity. It does address each of these topics in more or less detail, but these subjects do not define the study.

Above all, this book is not a history of how the Japanese Self was constructed vis-à-vis an Ainu Other. Again, it certainly speaks to this important topic, but I feel a keen need to emphasize from the outset that the "Othering" of the Ainu is not at all the linchpin of my argument. To be sure, one might reasonably expect a book about Japanese identity that devotes more than two chapters to the Ainu to argue that Japanese ethnic and national identity was forged mainly in the crucible of interaction with the Ainu. In fact, however, my aim is to illustrate how institutions that originated in the core polity embroiled the Ainu and other peoples on the peripheries of the polity, even when those peoples formally lay outside the purview of the Japanese state. If one were to insist on framing things in the vocabulary of Self and Other, I suppose the book tells the story of how the Ainu Other was tamed—made comprehensible, particularly in political and economic terms—and thereby integrated into the institutional and conceptual framework of the Japanese polity.

The Ainu were conceived as an Other, but one whose characteristics as Other were derived from the same list of attributes that situated subjects within the core polity's geographies of identity. The particular package of attributes that identified the Ainu as Ainu in Japanese eyes was unique, but no single characteristic decisively or permanently disqualified the Ainu from membership in the Japanese national community. There was nothing *meaningful* about the Ainu that was singularly and irrevocably Ainu and that could not be found somewhere among the community of people marked as Japanese; this includes their "race" and "culture," concepts mostly unfamiliar to the early modern Japanese in any case.

Of course, what was *meaningful* in this context was something for the Japanese to decide and apply to the Ainu; and they did so, with scant concern for the production of meaning within Ainu society itself. Ainu language, religion, oral tradition, social relations, knowledge of the land and its plants and animals, and so on—the various elements that made up what we would call Ainu culture—were of course unique and often differed greatly from their counterparts in Japanese culture. Tokugawa observers saw plenty of stark differences between themselves and the Ainu, and they freely commented on them. Nevertheless, those differences were not institutionalized in such a way as to impede a reconception of the Ainu as Japanese subjects in the latter part of the nineteenth century. Indeed, the category of *meaningful* difference consisted of an unexpectedly short roster of malleable, explicitly superficial attributes that could be manipulated to a surprising degree by administrative fiat.

The Ainu were an Other constructed from the spare parts of a Japanese Self that was itself constructed during the Tokugawa period. Because the Ainu were constructed from the same imaginary kit as the Japanese, they had a latent Selfness built into their character that could be invoked at critical junctures to make them and their homeland fully part of Japan. This is a roundabout way of saying that the institutions of the early modern state—particularly the status system and the distinctive notion of territoriality it nurtured—drove the mapping of identities onto the Japanese archipelago. Institutions preceded identities.

The process of delimiting *meaningful* differences cannot be reduced to the construction of an Other entirely separate from the Self. Insofar as the demarcation of status identities in the seventeenth century was largely a by-product of the political and institutional evolution of the early Tokugawa state, status identities were not imagined constructs but rather politically and institutionally defined categories, designed to meet the specific needs of a military regime that justified itself in terms of preparedness for war.

The same principles governed the drawing of status and civilizational boundaries, and in important respects status boundaries preceded civilizational ones as markers of politically meaningful difference. Consequently, the structuring of social difference through the status system helped to shape the way difference would be understood at the polity's edges. In other words, markers of status difference within the core polity also distinguished between the civilized and the barbarian on the polity's boundaries. It follows, therefore, that attributes that marked status difference in the core but had nothing in particular to do with ethnicity—hairstyle, for example—effectively served as the functional equivalent of ethnic markers on the border, albeit in a regime that generally did not see difference in "ethnic" terms.

The Meiji Restoration discredited this configuration of difference. The customs that had marked status and civilization lost their significance once the new regime embarked on its project of homogenizing the population of the archipelago as subjects of a modern nation-state centered on the emperor. This new project effectively ethnicized and even racialized the peoples of the archipelago's peripheries, for the malleable, explicitly superficial markers of identity that had prevailed in the early modern period were replaced with new criteria that required the subject to internalize identity more thoroughly than before, and which thus opened the door to essentialism.

Throughout the prewar period the Japanese state promoted the acculturation of domestic minorities, but it did not systematically require it. Similarly, the state provided incentives for Taiwanese, Koreans, and other newly incorporated colonial subjects to see themselves as Japanese, but until the wartime period—from the late 1930s onward—it did not attempt to impose new identities on them unilaterally except by treating them as Japanese citizens. Instead, a sinister sort of multiethnic ideology prevailed in which ideologues linked the diversity of the empire to the origins and vitality of the so-called Yamato people, the majority Japanese. Thus, for example, expansion into Korea was justified as the reunification of two peoples who had in ancient times enjoyed the beneficence of Japanese imperial rule.[9] Similarly, the supposed imminent extinction of the Ainu as a distinct people was celebrated as the culmination of a long process of ethnic amalgamation that had begun in ancient times.[10]

Ironically, however, the ethnicization and eventual racialization of difference on the peripheries occurred in tandem with policies of ethnic negation—that is, the systematic denial of the validity of ethnic difference in the realm of the politically meaningful. Imperial Japan may have been multiethnic, but the fundamental premises of the state's existence were not challenged by its multiethnicity. On the contrary, ethnicizing difference served mainly as a kind of dye to mark that which would be excised and those who in due course would be assimilated fully into the modern national community.

In the case of the Ainu, the state recognized the non-Japanese ethnicity only of those who remained in communities marked as Ainu communities; Ainu who left traditional communities *(kotan)* generally ceased to be seen as Ainu for administrative purposes. If they had been recognized as majority Japanese by society at large as well as by the state, one might argue that the state did not see them as Ainu because they had already been acculturated, or at least were well on their way toward acculturation (even if they retained a strong personal identity as Ainu). That was not the case, however. People living outside *kotan* who remained Ainu in their own eyes and in the eyes of the majority Japanese with whom they interacted nevertheless did not "count" as Ainu quite literally, for they do not appear in statistical records.[11] In this way the modern state acknowledged the existence of the Ainu as a non-Japanese ethnic group in the polity, yet it did so in a way that isolated them as transitory entities and did not consider them integral constituents of the national community.

Throughout the book I use *identity* as a relational term, meaning a way of distinguishing among groups of people based on their place in political and social institutions. Therefore, when I speak of identity I am not referring primarily to individuals' self-perceptions, although I suppose that externally marked identities and individual subjects' sense of self frequently overlapped. Rather, my principal concern is with identity from the outside looking in. How could one tell who was Ainu and who was Japanese in the Tokugawa period? What did it mean—as a question of political power, economic activity, and social relations—to be a commoner rather than a samurai or an outcaste? Who counted as an imperial subject in the Meiji period? Were all modern imperial subjects necessarily "Japanese"? For the most part, I can speak to such questions without presuming to look into anyone's heart; and in any case, the project of looking at identity from the outside—deliberately leaving the question of individual self-perception to one side—has a particular utility of its own.

This is not to say that individuals and groups have no agency in expressing politically meaningful identities, or that their agency is not important. But at a certain level, surely it matters that institutions mark people as members of this ethnic group or that, this nationality or that, this race or that, with little regard for how the people themselves feel about the act of marking or the particular form the marking takes. If the institutions that mark people are sufficiently powerful, their marks set the ground rules for future debate, often so effectively that people internalize identities they might not otherwise have embraced. In that sense, marked identity trumps felt identity when talking about the realm of the politically meaningful. Or, to express my aim in the idiom of current discourse on nationalism, I will not say much about how individuals imagined ethnic and national communities (in their own minds or through their discourse), but I will instead focus on the ways political, social, and economic institutions evolved to demarcate and hence contain the field within which communities could be imagined. After all, integral to the process of imagining a community of Japanese was the need to reach a rough consensus on where and what Japan was. The state, through its institutions, defined the terms by which such a consensus would be reached.

By focusing on externally marked identities, I do not mean to suggest that social groups were simply willed into and out of existence by the state. Indeed, my premise throughout the book is that identity is at heart the institutional manifestation of material forces, of economic ties and the power relations on which they are based. Actual social and economic relations gave rise to the institutional structure of group identities in the early modern period. For the people enmeshed in those relations, identity was not an abstract intellectual issue but rather a problem of livelihood played out in the arena of everyday life.

Having said that, I do not mean to argue that identity, even as I narrowly define it, can be reduced simply to economics or even to power relations rooted in certain economic practices. For one thing, the Japanese economy was already quite sophisticated when the status system came into being in the seventeenth century, and hence only some economic practices bore significance vis-à-vis the institutions of status. Moreover, status groups evolved significantly once they were defined institutionally, and in the course of their evolution they developed elaborate internal structures and became entangled in complex relations with other groups. At the same time, however, it is also true that the institutional structure of the Tokugawa state was founded on specific material imperatives, particularly the need of the shogunate and domains to marshal resources for war. In that sense, political power and the economic means to maintain that power drove the definition of identities. Concomitantly, the tensions that challenged the stability of the Tokugawa state were often rooted in the growing dissonance between the material needs of political power—and the institutions of status through which they were satisfied—and the ever-changing realities of a complex economy. Identity was politically meaningful, ultimately, because of its relationship to the material supports of the polity. Yet everyday life encompassed much more than the relatively narrow realm of the politically meaningful, and the Tokugawa state inevitably evolved as its own institutions became more complex. Material forces underlay the formation of identities, but they did not completely subsume them.

All sorts of groups existed beyond earshot of the state, at least as long as disputes among or within them did not grow too noisy to ignore. But the state had its own agenda, which it furthered by reifying certain social configurations in law, thereby plotting them onto the geographies of identity. The ways of distinguishing between Japanese and Ainu and between outcastes and commoners had this quality: groups that antedated the founding of the Tokugawa regime were nominally frozen but actually transformed by the early modern state as it defined itself and justified its power.

The externally marked identities rendered politically meaningful by the state always existed in tension with on-the-ground social and economic relations. In real life, people challenged and breached social boundaries all the time, in no small part because reality did not correspond with the idealized vision of polity reflected in the geographies of identity. Throughout the book I will reiterate this point by contrasting how the geographies of identity looked as they were conceived with the complexities of their actual operation. Insofar as social and economic relations both antedated institutions and challenged their premises, an element of tension is only natural. However, just because the system was always under assault does not mean that it did not have lasting meaning and real power.

Let us return briefly to the question of who "counted" as an Ainu to illustrate what I am aiming at with my use of *identity*. By applying the household-registration law to Ainu communities in 1871, the Meiji state declared the Ainu people to be, for most purposes, ordinary Japanese subjects. Individuals could and certainly did retain a strong ethnic and cultural identity as Ainu, but the Meiji state did not generally recognize an exclusively Ainu category of subjects. Ainu identity thus became a mostly personal matter contained within households, local communities, and elsewhere in the realm of the private. Within the largely private domain of Ainu identity there existed heterogeneous social configurations—based on residence and lineage, for example—that had profound meaning within the Ainu community but were invisible and hence invalid outside it.

As a matter of public concern, Ainu identity became in the eyes of the state and its ideologues a transitional and decidedly homogeneous condition for people on their way to a more genuine state of Japaneseness. As a result, even though there is no reason to believe that the Ainu marked as Japanese immediately embraced their new putative identity, in practice they had no choice but to deal with the state as if they had, in fact, become Japanese. During the decades after 1871, the Ainu and the Japanese state engaged in a protracted struggle over the precise nature of the Ainu's membership in the national community—and here is where we see Ainu agency—but all negotiations had to be articulated through the very legal and political institutions that had preemptively marked them as Japanese in the first place. "Japanese" was the only identity through which Ainu subjects could negotiate with the nation-state.

In the economic domain, Ainu labor, which had previously been accessible only to employers with a special relationship to the Matsumae domain, became free and unmarked: in other words, after the Meiji Restoration there was no longer a category of "Ainu labor," though there were many wage laborers in Hokkaido who happened to be Ainu. Likewise, whereas Ainu labor in the Tokugawa period was treated institutionally as a particular manifestation of the trade relationship between the Ainu and the Matsumae domain, after the Restoration there was no longer a category of "Ainu trade," though commodities continued to change hands between Japanese and Ainu. Of course, the Japanese who worked and traded with Ainu had a clear sense they were dealing with people different from themselves, but that sense of difference—even when expressed through lower wages or a contemptuous attitude—was no longer underwritten by the institutions of the state. As a practical matter, Ainu in the general labor force disappeared from official view as Ainu, while those who remained in upriver communities were targeted for state intervention into their economic lives through agricultural promotion policies. The latter were nearly the only people publicly marked as Ainu by the Meiji state after the early 1880s.

As with *identity*, I use the term *customs* in a distinctive sense. As noted above, *customs* is my rendering of the Japanese term *fūzoku*, which today includes the meanings captured by the English *customs* as well as other connotations (notably, it is used as a euphemism for sex work). In the period covered by this book, however, *fūzoku* referred more commonly to dress, hairstyle, and other elements of outward appearance.[12]

Hence, *demeanor, comportment,* or even the clunky *somatic markers* might be a better translation of the term. Nevertheless, I prefer *customs* to highlight a broader point about the vital importance of the external performance of norms in Tokugawa Japan. Using a term like *customs,* laden as it is with the connotation of representing the essential building blocks of culture and identity, accentuates this importance.

Both the Tokugawa and Meiji states concerned themselves with the inner lives and outward appearances of their subjects, but they weighed these aspects differently. The Tokugawa authorities were more concerned with exteriority—the visible compliance with norms—than with the internalization of the principles behind those norms. This is revealed most obviously in their obsession with sumptuary regulation, which was primarily expressed by exhortations that people dress and behave in accordance with their social station. To be sure, ideologues, often with the support of the state, tried hard to instill in the people the values that underlay the status order, and they succeeded to the extent that more or less Confucian notions came to permeate the value systems of people at every level of the status order. However, with the exception of its virulent attacks on heterodox ideologies that appeared to reject the premises of Tokugawa rule—such as Christianity, the Fuju-fuse sect of Nichiren Buddhism, and some of the so-called new religions that appeared in the nineteenth century—the state did not make much effort to police popular thought. (Matsudaira Sadanobu's famous proscription of heterodoxy at the end of the eighteenth century was directed mostly at intellectuals.)

Lacking the means to intervene systematically in the inner lives of their subjects—and skeptical at any rate of most commoners' ability to comprehend the ethical and philosophical bases of governance—officials necessarily focused on the external performance of proper deportment. But the problem was not simply one of technology. Rather, exteriority was at least as important to the maintenance of good rule as was the internalization of the ruling ideology. Consequently, a relatively weighty term like *customs* is an appropriate translation of *fūzoku:* for the people who concerned themselves with *fūzoku,* those practices did indeed carry the full weight of meaning that we would now want to see expressed by a wider and deeper range of practices.

The concern with exteriority survived through the opening years of the Meiji period, as the new regime targeted emblems of outward appearance that had been discredited with the collapse of the status order. At the same time, however, the Meiji state, working through its own institutions and with the enthusiastic support of ideologues, quickly evinced an ardor for the internalization of new norms through its attacks on a variety of popular beliefs and practices. It could hardly do otherwise, for it faced the pressing need to justify its own existence, which was necessarily predicated on a rejection of the bases of Tokugawa rule. The early Meiji period covered in this book, in other words, was a transitional period during which the old concern with exteriority gave way to an emphasis on interiority. With the development of schools, the modern military, and the modern imperial institution, the state turned its attention from the active policing of physical appearance to problems of moral suasion and outright indoctrination: this project, which was still in its initial stages at the time of the Meiji emperor's death in 1912, was central to the creation of Western-style modernity in Japan.

The chapters that follow are essays that build on one another, but they do not offer comprehensive, monographic coverage of the topics they address, either individually or severally. My treatment is schematic, even formalistic, and deliberately so. The advantage of making a schematic argument is that it allows me to present a broad vision of nineteenth-century Japan. My hope is that this book will serve as a statement of what held Tokugawa Japan together and how it worked, and what needed to change and why when Japan entered the modern international order in the latter part of the nineteenth century.

For example, I argue that *all* social relations in the Tokugawa period can be understood at some level as an expression of the institutions of the status system. But in doing so, I do not mean to suggest that status was the *only* medium through which identities could be expressed, or even that status always took precedence over all other ways of marking people. Gender, class, age, religion, ancestry, and many other criteria for sorting people into groups functioned robustly in Tokugawa Japan. Nevertheless, the institutions of status gave Tokugawa Japan its peculiar character as a unique social and political system. This ought to be a merely commonsensical point, but in fact scholars have failed to appreciate just how deeply status was embedded in social and economic relations in early modern Japan. Although my approach does not claim to explain the social and political fabric in its entirety, it does expose the institutional webbing that held the Tokugawa order together.

I take a similar approach in my treatment of the transition from Tokugawa to Meiji and the advent of Western-style modernity in Japan. This is an impossibly complex topic, and my discussions of economic change, the role of violence, and the reorientation of the content of civilization will do no more than highlight aspects of the transformation that have not been examined in detail by earlier scholars. I do not mean to suggest that the transition can be reduced to these elements. Rather, my discussion of these aspects of the transition is intended to reinforce my argument about the importance of the status system to the early modern order, on the one hand, and the traumatic character of its necessary dissolution as Japan self-consciously embraced modernity, on the other hand. My aim is to illuminate the nature of the transition below the level of political and diplomatic events.

Finally, a word about my use of ethnonyms and other labels. Throughout the book I call the majority population of the archipelago *Japanese;* the indigenous people of Hokkaido *Ainu;* and members of the main outcaste groups *eta* and *hinin* (in this last case I follow both my sources and the conventions of historical writing in Japan, although the terms are considered pejorative now). I do so fully aware that, like the identities they represent, names are products of the power relations that sustain their use. Applying labels unreflectively can validate those power relations, albeit often unwittingly. However, making a show of critiquing power by rejecting them entirely (or placing them in quotation marks to show that one is using them under duress) does little more than evade recognition of the force of politics in constituting identity as social reality. Accordingly, I have rejected the use of scare quotes around ethnonyms and normative markers like *barbarian* and *civilized,* a practice that has the added virtue of avoiding the clutter of pages filled with quotation marks.

The fact that power relations—and hence identities and names—are in constant flux does not diminish their force at any given time. To be sure, Japanese identity is a construct, and as such it is constantly subject to redefinition: to be "Japanese" does not mean the same thing in the twenty-first century as it did in the nineteenth, much less in the eighteenth. This is an important if obvious point, but in making it we invite intellectual paralysis. After all, how can we ever talk about "Japan" and the "Japanese" when we know that they are mere constructs, always changing and hence not objectively "real"?

My solution to this dilemma is simple if heavy-handed: however much a construct, "Japan" is nonetheless "real"; however fluid the content of the category of "Japan," it does indeed exist as a political entity, not only in the minds of its people, but also in its authority over them. After all, Japan as a geographically bound polity may have been new—and constructed and contingent—in the seventeenth century, but the state's power was very real nonetheless. Put starkly, the shogun could have a subject's head cut off if he broke the shogun's laws, just as the contemporary state can imprison people, dictate the language of instruction in its schools, and grant passports. None of this denies the constructedness of the polity, but it does remind us that even constructs have real power: a severed head is no construct, however arbitrary the polity that ordered it cut off. Real power over life, property, and livelihood is reality enough.

CHAPTER 2

The Geography of Status

In 1603 the military government of the Tokugawa shoguns, backed by about 260 autonomous daimyo, completed the reunification of Japan after nearly a century and a half of civil war and imposed a federalist order on the country while cutting most ties with the outside world.[1] The Tokugawa hegemony thus established prevailed until 1868, when the nascent Meiji regime brought Japan into the modern world. Because political authority and legitimacy before 1868 were dispersed among the shogunate, the imperial court, and the daimyos' autonomous domains, some scholars have questioned whether "state" (in the singular) is even an appropriate term to describe the Tokugawa polity.[2] In fact, the shogunate did indeed function as a state apparatus, as revealed in the way it had, by the middle of the seventeenth century, achieved a virtual monopoly over the formation of national political and social institutions.

At the same time, the state was not coterminous with the shogunate, or even with the amalgam of shogunate and domains (the so-called *bakuhan* system). Some territory fell under the autonomous administration of large temples and shrines or of the imperial court, creating space that was part of the Tokugawa state without belonging to either the shogunate or any domain. More important, multiple political authorities sometimes occupied the same physical space, staking claims to people, land, and other resources according to the rules of the status system. Rural outcastes, for example, enjoyed exclusive rights to animal carcasses within their territories, even when the beasts had been the private property of commoner cultivators and the land upon which they lay subject to the sole jurisdiction of a local daimyo. In that sense, the Tokugawa state transcended its constituent elements. The status system served as the framework in which political authority was articulated and territory allocated.

The status system was an institutional structure intended above all to ensure military preparedness in the service of the shogun. Formally, the shogun enfeoffed daimyo and lesser lords so they could provide sustenance to their men and horses; the land taxes and other levies paid by commoners were conceived at the outset as that sustenance. The emphasis on military preparedness remained intact throughout the Tokugawa period, despite the fact that for almost 230 years the shogunate had no occasion to muster troops for warfare, and that even samurai warriors were more likely to serve in a bureaucratic rather than martial capacity. But because the principle of military rule was never challenged, political and economic institutions retained their orientation toward military service.

The principle of military rule meant that the division of society into different status groups was not an end in itself, but rather an expedient that emerged in response to the concrete military needs of the Tokugawa house in the early seventeenth century. Once it was institutionalized, regularized, and elaborated for peacetime administration, this ad hoc division of society became the status system. The status system was therefore decidedly *not* a caste system in which birth permanently determined one's station in life, nor was status the Tokugawa era's functional equivalent of race.

The status system integrated the shogunate's "public" nature as a central state apparatus with its "private" character as the administrative organ of the Tokugawa house. Strictly speaking, feudal obligations were the product of the private ties of vassalage between the shogun and his retainers, including the daimyo.[3] Yet to fulfill those obligations, social groups of all sorts had to be mobilized: peasants and artisans to provide material support, merchants to oversee distribution, clergy to tend to spiritual and ideological matters, outcastes to regulate and contain social disorder and pollution, the imperial court to lend legitimacy to the shogun's rule, and so on. In exchange, the shogunate and domains promised benevolent rule *(jinsei)*, an obligation they and their subjects took quite seriously, if often only in the breach.

Such an all-encompassing order soon took on a public character. Indeed, the term most commonly used in the Tokugawa period to refer to the shogunate, *kōgi*, is generally translated as "public authority." Once the threat of civil war had receded (by about 1640), the shogunate and domains necessarily involved themselves with matters that extended far beyond immediate security concerns. (In any case, as anyone who lived through the cold war knows, "national security" is an infinitely pliable concept.) Social groups of all sorts found plenty of space in which to see to their own interests beyond the fulfillment of tax obligations or other feudal duties. Yet the fundamental premise of Tokugawa hegemony, expressed in terms of the personal ties between the shogun and his vassals, was never denied—nor, indeed, did it need to be for early modern society to function smoothly.

By ceding a measure of autonomy to status groups, including the domains, the shogunate abstained from intruding into those aspects of daily life deemed external to national concerns. This opened the door to a degree of dissonance between the interests of the state at the national level, as embodied in the shogunate, and its actual operation at the local level, as overseen by the domains and other status groups. Indeed, dissonance even manifested itself in the realm of foreign relations, as the interests of the shogunate and those of the domains charged with overseeing ties with Japan's peripheries did not always coincide. More generally, every domain's desire to maintain autonomy necessarily clashed with the shogunate's need to assert overall control. Yet throughout all but the very last years of the Tokugawa period, the domains' recognition of Tokugawa legitimacy ensured that all differences of interest would be resolved within broad parameters laid down by the shogunate. Consequently, Japan could safely maintain a multiplicity of "states" within the state.

This geo-institutional structure was designed to support the military and administrative needs of the regime through the expropriation of agricultural surplus and the provision of other goods and services. The *kokudaka* system, which expressed tax burdens and the domains' military obligations to the shogunate in terms of the putative productivity of agricultural land, was the institutional manifestation of the expropriative order.[4] Whether the *kokudaka* system worked well or not—and in fact, never perfect, it worked less well over time—is not the issue; the salient point is that institutions could develop and change only to the extent that the regime's imperative of military preparedness could be accommodated.

The *kokudaka* system permitted the efficient translation of obligations from agricultural production to a range of feudal duties. The daimyo, lesser lords, and other groups (such as the imperial court and major religious institutions) administered lands assigned a *kokudaka*, or putative agricultural yield expressed in terms of a quantity of rice. (A *koku* was a measure of rice, about 180 liters, nominally sufficient to support an adult man for a year.) Ten thousand *koku* was the minimum yield that qualified a lord as a daimyo; the biggest domain, Kaga, controlled territory worth about a million *koku;* and the shogun's personal lands produced more than three million *koku* of grain. The shogunate used *kokudaka* to calculate both the military forces a lord could reasonably expect to support and, concomitantly, the scale of public-works projects he could be called on to supervise. Similarly, *kokudaka,* in combination with other considerations, such as the antiquity of a lord's line and his ancestral relationship to the Tokugawa house, served as a marker of a daimyo's prestige, which determined ritually important matters like the seating arrangement at shogunal audiences and honorific court titles.

The extensive land surveys mandated in the 1590s by Toyotomi Hideyoshi and continued under the early Tokugawa shoguns were designed to ensure that the *kokudaka* of daimyo domains had a rough basis in actual productivity, but nothing about the system required that this be so. Rather, the *kokudaka* of a domain was above all a measure of its lord's standing within the community of daimyo and of the concomitant military obligations he could be expected to fulfill. Thus the high putative yield of the Tsushima domain—100,000 *koku*—reflected the domain's importance as an intermediary in relations between Japan and Korea; the fact that its core territory had practically no agricultural production at all was not an issue. Similarly, the Nanbu and Tsugaru domains both saw their putative yields rise substantially in the early nineteenth century as a reflection of their importance in defending Hokkaido against possible incursions from Russia. These increases, which enhanced the prestige of the two domains' lords, were perceived as rewards for loyal service, but of course they also carried with them heightened expectations for future military service.[5] Many other domains were content to enjoy the economic benefits of an actual yield far higher than the official figures according to which their obligations to the shogun were calculated.

Institution builders in early modern Japan showed great creativity in tailoring the *kokudaka* system to accommodate a wide range of economic activity, much of it utterly divorced from agricultural production, yet they never showed any inclination either to abandon it entirely or even to deny its putative basis in agricultural production. The idea that agriculture, and rice cultivation in particular, was the basis of the economic and social order was similarly universally accepted by thinkers and other social actors. Hence the expropriation of agricultural surplus

remained both the material and the ideological motor of Tokugawa institutions. This concern with production endowed Tokugawa institutions
with a character fundamentally different from that of the modern state,
which conducts its expropriation through the taxation of income and
consumption.

STATUS IN EARLY MODERN JAPAN

The linchpin of my inquiry in this chapter will be a conceptualization of
Tokugawa society in terms of the status system. Until recently, status did
not figure into many English-language discussions of early modern
Japanese history.[6] Until the mid-1980s the same was true of Japanese
scholarship as well, at least outside the small field of outcaste history.
Since then, however, scholars such as Asao Naohiro, Hatanaka
Toshiyuki, Tsukada Takashi, and Yoshida Nobuyuki have raised awareness of the centrality of the status system to the Tokugawa institutional
order. Although much of their work focuses on the history of outcastes
and other marginal social groups, unlike earlier scholarship (which was
mostly concerned with explaining discrimination against contemporary
Burakumin, or descendants of early modern outcastes), it reveals the
need to consider status in any treatment of social and political organization in early modern Japan.[7]

Before I proceed further, it is necessary to emphasize that by *status* I
am not referring to the hierarchical social taxonomy of four estates,
ranked by utility to polity and society, that appears in textbook accounts
of Tokugawa society. According to that taxonomy, the samurai *(shi)*
rulers of the country occupied the top position, followed in order by the
peasants *(nō)*, who produced food; artisans *(kō)*, who crafted articles of
practical utility; and merchants *(shō)*, who prospered despite producing
nothing, and were accordingly portrayed as parasites on the body politic.
Outcastes *(eta* and *hinin)*, when mentioned at all, are usually portrayed
in traditional accounts as existing in an inferior position outside the system entirely.

This *shi-nō-kō-shō* hierarchy prevails because it was prescribed by
Confucian thinkers and enjoyed a certain currency in Tokugawa and
later discourse; indeed, writers of all sorts often referred to the "four
estates" *(shimin)* when talking about Japanese society as a whole.[8]
However, the *shi-nō-kō-shō* ranking had no real basis in Tokugawa law.
For most purposes, peasants, artisans, and merchants composed a single
status group of commoners.[9] Thus, unlike priests and nuns, outcastes,

and other members of distinct status groups, merchants and artisans in peasant villages were not listed separately from cultivators in population registers. Similarly, peasants who went to the city to work as shop apprentices did not move down the status ladder either legally or socially. Moreover, although the Tokugawa shogunate applied distinct laws to the samurai and to the imperial court, commoners were generally covered by a uniform set of injunctions.[10] Nor was the status system strictly hierarchical: a horizontal division of social groups according to function was at least as important as vertical ranking. Finally, status categories were extremely fluid. Although most people indeed remained within the same status group their entire lives, occupation rather than birth was the principal criterion for categorizing people. The son of a samurai remained a full-fledged samurai only if he entered into service; likewise, a peasant youth could cross status boundaries by taking the tonsure or through incorporation into a lord's retainer band. To be sure, opportunities for social mobility were limited (though surprisingly common), but, with the exception of members of the imperial household, the *eta*, and some descendants of Christians (including apostates), mobility was not constrained by an ideology of essential identity such as race or caste.[11]

The status groups of early modern Japan were neither internally homogeneous nor unitary in their conception or operation, but they were nevertheless coherent markers of identity. The status category of samurai, for example, existed throughout the country, and it was salient as a marker of one's position in the general political order that transcended internal borders. A samurai was recognized as such whether he was in his home domain, in Edo, or anywhere else in Japan. The two swords he carried in public served as the most important outward emblem of that status. At the same time, however, the warrior would have had no horizontal ties with samurai from other domains beyond a shared public identity as samurai, with the general privileges and obligations that pertained thereto. The daimyo's retainer band was his immediate status group, and for most purposes his social identity was mediated through that group. Moreover, the samurai occupied a specific rank somewhere within the intricate hierarchy of the retainer band, and this rank largely determined his career and marriage prospects. The same principle worked throughout society: Buddhist priests were readily identifiable as such by their clothing and shaved heads, but beyond that they were divided along sectarian lines, and within sects by rank. Outcastes belonged to highly differentiated groups and were separated not only by status—as *eta, hinin,* and so forth—but also by residence and, again, by internal rank; yet they were identifiable as outcastes through their dress, hairstyle, and general comportment. The same applied throughout the status order and throughout the archipelago.

Commoners, who constituted the overwhelming majority of the people, were subject to multiple forms of classification beyond the general category of commoner. For rural commoners, the most immediately salient subgroup was the peasant village and, beyond that, the domain within which the village was located. Urban commoners were situated within the social landscape through a combination of their residence, property holdings (or, more commonly, lack thereof), and, most important, occupational group. Similar to members of other status categories, commoners occupied a specific position within their residential and occupational groups, a position that greatly influenced their everyday social and economic relations. Moreover, commoners were divided by wealth, with the result that the social position of a well-to-do merchant was quite different from that of a poor peasant. Occasionally, usually during times of crisis, rural commoners expressed a common identity as peasants *(hyakushō)* that transcended domainal boundaries as well as village ones, but for the most part the category of commoner was too large and too highly differentiated to allow for any kind of general solidarity.

Given that status categories were both broad and internally highly heterogeneous, one might wonder why I insist on invoking status as the basis of social and political organization. The chapter as a whole should answer this question, but here I would like to start with two points. First, however diffuse, the categories of status operated more or less uniformly throughout the early modern polity. The shogunate and 260-odd domains all maintained their own internal status systems, essentially the same despite minor variations (particularly at the margins of society): every domain had samurai, commoners, and so on. (Not every domain had legally instituted outcaste status, however, for reasons probably rooted in the medieval origins of so-called base social groups *[senmin]*.) Accordingly, status categories were portable: just as a samurai would be recognized as a samurai wherever he went, so too would a commoner or a priest carry his status identity with him when he left the confines of his residential or occupational group.

Thus, status was a universal construct despite the highly particularistic character of belonging to a specific domain, village, sect, outcaste organization, and so forth. No other institutional categories existed above status to unite all Japanese as members of the same political community. To be sure, within the confines of a single domain, people of all statuses shared an awareness that they belonged to a political community distinct from others, albeit within the context of a national polity headed by the shogun. Nonetheless, the fundamental nature of an individual's relationship to the daimyo depended on his status: the samurai was his vassal and others were his subjects. This distinction is neatly captured by the conventions of writing addresses: commoners were usually identified in terms of the old imperial provinces, while samurai were identified by their domains.[12] Likewise, at the national level, people certainly had a sense that the world was filled with countries beyond Japan, and that they shared an identity as Japanese in distinction to being Korean, say, or Dutch. But this was mostly an intellectual construct. In the realm of law and institutions, there was no generic category of "Japanese." The closest one could come was to be a subject of the public authority *(kōgi)*— that is, the shogun—or, more abstractly, of the emperor, but subjecthood was always mediated through the institutions of status.

The second point relates to gender. Everyone in early modern Japan belonged to a status group, but membership was generally mediated through smaller clusters of individuals. In the vast majority of cases, the smallest meaningful unit of organization was the household, not the individual. (The unit did not have to be the household, however: a temple organization or local outcaste band could serve the same function.) The status of women, minors, and other dependents was expressed through the position of the household head, who was almost always a man. Thus in matters of law, contracts, occupation, and other public interaction— into which status always came into play—women and other dependents were not usually seen as autonomous social actors. Similarly, if the head of a household changed status for some reason, his dependents' status changed as well, but if a dependent moved into a new status group— when a peasant woman married a samurai, for instance—the household she or he left behind remained unaffected. The expression of status through households helps to explain why adult men, as household heads or potential household heads, always displayed salient markers of status identity—swords or distinctive hairstyles or clothing—while women and children did not necessarily bear such clear marks. Thus as a practical matter status was effectively gendered as male, but this fact was the by-product of a social organization that operated through households that were normatively headed by men. This is particularly clear when one considers that the ultimate purpose of the status system was to marshal resources for the authorities: under such a system, it was only natural to privilege the household, which was seen as the principal unit of productive activity.

Status in Tokugawa Japan referred both to membership in a group (usually based on the occupation of the head of the household) and to the formal duties *(yaku)* that accompanied such membership.[13] Duties included the payment of taxes, the performance of various types of labor, the provision of services, and military service to a lord. Thus a peasant household was part of a village community, with which it shared an obligation to pay taxes and perform corvée labor; similarly, a samurai warrior served in battle and bureaucracy alongside other members of his lord's retainer band. Self-governing status groups (or, much more commonly, their constituent units) mediated relations between their members and higher authorities. The peasant village is the classic example of this, but samurai retainer bands and indeed the domains themselves similarly served to ensure the daimyo's ability to fulfill his military duties to the shogun (pragmatically reconceived to include and indeed center on administrative functions).

Perhaps 90 percent of the people in early modern Japan were commoners, called "peasants" *(hyakushō)* if they lived in the countryside and "townspeople" *(chōnin)* if they lived in major urban areas, but legally equivalent nonetheless. (In legal discourse, the term *chōnin* often referred specifically to men who directly bore responsibility for the fulfillment of status-based obligations through the ownership or management of urban property; similarly, *honbyakushō,* or "full-fledged peasant," referred to rural landowners. The obligations of landless commoners were mediated through their residential communities.)[14] Of the rest, the samurai, or warrior class (usually called *bushi* or *buke*—"warriors" or "warrior houses" —in early modern documents), was the biggest group, accounting for about six percent of the population.[15] Other major status groups included the imperial house and the court nobility (which together numbered around a thousand people), Buddhist and Shinto clerics and mountain priests *(yamabushi)* (several hundred thousand altogether), and outcastes (who accounted for two or three percent of the national population—up to about a million people).

Outcastes *(senmin)* did not compose a single status group, but rather occupied a variety of statuses that were linked by a perception of their baseness and often by interconnected hierarchies of authority.[16] The great majority of outcastes were *eta,* who disposed of animal carcasses, worked with leather, and performed various police and jailhouse duties for the authorities. The other major outcaste group was the *hinin*, whose members begged, served as village and urban-ward guards, and also performed police and jailhouse duties. In addition, there was a multitude of small outcaste groups whose names, duties, and social conditions varied from region to region.[17] Membership in an outcaste group was generally determined by birth, but commoners were sometimes absorbed into the ranks of the *hinin*, either as a consequence of their taking up begging or as a punishment *(hinin teka)* imposed occasionally on those for whom execution was inappropriate (most famously survivors of love-suicide attempts). In addition, people whose economic activities brought them within the orbit of minor outcaste groups also took on a base status. For instance, the *angya,* mendicant religious practitioners in Satsuma, absorbed new members in this way, as did other groups we shall encounter below.[18]

The Japanese population also included a number of marginal status groups whose members were officially considered to be commoners but were nonetheless forbidden to marry or engage in social relations with peasants and townspeople; in major cities the members of such groups sometimes came under the authority of *eta* and *hinin* leaders.[19] In Kyoto, marginal status groups included, among others, the *shuku,* who purified temple and shrine grounds by disposing of dead animals; *shōmonji,* who also purified religious sites and engaged in fortune-telling and performance at New Year's; *hachitataki,* lay priests who traveled around the countryside reciting prayers for the dead; and *onbō,* graveyard workers.[20] In other regions, groups like the *tani-hinin,* a group of beggars of the Tottori domain; the *ushikubi kojiki,* beggars and performers of the Kaga and Fukui domains; and some abalone divers *(ama)* along the Japan Sea coast also fell into this marginal category.[21]

Status groups typically functioned through their constituent units, such as the peasant village, urban ward, outcaste territory, Buddhist sect, or daimyo domain. Although laws typically applied to all members of a status group within a political jurisdiction (a domain, shogunal territory, and so on), the specific obligations accruing to members of a status group could vary depending on the group's location or size. Peasants living near major highways, for example, often found themselves saddled with post-station duties not imposed on other villagers in the same domain.[22] Being a member of a particular status group therefore implicated individuals at two levels simultaneously: it was a universal category that situated one within the Japanese population in general, so that under most circumstances an individual took his status identity with him away from home; at the same time, status was highly particularistic, for it carried specific obligations and a place within a community unique to that individual (or his household).

As a rule, group membership and the performance of duties went together, but exceptions were common. Sometimes group members could not fulfill their assigned duties, while other people performed various duties without belonging unambiguously to the relevant group. A landless peasant, for example, could not participate directly in paying land taxes and therefore did not merit full membership in the village community, while a masterless samurai who freelanced as a political consultant might serve a lord without being included in his retainer band. Such people occupied a vulnerable position in society, yet they retained a status identity nonetheless: a landless peasant was still a peasant, a masterless samurai still a samurai.

Status as an expression of group membership and duty encompassed all members of society, albeit often incompletely or indirectly. Indeed, the status system even incorporated people who neither belonged to an occupational group nor performed clear duties and were therefore without regular status. Efforts were made to gather such people together and assign them duties to perform on the margins of society and thereby ascribe to them the attributes of a status group. In effect, being without status itself became a type of status.

A brief example will illustrate this paradoxical point. The *hinin*, or "nonpersons," were a heterogeneous collection of beggars, entertainers, fortune-tellers, and other marginal people who existed beyond the bounds of commoner society, yet they composed a status group with an internal organization and explicit duties. Among the duties of urban *hinin* was the regulation of unregistered transients, called *nohinin* ("wild" *hinin*) if they begged or called *mushuku* (literally, "without lodgings") more generally. The unregistered were peasants or townspeople who had fallen on hard times; by dropping out of society (by virtue of being removed from village or town population registers and hence losing their place within the status order) they had effectively forfeited their commoner status, at least temporarily. *Hinin* were charged with removing the unregistered from urban areas by sending them back to their native communities, or at least running them out of town; failing that, the *hinin* might incorporate them within their own ranks as "official" *hinin* (*kakae hinin*; literally, "kept" *hinin*), in which case they would continue to live by begging, but now within a community of beggars obligated to perform a variety of mostly unsavory tasks for the political authorities.[23]

This example raises the issue of the nature of discrimination in Tokugawa society. Specifically, it prompts the question of whether relegation to *hinin* status was necessarily a bad thing for *nohinin* and other freelance beggars. On the surface it would appear to be so. After all, a "kept" *hinin* was placed permanently outside the rest of society, while an unregistered peasant or townsman might be experiencing nothing worse than a brief run of bad luck, after which he could return untainted to the ranks of commoners. Nevertheless, for many it was better to be officially despised than casually reviled. The tag *(fuda)* that marked one's membership in the ranks of the *hinin* was certainly a symbol of social stigma, but it also symbolized the right to beg and to deal with other people of all statuses according to the rules of the status system. To be sure, the privileges of *hinin* status came at a price: in addition to suffering from discrimination as outcastes, the *hinin* had to perform duties on behalf of the authorities. Yet the freedom from feudal duty enjoyed by the unregistered came at an even greater price: as unplaced persons they were left completely vulnerable to the predations of arbitrary authority, for Tokugawa Japan was, in John W. Hall's phrase, a "container society." The "containers"—status groups—"can be thought of as protected arenas within which all persons of a given status [could] expect equal treatment under the law."[24]

As Yamamoto Naotomo has argued, discrimination *(sabetsu)* was the principle behind all social organization in early modern Japan; equality in social relations was seen as neither natural nor proper.[25] The status system served as the structure on which social inequality—as well as orderly social relations—was produced and reproduced at the level of everyday interaction. Insofar as each status group performed a distinct function, all were equally important to the maintenance of social order. Status relations were thus guided as much by horizontal differences in social function as vertical distinctions in rank. Consequently, the outcastes existed outside of commoner society, but not necessarily below it—which explains why, for example, the headman of the outcastes in Edo (Tokyo) and the surrounding Kantō region, Danzaemon, was able to carry two swords and otherwise comport himself in a manner analogous to that of a minor domain lord. In short, the discrimination directed against outcastes in the Tokugawa period was qualitatively different from the racial and ethnic discrimination practiced in contemporary societies, including Japan.[26] In an era in which all social relations were characterized by inequality, the benefits of membership in an official outcaste group may well have outweighed the burden of the extra measure of contempt that accompanied it.

The picture of status in Tokugawa society that I have sketched thus far is a political one insofar as it takes for granted the power of political authorities to sort people into social groups on the basis of their utility to the shogun or daimyo, and because it assumes a rough equivalence between utility to political authority and utility to society at large. Not surprisingly, status was much more than a political construct, but it is worthwhile to pause here to consider its political dimensions more fully, as doing so will help clarify the relationship between status and civilization and, ultimately, the origins of the modern nation-state in Japan.

Status as a legal institution originated in the national unification of the late sixteenth and early seventeenth centuries. It was not a conscious creation but rather the product of an interconnected series of measures implemented under the hegemonic authority of Oda Nobunaga and, particularly, Toyotomi Hideyoshi and built on by the early Tokugawa shoguns.[27] Policies like the separation of the samurai from the peasantry (heinō bunri), sword hunts (katanagari) and other attempts to disarm peasants, land surveys, the founding of large castle towns with their merchant and artisan populations, and the compilation of registers of religious affiliation (shūmon aratamechō) all contributed to the formal delineation of the samurai and commoner populations as status groups. Furthermore, over the course of the seventeenth century the shogunate and domains institutionalized various other extant social groups, including the court nobility, the Buddhist clergy, and the outcastes as legal statuses.

To be sure, assigning legal statuses to groups of people was not the principal motive behind these policies, but the policies nonetheless came together as a system. The removal of most samurai from the countryside and the concomitant disarming of the peasantry, combined with the imposition of a federalist national order by Hideyoshi and the early Tokugawa shoguns, were intended to thwart challenges to the hegemonic order, but in doing so they effectively detached the warrior class from the mass of peasants and townspeople. Land surveys and the registration of the rural population were designed to secure the samurai's access to surplus agricultural production and to control Christianity, but in the process they marked the commoners as a distinct status group. Similarly, the shogunate's organization of Buddhist and other religious institutions under the commissioner of temples and shrines *(jisha bugyō)* was aimed most immediately at preventing a revival of Buddhist political power, but had as a corollary result the demarcation of the clergy as a distinct status category. The same was true of the shogunate's control of the imperial court and the attendant separation of the nobility from the rest of the population. Finally, the creation of a centrally sanctioned (albeit plural) authority structure for the outcastes was designed to maintain social order, but in the process imbued them with the characteristics of a single status group (or, more properly, a cluster of related status groups), despite their internal occupational heterogeneity.

The imperative to create an institutionally diverse yet centrally integrated political structure fueled a taxonomic revolution in late-sixteenth- and early-seventeenth-century Japan, so that the clarification of one group's function necessarily led to the clarification of other groups' functions as well. This revolution led by the middle of the seventeenth century to a structure in which every individual (through the medium of the household or its functional equivalent, such as the Buddhist sect) was placed into a social category with attendant obligations. This process was validated in Tokugawa law, which gave status groups or their constituent units a measure of autonomy in adjudicating internal disputes and treated members of different statuses differently in cases that crossed status boundaries.

Nowhere is the taxonomic urge more evident than in the case of the blind and other people with physical handicaps. According to Katō Yasuaki, most blind people in early modern Japan remained at home and therefore fit into the status system in the same manner as other members of their households; they retained their natal status identity even when living alone so long as the village or other community took responsibility for their well-being. Those who left home to beg fell under the authority of *hinin* bosses, while others who engaged in divination became affiliated with local Buddhist temples or, after 1783, the national Tendai sect organization. But when the blind left home to work as storytellers, acupuncturists, or masseurs they became subject to self-governing associations, complete with an intricate hierarchy of ranks, regardless of their original status. The principal association of the blind was known as the *tōdō* or *tōdōza*, a guild based in Kyoto with branches in Edo and numerous other cities. True to the principle of internal autonomy for status groups, the *tōdō* maintained its own justice system, including even the right to pass death sentences on members.[28] As Gerald Groemer has demonstrated, the *tōdō* in Edo fought vigorously and successfully to maintain its identity as a de facto status group in the face of assaults by the outcaste head-man, Danzaemon, who sought to bring the guild within his political and economic orbit.[29]

Other people with handicaps were organized into self-governing com-munities with the attributes of status groups as well. The best-known example is Monoyoshi village, a community of people afflicted with Hansen's disease (leprosy) on the outskirts of Kyoto. Ordinarily, the res-idents of Monoyoshi, who were subject to the authority of Hiden'in, Kyoto's principal *hinin* community, remained segregated within their own district, but at New Year's, midsummer, and the end of the year they would venture into town and perform *monoyoshi* (originally meaning felicitous words of celebration) in front of houses in return for cash and food. If the people did not reward them sufficiently they would take goods in an edgy version of trick or treat.[30]

As these examples reveal, social taxonomy was driven principally by occupation rather than some immutable characteristic such as heredity. Accordingly, it was often possible for people to change status (at least tem-porarily) by taking up a new occupation: thus male servants in warrior households carried swords and otherwise comported themselves as petty samurai while in service, while a blind person's status as a commoner, out-caste, or member of the *tōdō* depended entirely on his involvement in farming, begging, or storytelling. There were some exceptions to this gen-eral rule—it was nearly impossible for *eta* to escape outcaste status, and commoners could sometimes acquire nominal samurai status without changing occupation—but insofar as status was linked to the perfor-mance of feudal obligations, it follows that the means of such perfor-mance—occupation—was the key criterion of status identity, and that the exceptions involved statuses that carried special burdens or privileges.

However, *occupation,* meaning here the economic means by which one fulfilled his or her status obligations, was distinct from livelihood, or the means by which one actually made a living. This is a crucial distinc-tion that will be examined at length in chapter 3. Suffice it to say here that people who engaged in the same status-based occupation could and did engage in a wide variety of economic activities in addition to those that allowed them to fulfill their feudal obligations. As a result, the lives of individuals of equivalent status varied considerably, but so long as they performed their prescribed occupations, the integrity of the status system as an institutional order was not fundamentally threatened. At the same time, occupation was rarely a matter entirely of individual voli-tion, even in cases in which one took the initiative to make a change. For example, a commoner accepted into a Buddhist sect could take the tonsure and thereby take on a new occupationally defined status identity, but a villager who managed a vacant rural temple could not preemptively remove himself from his village registry.[31]

The existence of self-governing occupational groups in and of itself did not require that status be the organizing principle behind social relations. After all, all sorts of occupational groups had existed in medieval Japan, yet status was not systematized as an all-encompassing set of institutions. In contrast to groups in the early modern period, social groups in late medieval Japan—whether defined by livelihood, residence, or some combination of the two—functioned not to integrate the various parts of the polity into an institutional whole, but on the contrary served to shield their members, both individually and collectively, from the authority of the state and the predations of competing groups.

The late medieval state (here referring to the Muromachi shogunate, 1336–1573) recognized the autonomy of social groups, not as a means to tap into their productive power, but rather as a pragmatic reflection of its inability to do so. Examples of autonomous institutions abound: the so-called free cities, such as Sakai; merchant guilds; *Ikkō ikki,* or regional polities established by the Ikkō school of the True Pure Land sect of Buddhism; Buddhist institutions in general, which maintained independent economic and even military power; landed estates *(shōen)* controlled by nobles, religious institutions, and warriors; and indeed the imperial institution itself, which fostered ties with a variety of nonagricultural peoples as a counterweight to the agricultural power base of medieval warrior regimes.[32]

Conversely, the early modern state effectively marshaled its limited power—limited because it had neither the manpower nor indeed the need to venture often into the realm of individual (or household) affairs—to organize occupational groups as its self-governing agents. In short, although occupational and residential groups in late medieval Japan were truly independent of the weak and ineffective state, status groups in the early modern period surrendered true autonomy in favor of state legitimation while retaining a measure of control over their internal affairs. Social groups evolved to escape state power in medieval Japan; they were created or validated by the state in the early modern era. The Edo outcaste headman, Danzaemon, manipulated this fact when he extended his authority over a variety of marginal groups by inventing a counterfeit genealogy for himself, in which he claimed that the founder of the Kamakura shogunate, Minamoto no Yoritomo, had granted him authority over twenty-nine occupational groups at the end of the twelfth century; the shogunate validated his authority by recognizing the genealogy despite its obviously fraudulent provenance.[33]

As Sasaki Junnosuke and others have argued, the co-optation of autonomous social groups by the nascent early modern state was in part an organic process—that is, it was a reflection of the growing need of regional warriors to gain access to local productive power to support their military activities, on the one hand, and the need of the groups themselves to forge alliances with warriors for protection, on the other hand—and in part a deliberate policy of institution building once the basic contours of the new regime were fixed in the middle decades of the seventeenth century.[34] Once this process was complete, as it was by the late seventeenth century, Japan became a "status-system society" *(mibunsei shakai)*.

The formalization of legal status, even of groups that had long existed organically, was critical to the delineation of internal social and political boundaries within the early modern polity. An examination of the position of *eta* in agricultural districts reveals the complex nature of such boundaries. Although the *eta,* as outcastes, are stereotypically associated with professions entailing contact with defilement and death, in fact many if not most Tokugawa-period *eta* lived mainly by farming and engaged in outcaste activities primarily as by-employments or to fulfill their obligations to the authorities.[35] *Eta* farming communities were subject to the same obligations as commoner peasant villages, particularly the payment of land taxes *(nengu),* but they were not generally considered to be independent, self-governing entities. Rather, they were usually subordinated as branches *(edamura)* of neighboring commoner villages, and as such were subject to the authority of the parent village leadership—without, however, being accorded the privileges of membership in the peasant community.[36] In addition to their land-tax obligations as farmers, rural *eta* were responsible for the performance of duties as outcastes. Some of these duties—such as the disposal of animal carcasses, from which valuable leather and other products could be obtained—were lucrative, but others—such as guarding prisoners and executing criminals—were not, although they did enhance their practitioners' standing within the outcaste community. In either case, because these outcaste duties were unconnected to the *eta*'s identity as farmers, the commoner parent villages had no control over them. Instead, they were overseen by regional *eta* leaders, such as the elders of Amabe and Rokujō villages for residents of the vicinity of Kyoto, or Danzaemon for residents of the Kantō plain.[37] In this example the power of political authorities to dictate status disadvantaged the *eta* doubly, first by denying their communities the autonomy enjoyed by peasants of commoner status, and second by perpetuating discrimination against them by forcing them to maintain ties to activities considered unclean. At the same time, however, their status-based monopoly on outcaste occupations (particularly leather working) appears in at least some cases to have fostered a measure of economic prosperity, reflected in part in an *eta* population that rose steadily throughout the Tokugawa period.[38]

The example of the outcastes is particularly interesting because it reveals the overlapping geographies of status in the early modern period. Rural *eta* communities were part of the familiar scenery of peasant villages, daimyo domains, and shogunal territory that composed the political landscape of Tokugawa Japan; but at the same time they were also situated on a very different map—largely invisible except to outcastes—that allocated rights to animal carcasses and distributed obligations to perform prison duty without regard to boundaries of village or domain. For instance, Suzuki Jin'emon, the hereditary *chōri (eta)* headman *(kogashira)* of Wana village, Musashi province (Saitama), controlled a territory *(shokuba)* encompassing twenty-five villages with a total assessed yield of about 11,620 *koku*. As map 2 shows, eleven of the villages were under the sole jurisdiction of the Sakura domain, but the other fourteen were divided among some eighteen different suzerains (mostly lesser vassals of the shogun, or bannermen [*hatamoto*]).[39] The Kantō was divided into a patchwork of about fifty such outcaste territories, all under the ultimate control of Danzaemon.[40] Similarly, outcastes in the vicinity of Kitsuki, in northeastern Kyushu, freely crossed domain borders to conduct police investigations; the samurai authorities took advantage of the outcastes' alternative territoriality and deputized them to apprehend criminals who would otherwise have remained beyond their reach.[41] Other marginal status groups—such as the calendar makers, fortune-tellers and *manzai* performers tied to the noble *(kuge)* Tsuchimikado house, or the houseboat people *(ebune)* of the Inland Sea region, whose movements and social relations were unconstrained by political borders—subscribed to their own geographies.[42]

Institutionalized status categories were as obvious and apparently immutable to observers as a samurai's two swords, yet their boundaries were quite porous. Perhaps the closest analogy in contemporary society is gender. Just as most people bear their gender identities without reflection, so too did status constitute a "natural" part of the social selves of people in early modern Japan. And just as gender conventions can be

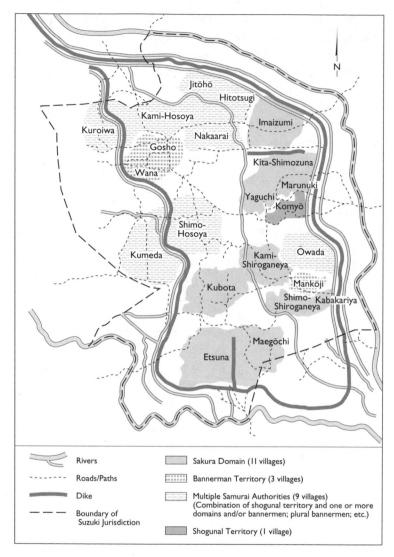

Territory of the outcaste headman Suzuki Jin'emon. Based on manuscript map, dated 13th day, 2nd month, 1794. Appendix to Saitama-
ken Dōwa Kyōiku Kenkyū Kyōgikai, ed., *Suzuki-ke monjo*, vol. 1.

challenged or even inverted, so too was status constantly subject to redefinition. But like gender, status was all-encompassing: it could be ambivalent or situationally defined but not eschewed entirely because it lay at
the core of social and legal identity.

Disruptions of status boundaries had to be rectified or at least regularized. The authorities usually sought to bring practice in line with status through such means as sumptuary decrees, which aimed at forcing commoners to behave in a manner appropriate to their station.[43] But discrepancies could also be resolved the inverse way, by adjusting status to fit social reality. For example, a commoner woman betrothed to a samurai could be adopted into a second samurai family to get around prohibitions of marriage across status lines.[44]

Some violations of status boundaries challenged the premises of Tokugawa social hierarchy and therefore attracted official concern. For example, the shogunal authorities punished eta caught attempting to pass as commoners in Osaka (conversely, however, commoners living in eta villages were not disturbed, although there seems to have been an implicit assumption that they would enter officially into eta status if the move was permanent).[45] Danzaemon also included prohibitions against passing in his orders to his underlings.[46] Similarly, in 1648 the Edo city magistrates prohibited townsmen from carrying swords in imitation of servants in samurai households, who assumed the trappings of samurai status while in service but were not considered true samurai.[47] This problem was not limited to major cities, however. In 1809, the Miyazu domain, north of Kyoto, issued the following edict:

> Peasants are forbidden to use surnames or carry swords without permission. In particular, peasants are not to send their children into light service in samurai households for a while, then bring them home to the countryside and let them wear swords, even if they continue to receive some small amount of assistance from their former masters.[48]

With official sanction, however, forays across status boundaries could serve as a necessary corrective to the contradictions built into the system. In all instances, status boundaries were defined situationally, and so movement was not necessarily permanent or even intended as genuine, as the following example from the Nanbu domain reveals. In 1836, Shōsuke, the peasant scribe at a rural intendant's office (daikansho), was sent by the authorities to the Mito domain to deal with the aftermath of a vendetta exacted by a local youth. While on his mission, he was permitted to use a surname and carry two swords, and thereby present himself as a samurai.[49] Shōsuke engaged in status transvestism, assuming a form appropriate to his task without the pretense of a more profound or lasting transformation. The artifice was necessary because his duties were of a sort suited to a village official, yet his role as an official representative of the Nanbu domain called for someone of samurai status.

The *gōmune,* a group of entertainers in Edo, epitomize the situational character of status identities. *Gōmune* were commoners who engaged in performance and begging; their standard repertoire consisted primarily of imitations of established arts—noh, religious storytelling, puppetry, and the like—which they performed on street corners, temple grounds, and other public places. The *gōmune's* begging, albeit disguised as performance, infringed on the outcaste map of Edo, in which territories for begging were carefully delineated. Accordingly, in 1651 their leader, Isoemon (later known as Nidayū), was placed under the authority of Kuruma Zenshichi, headman of the Edo *hinin,* who in turn answered to the *eta* leader, Danzaemon. Unlike other marginal groups under outcaste authority, however, the *gōmune* retained their commoner status, so that once an individual *gōmune* gave up his profession Zenshichi lost all claims to authority over him.[50]

The religious overtones of some status divisions further complicated the drawing of boundaries in early modern Japan. The institutionalization of outcaste status in the seventeenth century formalized an earlier distinction between the "base" people *(senmin)* and the "good" or "common" people *(ryōmin* or *heimin)*. Although the exact nature of the connection between the medieval base people and early modern outcastes is still a topic of spirited debate,[51] without question medieval attitudes about the pollution of death and the nature of people not bound to the land (Amino Yoshihiko's so-called free people *[jiyūmin]*) informed early modern attitudes toward status in general and the outcastes in particular.[52] At the very least, status as an expression of religious understandings of social relations helps to account for the castelike element in outcaste status: the pollution that devolved on *eta* by virtue of their status transcended the putative cleanliness or defilement of their actual livelihoods, which is why *eta* farmers were not treated as commoners even when they fulfilled the nominal criteria for inclusion in the peasantry.

The institutionalization of outcaste status by the early modern regime politicized the religious bifurcation of medieval society, and rendered the base realm of the outcastes autonomous yet clearly and in multiple ways subordinated to the quotidian world of samurai and commoners. The autonomy of the outcastes represented the drawing of a significant political boundary, for it rendered their largely invisible map of carrion and condemned prisoners exogenous to the visible map of shogunate, domains, and peasant villages, and explains the regime's readiness to defer to the outcaste authorities' judgment on matters pertaining to the status of outcastes.[53]

Tsukada Takashi gives an example of this phenomenon from Oshi, a small domain north of Edo. In 1823 and 1824, outcastes from Kumagaya and Omi villages asserted their right to guard the domain's jail in the castle town of Gyōda, a duty theretofore performed by outcaste residents of Mida village. Guard duty was coveted because it helped outcastes secure both higher standing within the outcaste community and economic privileges from the authorities. The Kumagaya and Omi outcastes based their claim on the fact that their villages lay within the Oshi domain, while Mida did not. However, Mida prevailed because its territory *(ba* or *shokuba),* as recognized by the regional outcaste authorities, included Gyōda. Under pressure from Danzaemon, representatives of Kumagaya and Omi eventually signed a document agreeing not to perform guard duty even if so ordered by domain officials, who were unaware of the contours of outcaste territoriality.[54]

Status, as a set of relationships between social groups and the state and among the groups themselves, determined how individuals and their communities participated in society. Status, and with it a relationship to the state, was so deeply embedded into the structure of communities that it is difficult to disaggregate political authority from the realm of everyday life. Whereas unilateral classification by the Japanese was largely responsible for the Ainu's barbarian identity, status groups secured their position through a measure of active participation in the creation (and constant re-creation) of the political order. This assertion holds despite the fact that the social groups later categorized by status antedated the institution building of the late sixteenth and early seventeenth centuries, and were thus products of an organic process similar to the one that shaped Ainu society in the early modern period.

The core polity had no space that was absolutely removed from the status system and hence the authority of the state. In other words, there was no space analogous to the Ainu's inland *kotan,* to which people could retreat to escape the institutions of status and the power that lay behind it. When people did in effect try to escape—by becoming unregistered transients, for example—the state sought them out and tagged them with a status identity, however tenuous, whether they liked it or accepted it or not, through such means as decrees directed against the unregistered.

At the same time, it is also true that status was not the sole focus of the social lives and economic activities of people within the core polity. Status was an inescapable mark of one's relationship to political authority, but political authority alone did not give meaning to daily life and identity. In other words, status blanketed social relations, but it was not the only factor to determine the content and context of economic activity and cultural production.

The state recognized and indeed embraced the internal diversity of status groups, for organizing society around status categories did not require complete homogeneity within status groups. Knowing that someone was a commoner tells us much about his relationship to feudal authority and the assumptions he and those with whom he interacted brought to social relations, particularly when they crossed status boundaries, but it tells us little about his daily life or standard of living. In particular, it tells us nothing about his place within his own status-based community (whether organized around residence, occupation, or service to an intermediary lord), for communities had complex political structures of their own. Indeed, within the context of the community—where the common status identity of its members was taken for granted—being a commoner (or samurai, outcaste, or priest) was not immediately relevant to the functioning of social relations like marriage, hospitality, commerce, and religion. Those affairs were products of the intricate network of ties within the community itself. Feudal authority ceded autonomy to the community and distanced itself from the social relations within it, provided the community met its status-based obligations, stayed clear of other communities' internal affairs, and preserved social order.

Herman Ooms points to the dual structure of political authority as a set of institutions transcending the community, on the one hand, and operating entirely within it, on the other hand, when he uses status both in the sense I have invoked here and, following Pierre Bourdieu, to refer to the internal hierarchies of peasant villages.[55] Ooms's strategy of conflating the two senses of the term effectively highlights the fact that the various dimensions of status were indeed inseparable in the eyes of individual peasants: a shared identity as the tax-paying residents of an agricultural community was the mostly unspoken precondition of participation in a complex and more immediately powerful hierarchy internal to the community itself. Even if one was simply considered a commoner by the domain's or shogun's officials, in the eyes of the community, one might be a village headman (and hence able to distribute tax obligations and adjudicate disputes), a descendant of a founding family (and hence eligible for preferential treatment in village affairs), a landless cultivator (and hence vulnerable to the predations of both landlord and village officialdom), and so on. Given the impact of internal status distinctions on the routines of daily life, it is only natural that it was these distinctions that mattered most to members of the village community. As Ooms demonstrates, moreover, those who ran afoul of the communal status order found themselves in an extremely weak position, even to the point of jeopardizing their lives and property.[56]

There is no need to stop at the level of the community, however, for yet another realm of status differentials existed within the household. Just as the feudal authorities were generally content to validate and supervise community affairs from a distance, so too did the community largely leave households to order their own internal power structures, provided they respected general rules that preserved community integrity, such as those that governed property disposition and hence the community's ability to meet its feudal obligations.

Real life is infinitely complex. Even with all the structures to classify and thereby constrain social relations—household, community, and national status order—people nonetheless found ample space to engage in all manner of activities autonomously of status, however defined. My invocation of status as a fundamental principle of the early modern state is not intended to deny the importance or immediacy of other dimensions of social identity. Rather, my aim is to expose the institutional framework that underlay society in all its complexity. However heterogeneous individuals' experiences were, at the broadest level status shaped and constrained their lives.

The status system therefore pervaded society, and thereby gave meaning to its internal structures, but it did not comprise the totality of social relations, particularly at the level of everyday life. Quite the contrary: the institutional structure of status ensured that the state would remain remote from the mundane joys and anxieties, alliances and rivalries— and naked power struggles—that preoccupied people as they went about their lives. The state did not care much whether Influential Peasant foisted part of his tax burden onto the shoulders of Downtrodden Peasant—at least not so long as the village met its tax bill and order prevailed. If things got out of hand, of course, the state cared a lot and took appropriate action to reestablish order. It could not do otherwise because, in addition to its need for the village's tax receipts, providing benevolent rule through the preservation of order was its end of the feudal bargain. The very pervasiveness of the status system freed the state from the need to intervene directly into community affairs because it could depend on internal hierarchies to take care of the details of administration. Of course, the community power structure mattered much more to Influential Peasant and Downtrodden Peasant than their shared status identity as commoners, for the former was what determined in most cases whether Influential would in fact pay his fair share, or whether Downtrodden's grudge against Influential would turn ugly. The fact that such matters were the community's internal concern does not detract from the centrality of the status order, for it was status that established the ground rules for their dispute and channeled its eventual resolution.

How different this was from the modern state, which feels compelled to look into every nook and cranny of social life—into the community, the workplace, the household, the very minds of its subjects. The modern state is the cop on his beat, the postman on his rounds, the brigadier at the parade grounds, the functionary surveying hygiene practices, the teacher at his lectern, the emperor in his carriage. But even the modern state does a poor job of implicating itself so thoroughly into individuals' lives and minds as to efface any distinction between individual and national identity. It strives constantly to achieve that effacement, for striving is its nature. It strives but never achieves, for never achieving is its nature, too.

In sum, if the modern state, with its busybody proclivities and formidable arsenal of technologies, cannot make itself the sole referent of identity, we can hardly expect the early modern state, with its institutionalized disinterest in individual and community affairs and limited—and largely symbolic—bag of tricks, to have achieved the same goal. But the early modern state's power, however limited, was very real.

CHAPTER 3

Status and the Politics
of the Quotidian

If the status system was the defining feature of the early modern order, surely its collapse marked the onset of modernity. Central to this transformation was a reconfiguration of the relationship between economy and social order. During the Tokugawa period, economic relations were given social expression through the status system, then subsumed within it. For example, although a compelling economic imperative—hunger—drove the original *gōmune* into the streets to sing and dance for a few coppers,[1] once the *gōmune* were imbued with an identity as such and placed under the authority of outcastes, the strictly economic nature of their activities was thoroughly subordinated to their social identity as members of a particular status group. Their livelihoods as performers, in other words, could be comprehended only in the context of the status system. The example of the *gōmune* is particularly striking because of the close relationship between their economic activities and their status—once they gave up performing and begging they returned to being commoners—but the same general principle obtained throughout early modern Japan: livelihood had no meaning as an economic activity divorced from status.

The ordering of social groups through the status system was a political act. The transition from the early modern to the modern therefore entailed a reorientation of the politics of the quotidian, by which I mean the political significance attached to the ways people led their everyday lives. For instance, many people in Tokugawa Japan supported themselves through handicraft production, but while the daily routines and living standards of the craftspeople may have been generally similar, political understandings of their production varied considerably. Hence the everyday existence of an outcaste maker of leather-soled sandals (setta) was perceived as being qualitatively different from that of a commoner weaver, while both lives differed radically from that of a samurai who constructed umbrellas to make ends meet. The status system did not, however, distinguish among different ways of organizing production: the weaver's formal status identity as a peasant (hyakushō) remained fixed whether she worked alone at home or in a manufactory with two dozen other women.

Through the subordination of economic activity to social status, the Tokugawa order could absorb a certain degree of economic-structural change without experiencing a fundamental threat to feudal institutions. Absent the status system, economic relations in the Meiji period and after achieved greater influence on the ordering of society: put starkly, class came to affect social relations more immediately and more obviously than in the past. The emergence of a new politics of the quotidian was fraught with difficulty and disruption. Its roots lay in the economic growth and structural change that began well before the Meiji Restoration, and particularly in the widening gap between the network of occupations defined by the demands of the status system, on the one hand, and the increasing diversity of livelihoods pursued by Japanese people of all statuses, on the other. Under the new, modern politics of the quotidian, the locus of political meaning in everyday life shifted from the corporate status group to production and the individual's (or household's) relationship to it.[2]

OCCUPATION AND LIVELIHOOD

In this chapter I will discuss the relationship between status and economic activity in the Tokugawa period and outline the mechanism by which economic activity was detached from status during the transition to the Meiji order after 1868. To elucidate the relationship between status and economy, I shall distinguish between occupation, which refers to the economic activity linked to a household's formal status, and livelihood, or the economic means by which households actually supported themselves. This analytical distinction between occupation and livelihood is mine, but it does to an extent reflect a conceptual framework that would have been familiar in early modern Japan. Occupation, with its reference to political institutions, recalls the Japanese shokubun, a lot or station in life (*bun,* an element found also in *mibun,* or social status) tied to a specific type of work *(shoku),* while livelihood is similar to such terms as *tosei* (literally "crossing the world," the most common way to describe making a living at something) and *nariwai* (also read *seigyō*), the business *(gyō)* of life *(sei).*

The politics of the quotidian in early modern Japan was bifurcated between the explicitly political (in the sense of being linked to governmental authority) realm of status-based occupations and the explicitly economic realm of livelihood. The two elements were by no means equal for, as we just saw in the example of the handicraft producers, occupational status identities alone situated individuals within the political structure. At the same time, however, the actual means of livelihood allowed for a great deal of diversity in the everyday lives of members of status groups, including even residents of the same local community. The creation of a new politics of the quotidian in the Meiji period supplanted occupation (in the early modern sense) with the new category of imperial subjecthood. That is, whereas subjects in early modern Japan served the state through their status-specific economic activities, after the Restoration serving emperor and nation became every subject's "occupation" insofar as economic activity in general contributed to the project of building a modern nation. Under this new order livelihood gained free rein to express itself in the nominally extrapolitical realm of economic class.

Although the occupation and means of livelihood of most Tokugawa households overlapped considerably, the two were almost never entirely identical, and they were often quite distinct. The gap between occupation and livelihood endowed the early modern political economy with an element of flexibility, allowing the system to bend but not break in the face of economic-structural change. This elasticity may help account for the relatively smooth transition from Tokugawa to Meiji, although we must nevertheless take seriously the very real disruptions that accompanied the transition. My argument, in brief, is that the Tokugawa system accommodated the distinction between occupation and livelihood, although at the cost of considerable institutional complexity. The Meiji regime eliminated the distinction by monetizing the obligations owed by its subjects through collecting taxes in cash and the abolition of status categories, a disruptive move that nonetheless benefited many Japanese. Although my goal here is not to account for the causes of the collapse of the Tokugawa regime per se, distinguishing between occupation and livelihood does help to clarify the role of economic change in bringing about the Meiji Restoration.

A brief examination of the status category of "peasant" (hyakushō) will illustrate the distinction between occupation and livelihood in early modern Japan.[3] Both stereotypically and typically, peasants grew rice, which was both the staple grain and the principal means to calculate the productivity of land and its attendant tax obligations. Rice is a labor-intensive crop, so many peasants devoted the bulk of their time to its cultivation. Occupation and livelihood were nearly identical for such persons: their occupations (shokubun) as peasants (hyakushō) obliged them to pay land taxes to their domainal lords, while as subsistence farmers, they derived their livelihoods (nariwai) from the production of the same rice with which they paid their taxes.

For much of the Tokugawa period, a great many peasant households came close to this archetype, but with the development of a market economy the gap between occupation and livelihood began to grow. After the middle of the eighteenth century, peasants throughout Japan commonly engaged in a variety of by-employments; moreover, in areas where it was ecologically feasible, sericulture and the cultivation of a wide range of cash crops came to dominate the agricultural economy. The production of silk textiles, handicrafts, and processed agricultural products became an important source of supplemental income for peasant households and the engine of protoindustrial development.[4] As an example of the importance of by-employments to the late Tokugawa peasant economy, Thomas C. Smith notes that in 1843 farm households constituted 82 percent of the commoner population of Kaminoseki district in Chōshū, in westernmost Honshu, but nonagricultural pursuits supplied 55 percent of the district's income.[5] This example—bolstered by a wealth of similar evidence from around the archipelago—suggests that by the end of the Tokugawa period a significant discrepancy had developed between the occupational definition of peasants as land tax–paying cultivators and their actual livelihoods, in which grain production was but one item in a diverse portfolio of economic activities.

Many people legally classified as peasants led economic lives even further removed from agricultural production than the part-time handicraft producers just described. By the nineteenth century, village populations frequently included a number of artisans and merchants who neither owned land nor farmed but were considered peasants all the same because they contributed through their village communities to the fulfillment of status-based obligations.[6] Within these same farming districts a class of rural entrepreneurs, the gōnō (literally "rich farmers"), emerged over the course of the late eighteenth and early nineteenth centuries. As

Edward Pratt has shown, *gōnō* in centers of cotton, silk, tea, and sake production oversaw substantial commercial, manufacturing, and financial enterprises even as they retained a formal occupational identity as peasant cultivators.[7] In fact, Pratt's *gōnō* often owned substantial tracts of land, but farmed little of it themselves.[8] In fishing and mountain communities, entire villages supported themselves without recourse to farming beyond small kitchen gardens. In such cases, marine and forest products were generally substituted for grain in the payment of taxes, but the status-based designation "peasant" applied to the villagers nonetheless.[9] In short, plenty of peasants made a significant part of their livings at things other than farming, and some "peasants" did not farm at all.

One might expect a peasant intent on interrogating the bases of Tokugawa rule to chafe at an institutional structure that bound him to an increasingly obsolescent ideology of a rural economy centered on agricultural production. However, that seems to have rarely been the case. Students of popular contention in early modern Japan have found ample evidence that peasants subscribed to a moral economy in which they fulfilled their status-based obligations in exchange for their lords' promises of benevolent rule *(jinsei)*.[10] Peasants might rise up in reaction to economic change—sometimes because they were hurt by its consequences, other times because they wanted to enjoy more of its fruits—but their calls for reform were always predicated on the legitimacy of the status order as the basis of political economy.

Even peasants who had lost faith in the moral covenant of benevolence argued for the integrity of peasanthood as a social category. A famous example is Miura Meisuke, a village official in northeastern Honshu who was imprisoned for leading the Sanheii Rebellion of 1853, a massive protest against the Nanbu domain's commercial policies. His "prison notebooks" *(gokuchūki)* close with an exhortation to his family to emigrate to Hokkaido, where they might flourish under the benevolent rule of the Tokugawa shogunate. Miura's defiant attitude toward the Nanbu authorities has made him the darling of historians eager to find a revolutionary tradition in the early modern countryside; however, the panegyrics to him neglect to mention that the bulk of his "notebooks"—actually a series of letters to his wife and children—are in fact filled with pointers on success in commerce and secret recipes for the homemade remedies Miura sold to supplement his agricultural income.[11]

Less well known but even more striking is the story of Hayashi Hachiemon, a sixty-year-old village headman who was imprisoned by the Kawagoe domain in 1822 for leading a protest against a tax increase during a period of crop failures and rural depopulation. While in jail Hayashi wrote a remarkable document he entitled "Instructions for the Promotion of Agriculture" *(Kannō kyōkunroku)*, which was partly a detailed account of the uprising that had landed him in jail, and partly a testament to his children.[12]

By the time he wrote his "Instructions," Hayashi had been in jail for five years. He insisted that domain officials eager to pin responsibility for the protest on a scapegoat had framed him. As an elderly man who had endured a three-hanky tearjerker of a life before surviving five years in the notoriously squalid conditions of a Tokugawa jail (where incarcerated suspects often died before being formally charged), Hayashi had ample cause to feel bitter toward a system that expropriated the wealth of peasants to support an often idle ruling class.[13] His bitterness is palpable in his dismissal of domain officials as "tremendous fools" *(ōbaka)*.[14] Yet his testament offers nothing but support—guarded, to be sure—for the status system and his own place in it. It is worth quoting at length:

> A peasant's work *[gyō]* is filled with hardship and poverty, and it is difficult for even the young to endure, but one should put up with it nonetheless. Of course, young people want to dress finely and eat well, but such an attitude would bring ruin on a peasant household, making it a laughingstock living in unsightly hardship. Yet on reflection it is clear that no one's work is as easy as a farmer's *[nōka]*. Warriors have the difficulty of outfitting and comporting themselves properly, and they must serve [their lord]. Moreover, even if they are careful, unexpected problems can arise and cause embarrassment, and their distinctions of rank *[jōge no kakushiki]* are troublesome *[mendō]*. Artisans and merchants must depend on others to make their living, with the result that in public they must be circumspect and cannot freely speak their minds. Their lives may be comfortable, but in exchange they must endure all measure of mental hardship *[shintsū]*. Monks, priests, and doctors all have to live up to the dictates of their chosen paths.
>
> Farmers need only stave off poverty and they are free *[jiyū]* to do as they please. Among farmers, ordinary peasants *[hirabyakushō]* have it the best: they need not concern themselves with differences in rank *[kakushiki]*, nor do they have to lower themselves before anyone other than village officials. Even then, so long as they pay the land taxes and other levies due to the village headman and otherwise keep a low profile, they can avoid contact with officials entirely. Sending servants to perform corvée and post-station duties makes it possible for them to elude that sort of thing as well. The cultivator *[sakujin]* alone can get by without dealing with anyone else: so long as he can get to his paddies and fields to work, he can make his living without hardship. The only one who can stay in his house and say whatever he pleases is the peasant.[15]

Hayashi's prophylactic against poverty is diligence, particularly between the ages of twenty-five and forty. At forty a farmer can retire, avoid participating directly in agricultural labor, and pass his days in comfort. The secret to success, then, is to resolve to work hard for fifteen years in the prime of life. Although Hayashi's injunctions include the usual moral exhortations against gambling, fighting, drunkenness, debauchery, and sumo wrestling, they are appended to the document almost as an afterthought.

Clearly, many peasants would have had difficulty following Hayashi's advice. Notwithstanding his complaints about the hardship and sorrow of his own life, his household must have been quite well off for him to assume that one could leave the backbreaking routine of farming behind at middle age and settle into a quiet life of free speech. No doubt his experience languishing in jail as a framed headman made the lives of the rank and file appear especially attractive to him, but Hayashi's poor neighbors, struggling their entire lives to put millet gruel on their dinner tables, never enjoyed the sort of leisure he holds out as life's due reward.

For our purposes, however, Hayashi's advice is fascinating precisely because of its impracticality. He favors the peasant's station in life because peasants alone can avoid both the troublesome rules of social interaction that govern the lives of warriors, clergy, and doctors and the groveling subservience demanded of townsmen and officials of all statuses. At the same time, he clearly distinguishes between occupation and livelihood: his use of the term "ordinary peasant" (hirabyakushō) alludes not to income, but rather to office holding; it refers to middling villagers who owned land (and thus enjoyed the rights of full-fledged members of the peasant community) but were not encumbered with the responsibilities of service as village officials. He generally uses the term "peasant" (hyakushō) to refer to status, but, significantly, he prefers "farmer" or "cultivator" (nōka or sakujin) to refer to livelihood. In other words, his ideal is to have an undistinguished occupational status but to amass wealth through the diligent pursuit of livelihood during the prime of life.

Although the status system insulated Tokugawa institutions from the immediate effects of economic change, it is nonetheless true that commercialization and eventually the beginnings of capitalist production undermined the integrity of status boundaries. As an example of the increasing dissonance between the political-institutional and social-economic natures of status groupings, Tsukada Takashi has examined the transformation of Watanabe village, the principal eta community in Osaka, over the course of the Tokugawa and early Meiji periods. He argues that prior to the late eighteenth century the elders of the village, who controlled the leather trade throughout western Japan and had authority over *eta* in the greater Osaka area, put the fulfillment of their (and their community's) feudal obligations as *eta* ahead of independent economic activities, but by the end of the Tokugawa era many of the same families (as well as new ones that had risen to prominence) favored business ventures over their official duties. By the 1880s, the community's leading citizens—now officially commoners—had invented for themselves an entrepreneurial past in which their former role as custodians of relations between the outcaste community and society at large played no part.[16]

The example of Watanabe is particularly striking, but in its essence the case is not unusual. Throughout the countryside, commercialization undermined the economic insularity of peasant villages, often leading to tensions between a small group of relatively well-to-do families at the top of village society and a larger number of their less fortunate neighbors.[17] In a strict, institutional sense, the nature of peasant status did not change whatever the consequences of economic change, for the levying of tax obligations and the registration of villagers remained essentially the same. Yet the reality of social and economic relations made peasanthood a complex status category. In particular, the spread of protoindustrial manufacturing during the last half-century or so of the Tokugawa era led to the appearance of a class of entrepreneurs whose place in an emergent (if not yet fully articulated) capitalist mode of production was fundamentally different from that of both peasant cultivators and the rent-seeking merchant capitalists who oversaw distribution and finance under the feudal regime.[18]

As Hatanaka Toshiyuki has demonstrated in his analysis of the leather-soled-sandal trade in the Osaka area, protoindustrial development could sometimes even transcend the distinction between commoner and outcaste status, leading commoners to take up residence in outcaste villages in order to oversee their entrepreneurial interests. In such cases, the economic imperatives of sandal production clearly took precedence over the political and social barriers to intimate contact between outcastes and commoners.[19]

Economic and social conflict within peasant villages was as old as the Tokugawa period itself, but by the end of the era dislocation had spread well beyond the confines of the village community into the public realm, where it became the pressing concern of the feudal authorities. Tsukada points to this development when he differentiates between status and condition *(jōtai)*, referring to the increasing appearance of people whose social condition did not fit their status, particularly after about 1790. This distinction is similar to the one I make between occupation and livelihood, though Tsukada uses *condition* to describe social relations in general rather than economic activity in particular. Tsukada discusses the apparently rapid expansion of the population of unregistered transients *(mushuku)* as a case in point.[20] Although many *mushuku*—literally "without lodgings"—were indeed homeless, it was their absence from population registers rather than residence or lack thereof that marked them as unplaced persons.[21] They were thus the commoner counterparts of masterless samurai *(rōnin)*, and the shogunate often paired the two in its calls for the restoration of social order. As we saw in chapter 2, the shogunate sometimes called on *hinin* in Edo and other major urban centers to deal with *mushuku*, either by returning them to their home villages or by incorporating them within their own ranks. However, the problem was by no means limited to cities, nor indeed were *mushuku* necessarily the down-and-out sorts who would come within the outcastes' orbit. This was because villages removed peasants from their registers for any number of reasons, of which absconding was but one.

There were many cases in which village authorities knew exactly where an errant peasant was but removed him from the register nonetheless to avoid the burden of communal responsibility if he were found guilty of a crime. For example, in 1849, the leaders of Mishuku village in Suruga province (Shizuoka) found themselves faced with the aftermath of a messy case in which a *mushuku* staying at an unlicensed inn run by a local peasant was killed by a band of outlaws, apparently in retribution for an earlier murder. Although the villagers knew who this man was and where he had come from, his status as a *mushuku* meant that he was officially unplaced and hence unknown. The man's death per se was not the problem; instead, the difficulty arose out of the fact that the peasant, Gen'emon, was not supposed to have been offering lodging to an unregistered commoner in the first place. If the village leaders had reported the incident, their failure to oversee Gen'emon's activities would have prompted a criminal investigation. They accordingly buried the body in a local temple cemetery, hoping that no one would miss the dead man. In the meantime, they removed Gen'emon from the village registry—and thus made him a *mushuku*—as a precaution, on the premise that he had absconded. (In fact, he likely remained in hiding in or near the village.) Unfortunately, however, because the dead man was a casualty in an outlaw war, officials from the domain and the shogunate came to investigate, causing the whole cover-up to blow up in the faces of the embarrassed village officials. In the end, the headman and Gen'emon's relatives were subjected to a lengthy and devastatingly expensive inquiry in Edo, but by keeping to their story that Gen'emon had disappeared they were able to limit their penalty to fines and administrative punishment, saving themselves and Gen'emon from criminal charges.[22]

Although this particular example may appear to be little more than a curiosity, in fact at the time such incidents were rightly perceived to be a consequence of economic change. Gen'emon took advantage of his village's location on a pilgrimage route to Mt. Fuji to run an illegal inn, an enterprise that would not have been possible were it not for the economic growth that ensured steady traffic on the road. Gang warfare was viewed as a by-product of economic dislocation and its attendant moral decline, for a stable agrarian economy should not have produced recruits into the ranks of outlaws and gamblers. Accordingly, officials and ideologues saw widespread disorder as evidence of the collapse of the rural economy, and with it instability in status-based social institutions. Moreover, the village officials were able to bring the incident to a more or less favorable conclusion in part because the headman's elder brother had been adopted into the household of an influential bannerman's needy retainer.

The status system was flexible enough to absorb a degree of social change without disrupting the integrity of status groupings. As such, it was compatible with the institutional structure of the Tokugawa economy, which provided an environment amenable to growth and the beginnings of structural transformation. But neither social nor economic institutions could contain change forever. By the end of the Tokugawa period, the status system had grown heavy on duty but light on privilege as the demands of a collapsing regime put a tremendous burden on society while the autonomy of status groups rapidly eroded in the face of economic change.[23]

The regime did what it could to respond to the situation. For instance, in 1805 the shogunate established the Kantō Regulatory Patrol (Kantō torishimari shutsuyaku) in an attempt to coax unregistered peasants, masterless samurai, and other unplaced persons back into the status fold. Although it began with a limited mandate to round up disorderly elements, a reform in 1827 put the patrol at the center of an ambitious plan to revitalize rural society. One of the new policy's goals was to bring fallow land back under cultivation and thereby reestablish peasant villages as viable economic units.[24] Not surprisingly, the endeavor achieved little lasting success, but the imperatives of the feudal order made it difficult for the authorities to come up with a more creative or effective response.

The turmoil immediately following the Restoration created similar problems for the nascent Meiji regime. In Kyoto, local officials tried for a time to maintain the distinction between *hinin* and commoner beggars *(kotsujiki)* who had taken to the streets in the aftermath of the Boshin War, the conflict that followed the proclamation of imperial rule. Ordinarily, all such persons would have come under the authority of the *hinin* leaders of Hiden'in, but the sheer number of people dislocated by the war overwhelmed the outcaste authority structure. Accordingly, the city gathered vagrants *(ryūmin)* of all sorts, including those with physical handicaps, into a workhouse in the eleventh month of 1868. True to the logic of the status system, *hinin* in the facility remained under the control of the Hiden'in elders. However, all inmates participated in the cleaning and police duties historically delegated to outcastes. All, moreover, learned handicrafts and other useful skills while being subjected to a disciplinary regime of early rising and clean living. A government report commented that although some inmates were indeed the victims of misfortune, most had brought their sorry state on themselves through gambling, debauchery, and laziness. Given the turmoil of the period immediately after the Restoration, this explanation is scarcely credible, but it fit well-established understandings of the causes of dislocation. In any case, beggars received tags marking them as *hinin* or commoner vagrants; those without tags were not to receive alms, regardless of status. By taking direct control over beggars and other displaced persons, city officials paved the way for the elimination of Hiden'in's residual authority after the abolition of outcaste status in 1871.[25] Although the perception of unprecedented disorder was similar, the officials in Kyoto transcended status in their response in a way that the shogunate could not when it instituted its patrols of the Kantō. The dissonance between status and condition was too great for them to do otherwise.

The policies of both the Kantō Regulatory Patrol and the Kyoto officials toward beggars and vagrants were products of the need to control and contain disorder at the lower margins of society. At the other end of the social spectrum, the feudal authorities worked to avert disorder by manipulating the distinction between occupation and livelihood among samurai. The occupation of the samurai, of course, was "warrior," with the attendant duty of providing military service to their lords. In practice, service usually meant some sort of administrative post, but the concept was sufficiently flexible to accommodate a surprisingly wide range of activities. For example, Mark Ravina has described the attempts of two domains in northeastern Honshu, Tsugaru (he refers to it as Hirosaki) and Yonezawa, to revitalize their finances in the eighteenth century by putting some of their samurai to work farming (in Tsugaru) or weaving silk textiles (in Yonezawa). Here we see samurai whose livelihoods depended in large measure on the income they earned from farming or weaving; indeed, their participation in economic activities generally associated with the peasantry might lead one to question whether they remained samurai in a meaningful sense at all. In fact, they did. The Tsugaru and Yonezawa domain authorities cleverly reinterpreted the status-based duties of the rusticated samurai to include tilling and weaving. The affected samurai in these domains thus remained secure in their samurai status because the domains treated their economic activities as the functional equivalent of military service.[26]

Within the samurai status group ranks were intricately delineated, but imperfectly coordinated with the peacetime needs of the shogunate and domains. This gave rise to a situation in which rank and position within a lord's retainer band functioned similarly to status-based occupation and livelihood in society more broadly. In brief, rank determined one's hereditary stipend and the range of official posts one could fill. Samurai ranks were minutely ordered, with the result that the pool of men with a rank appropriate for a given position could be quite small, especially at the highest levels of domain administration. Domains could and did elevate men permanently to higher rank, but they were reluctant to do so because of the fiscal strain and inflexibility that would result from creating a top-heavy retainer band. As an alternative way to get talented men into important positions, many domains adopted the expedient of paying supplemental stipends *(tashidaka* or *yakuryō)* that temporarily raised their recipients to a rank sufficiently high to serve in a particular position. The recipient benefited from the extra income and the access to a position higher than his hereditary rank would normally permit, while the domain benefited from his service.[27] For our purposes, the salient point is that for a samurai, hereditary rank determined the type of service he provided to his lord, but his rank could be adjusted nominally upward to satisfy the needs of the domain. In such cases, the officeholder's "real" (that is, hereditary) rank did not change: on dismissal from his high post he would revert to his normal stipend. The status system could accommodate the exigencies of practical administration, provided it was accommodated in turn: hence, because ranks ("occupations") and posts ("livelihoods") were distinct, a domain could not simply appoint a man of low rank to a high post without first temporarily elevating him to an appropriately high nominal rank.

As the Tokugawa period progressed, a combination of increasing expenditures and flat tax revenues left many domains unable to pay their rank-and-file samurai adequate stipends.[28] Moreover, because the shogunate and most domains had more low-ranking samurai than posts for them to fill, there were large numbers of unemployed and underemployed warriors. These men received meager stipends as their birthright but were forced to take up handicraft production or other wage work to support themselves. By the eve of the Meiji Restoration the impoverished warrior who assembled umbrellas to support himself had become a stock figure in depictions of life in Edo. So long as they remained in the pool of men available for active duty, however, they retained their status as samurai notwithstanding their actual condition as marginal artisans. By the same token, however, younger sons of low-ranking samurai who were neither adopted into other households as the heir nor given service appointments of their own dropped out of samurai status entirely. In the lowest ranks of the samurai, then, we see some men whose occupations (as warriors) and livelihoods (as artisans) were almost completely divorced, and others whose loss of samurai status brought the two into proximity because their livelihoods as artisans or wage workers provided the means to fulfill the status-based duties of their new occupations.

Although the boundary between samurai and commoner status was quite porous, it remained meaningful thanks to the powerful symbolic value of the use of surnames, the right to carry two swords, and other markers of warrior status. Enough men opted for membership in a lord's retainer band to maintain the boundary, even when life as a commoner offered greater freedom and material comfort, but not all did so: the author Takizawa Bakin, for example, famously relinquished his samurai status to devote himself to his writing, but he had a change of heart and spent the final years of his life trying to raise enough money to buy a commission for his son or grandson.[29]

The authorities understood the value of samurai status and often took advantage of that value, sometimes to the extent of putting a price tag on it, as Bakin knew. Both the shogunate and the domains frequently rewarded peasant officials, privileged merchants, and other commoners who had rendered meritorious service or financial assistance with the right to carry two swords and publicly use a surname. This practice—which dates to the seventeenth century—did no violence to the status order; if anything, it reinforced it by affirming the inherent desirability of the warriors' status privileges without pretending that the commoners so rewarded had become genuine samurai. During the latter part of the Tokugawa period, however, the emergence of an expanding class of wealthy merchants and financiers, combined with financial crisis in the shogunate and domains, prompted many domains to grant nominal samurai status to commoners who made monetary contributions to the regime (sometimes according to a fixed price schedule). The shift was subtle—purchasers of samurai status did not necessarily enter into service—but extremely significant nonetheless, in part because the nominal samurai effectively removed themselves from their status-based communities. Among the most serious complaints of Miura Meisuke and his fellow rebels in Nanbu in 1853 was the charge that rural merchants who had bought samurai status used their privileged position to evade taxes and exploit local cultivators. They accordingly demanded the return of all such persons from the past half-century to their previous status immediately. The domain rejected the demand, although it did institute reforms to curb the nominal samurai's most egregious abuses of their purchased status privileges.[30]

The gap between occupation and livelihood was especially stark for many outcastes. As we have seen, the principal group of outcastes, the *eta,* fulfilled obligations to the authorities in the form of prison guard duty, low-level police work, and the disposal of animal carcasses. Although in some domains these duties could occupy a great deal of the *eta*'s energy, in most areas outcastes lived mainly by farming, the manufacture of footwear and leather goods, or commerce, with their status-specific duties at most a part-time pursuit. Thus, for example, Suzuki Jin'emon, the outcaste headman of Wana village, devoted most of his household's labor to farming (which served as a secondary "occupation" insofar as he paid land taxes) and to a side business manufacturing and selling medicines.[31] Jin'emon's pharmaceutical business was not marked as an outcaste livelihood (recall that Miura Meisuke also manufactured drugs), but even those outcastes who engaged in tanning and other activities over which the outcastes maintained a monopoly did not do so to fulfill status-specific obligations. (It is important to stress here that although the disposal of dead animals was a feudal obligation of outcastes, the production of commodities such as leather from carcasses was not, except to the extent that some outcastes provided saddles and other leather goods to the samurai authorities as taxes.) Status often channeled people into a particular livelihood, but even outcastes enjoyed some agency in deciding how to make a living.

As the above examples show, the relationship between occupation and livelihood was a complex one. It appears that the gap between the two generally widened during the late Tokugawa period, particularly within the commoner population. However, it is difficult to generalize, not least because the authorities sometimes sought to bring the two into alignment by devising ways to tax or otherwise corral entrepreneurial activities (and thereby translate livelihood into occupation) or by altering status categories themselves to create new occupations with their attendant duties. Thus, commoners who engaged in approved land-reclamation projects typically received tax breaks on the farm land they opened, a measure that accommodated both the commoners' entrepreneurial desire to improve their livelihoods and the regime's desire to harness new wealth by eventually bringing the land under the purview of feudal obligations. Conversely, unauthorized projects alarmed the authorities, particularly if it appeared that the cultivators who worked the new land would remove themselves from the tax rolls.[32]

In any case, my purpose in distinguishing between occupation and livelihood is not to suggest a simple story of unidirectional development. Rather, making the distinction clarifies the circumstances in which economic activity posed a threat to feudal authority. The authorities seemed to be perfectly willing to accept the fact that for most people a gap of some sort would exist between the occupation that provided their means to fulfill status-based obligations, on the one hand, and the economic activities in which they engaged to support themselves, on the other. With the development of the commercial economy, the shogunate and domains frequently tried to tap into the new livelihoods created by growth, by such means as levying new taxes, mandating the creation of commercial guilds, and imposing domainal monopolies and monopsonies. The authorities also frequently issued sumptuary laws designed to curtail ostentatious displays of consumption, and perhaps thereby keep commoners more uniformly common.

The authorities did not, however, try to curtail the accumulation of wealth per se, nor did they attempt to prohibit by-employments or commerce, so long as these pursuits did not adversely affect a subject's ability to fulfill the obligations of his formal occupation. This makes perfect sense: so long as we recall that the status system, rooted in the fiction of a society mobilized for military preparedness, was concerned foremost with the delivery of services to the shogunate and domains, it follows that the authorities would not concern themselves with extraneous economic activity provided it did not threaten social order. At the same time, however, the same principles that allowed the authorities to remain disinterested in much economic activity made it impossible for them simply to cede regulation of the economy to the market and thereby set people free to pursue their livelihoods unconstrained by the demands of feudal obligations. Here we see the Tokugawa political economy as one in which robust markets for goods and labor thrived within an institutional structure that appeared to be inimical to such markets.

The separation of occupation and livelihood through the status system and the Tokugawa state's concomitant disinterest in the accumulation of wealth per se had tremendous implications for the nineteenth-century economy. In other early modern societies, commoners often accumulated wealth with the express purpose of using it to gain entry into the ruling class. Sometimes this could be accomplished by outright purchase, as in the case of French holders of venal offices, or it could take an indirect form, as with Chinese families that invested fortunes to educate their sons for the civil service examinations. Although, as we have seen, many domains in the late Tokugawa period were forced to sell nominal samurai status—often with disruptive effects on social relations—the practice never became so widespread as to undermine the integrity of the status order, and in any case the ranks sold tended to be at the bottom of the samurai order. Meaningful offices remained reserved for those born into samurai status, except for a few technocratic positions in financial affairs, into which successful merchants might be recruited.[33]

A number of explanations for the anomaly of the Japanese case suggest themselves. First, the domains generally had more samurai than positions for them, and the sale of offices would have violated the daimyos' obligation to look after their hereditary retainers. Second, well-to-do commoners in fact had access to political power at the local level, as village officials or, in some domains, as the heads (called ōjōya, tomura, and so forth) of various regional groupings of villages. Moreover, office holding often came with coveted trappings of samurai status—such as the right to bear swords and publicly use a surname—without, however, suggesting a genuine change in status. Third, and most important, taking on genuine samurai status would have cost commoners much more than the price of an office, for their landed wealth would have become problematic in an institutional structure predicated on the separation of warriors from the land. So instead of aspiring to samurai status themselves, wealthy patriarchs more often sought to place their children into samurai households (through the marriage of their daughters and the adoption of noninheriting sons) while maintaining their own household's wealth and securing their status as prominent commoners. This strategy served to maintain the integrity of the samurai class because new entrants generally entered extant warrior households, and the strategy had the additional advantage of providing impoverished samurai with a means to tap into some of the wealth generated by commerce, manufacturing, and agricultural development.

The separation of occupation and livelihood thus gave well-to-do commoners an incentive to remain where they were in the status order. Rather than use their riches to seek access to samurai status, they invested their wealth in production, commerce, and money lending, which fueled protoindustrial development in the late Tokugawa period and established the base from which the Meiji economy would take off into capitalism. This development was fostered by the feudal preoccupation with the expropriation of agricultural surplus, which left commerce and manufacturing free from regular taxation. To be sure, the authorities tried to tap into nonagricultural wealth through the levying of extraordinary fees and the imposition of forced loans, but these sources of income were never regularized effectively, and in any case they did not impede entrepreneurial activity until the chaotic years of the Restoration period. By distinguishing entrepreneurial activity from the fulfillment of status-based obligations, Tokugawa institutions freed commoners to pursue wealth, and that is what they did.

The exception that proves this rule is the Satsuma domain, which had an extraordinarily large samurai population—perhaps 25 percent of the population—much of it living on the land. As Hidemura Senzō has noted, the samurai and peasant populations in Satsuma were only imperfectly separated during the formative decades of the Tokugawa period— that is, in contrast to the usual pattern, low-ranking warriors in Satsuma were never pressed to choose between remaining on the land as peasants and leaving for the castle town as samurai.[34] Rural samurai *(gōshi)* in the domain served as village headmen, and their control of the land—much of it developed by peasant labor under their control—inhibited the emergence of significant numbers of wealthy peasants *(gōnō)* of the sort found elsewhere in Japan. Excluded from even the lowest rungs of the ruling hierarchy, those peasants and merchants who did accumulate capital tended to purchase *gōshi* status and remain on the land as low-ranking samurai.[35]

Significantly, the institutional structure of Satsuma inhibited the development of an internal market economy, as most peasants were too poor to invest in cash cropping or other entrepreneurial activities. Commercialization in Satsuma, rather than consisting of economic growth rooted in agriculture and ancillary manufacturing and commerce in its core territories, instead centered on the marketing of sugar and other nongrain crops produced in Ryukyu and the islands south of Kyushu. As a result, the richest commoners in the domain tended to make their fortunes in shipping.[36]

Hidemura attributes Satsuma's anomalous situation to the antiquity of the Shimazu house's control over southern Kyushu—the house had ruled over the area's core territory since the late twelfth century—the domain's large size, and its remoteness from the center of Tokugawa power.[37] In other words, feudal institutions owed much more to the medieval past in Satsuma than in other domains. But even in Satsuma institutional anomalies served mostly to give purchasers of *gōshi* status access to the sort of local political power they would have had anyway as commoners in other domains: beyond the local level the political structure and access to it fit the same broad patterns found elsewhere.

Let us examine the hairdressers' guild of Edo as a specific example of the complexity of the relationship between markets and institutions as mediated by the status system. Yoshida Nobuyuki has described the intricate system by which rights to dress hair were allocated in the city of Edo.[38] To simplify the story a bit, two sets of authorities had an interest in hairdressing as an occupation with attendant duties. On the one hand, self-governing urban commoner wards *(chō)* granted permission to hairdressers to ply their trade within ward precincts in exchange for their service as guards at the entrances to the wards. On the other hand, the shogunate imposed two duties on hairdressers specifically: first, they were expected to shave the pates of jail prisoners once or twice a year (*yakuzori*, or "duty shaving"), and, second, during fires they were expected to run *(kaketsuke)* to government offices to try to save official documents from incineration. Because these duties were specific to them, Edo hairdressers took on a character akin to a status group; indeed, shogunal officials debated whether to treat hairdressers as a distinct status group, but in the end concluded that they should be considered urban commoners with special duties. By the 1850s, licenses to engage in hairdressing had become completely commodified and were traded among men who for the most part had no personal connection to hairdressing whatsoever. Licensees contracted with actual hairdressers—formally considered apprentices of the license holders—who used their connections with their putative masters to gain access to space to pursue their trade.

Thus in Edo a limited number of men held licenses that officially designated their occupation as hairdresser, yet few of them had ever actually dressed anyone's hair. Nevertheless, they bore responsibility for the fulfillment of the hairdressers' duties, the actual performance of which they often contracted out to their nominal apprentices , men who were generally classified occupationally as "peddlers" *(furiuri)* —that is, petty traders who occupied a position in urban society akin to that of landless peasants in agricultural villages. These actual hairdressers gained exclusive rights to practice their trade in urban wards by virtue of their "apprenticeship" to the licensees. This complex arrangement worked well for all the parties involved: the shogunate received licensing fees and the status-based services of those officially occupied as hairdressers; urban wards got help in maintaining social order within their precincts; the license holders earned a healthy return on their investments; and the men who actually made their livelihoods from hairdressing were protected from the competition of wildcat hairdressers who tried to break the monopoly of the licensees' guild by working outside the system entirely.

It is particularly interesting to note how hairdressers were able to manipulate the concept of feudal duty *(yaku)* to their own advantage. In the city of Sunpu (Shizuoka) (which, like Edo, was administered directly by the shogunate), hairdressers asserted that their performance of unique, occupationally defined duties (such as jailhouse pate shaving) distinguished them from ordinary urban commoners and thereby validated their attempt to prevent others from taking up hairdressing as a by-employment *(naishoku)*. In other words, the hairdressers were keen to assert that the performance of feudal duties carried with it commensurate status privileges.[39]

The distinction between occupation and livelihood in early modern Japan reminds us that economic relations in the early modern world did not operate according to the logic that we now take for granted. William Sewell gives a parallel example in his consideration of property in prerevolutionary France. As Sewell explains, three distinct types of property were recognized in the Old Regime. In addition to absolute private property in the form of personal possessions, buildings, and the like, there also existed property that belonged to its owner but did not lay under his absolute dominion; "rather, it was held by the owner under the supposition of detailed regulation by the community for the public good." Much productive property in agriculture, industry, and commerce fell into this category. The third form of property "was derived from and had no existence apart from public authority. This was property in public functions," such as venal office and the *seigneurie*.[40]

Individuals could hold all three types of property simultaneously. Sewell gives the example of a master in a corporate trade, who held personal property, such as cash and perhaps his house; productive capital, such as his tools, which he owned but could not dispose of freely; and his mastership, which was "a share in the public authority granted to the corporation by the king; like a seigneurie or a venal office, it belonged to him by legitimate title and it empowered him to carry out certain publicly authorized functions."[41] For our purposes, the artisan's mastership is particularly interesting because membership in a trade corporation carried with it a particular set of obligations and privileges—quite different from the occupational duties borne by members of status groups in Japan, to be sure, but in some ways analogous to them nonetheless. It is not surprising, then, that just as one could not freely shed one's occupation in Japan, the master could not freely dispose of the property that his mastership represented.

The sumptuary regulations issued repeatedly during the Tokugawa period indirectly illustrate the primacy of occupation over livelihood. The authorities were constantly on the lookout for commoners who indulged in luxury *(ogori* or *shashi)*, and they repeatedly issued injunctions against the wearing of silk garments and ostentatious public displays of wealth, particularly during festivals and at weddings, funerals, and other family and community rituals. A questionnaire circulated among village leaders by officials of the Shibayama domain of Kazusa province in territories they took over at the very outset of the Meiji period (before any significant institutional changes had been implemented) began with a request for advice on how best to curb peasants' wasteful habits, thus illustrating that even in a period of considerable political turmoil sumptuary laws were seen as a major tool of reform.[42] Significantly, the authorities did not attempt to use sumptuary measures to regulate the accumulation of wealth, but only the display of it. Thus, livelihood (as the source of wealth) was not a concern of the laws. Conversely, occupation was addressed through sumptuary regulations explicitly concerned with breaches of status boundaries, such as prohibitions on the unauthorized wearing of two swords by commoners.

The authorities' disinterest in wealth is true even of the attempts to curb the wearing of silk by commoners. As noted previously, the sumptuary regulations had implications for the status system, insofar as wearing silk garments was seen as a privilege of samurai status, but at the same time a well-to-do commoner woman wearing silk would not ordinarily be mistaken for the wife of a high-ranking warrior, for elite samurai women rarely ventured into public. In that sense, clothing regulations can be seen as having two purposes that perhaps superseded the maintenance of the boundary between commoners and samurai. First, they encouraged commoners to focus on the pursuit of their status-based occupations rather than on extraneous displays of luxury; second, they helped to minimize the obvious distinctions among commoners, and as such they may be seen as an (admittedly self-serving) attempt by the authorities to engage in "benevolent rule" by preventing the resentment of wealthy commoners by their poorer fellows. At the very least, it is clear that sumptuary laws were concerned more with consumption—a problem ultimately of occupation—rather than with accumulation or production—issues of livelihood.

The situational use of names helped to mark the distinction between occupation and livelihood.[43] The classic example is the practice of merchants to use a shop-name *(yagō)* in commercial dealings but not necessarily otherwise. Similarly, a given name often served as a symbol of a man's place in his household, and hence revealed its bearer's responsibility for the fulfillment of feudal obligations. Thus it was common practice for households to use specific names for their heads (either the same name or two names that alternated by generation). For example, the headman of Tomida village, Kazusa province, always used the given name Zenbei in his capacity as head of the Ōtaka house, but he used his personal name in private; the household head at the time of the Meiji Restoration was supposedly the forty-fifth Zenbei in his line.[44]

The role of names in distinguishing occupation and livelihood was especially clear among the *hinin* of Edo, as Tsukada has demonstrated through his analysis of a document produced in 1856. The residents of a group of commoner wards hired a local *hinin* boss to clean the streets, keep a lookout for fire, and ward off unregistered beggars. This man was always known as Shirōbei in his dealings with the commoners. Within the local *hinin* community, however, Shirōbei was identified by his actual personal name, Otojirō. According to Tsukada, the local commoners did not particularly care about the personal identity of the *hinin* who performed services for them; "Shirōbei" was their generic label for the ward *hinin*. The *hinin* authorities accommodated the commoners' naming practice, so that a request for assistance to rebuild Otojirō's hut *(koya)* was presented to the wards in the name of Shirōbei, despite the fact that the Edo *hinin* headman, Kuruma Zenshichi, had obviously drafted it. In other words,

Zenshichi wrote a request in the name of Shirōbei on behalf of a man whose actual name was Otojirō. To the commoners, "Shirōbei's" standing within the outcaste community—and indeed his very humanity—was immaterial. Within the outcaste community, of course, the man was not a generic *hinin*, but rather an individual with a specific rank with its attendant privileges and obligations—and a family, friends, and a social network.[45] For our purposes, "Shirōbei" was the name the man used when pursuing a livelihood as the employee of the commoner wards, while "Otojirō" situated him within the occupational group of *hinin*.

The Meiji state granted all Japanese the right to use surnames publicly in 1870. The measure and responses to it reveal the importance of naming practices in the early modern status order. For one thing, it marked all Japanese with a uniform identity as imperial subjects insofar as the use of a surname no longer suggested a privileged position in society. Moreover, in conjunction with the implementation of the household-registration system, it made the situational use of names impractical. Accordingly, although shop-names did not disappear, they were now used to refer to enterprises as corporate units rather than as surnames. (Some commoners adopted their shop-name as their surname, which they then used in all social relations.) Similarly, the practice of changing given names to mark one's position within the household became obsolete, although some individuals did continue to use distinct names in specific circumstances, such as within poetry circles or when writing or painting.

An inquiry from the Tsuyama domain in the intercalary tenth month of 1870 reveals the confusion engendered by the creation of a uniform roster of subjects. Domain officials apparently could not believe that the surname law indeed covered all commoners. Thus they asked if the law applied to commoners who did not bear their occupational obligations directly, such as landless farmers, tenants in the countryside and towns, servants, and the like. (The answer was yes.) What about members of marginal status groups, who were officially commoners but were nonetheless barred from intermarriage with peasants? (Yes, but the other constraints on their behavior would remain in place.) Was it permissible for commoners to carry short swords and to wear formal garments *(kamishimo)*? (Yes; here we see the linkage between surname use and other status privileges.) And, finally, was it correct that *eta* and *hinin* were outside the category of commoners (and hence, presumably, not allowed to use surnames)? (Yes.)[46] The abolition of outcaste status the following year concomitantly eliminated the remaining constraints on surname use and other public behavior.

THE MONETIZATION OF DUTY

The Meiji state signaled its embrace of a new politics of the quotidian in a series of measures that eliminated the institutions of the status system. Reforms like the granting of occupational freedom to samurai, commoners, and outcastes, combined with the abolition of the domains, commutation of samurai stipends, and the land-tax reform, established a direct link between individual households and the state, thus fully severing livelihood from status.

In addition to the elimination of restrictions on occupation, the abolition of the early modern status system was most clearly marked by the implementation of the household-registration law of 1871.[47] The measure did not completely abandon the principle of status, but it did change it. It confirmed an earlier set of reforms that had divided society into four broad categories: the imperial household *(kōzoku)*, the peerage *(kizoku)*, the gentry *(shizoku)*, and commoners *(heimin)*. The peerage comprised the court nobility, former daimyo, and, after 1884, a handful of persons who had rendered extraordinary service to the state. The gentry consisted overwhelmingly of former samurai. Originally, people of marginal warrior status (foot soldiers, pages, rustic samurai *[gōshi]*, rear vassals, and the like) composed a separate category known as the *sotsu* or *sotsuzoku,* but in 1872 that status was abolished, with most *sotsu* becoming commoners and the remainder (mostly from domains that had been prominent in the Restoration movement, notably Satsuma) being incorporated into the ranks of the gentry. Everyone else, regardless of previous status, was legally considered a commoner, though the officials maintaining the actual registers occasionally listed former outcastes as "new commoners" *(shinheimin)* and Ainu as "former aborigines" *(kyūdojin)*.[48] In fact, the original version of the law included a provision to list outcastes separately, but by the time the registers were actually compiled in early 1872, outcaste status had been abolished and the law revised accordingly.[49] The imperial household existed completely apart from the rest of society, and the peerage enjoyed a few, mostly financial, perquisites, but together these two groups accounted for only a tiny percentage of the national population. Conversely, membership in the gentry, although coveted, was largely honorary, as it carried (after 1876) none of the privileges formerly accorded to the samurai.

The new categories thus marked a fundamental departure from the early modern status system, for rather than representing a relationship to political authority based on the performance of feudal obligations, they symbolized their members' relative distance from the emperor, as Hirota Masaki has noted.[50] Being the emperor's subject carried all sorts of obligations, too, of course, but individuals bore them directly rather than channeling them through the medium of an intermediary social group above the level of the household. If anything, the status categories of Meiji Japan emphasized the unity of the nation, for a central myth of the modern regime was the notion that Japan was a family-state, with the father-emperor at its head. The clear hierarchy of the new status categories therefore replicated the vertical organization of a household, which maintained an essential coherence despite internally demarcated differences of status and power. Most important, modern status identities connected people only to the emperor, and not to one another except as fellow members of the Japanese nation, whether horizontally within status groups or vertically within a chain linking the individual or household to the lord through intermediate tiers of authority.

Like the Tokugawa status system, however, the household-registration law was predicated on the assumption that it would encompass every member of society. Indeed, as Yamamuro Shin'ichi has noted, Japan did not have a citizenship law until 1899, and even today, listing in a household registry is the main criterion of Japanese citizenship. People excluded from registration for one reason or another face cumbersome obstacles to attending school, marrying, voting, obtaining a passport, and gaining access to other privileges of membership in the national community.[51]

Meiji officials administering the household-registration law evidently hoped to solve once and for all the problem of the unregistered. Thus, in the period immediately following the implementation of the registration system, authorities in western Japan proceeded to round up mountain people (sanka), who led itinerant lives of swidden agriculture, lathe working, and begging, while their counterparts in Chiba issued an order prohibiting the provision of alms to beggars on the grounds that the law was supposed to have eliminated all unregistered and destitute persons from the prefecture.[52] The latter injunction is particularly suggestive, for it reveals the equivalence accorded to registration and economic activity: registration suggested a livelihood of some sort—pursued by the household if not the newly registered individual himself—and thus should have eradicated the sort of economic free agency suggested by the presence of beggars in the prefecture.

The collapse of the status order did not simply free economic activity, for as we have seen, livelihood was only minimally regulated under the

Tokugawa. Rather, it transformed the obligations owed by subjects into explicitly economic transactions—taxes paid in exchange for government services and the maintenance of order. In other words, the Meiji state monetized the obligations owed to it by its subjects. Instead of providing goods and services in kind (tax rice, garrison duty, pate shaving, and so forth), subjects paid cash to the state in the form of property and income taxes. This policy effectively institutionalized what many people were already doing in practice, and it cleared away the intermediary layers of authority between individual households and the state.

Monetizing obligations in this way was for many subjects a liberating reform because it rationalized and simplified the relationship between earning a livelihood and providing services to the state. At the same time, however, the shift had a number of deleterious effects for many Japanese, insofar as it left them more vulnerable to short-term economic ups and downs than they had been under the Tokugawa, when the corporate village or other social group had served as a buffer between the economy and individual households. Giving livelihood completely free rein meant that people's fortunes hinged *entirely* on their livelihoods, so that bad luck and bad choices could leave households in financial ruin, as many peasants discovered during the Matsukata Deflation of the mid-1880s. Moreover, the monetization of obligations helped to create a governmental structure in which the state had a great deal more direct control over its subjects than the Tokugawa state had ever had. At the same time, although the Meiji state did not repudiate the notion of benevolent government, subjects found themselves progressively less able to invoke benevolence as a *quid pro quo* for the fulfillment of obligations.[53]

In general, the people whose occupations and livelihoods diverged to the greatest degree welcomed the monetization of obligations most ardently because it freed them from institutional encumbrances without affecting their immediate economic condition. For example, the *gōnō*, the well-to-do peasants whose entrepreneurial activities were the engine of protoindustrial growth, had every reason to embrace the new regime's institutional reforms because they allowed them, if they so wished, to abandon the fiction that rice production was the focus of their livelihoods. At the same time, the regularization of commercial taxation liberated them from the sort of arbitrary and often devastating exactions that had ruined many of their number during the Tokugawa-Meiji transition.[54] Many *gōnō* exercised their freedom by becoming absentee landlords. Conversely, those who resisted most stridently were those whose feudal obligations were the least readily monetized. Thus participants in early Meiji samurai uprisings joined in because their livelihoods had nearly coincided with their occupations as warriors. Interestingly, for many participants the coincidence between occupation and livelihood did not mean that they had been full-time warriors. Quite the contrary: rural samurai *(gōshi)* in Satsuma lived mostly by farming, but their farming activities were conceptualized as a form of martial service. The monetization of obligations for such men meant the loss of both the symbolic value of membership in the lord's retainer band and important economic privileges like land-tax exemptions.

The abolition of outcaste status in the eighth month of 1871 illustrates both the benefits and anxieties fostered by the monetization of duty. As we shall see in detail in the following chapter, abolition alarmed commoners in many parts of the country, and in western Japan the Ministry of State's decree sparked several outbursts of sometimes-deadly violence. To give just a couple of examples here, in the former Hiroshima domain, peasants called for a return to the status order in part out of fear of the chaos they assumed would prevail once former outcastes were freed from their obligation to perform police duties.[55] Even more striking is the response to abolition of peasants in the former Tosa domain. When they discovered that a group of Burakumin had entered a river to purify themselves of the pollution that had adhered to them as a result of their outcaste status, they countered with a two-pronged assault: they took night soil buckets to the river, declaring that they would "purify the buckets just as the *eta* had purified themselves," and they proclaimed a boycott of all enterprises run by Burakumin.[56] If the Burakumin insisted on washing away the stain of their former occupations, the commoners would undermine their livelihoods and thus perhaps force a return to the previous order.

Even in areas in which the abolition order was greeted peacefully, commoners and Burakumin expressed uncertainty about the implications of the new order. For instance, officials in Komoro, Nagano prefecture, sent a series of inquiries to Tokyo concerning the performance of guard duty at the local jail. On receiving word of abolition, the officials summoned local Buraku leaders, who readily volunteered their community's continued service. However, the rank and file among the Burakumin refused to serve, saying that if they did so they "would not be able to shed the name *eta*." The commoner officials countered with an offer to transform "occupation" into "livelihood"—that is, they would pay the former outcastes for their services. At the same time, the Buraku leadership noted that hairdressers and bathhouse owners in nearby

Kōzuke province (Gunma) had folded up shop rather than serve Burakumin, apparently to make the point that a government order was not sufficient to change longstanding attitudes about the proper place of outcastes in local society. The same officials assured the authorities that the services would be performed, but in the twelfth month another group of Burakumin showed up at the local government office to return the tools they had used as prison guards. Moreover, in a symbolic assertion of their new standing as commoners, many members of the local Buraku community refused to appear at the office at New Year's for their customary ceremonial greetings.[57]

The situation in Komoro illustrates a number of important points. First, whatever local officials thought about the abolition of outcaste status, they saw the performance of guard duty as a function tied so intimately to the outcastes that they apparently could not think creatively about a solution to their problem, by recruiting commoners to serve, for instance. This is no surprise, and in any case there is no reason to think such a solution would have worked. Central officials encouraged prefectural governments throughout the country to hire recently unemployed samurai to man their new, Western-style police forces, but they ran into severe problems when they tried to impose the uniform title of *bannin* (guard) on the officers: men otherwise willing to serve demurred because the title of *bannin* had been used exclusively by *hinin* guards in many localities. After much wrangling the central authorities relented and chose the status-neutral neologism *junsa* (patrolman) instead.[58] The officials in Komoro thus tried to recruit former outcastes with promises of remuneration, a solution that seems to have worked in some locales. Meanwhile, leaders of the Burakumin tried to maintain their community's special standing, presumably because their positions of authority hinged on their ability to provide needed services to local officials. They thus had a vested interest in maintaining the distinction between occupation and livelihood in Komoro; conversely, the ordinary Burakumin welcomed their elevation to commoner status and with it, perhaps, the chance to liberate themselves from their leaders' control over their livelihoods.

Within a few years of the abolition edict the tensions within the Buraku community had been inverted, with the result that the pursuit of a livelihood related to the old outcaste occupations was marked by discrimination. We have already seen how the elders of Watanabe village in Osaka had edited the performance of outcaste duties out of their community's history by the 1880s. Similarly, in 1876, officials in Hōjō prefecture (the site of the anti-Buraku violence described in the following

chapter) issued an order in which they decried the practice of distinguishing between those Burakumin who had given up livelihoods dealing
with animal carcasses and those who had not. Burakumin involved in
slaughtering and rendering animals "are merely contributing to their
own livelihoods *[seikatsu no ichijo]* and thus should not be the object of
disparagement *[keibetsu]* that might hinder their work" by any members
of society, whether "new commoners" or not. Thus, when an ox or horse
died, the owner should "courteously request someone in that line of
work" to dispose of the carcass.[59]

The monetization of duty affected all Japanese, regardless of previous
status. The most significant economic measure of the early Meiji period
was the land-tax reform of 1873, which divested the village community of
its previous role as intermediary between individual subjects and the state.
As discussed in chapter 2, feudal obligations during the Tokugawa period
were allocated through the medium of the *kokudaka* system. It was an
institution that served the military needs of the shogunate reasonably well
but only imperfectly reflected the actual productivity of agricultural landholdings, in part because accurately gauging productivity was not its sole
purpose, and in part because official *kokudaka* remained generally stag-
nant during two and a half centuries of economic growth. Under the
Tokugawa, *kokudaka* were assigned to villages as corporate units, with
the result that the distribution of tax obligations to individual households
was left to communities to decide for themselves. This arrangement suited
the needs of the poorly staffed feudal regime, for it concentrated the
responsibility to oversee the payment of land taxes on a few hundred
thousand village officials rather than dispersing it among millions of peasant households. Moreover, it allowed the authorities generally to remain
aloof from the consequences of rural economic change: so long as peasant
officials paid the annual tax bill and contained disorder, the samurai could
remain disinterested in villages' demeanor toward their impoverished residents.[60] In the economic realm, they demonstrated this disinterest by
acquiescing to the existence of numerous loopholes in the official prohibition on land sales and the concomitant spread of tenancy.

In contrast, the Meiji state drew up a roster of individual households,
each responsible for the payment of land taxes in cash. This was achieved
through a series of policies, beginning with the household-registration
law of 1871 and continuing with the recognition of land sales in 1872
and the land-tax reform of 1873. The land-tax reform ensured the hard-
pressed Meiji state a predictable flow of revenue, because taxes were
assessed on the value of land rather than on its often-fluctuating produc-

tion. Furthermore, the new system was at least theoretically equitable because the land surveys conducted between 1873 and 1876 brought previously hidden landholdings under government purview. Equity did not mean, however, that peasants welcomed the reform. Some wealthy peasants opposed the new land tax because they were more likely than their poor neighbors to have hidden or underassessed fields, while impoverished farmers were disillusioned by the fact that tax rates remained steady or even rose, and were angered by the requirement that they pay their taxes in cash, which made them vulnerable to the vagaries of the rice market. The state's refusal to grant tax remissions in times of poor harvests or bad weather—a cornerstone of the Tokugawa principle of benevolent rule—both galled cultivators and rendered them insecure.[61]

Village officials remained responsible for the collection of taxes, but not, significantly, for their allocation. Now, instead of being representatives of their local communities they were reconceived as agents of the central government, even when, as was often the case, local property owners elected one of their own (often the old village headman) to serve. The first significant change in local administration came when several villages each were grouped together for purposes of enforcement of the household registration law of 1871. These new units briefly coexisted with preexisting village administrations, but competition between the overlapping sets of officials soon led to the infiltration of the new units to the village level.[62] By the mid-1870s, village officials throughout Japan bore a uniform set of titles as "mayors" (kochō) and "vice mayors" (fukukochō), and they were charged specifically with implementing the central government's major policies, such as conscription, universal education, household registration, and the land-tax reform. Thus, instead of serving as intermediaries between the village community and the authorities, they functioned as the local representatives of state power.

The symbolic import of this shift is captured in "A Tale of Enlightenment" ("Kaika no hanashi"), a didactic tract written in 1872, in which the author describes an encounter between a "stubborn" old peasant, Ganbei, and the "enlightened" young mayor of his village, Kaisuke. Not only does Ganbei fail to recognize the mayor—whom he insists on calling nanushi, a Tokugawa term for village headman—in his Western hat and overcoat, but Kaisuke complains that he is overwhelmed by all his official duties.[63] Notwithstanding the onus of his job, however, Kaisuke is an enthusiastic advocate of the Meiji reforms, for after greeting his neighbor he launches into a lengthy exaltation of the benefits of the new "politics of civilization" (bunmei no goseiji), among which were the opening of new land, the production of a variety of commodities, and the creation of considerable wealth.[64]

Ogawa Tameji, the author of another didactic tract, "A Dialogue on Enlightenment" ("Kaika mondō") (1874), argued for the benefits of the Meiji state's reforms through the conceit of a question-and-answer session, this time between the "enlightened" Kaijirō and his "backward" neighbor, Kyūsuke. (As in "A Tale of Enlightenment," the characters' names telegraph their attitudes toward the reforms. *Kai* is "enlightened," *gan* is "stubborn," and *kyū* is "old" or "backward.") Kyūsuke complains that the land-tax reform is a feeble imitation of the policies of the "hairy Chinamen" *(ketōjin)*—the Western powers—and that the payment of taxes in cash will bring unspeakable hardship on peasants, who are already poor. Kaijirō responds that the new policy will not only eliminate the corruption and inequities of the old order, but it will benefit cultivators by granting them unfettered control over their means of production and by giving them a sense of security in knowing their tax obligations in advance. The land, he argues, is analogous to the artisan's tools and the merchant's trade commodities and should thus properly be the private possession of its cultivator.[65] Ultimately, Kaijirō envisions a rational-choice utopia in which farmers, secure in their ownership of the land, redouble their efforts to maximize their profits, with the happy result that the volume of commodities increases, prosperity reigns, and "the people naturally come together and evil-doers disappear from the face of the earth. . . . Making people secure in their rights of private property is the best route to bringing the world to a state of civilization and enlightenment."[66]

In fact, once the new system was put into place, many peasants profited handsomely, if only for a time. Japan experienced considerable inflation during the late 1870s and early 1880s, with the result that cultivators enjoyed steadily rising incomes from grain sales. Because land values were not reassessed, the average farmer's tax burden fell steadily for the better part of a decade. Unfortunately, rice prices eventually fell—precipitously—as a consequence of finance minister Matsukata Masayoshi's deflationary policies in the mid-1880s, and many peasants lost their land. Conditions became so bad that even one of the Meiji state's principal architects, Inoue Kowashi, expressed dismay at the sight of hordes of beggars in Osaka and the surrounding countryside, where, in 1886, the police reported that 556 people had died of starvation.[67]

The long-term result of the land-tax reform, therefore, was a pronounced increase in tenancy rates and the growth of a desperately poor underclass in the Japanese countryside. However, the combined effects of the short-lived prosperity that followed the reform and the fact that the wealthiest and most powerful villagers profited from both the reform and the deflation (because they were their poor neighbors' creditors) meant that by the time the full implications of institutional change were clear there was no question of returning to the old taxation regime. Peasants continued to appeal for government assistance, but they did so increasingly through the medium of political parties and, eventually, tenant unions that employed a class-based rhetoric of poverty relief. [68]

For samurai the monetization of duty occurred as a consequence of the abolition of the domains in 1871. Most men of marginal samurai status, such as foot soldiers and rear vassals, legally and symbolically ceased to be warriors when the government eliminated the short-lived status category of *sotsu* the following year. The rest, reclassified as gentry, continued to receive stipends from the state and enjoy the perquisites of samurai status for another five years. However, the payment of stipends was little more than a palliative intended to wean the former samurai of their dependence on the state without stirring up disruptive opposition, for the abolition of the domains disengaged the former samurai from their occupations as providers of military service.[69] For a few years, then, there was a considerable population of men who had lost their occupations as warriors and instead pursued livelihoods as the privileged wards of the state.

Disenfranchised samurai without marketable skills experienced considerable hardship once all stipends were converted to bonds in 1876. The government implemented a number of policies—particularly land-development projects—to help them, but very few of these schemes succeeded: not only did few samurai know anything about farming, but the land allocated for development tended to be poor. A number of samurai groups emigrated to Hokkaido to make livings exclusively from farming or, in some cases, to combine agriculture with military duty as farmer-soldiers *(tondenhei)*. However, aside from a few settlements founded by former rear vassals of the Sendai daimyo, who had farmed extensively in Honshu and who had received relatively productive tracts in Hokkaido, these projects fell apart after a few tough winters.[70] However, many other former samurai were able to find a place for themselves in the new regime as government officials, teachers, police officers, entrepreneurs, and salaried members of the new Western-style military. Whether they prospered or not, the samurai were brought unequivocally into the new politics of the quotidian, for their livelihoods were taxed in the same manner as other subjects'.

The state accorded the former samurai special treatment because it was afraid of the disruption that would occur if the warriors were cut off too precipitously. As might have been expected, the greatest threats to the new order came from warriors, particularly those in domains that had been instrumental in bringing about the Restoration and who therefore felt entitled to special treatment. The regime was buffeted by a series of samurai uprisings beginning in earnest around 1870 and culminating in the Satsuma Rebellion of 1877, which was put down only after the government threw nearly all of its military and financial resources into its suppression; even then it might not have prevailed had the rebels, led by the disillusioned Restoration leader, Saigō Takamori, not made a series of strategic errors.[71] Defeating the rebels eliminated the status system once and for all, and the Meiji oligarchy was able to proceed confidently on its chosen path of military and industrial development.

Within a decade of the Meiji Restoration, the principal institutions of the old regime had been abolished and replaced by new ones that utterly transformed relations between individual Japanese subjects and the state and among different segments of Japanese society. Despite the revolutionary upheaval, however, people did not generally behave as though they were experiencing a social revolution. To be sure, there was a brief civil war in 1868–69, followed by hundreds of (mostly minor) peasant protests and a number of sizable samurai uprisings, but with the exception of the Satsuma Rebellion, none seriously threatened the stability of the new regime. In sharp contrast to the trauma of the French and Russian revolutions, "nothing happened"—or at least nothing catastrophically disruptive happened—in much of the country.[72] Indeed, the apparent passivity of the populace led one prominent historian of Japan to conclude in 1960 that the Restoration was an "aristocratic revolution," imposed from above.[73] Today few specialists would concur wholeheartedly with that assessment, but the fact remains that the Meiji state faced few fundamental questions concerning its legitimacy and encountered comparatively little concerted opposition to its policies, particularly after its major institutional reforms had been implemented by the mid-1870s.

The regime's quick achievement of legitimacy had important political and ideological roots. At the very least, the widespread perception that the shogunate had bungled its responsibility to cope with Western imperialism opened many political actors to the idea of nominally direct imperial rule. Ideologues of many persuasions accommodated themselves with surprising alacrity to the idea that Western-style modernity was Meiji Japan's proper destiny, even as they hotly debated its nature.

In emphasizing the smoothness of the transition, I do not mean to deprecate the very real disruptions of the Restoration period. On the contrary, my aim is to contextualize them as a first step toward understanding their long-term significance more clearly. Indeed, in the next chapter I will take up in detail the question of violence—particularly murderous violence against former outcastes—during the period immediately after the Restoration. However, focusing here on the relative smoothness of the transition is more productive than following the lead of a long tradition of previous scholarship, which has tended to focus on the ideological disruptions of the period with the goal either to dismiss the violence and disorder that did occur as the product of inchoate, even irrational, anxiety, or to frame it within a narrative of class conflict that somehow fizzled out. Changes in the structure of the economy certainly contributed to the collapse of the Tokugawa regime, yet analyses of the causes of the Restoration that privilege economic factors fail to account for the relative ease and rapidity of the Meiji state's reimposition of order.

In summary, I would like to suggest the following interpretation of the economic aspects of the Meiji Restoration as they relate to issues of occupation, livelihood, and status. During the late Tokugawa period, the Japanese economy underwent considerable growth and even structural change. This change had numerous disruptive effects, but the institutions of status were crafted in such a way as to ensure that it did not fundamentally undermine the political institutions of the state. The key here is the separation of occupation and livelihood, for political institutions could remain stable so long as people continued to fulfill the obligations attendant on their occupations, while in the meantime society and economy could express considerable dynamism in the realm of livelihood. The state did not remain aloof from the workings of markets and labor—quite the contrary—but its institutions were structured in such a way as to allow it to intervene without staking its fundamental premises on the issue.

The widening gap between occupation and livelihood thus formed the economic background to the arrival of the Meiji Restoration, but economic developments per se did not "cause" the collapse of the Tokugawa shogunate. Once the old regime did fall, for reasons most immediately linked to foreign diplomatic pressure, the state that succeeded it repudiated the institutions of status and instead embarked on a series of policies that had the effect of monetizing the obligations owed by individual Japanese to the state. For many people, particularly in the countryside, this approach to governance was liberating because it freed them from the encumbrances of participating in the status system. Many others fared less well, but the point is that the monetization of obligations was a sufficiently welcome reform to a sufficiently large segment of the population to smooth the way into the Meiji period and the eventual beginnings of a capitalist economy.

From its inception the Meiji state expected much more of its subjects than their money, and over time it translated expectations into demands ever more effectively. People got the message: certainly by the conclusion of the Sino-Japanese War in 1895 they knew that the state would readily call on them to pledge their loyalty and perhaps their lives as the price of belonging in the nation as imperial subjects. They generally responded willingly, even eagerly, to such demands: their ardor was a mark of their embrace of nationalism and with it modernity. That said, the Japanese people understood how radically their situation had changed and behaved accordingly. As Makihara Norio has demonstrated, they forsook their entitlement to Tokugawa-style benevolent rule only very reluctantly.[74] More generally, the political history of Japan from the Freedom and Popular Rights Movement of the 1870s and 1880s through the fierce struggles over "imperial democracy" in the early twentieth century can be read as a long and ultimately irresolvable negotiation over the precise terms of a modern subject's obligations to the state.[75]

Perhaps a revitalized Tokugawa regime would have reinvented Tokugawa status to fit the needs of a modern nation-state. Perhaps a conquering Western power would have discovered and imposed a rigid four-class status hierarchy on Japan, along the lines of the British discovery and reinvention of caste as a form of colonial knowledge in India.[76] The Meiji state, having repudiated the logic of differentiation .through status, could not attempt any such experiment. It had no choice in the realm of economic institutions but to free livelihood through the monetization of duty; once this was done it proceeded to address the politically fraught project of creating an ideology for a modern Japanese nation-state. Demanding cash instead of goods and services was on one level nothing more than an accounting maneuver perfectly palatable to an important segment of the population. At the same time, however, it permitted the state to assert the fundamental homogeneity of its subjects as a people who equally enjoyed the emperor's benevolence and who equally fulfilled their obligations through the payment of monetized taxes. Soon enough money alone would cease to suffice to meet the demands of subjecthood, but all further developments proceeded from this first, critical step.

CHAPTER 4

Violence and the Abolition of Outcaste Status

When the Meiji regime came to power in 1868 it immediately repudiated the fundamental logic that had informed the Tokugawa status order. Rather than a military regime organized in the first instance to support the mobilization of troops, the Meiji state presented itself as returning to the institutions and ideas of Japan's distant past, when the emperor ruled the entire archipelago directly. It does not matter that regime's logic did not accurately reflect actual conditions; the Tokugawa state was much more than a simple military machine, and the celebration of the past by the Meiji state was in fact a roundabout embrace of Western-style modernity. The important point is that the creation of a centralizing regime rendered obsolete the status order that underlay Tokugawa institutions.

The abolition of outcaste status in 1871 was a central part of the Meiji state's nation-building project. Unlike other Meiji policies, however, it has received little sustained attention from scholars.[1] This neglect may reflect a feeling that since discrimination against the Burakumin has persisted to the present, abolition was essentially an empty reform and therefore not worthy of careful consideration; in studies written from this standpoint, the real story of Buraku "liberation" does not begin until the founding of the Suiheisha (Levelers' Association) in 1922. In any case, the scholarly neglect of the 1870s is unfortunate, for the abolition policy and reactions to it tell us much about how the politics of the quotidian—the political significance attached to the ways people led their everyday lives—were transformed during the transition from Tokugawa to Meiji.

I will begin this chapter by briefly surveying the background to and immediate effects of the abolition edict. Then I will proceed to a lengthier consideration of one incident in particular, the Mimasaka Blood-Tax Rebellion of 1873. Although I will focus principally on matters related to the abolition of outcaste status, my broader goal here is actually to assess the significance of the disintegration of the status order in the realm of social relations. I will look at murderous violence in late Tokugawa and early Meiji popular protest as the medium for that assessment. I will argue, first, that the sudden incidence of murderous violence in the first decade of the Meiji period was a by-product of the dissolution of the status system and its ideological supports, and second, that even apparently random violence was subject to rules that had their origins in the performative conventions of Tokugawa protest. Even as I frame this part of the discussion in terms of popular protest, I will do so with an eye to capturing the breakdown of the status system in action. Thus, whether I am addressing the elimination of outcaste status or the murder of Burakumin, my main interest is in the place of status in the social fabric of nineteenth-century Japan.

MAKING COMMONERS OF OUTCASTES

The position of outcastes in Tokugawa society was complex. Their base status was rationalized by reference to their supposedly frequent contact with ritual pollution, yet in fact many outcastes led everyday lives nearly identical to those of commoners. Outcaste status thus had little necessary connection to actual livelihood, but rather was reproduced through the structure of status-based duties. Outcastes suffered discrimination in their social relations as a result of their status, but they also enjoyed a degree of autonomy within their own communities, which were perceived to be largely immune to the interference of outside authority, samurai and commoner alike. Moreover, outcaste status was grounded in regional histories to a far greater extent than other status categories, with the result that the terminology and precise nature of base status varied considerably around the archipelago. Some regions, particularly central and western Honshu, Shikoku, and northern Kyushu, had large outcaste populations, while others, such as northeastern Honshu, had very small ones. This parallels the concentration of base social groups in central and western Japan in the medieval period.

Integrating the outcastes into the new politics of the quotidian after the Meiji Restoration of 1868 was particularly difficult because of the burden of discrimination that adhered to them and their nominal occupations. The *eta*'s status in particular was perceived to reflect essential differences between them and the rest of the populace. Accordingly, Tokugawa commentators generally dismissed them as unassimilable. For example, in an essay written in 1817, the merchant ideologue Kaiho Seiryō developed an elaborate rationale for discrimination against the outcastes. First, he attributed their origins to barbarians *(iteki)* and thereby asserted that they were not descendants of the sun goddess and hence were ineligible for membership in the Japanese national community. Koreans, Ryukyuans, and the Dutch were similarly alien, but because they had true hearts they were not to be despised. The problem with *eta,* he argued, was that although their faces were indistinguishable from those of Japanese, their hearts were irredeemably bad, making assimilation impossible. This raised the pressing issue of devising clearly visible markers of separation. Seiryō found the fact that *eta* in Edo did not bind their hair to be laudable, but he concluded that because *eta* in Kyoto and Osaka wore theirs like commoners, hairstyle was an inadequate symbol of difference. He therefore proposed that the authorities tattoo all adult outcastes' foreheads and bar all juvenile outcastes from leaving their home communities. In addition, he suggested that requiring them to take "Dutch" names like Heito and Rinki, written in the kana syllabary rather than characters, would help to maintain the distinction between them and commoners.[2]

Writing at about the same time as Seiryō, Buyō Inshi, the pseudonymous author of the "Observations of Worldly Affairs" (Seji kenmonroku), a polemic on the collapse of social order, focused his denunciation of the outcastes on their supposed distaste for labor, love of wasteful luxury, and flagrant disregard for status-based rules of propriety.[3] Policy makers took such worries seriously, and indeed imposed many restrictive policies governing the outcastes' customs in response to them during opening decades of the nineteenth century. Thankfully, they never went so far as to adopt Seiryō's suggestion that they tattoo outcastes' foreheads, but they did introduce rules requiring them to tie their hair with straw or wear leather patches on their kimono.[4] Similarly, the Sonobe domain, near Kyoto, issued a notice to villages under its control in 1858, in which it pointed to the *hinin* village guards' practice of shaving their pates as the cause of disorder in the countryside, for although the guards were of a different status from commoners and hence forbidden to have social relations with them, "if they shave their pates they naturally take liberties and the distinction between *hinin* and peasants" is imperiled.[5]

By the end of the Tokugawa period, however, some commentators attempted to undermine this discourse of essential difference because they saw it as a hindrance to the promotion of the national interest. The most thorough such attempt was a short tract written in 1864 by Senshū Tōtoku, a scholar and imperial loyalist from the Kaga domain, who proposed that the authorities gradually elevate the *eta* to commoner status. Although he did not dispute the widely accepted grounds for their despised status—that they were descended from Koreans and other foreign immigrants and were defiled by their engagement in unclean professions—he saw neither of these grounds as an insurmountable barrier to eventual assimilation into the commoner population. His advocacy of the promotion of particularly worthy *eta* to commoner status followed from his assumption that they and their children would gradually blend into the mass of the "good people" *(ryōmin)*. His rationale combined Confucian physiocratic thought—only as commoner farmers would the *eta* contribute fully to the greater good of the nation—and an argument for the essential equality in the sovereign's gaze *(isshi dōjin)* of all the emperor's subjects, which he interpreted as including even "birds and beasts" and people like them.[6]

In the first month of 1868, the shogunate in fact elevated the Edo outcaste headman, the thirteenth Danzaemon, to commoner status in reward for his meritorious actions in the aftermath of a fire in the Edo city jail in 1864 and service to the shogunate during the second punitive expedition against the Chōshū domain in 1866; the idea is said to have originated with Matsumoto Ryōjun, the shogun's personal doctor. The shogunate similarly rewarded nearly seventy of Danzaemon's major underlings shortly thereafter.[7] At this stage it seems to have been the shogunate's intent to maintain the former outcastes as a distinct community—now officially labeled *chōri* rather than *eta*—under Danzaemon's continued authority. The use of terminology here is particularly interesting, insofar as *chōri* was the term *eta* in Edo and its hinterland had long used to describe themselves in preference to the blatantly pejorative *eta*.[8] Under the logic of the status system it would have been difficult for the shogunate simply to incorporate Danzaemon and his subordinates into the undifferentiated mass of Edo commoners and still expect them to fulfill status-specific duties. It thus appears that the aim of the shift in terminology was to designate the former *eta* as commoners with special duties, similar to several types of urban tradesmen, such as the hairdressers examined in the previous chapter.

Perhaps emboldened by his new status, Dan Naoki (as Danzaemon now called himself) made a proposal similar to Tōtoku's to the new regime shortly after the Restoration. In 1870, he submitted a memorial to the Tokyo prefectural authorities recommending that the outcastes be integrated into commoner society and offering his services in overseeing the process. In an attempt to preserve his feudal privileges while superficially embracing the new politics of the quotidian, he proposed that he be given authority over all the outcastes in Japan as a means to guarantee the greatest possible productivity from outcaste labor. He framed his plea for broadened powers in terms of the state's need for rapid industrial and military development. He argued that integrating all of Japan's outcastes under his authority was necessary to ensure the smooth development of a modern leather-working industry, which he saw as central to the creation of a modern military establishment. Giving him the power to allow particularly diligent outcastes to join him in the ranks of commoners would ensure both industrial success and a steady stream of revenue into government coffers, in the form of both taxes and donations from grateful former outcastes.[9]

The memorial epitomized the contradictory nature of Dan's position in the feudal order; he was privileged and powerful but despised nonetheless. His attempt to create a commoner elite, with himself at its head, to control the outcaste population was not only self-serving but unacceptably conservative as well. That is, he did not—could not—accept the basic premise of the new regime, the establishment of a direct link between itself and all of its subjects. Maintaining an intermediate stratum of independent authority was incompatible with that imperative. Tellingly, the government separated Dan's status privileges from his expressed desire to contribute to industrial development. That is, it did not grant him the broad administrative powers he had asked for, but did allow him to hire European technicians to help establish a modern tannery to supply boots and other leather products to the military. Just as tellingly, however, once Dan lost his monopoly over access to outcaste labor in the Kantō in 1871, his career as an industrialist went into precipitous decline. After numerous setbacks, the tannery fell under the control of the Mitsui cartel.[10]

Soon after the Restoration officials began considering various proposals to abolish outcaste status. The liberal intellectual Katō Hiroyuki submitted a memorial calling for emancipation in the fourth month of 1869; in it he decried the practice of treating outcastes as nonhumans as a national embarrassment *(kokujoku)* that would adversely affect Japan's relations with foreign countries. (He is said to have been inspired to submit his memorial after seeing a desperately poor outcaste village near the treaty port of Hyōgo.)[11] The following month, a samurai from the Matsumoto domain, Uchiyama Sōsuke, suggested that the nation would benefit if outcastes were granted a status equivalent to that of commoners and allowed to marry freely. He called for the creation of a new label that referred explicitly to the outcaste's livelihood of leather working (such as *kawayagumi* or *kawayashoku*) to replace the occupational labels of *eta* and *hinin*.[12]

The individual perhaps most directly responsible for pushing forward the emancipation of the outcastes was Ōe Taku, a Tosa samurai who submitted a pair of proposals to the Ministry of Civil Affairs (Minbushō) in the first and third months of 1871. In his memorials, Ōe called for the government to undertake a program of gradual abolition tied to economic development. He proposed that outcastes remain one rank below commoners under a new label, such as "base people" *(senmin)*, and be put to work in tanning, agricultural development, and animal husbandry. Those who put up money for this work would be elevated to commoner status immediately, while the rest would be folded gradually into the ranks of commoners over time. The proposal impressed the oligarch Ōkuma Shigenobu and the civil affairs minister Ōki Minpei enough to win Ōe a position in the ministry. As a result, in subsequent months the Ministry of Civil Affairs took a position very close to Ōe's in its negotiations with the Ministry of State over the best way to proceed with the abolition of outcaste status.[13] In the end, however, Ōe's elaborate proposal to link abolition directly to participation in economic development programs was rejected in favor a simpler and more direct approach.

The Ministry of State's so-called liberation edict, issued on the twenty-second day of the eighth month of 1871, stated merely, "The names *eta, hinin,* and so forth are hereby abolished. Henceforth in their status and occupation [former outcastes] shall be treated as commoners."[14] In other words, although it is often referred to as the "liberation edict" *(kaihōrei)* in the scholarly literature, from the state's perspective, the measure was not designed to free the outcastes from the bonds of their despised status so much as to eliminate one of a series of barriers between itself and its subjects. Nevertheless, "liberation edict" is not entirely a misnomer, inasmuch as both commoners and the Burakumin themselves saw it as an emancipatory measure. Of course, the same could be said of the abolition of the status system more generally, as it liberated people of all statuses from their feudal duties—and imposed the new obligations of imperial subjecthood in their stead—to the same degree that the liberation edict freed the outcastes. However, the abolition of outcaste status took the bottom out of the early modern social order, thereby destabilizing the position of commoners. In other words, by elevating the outcastes to commoner status, the edict effectively demoted commoners to the same level as the former outcastes, or at least many commoners viewed it in those terms. By the same token, many former samurai expressed similar anxieties about the loss of their privileged position in the status order. It comes as no surprise, then, that the elimination of both outcaste and samurai status provoked violent outbursts.

Evidence suggests that the Burakumin joyously welcomed the abolition edict, and particularly its formal elimination of terms like *eta* and *hinin*.[15] Unfortunately, however, the homogenizing neologism "new commoners" *(shinheimin)*, though never officially mandated, soon came into public discourse as a marker of continuing discrimination. In the realm of everyday life, the most immediate changes for most Burakumin resulted from the dismantling of the status-based authority structure. Many no doubt benefited from their liberation from the financial and other demands of the old outcaste elite and gladly gave up participating in such duties as holding condemned prisoners down while their heads were cut off. At the same time, however, abolition meant the loss of institutions to deal systematically with commoner society; under the new order individual Burakumin (or groups of individuals) had to go through the same channels as other Japanese to redress grievances, a situation that left them extremely vulnerable to mistreatment.

Abolition had a direct impact on the livelihoods of Buraku communities, and particularly the elites within them. The Kyoto authorities informed the elders of Amabe and Hiden'in that, as a consequence of the elimination of outcaste status, they would lose access to income linked to their status privileges, including dues from underlings and village guards, a share of receipts from public urinals (whose contents were sold as fertilizer), and an annual grant of 300 *ryō* from the city. The authorities also prohibited certain outcaste livelihoods, such as street performance and the lending of lodgings to unregistered *(museki,* formerly *mushuku)* persons (the latter livelihood had long been illegal but widely tolerated). At the same time, Burakumin who continued to perform police duties would be remunerated individually, while village guards were free to enter into individual contracts with their employing villages. However, the order made no mention of the outcastes' leather working and other entrepreneurial activities, which presumably would form the basis of their livelihoods under the new regime.[16] This neglect is not surprising, given the official disinterest in livelihood during the Tokugawa period. In any case, despite these changes, the Kyoto authorities hastened to add that "the livelihoods in which you have engaged are henceforth commoner livelihoods: there is no need for you to change them. Indeed, you are to work hard to achieve ever greater success [at them]."[17] In other words, although, like other Japanese, they were free to change livelihood if they so chose, nothing about the outcastes' actual everyday lives would necessarily change.

By focusing their policy on the disestablishment of the outcastes' institutionalized status, the authorities may have hoped to circumvent the problem of discrimination. However, discrimination was so firmly embedded in social relations that conflict with commoners frequently undermined the state's attempts to establish the Burakumin as autonomous economic agents. Indeed, the Buraku community itself was riven by internal discrimination, as Burakumin who gave up traditional outcaste occupations sometimes shunned those who, for economic reasons, did not. In one such case, in Hōjō (later part of Okayama) prefecture, officials issued a call for mutual courtesy, saying that those Burakumin who continued to deal with livestock carcasses were merely "contributing to their own livelihoods," and so ought to be left in peace.[18] The emphasis on livelihood over discrimination is more explicit in an admonition issued to the residents of Chiba prefecture, which stated that, insofar as the carcasses of livestock were the source of valuable commodities, peasants were not to abandon them on dry riverbeds or secretly bury them, but rather were to sell them to people in "that line of work."[19]

The dismantling of the early modern status system stripped the village of its role as the intermediary institution overseeing relations between feudal authority and the peasantry. In its place, the state created a nearly uniform roster of subjects regardless of previous status or domain affiliation and made individual households (rather than corporate villages or other previous status groups) responsible for the payment of taxes. According to the logic of this policy, rural Buraku communities, which had been subordinated as branches of commoner villages, ought to have been recognized as autonomous administrative units and their residents should have been given clear title to their agricultural lands. In practice, however, Buraku villages often received nominal autonomy only to see their land distributed among the residents of the former parent village. In other words, many Buraku villages existed in name only, with household registries but no landholdings and hence no tax base, and were populated by formerly self-sufficient residents now reduced to tenancy. Aside from the financial hardship this caused Buraku farmers, the lack of a tax base made it impossible for their communities to establish primary schools. With schools in neighboring villages open only to locally registered residents, Buraku children were sometimes left ineligible to attend school at all. Some particularly egregious inequities were resolved after 1884, when the government undertook a major reform of local administration, merging villages and towns throughout the country to reduce expensive bureaucratic duplication, but even then reform met with determined opposition.

For example, Suzuki Ryō has examined a dispute between Kashihara and Iwasaki villages in Osaka (later Nara) prefecture. Iwasaki had been Kashihara's branch village during the Tokugawa period, but after the Restoration it became independent, though landless. Prefectural officials gave the residents of Kashihara a choice: either merge with Iwasaki or cede land to it so that it might become economically viable. The Kashihara officials responded by offering to grant Iwasaki just under six *chō* (fifteen acres) of flood-prone wasteland (out of a total holding of about 122 *chō* [305 acres] between the two communities)—hardly a fair deal under any circumstances, but especially outrageous considering that Iwasaki had 150 households, compared to 130 in its former parent village. In this case, the Burakumin successfully forced a merger by pointing out that since their homes stood on land belonging to Kashihara, their household registries should likewise be located in that village. In other instances, however, prefectural and local officials colluded to draw school-district lines within newly amalgamated administrative units in such a way as to isolate Buraku hamlets. They justified their actions by referring to the Burakumin's poverty, backward customs *(rōshū)*, and alien race *(jinshu)* as incompatible with integrated education.[20]

Conflict between Burakumin and their neighbors extended well beyond strictly economic issues. Festivals are a case in point. During the Tokugawa period, outcastes and commoners were often parishioners of the same shrines, but during festivals the outcastes found themselves relegated to marginal roles that emphasized their inferior status, such as cleaning, beating drums at the head of the festival procession, and the like. This situation was of course consonant with their low standing in society more generally. In that sense, discrimination was written into the status order in such a way as to make its operation predictable and therefore normal, with the result that it did not ordinarily need to be articulated explicitly. After the promulgation of the abolition edict, however,

Buraku communities frequently asserted their right to participate in festivals on the same basis as other parishioners, by carrying their own portable shrines *(mikoshi)*, for example. These efforts met with strenuous opposition, resulting in a number of lawsuits, which the Burakumin usually (but not always) lost.[21]

Discrimination had assumed a new character. Unable to shield their loathing behind the institutions of the status system, the Burakumin's commoner neighbors were forced to enunciate it clearly: the Burakumin had to play a marginal role in the festivals not because their place in the political order so demanded, but rather because the commoners feared the Burakumin and the pollution that they assumed adhered to their participation. Despising the Burakumin, in other words, was no longer a mostly unspoken response to their political identity as outcastes; instead, contempt had to be constantly articulated and thereby reaffirmed, for it had no basis other than its constant reaffirmation. Therein lay the virulence of modern discrimination: instead of saying, in effect, "We *have* to hate you because you are outcastes," the commoners said, "We *choose* to hate you because you defile our community."

Which sort of discrimination was worse? The Burakumin's ardent desire to escape from status-based discrimination is obvious from their immediate embrace of their new standing as commoners. Moreover, the desire for liberation transcended internal divisions within the Buraku community. Wealthy and powerful elites like Dan Naoki and the elders of Watanabe village expressed as strong a desire for equality as the ordinary Burakumin who fought for the right to participate fully in festivals. All welcomed the nominal equality represented by the elimination of status labels like *eta*. Yet it is not clear that the Burakumin appreciated what they were getting into by being granted the status of commoners. That is, they behaved as though the status system had remained intact and they had become commoners in the same sense that their peasant neighbors had been before the Restoration. In fact, however, rather than entering into a new relationship with political authority as part of a broader community of commoners, they found themselves cut loose from the protective (albeit discriminatory) structure of the status system and left to cope as best they could as a disparate amalgamation of individual households.

Of course, the same was true for commoners. Everyone in Meiji Japan was a new commoner insofar as commoner status as it had functioned under the early modern regime no longer existed. The institutionalized discrimination of the status system gave way to a less formal structure, in which individuals (or groups of individuals in a household or community) had to express their biases explicitly and repeatedly if those biases were to have force in the realm of social relations.

Eliminating the protective structure of early modern discrimination left society vulnerable to unprecedented violence. The modernized discrimination directed against Burakumin was one expression of the apprehension felt by ordinary people throughout Japan during the tumultuous reforms of the immediate post-Restoration period. They gave voice to their anxieties in a wave of protest movements throughout the first decade and a half of the Meiji period. Mostly they articulated dissatisfaction with policies affecting their livelihoods, such as the land-tax reform, conscription, and universal education (which strained local finances and removed children from the household labor force), though some movements, including protests against the quarantining of cholera patients, reflected popular fears of official intrusion into household affairs. Of the 650 or so cases of rural contention during the period between 1868 and 1877, twenty-two are known to have included protests against the abolition edict and other anti-Buraku elements, including ten that involved direct conflict between commoners and Burakumin.[22]

As we have seen, the elimination of outcaste status was a complex process. From the standpoint of the men who pushed the state to consider abolition and the officials who actually enacted it, the policy was necessary for three reasons: first, as a matter of fairness in keeping with the principle of the intrinsic equality of the emperor's subjects *(isshi dōjin)*; second, as a matter of national pride; and third, as a means to unleash the economic potential of former outcastes in the development of new lands and new industries useful to the state, particularly tanning and animal husbandry. The outcaste leaders who pushed for abolition had their own economic and even patriotic reasons, too, but above all they seem to have been sincerely motivated by a desire to shed such discriminatory labels as *eta* and *hinin*. Ordinary Burakumin found themselves faced with new opportunities and new challenges after 1871, but there is no question that they welcomed their elevation to commoner status as a truly liberatory measure, even in the face of continued discrimination—and, indeed, as we shall see, even in the face of the threat of murderous violence.

VIOLENCE: THE MIMASAKA BLOOD-TAX REBELLION

The years before and after the Meiji Restoration were violent ones. Emblematic is the terror of the Restoration movement itself, in which "men of high purpose" *(shishi)* and other activists cut down officials, foreigners, and one another in the name of loyalty to the emperor. Peasants and townspeople rose in protest with especial frequency during this time, and urban riots *(uchikowashi)* and other large-scale incidents often resulted in the destruction of considerable property. Although surveys of the period devote due attention to this violence, they tend nonetheless to portray the Restoration as a generally peaceful revolution. Even scholars who emphasize the radical transformation of social relations and thought over the Tokugawa-Meiji divide focus less on murderous violence than on sporadic inversions of hierarchy, such as the carnivalesque revelry of the *eejanaika* (ain't it grand!) disturbances of 1867–68, as evidence of the tumult of the times. Violence thus appears to be an incidental feature of the transfer of power, rather than an integral characteristic of Japan's initial encounter with modernity.

In this portion of the chapter I will focus on one particular type of violence in the Restoration period, bodily attacks by commoners inflicted in the course of protest. I refer here to cold-blooded murder committed to make a point about the condition of the economy, the state of social relations, or the direction of government policies—in short, political violence, broadly construed. Violence in this instance is not the tragic outcome of a family dispute, commonplace thuggery, or crime, nor is it personal—or if it is, it is transformed into something universal by virtue of the politically charged moment in which it occurs.

My main topic here is the Mimasaka Blood-Tax Rebellion of 1873. This incident, like other instances of violence against Burakumin in the early Meiji period, is usually treated as an expression of generalized anxiety over the course of political change. Here I will depart from previous scholarship and approach it as a function of the dissolution of the status order and the concomitant loss of mechanisms to contain physical violence in society. That is, rather than look at anti-Buraku violence in isolation and argue merely that the Restoration and its reforms so thoroughly frightened commoners that they lashed out in violence against the former outcastes, I will examine the broader context of anti-Buraku violence to understand how it was specifically a function of the downfall of the status order.

Murderous violence as an instrument of protest deserves a central place in our narrative of nineteenth-century Japanese history, and the way to accord it that centrality lies, ironically, in setting aside—for a time, at least—our model of peasant contention *(hyakushō ikki)*. By disengaging the discussion of popular uses of violence from the analysis of peasant contention, we can expose the tensions that led to its eruption without reducing it entirely to a function of class conflict. That is, by looking at violence separately from the historiographical category of peasant contention, we are reminded that a tenuous balance between conflict and harmony—weighted ever so slightly in favor of harmony—is the usual state of affairs in any community. Conversely, focusing on moments of clearly articulated protest encourages us to overlook the tensions related to participation in community activities and access to resources, and indeed related to the rhythms of everyday life. Although these tensions were often quite minor when considered in isolation, they sowed the seeds of an anger more gnawing, by virtue of its integration into the fabric of daily life, than the major crises that led to the incidents that survive in our log of peasant contention. This is not to say we should ignore peasant contention or overlook the pressures that arose in the face of economic-structural change. Quite the contrary: my point is merely that only by recognizing that conflict was endemic to Japanese society in the middle of the nineteenth century can we proceed to a consideration of the social and political conditions that governed the translation of conflict into physical violence.

To that end, I propose to perform a methodological sleight of hand in an effort to circumvent familiar binaries of uprising versus normality, discord versus harmony, and the like. As noted above, I shall organize my discussion around one specific incident from the early Meiji period, the notorious Mimasaka Blood-Tax Rebellion of 1873. However, my principal aim is not to offer a new interpretation or even a detailed account of the incident itself, but rather to focus on several telling details of the rebellion that suggest ways to think about murderous violence beyond the analytical framework of studies of peasant rebellion. By the same token, this discussion is not intended to be a comprehensive analysis of violence in the Restoration period, but an illustration of an approach to the study of violence, cast in the context of one particular incident and framed in the context of abrupt institutional change.

Violence in early Meiji Japan was intimately connected to the collapse of the status system. In the long run, the dismantling of the institutions of status was for most people a liberating process, for it permitted individuals to engage in economic, intellectual, and political activities previously barred to them. At the same time, however, the disruptions attendant on the collapse of the status order gave rise to new patterns of physical violence: individuals briefly became free to express violent impulses, not at will, perhaps, but certainly in accordance with principles that neither the early modern regime nor the Meiji state would have accepted as valid. For a few years, the individual impulse to violence was like a free electron, liberated from the orbit of the status system but not yet captured by the disciplinary order of the modern regime.

The murderous violence of the Mimasaka Blood-Tax Rebellion and other early Meiji incidents occurred during this unstable interval.[23] Mimasaka province, in the hilly interior of present-day Okayama prefecture (at the time of the incident it was under the administration of Hōjō prefecture), was the site of a number of major peasant protests in the late Tokugawa period, some of which featured *hinin-goshirae,* the practice of peasants dressing as beggars for their procession to government offices. Although the term *hinin* here refers to beggars generically and is not a status label, oral traditions in the contemporary Buraku community suggest that outcastes participated alongside commoners in a massive protest in 1866, and in other incidents as well.[24] The region was also the site of intermittent unrest in the aftermath of the abolition edict. Two groups of villages submitted petitions demanding repeal of the abolition edict in the tenth month of 1871, just two months after a Burakumin had been assaulted by a mob during the course of a protest calling for the reinstatement of the former daimyo as governor of Majima prefecture, a short-lived administrative unit.[25] Later that year, commoners in one village entered into a compact promising to join in any protests that might occur in response to abolition.[26] Thus it is not surprising that the province would be the site of anti-Buraku violence. In any case, combine this animosity toward Burakumin with persistent rumors that villages would be forced to turn over oxen and young women to the government so that their blood might be given to foreigners, and with attempts to subvert implementation of the household-registration system—seen as the mechanism by which such levies would be assessed—and it is clear that peasants in the region were overcome with anxiety in the first years of the Meiji era.[27]

The authorities in the area responded by issuing official denials of the rumors of blood collecting.[28] They also urged mutual courtesy in relations between commoners and Burakumin, though peasants interpreted this exhortation (perhaps correctly) to mean that the authorities intended for the Burakumin to respect previous standards of deferential behavior; some of their Buraku neighbors agreed with this interpretation, for one village drafted a document refusing to honor the exhortation.[29] At the same time, officials mandated the monetization of outcaste duties related to the disposal of animal carcasses in the third month of 1871, but then ordered the Burakumin to continue to perform such duties eight months later.[30] Note that this reversal came after the Burakumin had been made commoners and was thus in clear violation of national law.

The Tokugawa roots of antipathy toward the Burakumin in Mimasaka are not clear. In 1864, *eta* accounted for about 7 percent of the Tsuyama domain's nonsamurai population of sixty thousand.[31] This was higher than the 2 or 3 percent estimated for the archipelago as a whole, but was probably similar to the figures for other regions in western Japan, which had far more outcastes than areas east of Edo. Outcastes in Mimasaka were scattered about the region according to the usual pattern for rural outcastes, and were subject to the control of headmen from the Kaiami house of Miho village.[32] As mentioned previously, evidence from the late 1870s suggests that the outcaste community was riven by disparities in wealth—and concomitant tensions—similar to those that affected commoner villages throughout Japan.[33] In addition to performing status-based duties, outcastes in Mimasaka farmed and produced charcoal, the latter a common enough livelihood in the heavily forested province.[34] In any case, available collections of early modern documents contain few references to outcastes, but it is possible that relevant materials either remain in private hands or have remained inaccessible because archives tend to limit public access to materials that contain discriminatory language or genealogical information.

The Mimasaka Blood-Tax Rebellion was one of the bloodiest conflicts in the early Meiji period; eighteen of the twenty-four people killed and eleven of the twenty-one injured were Burakumin.[35] The rebellion began when a thirty-three-year-old resident of Teieiji village in Hōjō prefecture, Fudeyasu Utarō, disillusioned with early Meiji state-building policies, manipulated popular misunderstanding of the term "blood tax" *(ketsuzei)* to launch an uprising against the new regime. The term, which was used in government pronouncements concerning the new conscription law, resonated with a long-standing belief in the existence of figures who roamed the countryside in search of human blood and fat, and was connected as well to fears raised by the Western presence in Japan.[36] Under repeated torture Fudeyasu confessed to having spread rumors that a man in white was making his way around the area draining the blood of men aged seventeen to forty, and to having staged an incident in which such a figure showed up in Teieiji. The appearance of the man in white provided the desired impetus for an uprising, but Fudeyasu almost immediately dropped out of the picture. Instead, several bands of peasants from neighboring villages, acting without identifiable leadership, rampaged around the countryside for six days from May 26 to 31, 1873.

During the course of the disturbance a group of protesters marched on the Hōjō prefectural capital of Tsuyama, and a list of demands—perhaps composed after the fact—denouncing every major Meiji reform eventually appeared. Nevertheless, it is clear that the incident was driven by its violence, rather than by specific grievances the protesters hoped to rectify. The rioters identified their two principal targets within the first hours of the uprising: local officials charged with carrying out government reforms and the recently "liberated" outcaste community. They treated their targets quite differently: on the one hand, they destroyed government property but avoided harming officials. On the other hand, the protesters brutally attacked the residents of Buraku communities, killing eighteen and injuring many more; in addition, they burned down 263 houses in Buraku villages. Moreover, the nature of the rebels' violence changed over the course of the disturbance. The protesters began with one technique of late Tokugawa contention, the "smashing" (uchikowashi) of buildings and other property, in their attacks on government property and several Buraku villages. As the disturbance progressed, they turned increasingly (but not exclusively) to arson—an indiscriminate form of destruction that departed significantly from the focused anger of the selective wrecking of property—when attacking Buraku villages. It was in the context of this escalating violence against property that the murder of the Burakumin occurred.

In the aftermath of the uprising nearly every commoner household in the province was fined for participating in the disturbance. Several hundred people faced punishments ranging from flogging to imprisonment, and fifteen men were beheaded, Fudeyasu for instigating the rebellion, the others for participating in the massacre of former outcastes in the village of Tsugawahara.

The Mimasaka rebellion is one of the most thoroughly researched incidents of the early Meiji years.[37] To oversimplify a bit, interpretations have split over the question of how central the attacks on the Burakumin were to the rebellion's greater significance. On the one hand, there is an impulse to valorize the rebels' opposition to the Meiji state's heavy-handed centralizing policies; historians on this side of the debate tend to downplay the significance of the Buraku attacks, treating them as spontaneous incidents or even the product of goading by disaffected samurai. On the other hand, scholars who situate the incident within a narrative of Buraku resistance against discrimination tend to cast the murdered Burakumin as heroic martyrs to the cause of Buraku liberation, but offer little further insight as to why the attacks occurred at that particular historical moment. (Raw violence of this sort directed against outcastes was virtually unknown in the Tokugawa period, and ceased after about the mid-1870s.)

Of course, the best studies of the rebellion offer subtler analyses than this summary suggests, but the fact remains that the incident is inevitably subordinated to a broader literature of peasant contention or of Buraku resistance. As a result, it has been difficult to discuss events like the Mimasaka rebellion outside the context of a predetermined narrative of class conflict and state repression. Rather than dwell on these important but familiar themes, I would like instead to consider the conditions that pushed the conflict over the edge into the realm of murderous violence.

First, let us consider the motives of the men who participated in the massacre of Burakumin at Tsugawahara village. The official history of Hōjō prefecture includes the confessions of the fourteen men who were executed for their role in the massacre, as well as that of Fudeyasu Utarō.[38] The documents must be used with care. They are composed in highly stylized language, with considerable overlap in phraseology. Moreover, judicial torture was used to extract some of the confessions, most notably Fudeyasu's. Nonetheless, they offer important insights into the motivations of the rebels.

From the confessions it is clear that the fourteen men sentenced to death for the Tsugawahara massacre were not the only participants in the killing of Burakumin. Indeed, reading through their confessions leaves one with the impression that most of them just happened to have been identified as participants. It is reasonable to suppose, then, that their fellow rioters shared their attitudes toward the Buraku community. In any case, the message that comes through the confessions is anger with the Burakumin's lack of deference toward commoners. In the eyes of the defendants, the elimination of formal status distinctions had emboldened the Burakumin, liberated from the burdens of their previous status, to behave as commoners themselves. As one of the defendants, Uji Teizō, put it, "Ever since the abolition of the label *eta,* the former *eta* of Tsugawahara village have forgotten about their former status and have in many instances behaved impertinently *[furei no shimuki sukunakarazu].*"[39]

This sort of resentment appears repeatedly in accounts of the tensions that emerged in the aftermath of the promulgation of the abolition edict. In western Japan in particular, commoners took measures to contain social interaction between Burakumin and themselves, especially in matters that exposed commoners to the Burakumin's supposed pollution. Thus hairdressers, bathhouse owners, and publicans posted notices that

their services were available only to residents of the immediate neighbor-
hood. They did so at the cost of considerable economic hardship, for to
prevent the occasional Burakumin from patronizing their businesses they
were forced to turn away commoner travelers and other unfamiliar customers. As we have seen, other conflicts arose over rights to participate
in Shinto festivals, the drawing of school-district boundaries, and the disposal of animal carcasses.[40]

In short, the reasons given by the defendants in Mimasaka for attacking Buraku villages and killing their residents were identical to those
expressed in other conflicts—some violent, most not—between commoners and Burakumin in the early Meiji period. As a result, the attacks
cannot be explained entirely within the context of the uprising, but
rather must be considered more broadly as part of the general reaction to
the elimination of the status distinction between commoners and outcastes. In other words, the uprising served as the medium in which tension and resentment escalated into murderous violence, but it did not
cause the underlying conflict. At the same time, the uprising was sparked
by the fear and confusion engendered by the imposition of conscription
and other early Meiji reforms; hence, opposition to the abolition of outcaste status—a policy announced nearly two years previously—did not
alone cause the rebellion. Furthermore, the uprising served as the
medium in which the resistance of Buraku communities took place, but it
did not cause their resistance, which must be attributed to the ardor with
which they welcomed the abolition edict. This is not to deprecate the
importance of the uprising as medium—after all, it is unlikely the attacks
on the Burakumin would have occurred independently of the more general antigovernment disturbance. At the same time, however, there is no
necessary progression from uprising to murder; indeed, it is the very rar-
ity of killing in peasant contention that makes the Mimasaka incident so
distinctive.

Killing is a funny business, utterly unimaginable in normal times,
utterly mundane under certain peculiar circumstances. Here we are faced
with the question of what pushed preexisting conflict over the edge and
made deadly violence mundane, if only briefly. It is tempting to attribute
the killings to the rage of the moment: after all, manslaughter in a fit of
emotion was common enough in Japan in the 1870s. Yet to dismiss the
massacre in this way begs the question of why killings in the heat of an
uprising were so rare in general, and yet were concentrated in the period
immediately following the Restoration. Obviously, weaponry is an
important issue here, for the presence of deadly weapons facilitates the

translation of rage into murder. In the Mimasaka rebellion, as in other early Meiji uprisings, the peasants armed themselves with bamboo spears, guns, and swords. The rioters in Tsugawahara relied mostly on bamboo spears (and, in one case, a gun) to kill their victims, though they battered a number of Burakumin with stones first, and set at least one woman on fire.

Bamboo spears don't kill people—people kill people—but killing is so much easier when one is armed. The presence of deadly weapons in early Meiji uprisings was a novel development in the history of peasant contention, as Yabuta Yutaka and others have demonstrated. Protesting peasants in the Tokugawa era rarely armed themselves, but rather carried agricultural implements such as sickles, hoes, and axes; during urban riots peasants and townspeople added carpenters' tools like saws and awls to facilitate the destruction of property.[41] These implements were known as *emono,* a term that normally refers to a weapon one is particularly adept at wielding; in the context of peasant contention, however, "tool" rather than "weapon" better captures the sense in which the word was used.

This particular use of the term *emono* dates to about the middle of the eighteenth century and is one manifestation of a distinctive etiquette of protest that evolved over the course of the seventeenth and early eighteenth centuries.[42] In accordance with this etiquette, peasants deliberately avoided carrying deadly weapons, and their use of sickles, hoes, and other farm tools was intended explicitly to emphasize their status as peasants.[43] Yabuta attributes this eschewal of bodily violence to a series of adaptations during the seventeenth century to Hideyoshi's disarmament edicts *(sōbujirei).* To be sure, weapons designed primarily to inflict bodily harm—guns, swords, bamboo spears—do occasionally figure into protest narratives, but they never predominate, particularly in accounts written by people close to the events.[44]

In any case, bloodshed was rare in early modern peasant contention. Although protesters often destroyed property, and the samurai authorities frequently threatened to use force to put down protests, only rarely did people actually get killed during the course of a rebellion, and when they did it was often accidental. This remained the case up to the onset of the Meiji regime, even as the conventions governing peasant protests evolved into a new form in which symbolic assertions of the burdens and privileges of peasant status took a back seat to graphic demonstrations of outrage. In the early nineteenth century, an increasing number of incidents occurred in which the protesters failed to present specific demands to the authorities, but rather destroyed property as an end in itself. By the

last two or three decades of the Tokugawa period, references to bamboo
spears and other weapons gradually became conspicuous in descriptions
of protests. Nonetheless, cases of weapons actually being used against
other humans remained quite isolated, though they could be quite spec-
tacular when they did occur, as in a case in which angry peasants murdered their lord, a profligate and corrupt bannerman *(hatamoto)*.[45]

To some extent we can disengage weapons from the question of the
etiquette of protest. Weapons were in fact quite common in the countryside: Hideyoshi's sword hunts did not extend to short swords *(wakizashi)*, or for that matter to firearms *(teppō)*, with the result that peasants
could arm themselves if they so chose. Tsukamoto Manabu has demonstrated that guns were surprisingly common in the countryside. Aside
from Tokugawa Tsunayoshi's reign at the end of the seventeenth century
and the 1850s and 1860s, the authorities rarely attempted to restrict
their ownership, though they did try (without much success) to encourage peasants to register their weapons.[46] Incidentally, although guns in
early modern villages were used occasionally by hunters to kill game,
they were more commonly employed to scare off wild boars, deer, and
other animals that harmed upland fields. This helps to explain why the
guns that occasionally appear in early modern protest narratives seem to
have functioned mostly to sound signals.[47] In Mimasaka, however, at
least one Burakumin was shot to death by a peasant who had brought
along his gun.

Perhaps the most suggestive evidence about weapons comes from the
Kantō region in the 1860s, where social disorder was a severe problem
for the shogunate. As we have seen, efforts to reestablish order in the
Kantō began systematically in 1805 with the creation of the Kantō
Regulatory Patrol, a police force with the authority to arrest gamblers
(bakuto), masterless samurai *(rōnin)*, and unregistered commoners
(mushuku) without regard to domainal or other political boundaries.[48]
The patrol and related efforts to impose order—never very successful in
the first place—proved particularly inadequate in the face of the political, economic, and intellectual dislocation of the final years of the
Tokugawa period.

During the last decade or so of Tokugawa rule, injunctions from the
patrol magistrates to Kantō villages included instructions to set up a system by which local temple and fire bells *(kane, hanshō)* would be rung to
alert residents of neighboring villages to the presence of "bad guys"—an
amorphous category of disorderly elements, referred to in contemporary
documents as *akutō, akuto, warumono,* and so forth—whom the peas-

ants were to apprehend and hold until the arrival of the patrolling mag-istrates.[49] When summoned, the villagers were to follow the orders of the local village officials regardless of their own place of residence; in the Kantō this could easily mean that peasants would be hurrying to enforce the law not only in another village, but indeed in another domain entirely. Some injunctions included calls for the peasants to arm them-selves with guns (whether registered or not) and gave leave to villagers to use deadly force to stop "unwieldy" *(te ni amarisōrō)* outlaws.[50]

These injunctions are important for a number of reasons. First, telling peasants to grab a weapon and come running at the sound of a nearby temple bell—perhaps summoned by an official with whom they had no formal relationship—marked a significant departure from the normal principles of governance in early modern Japan. Yet the routine would have been familiar to anyone who had participated in a peasant uprising, for the ringing of bells as a call to action was a standard feature of protests, including the Mimasaka Blood-Tax Rebellion, which began with the sounding of bells and blowing of shell horns.[51]

More serious was the shogunate's abdication of its monopoly over the legitimate use of force.[52] Giving peasants free rein to use deadly force against an ill-defined population of unwieldy "bad guys" threatened to dissolve the distinction between legitimate and illegitimate violence, for "bad guys" roamed around the Kantō plain (and everywhere else) in great abundance in the 1860s. Adding to the confusion was the fact that the Kantō Regulatory Patrol—like all law enforcement agencies in early modern Japan—relied heavily on the service as deputies of marginal characters, including the very sorts of gangsters and gamblers it was charged to control. In fact, as the regulatory patrol itself made clear in its various exhortations to good behavior, the line separating the law-abid-ing peasant from the dangerous outlaw could be quite fuzzy, as attested by the popularity of fencing lessons and other inappropriate activities among the peasantry and the more general tendency of young men to imitate "bad guys."[53]

The confusion and disorder of the last years of the Tokugawa period thus forced the shogunate to compromise some of the basic principles of the status order in an attempt to maintain control over the countryside. Not only did this foster considerable uncertainty among the peasantry, but it signified that the authorities had surrendered to the reality of a heavily armed countryside.

Legitimating the presence of weapons and their use in the name of preserving order may have had the further effect of disrupting the etiquette of peasant contention by blurring the distinction between protest and normal vigilance: the ringing of a temple bell could be a call to action in righteous anger against rapacious merchants and corrupt officials, or it could be a plea for the good denizens of the community to gather in defense against the forces of criminality. Or in an instance like the Shinchūgumi uprising of 1864, in which a motley band of masterless samurai, unregistered commoners, and local farmers banded together to take from the rich and give to the poor in Kazusa province, peasants may well have asked themselves for whom the bell tolled.[54]

The shogunate's policy of giving peasants permission to use deadly force to control disorderly elements is particularly interesting when considered in light of its official attitude toward peasant participation in fencing and other martial arts. In 1804 and 1805 the shogunate issued prohibitions against commoners' taking up martial arts; the first was directed at urban commoners and the other at both urban and rural commoners. Both were reissued several times during the remainder of the Tokugawa period. These prohibitions notwithstanding, it is clear that peasants throughout the countryside in late Tokugawa Japan participated in fencing and other martial arts.

For example, Sugi Hitoshi has examined the spread of a regional school of fencing, the *tennen rishin-ryū*, in the Tama region of Musashi province west of Edo. He finds that before the 1840s fencing practitioners in the area were overwhelmingly members of a group of rusticated marginal samurai retainers of the shogun (the Hachiōji sennin dōshin), but fencing came to attract the young heirs of village headmen and other prominent peasants (typically men in their teens or early twenties). By the 1850s, nearly 80 percent of the practitioners at the local *dōjō* were commoners.[55]

Sugi argues that participation in fencing was part of the *gōnō's* response to "world renewal" *(yonaoshi)* movements, or the threat of such movements, in the countryside west of Edo. Indeed, the area was the site of a number of large uprisings, particularly the Bushū Rebellion of 1866.[56] Many of the peasant fencers later became involved with peasant militias, though none enjoyed much martial success.[57] Sugi further notes that participation in fencing was, along with participation in poetry circles, one of the two main axes around which peasant cultural networks in the Kantō revolved at the time.

In the orders prohibiting martial arts practices among the peasantry at the beginning of the nineteenth century, the shogunate expressed a fear that commoners who took up swordsmanship would lose sight of their proper place in society, either by "losing their occupations" *(sono shoku-bun o ushinai)* or by assuming a bravado *(kigasa)* inappropriate to commoners. This feeling is echoed in one official's opposition to the formation of peasant militias in the 1860s: he was afraid that the peasant soldiers would not defer to samurai officials and that bosses would emerge from their ranks, leading the peasants to roam around the countryside without fear of the authorities. The wealthy among them would aspire to independence, the poor would turn to thievery, and all would shun agricultural labor.[58]

Thus the shogunate's calls for peasants to use deadly force against "bad guys" were issued against the background of its own repeated prohibitions of commoners' participation in martial arts organizations. No doubt this contradiction is a measure of the authorities' desperation at the end of the Tokugawa period. At the same time, the shogunate may have distinguished between peasant participation in fencing groups, which it saw as an inappropriate emulation of the samurai, and proper defense of the village community in the absence of members of the Kantō Regulatory Patrol. Well-to-do peasants may not have made such a distinction: whether practicing their swordsmanship or shooting down marauding outlaws, they were protecting themselves because they could not count on the samurai authorities' protection. In any event, it is clear that the shogunate's claims to monopolize the legitimate use of violence were being undermined from within and without during the final years of the early modern era.

Of course, the Kantō and Mimasaka are hundreds of kilometers apart, but the shogunate's fear of disorder in the hinterland of Edo appears to have been an exaggerated version of an anxiety felt by political authorities throughout the country. In any case, my purpose here is not to establish a causal link between the Kantō and Mimasaka, but rather to suggest that one by-product of the turmoil of the 1860s and 1870s was a simultaneous normalization and diffusion of force—or at least the threat of force—in response to conflict and disorder. Needless to say, were it not for assassinations, urban disturbances, civil war, the threat of foreign invasion, and so on, we would not speak of the "turmoil" of the Restoration period at all. But below the surface of such obvious tumult was a subtler problem: the normalization of the use of force effaced the distinction between "good people" *(ryōmin)* and outlaws.

During the Tokugawa period, the samurai authorities theoretically maintained a monopoly over the legitimate use of force, and they justified that monopoly by protecting the public peace. In reality, of course, violence occurred frequently in early modern Japan, as it does in every society. Habitually violent members of society—gangsters, gamblers, sumo wrestlers, and other outlaws and ruffians—existed on the margins of the polity, often in an ambiguous state as masterless samurai or unregistered commoners. To police this violent margin, the authorities deputized members of a variety of groups on the periphery of society, including some members of the outlaw community itself. This approach to preserving order was cumbersome and inefficient,[59] but it meshed well with the technological and political conditions of the times, with the result that Japan was a reasonably orderly society by the standards of the early modern world.

In the last years of the Tokugawa period, however, the shogunate, in response to its inability to control the violent margin in places like the Kantō, took the further step of deputizing the commoner populace in its entirety. In doing so, the authorities effectively admitted that they could no longer distinguish between the violent margin and the law-abiding core of society, for every member of the core—and particularly its young men—was a reserve member of the forces of the "bad guys," tottering on the precipice of criminality. In openly accepting the widespread presence of weapons in the countryside, and in attempting to harness elements of the peasantry's etiquette of protest in the service of law enforcement, the shogunate effectively enjoined the entire countryside to suspect and police itself, for the entire countryside threatened to descend into the violent margin.

This brings us back to Mimasaka and another telling detail of the incident there. The man who by his own confession opened the door to the most brutal violence in Mimasaka was Kobayashi Kumezō, a fifty-one-year-old former sumo wrestler and local boss (oyakata) who lived in Myōbara, a commoner village near Tsugawahara. Let us consider his role in the massacre in some detail. In his confession, Kobayashi said that people had always come to him for advice whenever disputes (motsure-goto) arose, and that they did so once again when news of the rioting arrived. His advice was to avoid joining the rebellion if possible, but to go along if the protesters insisted. On May 28, the protesters arrived in an insistent mood, and so a group of villagers duly joined the crowd.[60]

Kobayashi himself remained in the village, however, and used the opportunity to try to persuade the leaders of Tsugawahara to submit a formal apology for their supposed effrontery toward commoners in the months following the promulgation of the abolition edict. (A number of Buraku villages in Mimasaka avoided attack by presenting such apologies to the protesters; in the aftermath of the violence, the prefectural authorities ordered that all such documents be burned.)[61] In addition, he advised the Burakumin to honor the customary protocols of status difference—to go barefoot when business took them to commoner villages, bow their heads to the ground when encountering a commoner on the road, and so forth—and, as a sign of their sincerity, to agree to take up a position in the vanguard of the procession to Tsuyama. The Buraku leaders refused, saying they had no interest in participating in the rebellion and that they were determined to stand up to any attack that might be launched against them.[62]

Soon thereafter the rioters returned to Myōbara, vowing to attack Tsugawahara unless an apology were forthcoming from the villagers. Kobayashi and another man went once again to negotiate, this time with a different group of village leaders, but the result was the same as the first time. Disgusted by what he saw as the Burakumin's intransigence, Kobayashi urged the rioters to proceed into the village and "attack as they pleased" (katte shidai ni rannyū itasubeshi).[63]

Although Kobayashi makes no mention of it in his confession, other accounts of the massacre state that one reason for the extreme brutality of the attack on Tsugawahara was the crowd's anger at the residents' overt resistance. The Burakumin constructed a series of false fortifications to give the impression that cannons and other firearms were trained on the crowd, ready to fire in case of an attack. Once the protesters saw through the ploy, they poured into Tsugawahara and destroyed it completely, burning down every one of the hundred or more houses in the village.[64]

Kobayashi claims to have remained at home during the initial attack. The following day, May 29, he learned that the village had been destroyed and that a number of residents who had fled to the hills overnight had been caught and brought down to the bank of the Kamo River to be killed. He went back to Tsugawahara at that point, this time with the intention of settling old scores: "It was a chance to kill some people and clear up my longstanding hatred of them, and so I went down to lead the crowd myself."[65]

Going down to the riverbank, he did not see the men he particularly hated, but he did find seven or eight women and children being held near the riverbank. He got the guards to turn the prisoners over to him after agreeing to provide them with a receipt for the women and children they had captured. As a list of names was being drawn up more prisoners were brought to the riverbank, bringing the total to about thirty.[66]

At that point the crowd captured two prominent members of the community, Saimu Kiichirō and his son, Ryūtarō. The crowd called for their immediate deaths. Kobayashi thought this fortunate because the two had long been contemptuous of nearby commoner villages.[67] The mob dragged the two off to the riverbank. Kobayashi claimed to have left the area at that point because he thought he might be recognized if he accompanied the crowd, which could cause him problems later. By the time he returned, the two had been killed along with six or seven other villagers. He told the crowd to spare the remaining prisoners—all women and children—and went home.

In his confession, Kobayashi said that the following day, May 30, he "felt rather bad" *(nantonaku sokokimi ashikusōrō)* about his involvement in the massacre, even though his actions were the product of the heat of the moment.[68] Worried about repercussions from the attack, and about the possibility of the protesters returning to the Buraku village, he went to Tsugawahara to survey the damage and see the survivors. He persuaded one of the surviving villagers to draft a promise that the Burakumin would return to their previous status, which he then delivered to the mayor of his own village.

As a former sumo wrestler and local fixer, Kobayashi was the sort of person whom the authorities might have labeled a "bad guy," but even more, he was the sort of well-connected man of local influence whom the same authorities would have wanted to enlist in their efforts to control disorder. Indeed, if his confession is to be believed, Kobayashi could have prevented the massacre at Tsugawahara. In any case, his role suggests that elements of the etiquette of protest survived even in the darkest moments of the uprising, elements reflected in the crowd's deference to Kobayashi in launching the initial attack against Tsugawahara, in the negotiations with the Buraku leadership over the presentation of apologies for past behavior, and indeed in the exchange of receipts for captive Tsugawahara villagers.

In Mimasaka, the rules that had governed social relations between commoners and outcastes collapsed with the formal abolition of the outcastes' base status—rules that had given structure to discrimination and channeled aversion and interaction in ways recognized and accepted (or at least tolerated) by both sides. Kobayashi's inability to influence his Buraku neighbors reflected the collapse of those rules. At the same time, the dismantling of the status system and the political order of which it had been a part rendered invalid the script by which Mimasaka peasants could present grievances to the state. (In his confession, Fudeyasu stated

that he was against all the early Meiji reforms and had considered presenting a petition to that effect, but he abandoned the idea because he
knew it would be futile—as indeed it would have been.)[69] The collapse of
the early modern order took the petition out of the peasant's hand and
replaced it with a bamboo spear.

In their confessions, the Mimasaka defendants gave a very personal
view of their actions. One said that he had decided not to participate in
the uprising, but on hearing that the mob was headed to a Buraku village, he grabbed his bamboo spear and joined the rioters; most mention
a sudden welling up of murderous desire *(kotsuzen satsunen shōji)* that
led them to plunge their spears into the helpless Burakumin lying before
them.[70] Of course, people have been killing one another for millennia,
and early modern society had its share of murders. Here, however, we
have people killing strangers—or directing others to kill old acquain-
tances—for reasons explicitly political, yet at the same time rooted in
resentments and tensions that had built up in the course of everyday
interaction and everyday aversion. It is telling in this context that except
for Kobayashi and one other resident of Myōbara, the other men condemned for participating in the massacre simply went home after the
killings: for them, the rebellion had served its purpose.

The Mimasaka Blood-Tax Rebellion suggests that murderous violence
underwent a process of "modernization" in the years following the
Restoration. As we have seen, the shogunate's abdication of its monopoly over the legitimate use of force undermined the "feudal" mode of
violence in Japan. Violence became detached from state power, a development that simultaneously undermined the legitimacy of the early modern state and obscured the distinction between the law-abiding core of
society—that is, those secure in their status as peasants—and the violent
margin.[71] At the same time, the rules that had governed the peasantry in
the resolution of disputes broke down during the final decades of the
Tokugawa period, as Yabuta and other students of protest etiquette have
demonstrated. Or rather, the rules changed, so that protest, like violence
more generally, was detached from the confines of the status system and
allowed greater play within society.

In places like Mimasaka, the result of this combination of developments was a further evolution of the protocols of protest, such that the
individuated murderous impulse of the participants in the Tsugawahara
massacre found release. Mimasaka was not the only place to see such
violence, however. Other protests in the early Meiji years saw a similar
escalation from the controlled, collective violence of the crowd, to arson,

and in some cases, to the killing of individuals. During the 1879 cholera epidemic, for example, a mob in the town of Numatare, Niigata prefecture, killed Yasuda Hannosuke, a former samurai *(shizoku)* who had been seen pouring a mysterious substance—stomach medicine, it turned out—into the river. The crowd turned on Yasuda and a peddler who happened to be passing by after the police refused to arrest Yasuda as the person responsible for the epidemic. The police apprehended the killers, but only after battling a crowd of about seven hundred—many armed with bamboo spears—that had been summoned to the scene by fire bells.[72] The fire bells were remnants of an etiquette of protest rooted in the early modern status system that survived only to call the mob to do battle with the police.

The collapse of the early modern order rendered systematic expressions of the sanctity of peasant status meaningless. Without recourse to valid, traditional means of collective political expression, peasants turned increasingly to violence, killing to make statements about Meiji policies ranging from conscription to public sanitation, and killing to assert their liberation from the status-based strictures of membership in the law-abiding core of early modern society.

VIOLENCE AND THE COLLAPSE OF THE STATUS ORDER

The appalling violence of the Mimasaka rebellion fits into a familiar pattern of popular response to uncontrollable social dislocation, in which vulnerable groups direct their anger and fear against society's weakest elements. Although this no doubt explains much of the motivation for the attacks on Burakumin, it is worthwhile to consider the matter more closely. During the Tokugawa period, peasant contention often occurred when cultivators felt the feudal authorities had abrogated their moral covenant to provide benevolent rule. Protesters commonly referred to themselves as "august peasants" *(onbyakushō)* and rationalized their actions by asserting the centrality of their contribution to the stability and prosperity of the realm.[73] The Mimasaka protesters implicitly replicated this strategy by complaining that, in sharp contrast to the former daimyo, the Meiji leaders were behaving in all respects like "Chinamen" *(tōjin—* a generic term for foreigners). Recognizing that the new regime would no longer honor the moral covenant of the early modern period, the peasants struck out, lest they "be treated no differently from the *eta*."[74] Hence the virulence of their anger against the Burakumin and their insistence on the restoration of the norms of deference that had applied during the previous regime. If the protesters could not be "august peasants" in the eyes of the authorities, they could at least force the Burakumin to reaffirm their status as such. (Unfortunately, because of a lack of evidence, we cannot know whether the norms of deference the commoners tried to "reimpose" on the Burakumin had ever, in fact, been practiced: it was an excellent opportunity for the commoners to attempt to invent a tradition of extreme subservience on the part of the Burakumin.)

As we have seen, the exchange of obligations for benevolent rule was a cornerstone of the early modern status system insofar as it provided the rationale for the authorities' exactions of tax grain and corvée labor. Let us briefly examine the transition from occupation to livelihood and its relationship to early Meiji violence in light of the moral covenant of feudal rule. At the close of the Tokugawa period, the status-based occupation of the peasantry in places like the Kantō plain had come to include new obligations in addition to the payment of land taxes and the performance of normal corvée labor such as construction work and post-station duties. Because the authorities abdicated their monopoly over the legitimate use of violence, the maintenance of order became, in effect, part of a peasant's occupation.

The shogunate and domains that followed its lead may not have seen the delegation of violence as a fundamental departure from the principles of status: keeping a lookout for "bad guys" and serving in the various peasant militias organized in the waning years of the Tokugawa period were simply ways of ensuring the military preparedness of the regime and thus not intrinsically different from such indirect means as the provision of warriors' sustenance. The problem, of course, is that assigning peasants the duty of maintaining order raised questions concerning the obligations of those groups whose monopoly that duty had been—the samurai as a military class and the outcastes as agents of law enforcement. Thus, although it was hardly the intent, giving peasants leave to engage in violence undermined the moral covenant that lay at the heart of the status order, without, however, negating a basic premise of that order, which called for the peasantry to assist the authorities' attempts to provide benevolent rule.

In the early Meiji period, peasants in Mimasaka and other sites of antigovernment protest took it on themselves to recalibrate the status order through the exercise of the very technique—murderous violence—that had undermined it in the first place. That is, the authorities, deluded by Western "Chinamen," had clearly abdicated their duty by enacting policies that upended the proper order of things. The abolition of outcaste status ruptured the containment field that had regulated the violence of killing—who would oversee the deaths of animals and criminals if the outcastes were liberated from such duties?—and was thus particularly disturbing. But other early Meiji reforms had the same effect, too. Conscription was all about violence, after all, though in the eyes of many peasants it was not the instruments of violence soldiers wielded that were so scary, but rather the prospect that conscripts themselves would be killed for their blood. Public health policies prompted a similar anxiety, as seen in the fears of protesters in Kōchi prefecture, who were convinced that the metal beds used in quarantine hospitals were actually grills designed to drain off the fat of the hygienists' victims.[75] Universal education imperiled peasant livelihoods and the performance of status-based duties by removing valuable labor power from the fields and moving it to the classroom. The land-tax reform both undermined agriculture as an occupation and, through its corollary practice of household registration, created a roster of potential victims of the draining of blood and fat. Thus, violence against Burakumin can be seen as a way to reinstitute the normal balance between occupation and livelihood by forcing outcastes back into their proper place, thereby alerting the authorities to the errors of their ways.

On a national scale, the Burakumin and their problems were a relatively minor concern, as much larger and more powerful social groups voiced their opposition to the new politics of the quotidian. The wave of peasant movements during the years right after the Restoration—the vast majority of which had nothing to do with Buraku liberation—fit into this category. Perhaps the greatest threat came from dispossessed samurai, who rose repeatedly and sometimes extremely destructively in opposition to the loss of their status privileges. Indeed, the largest such incident, the Satsuma Rebellion of 1877, took seven months to suppress and nearly bankrupted the government.[76]

The Meiji state prevailed through these and many other difficulties, however, so that by the end of the 1870s, debate—even in its insurrectionary guise—had largely shifted from the question of whether Japan ought to embrace Western-style modernity to specific issues of the means by which modernization would be attained. No doubt the rapid economic growth of the late 1870s and early 1880s helped peasants to accommodate themselves to the monetization of obligations. After all, their lives had improved, at least temporarily, as a result; and if they did not, the fact that the state eagerly reclaimed its monopoly over the legitimate use of violence through the creation of a modern police force and a shoot-to-kill approach to quelling unrest surely encouraged dissatisfied elements of society to make their peace with the modern nation-state.

Although the samurai participants in the Satsuma Rebellion and similar movements preceding it had a clear counterrevolutionary intent, peasant protesters had largely given up their calls for a restoration of the Tokugawa status order by the mid-1870s. Peasants did keep rebelling: they launched a number of serious challenges to the state during the economic dislocation of the Matsukata Deflation of 1881–85 in particular. In incidents like the Chichibu Rebellion of 1884, protesters loaded their plates high with condiments from the salad bar of nineteenth-century discourse—a traditional insistence on the right to benevolent rule, world renewal *(yonaoshi)* from late Tokugawa uprisings, and democracy and even revolution from the Meiji Freedom and Popular Rights Movement—to express their sense that in placing so much emphasis on economic development the state had neglected its obligations to the people.[77] But it was clear both from their entrepreneurial behavior before the rebellion and the tenor of their demands during it that they had largely accommodated themselves to the idea of the individual as an autonomous economic and political actor.

CHAPTER 5

Ainu Identity
and the Early Modern State

As a consequence of the formation of the early modern state in the seventeenth century, Japan established clear political boundaries for itself for the first time. One such boundary lay in the southern part of Hokkaido. Everything south of a sometimes shifting but nonetheless clear line was part of the Tokugawa state, while the territory to the north of it was seen as the Ezochi, a nominally autonomous appendage of the state whose Ainu inhabitants were bound by trade and ritual to the Matsumae domain, the Japanese political entity in southern Hokkaido.[1] The most important by-product of the drawing of that political boundary was the creation of a civilizational boundary between the Ainu and the Japanese, articulated through the medium of customs.

The delineation of a boundary between the Ainu and the Japanese in Hokkaido was paralleled on early modern Japan's other frontiers. The invasion of the Ryukyu kingdom by the Satsuma domain in 1609 established a border in the south, with Ryukyu enjoying formal independence while being bound politically to the Tokugawa state. Likewise, Toyotomi Hideyoshi's disastrous invasions of Korea in 1592 and 1597 and the subsequent reestablishment of diplomatic relations with Korea by the Tokugawa regime, combined with the expulsion of most Europeans from Japan by 1639, clearly separated Japan from its neighbors across the Japan and East China seas. As in the case of the Ainu, the drawing of political boundaries was accompanied by the demarcation of civiliza-

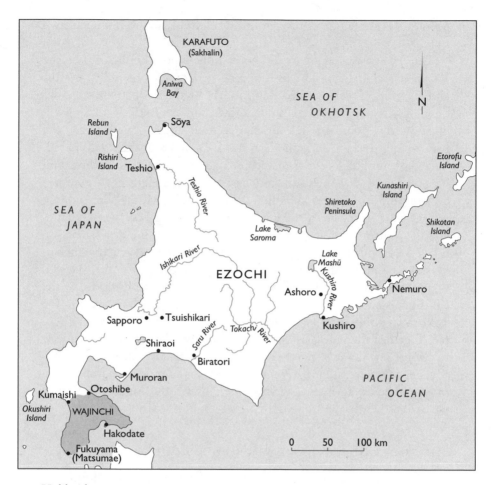

Hokkaido

tional boundaries between the Japanese and other East Asian peoples. As a result, by the late seventeenth century Japan had for the first time in its history unambiguous political borders, albeit ones drawn according to different principles than those in the modern world. One consequence of their establishment was the notion that the people living within those borders were part of a distinctive realm of Japanese civilization and those outside them were not. But because Chinese and other realms of civilization existed outside the Tokugawa polity, not everyone beyond Japan's borders was barbarian: the barbarism of the Ainu and other peripheral peoples was a function of their political subordination to the Tokugawa state.

The Tokugawa shogunate did not simply impose boundaries on the Japanese archipelago. The overlapping geographies of polity, status, and civilization were shaped importantly by the people whose livelihoods and social identities straddled their borders. In this chapter I will illustrate this point through an examination of relations between the Ainu people and the early modern state. The relationship was characterized by mutual dependence and constructive misunderstanding, and by policies of dissimilation and assimilation under the Matsumae domain and Tokugawa shogunate, respectively. Mutual dependence refers to the Ainu's need for Japanese commodities, on the one hand, and the Matsumae domain's need to maintain the Ainu as a barbarian people exogenous to the core polity, on the other. Constructive misunderstanding allowed each side to maintain agency: the Ainu viewed their dependence on Japanese commodities as simple trade, while Matsumae sublimated its need to legitimate its place within the Tokugawa polity into its self-image as suzerain over a barbarian people. Together, these discussions will show how long-standing economic relations on Japan's northern frontier were ritualized to secure Matsumae's place in the early modern polity, and how the combination of economic engagement and ritual determined the Ainu's position as barbarians within the status system.

THE ROOTS OF MUTUAL DEPENDENCE IN HOKKAIDO

Ties of mutual dependence joined the Ainu and the Japanese during the Tokugawa period. The Ainu's dependence on the Japanese was economic: they relied on their southern neighbors for commodities they could neither produce for themselves nor acquire by any other means. Conversely, for the Japanese, the Ainu occupied a critical bit of political space that at once defined the position of the Matsumae domain within the Tokugawa state and, more broadly, clarified the nature of state authority. In other words, Matsumae's place in the Tokugawa order was predicated on its continuing relationship with the Ainu people. Indeed, the Ainu were so important to Matsumae that the domain proved willing to create them if there were not enough "real" Ainu to go around.

In 1593 the founder of the Matsumae domain, Kakizaki (later Matsumae) Yoshihiro, submitted to Toyotomi Hideyoshi in exchange for Hideyoshi's recognition of his monopoly over access to trade with the Ainu. In asserting his role as an intermediary between the Japanese and the Ainu, Yoshihiro followed the precedent established by his forebears, who had dominated southernmost Hokkaido since the middle of the fifteenth century. The Kakizaki house differed from other military houses in its lack of economically significant agricultural production in its territories. Instead, its power derived entirely from its dominance over the valuable commercial traffic between Hokkaido and Honshu. Hokkaido Ainu exchanged marine products, gold, furs, feathers, and Chinese textiles (procured from Manchuria via Sakhalin) for ironware, lacquerware, rice, sake, tobacco, and other Japanese commodities.[2] It was control over the terms and volume of this trade, rather than dominion over physical territory, that Hideyoshi acknowledged and Tokugawa Ieyasu later confirmed. (In practice, the Matsumae domain as a geographical entity was eventually identified with the Wajinchi, the section of southern Hokkaido open to permanent Japanese settlement.)

Yoshihiro's pledge of loyalty to Hideyoshi brought the Japanese in Hokkaido fully within the purview of the emergent early modern Japanese state and, simultaneously, excluded the Ainu from the core Japanese polity. Kamiya Nobuyuki argues that Hideyoshi was pleased by Yoshihiro's submission because it secured a buffer against possible incursions from the north—not from the Russians, who were still a continent away from the Pacific, but rather from the expansive Jurchens of Manchuria, whose territory was thought to be contiguous with Hokkaido.[3] Yoshihiro represented himself to Hideyoshi and, later, to Tokugawa Ieyasu as suzerain of the Ainu by including Ainu troops in a force he led on Hideyoshi's behalf and by wearing Chinese brocades (Ezo *nishiki*) obtained through Ainu trade contacts in the Amur River basin to a meeting with Ieyasu.[4]

Shakushain's War of 1669 was the Ainu's final concerted effort to assert their independence from Matsumae and reestablish trade with Japan on their own terms.[5] The conflict was caused by a combination of economic factors, including competition among Ainu chieftains for access to fish and animal pelts to trade with the Japanese, conflict over Ainu access to markets outside the Matsumae domain, and discontent concerning the size of rice bales used by the Japanese in trade. It sparked a major crisis within the Matsumae domain leadership and caused concern in the Tsugaru domain and the shogunate, both of which assisted Matsumae in the struggle. Although rarely discussed outside the specialist literature, it was a seminal episode in the history of early modern Japan, for it reflected the Ainu's rejection of the basic premises of the Tokugawa order, particularly the state's authority to delineate Japan's political boundaries and order its contacts with alien peoples. Kikuchi Isao thus likens Shakushain's War to the Shimabara Rebellion of 1637, which, with its mixture of Christian and disaffected masterless samurai participants, similarly challenged the fundamental principles of the early modern regime.[6]

Some 150 Japanese and an unknown number of Ainu died in the fighting, which peaked during the summer of 1669. In the winter of that year the Ainu chieftain Shakushain was murdered by Japanese posing as peace negotiators. The Ainu war effort collapsed quickly after that, although a few groups in eastern Hokkaido continued to fight sporadically until 1672.[7] The conclusion of hostilities was marked by a conflict-resolution process that incorporated both Ainu and Japanese elements. Within Ainu society, disputes were resolved through a meeting of the hostile parties at which an indemnity *(tsugunai)* was negotiated. The peace talks between Shakushain and Matsumae representatives in the tenth month of 1669 conformed to Ainu cultural expectations; Shakushain had even agreed to an indemnity before being murdered. After his death his followers in eastern Hokkaido gave the domain 252 indemnity items with a promise to pay 247 more later; the following year Ainu leaders in western Hokkaido turned over an additional seven or eight hundred items. Although a few Ainu chieftains refused to comply with the domain's demands, most paid rather than risk being cut off from all access to trade.[8]

In accordance with Japanese practice, the domain extracted an oath of submission from the Ainu leadership in the fourth month of 1671. In addition to agreeing to comply with domain directives and inform the authorities of any plots against Matsumae, the Ainu promised to trade according to rules established by the domain. In practice, this meant that they acceded to higher prices for Japanese commodities, which they could obtain only at designated trading posts *(akinaiba)* within the Ezochi. The agreement thus forced the Ainu to sever their long-standing commercial ties to Tsugaru and other Honshu domains.[9]

After the Ainu's defeat, the broad political structures that had been evolving among them disappeared, only to be replaced by a new and much weaker political organization that was tied very closely to the patronage of the Matsumae house and its leading retainers. Thereafter all trade was conducted at outposts managed by the daimyo and his leading retainers or at Fukuyama castle. Management of the trading posts was later entrusted to merchants, an arrangement that formed the basis for the emergence of the contract-fishery system *(basho ukeoisei)* in the eighteenth century. A key result of Shakushain's War was the prohibition of travel by the Ainu beyond the Ezochi and the concomitant demarcation of southernmost Hokkaido as the Wajinchi, an area of nearly exclusive Japanese habitation, an arrangement validated by the shogunate in 1682.[10]

Shakushain's War was a critical turning point in the history of the relationship between the Ainu and the Japanese state. Before Toyotomi Hideyoshi's attainment of hegemony throughout the archipelago, the head of the Kakizaki house had behaved in many respects like an Ainu chieftain, albeit a particularly powerful and influential one, in forging alliances with and mediating disputes among the various broad, regional groupings in Hokkaido. Renamed Matsumae and backed by the power of the Tokugawa regime, the daimyo house in southern Hokkaido steadily arrogated control over regional trade during the first decades of the seventeenth century, but it was not able to prevent the Ainu from traveling south to trade in Honshu, nor did its growing power compromise the integrity of the Ainu chiefdoms. Shakushain's War decisively changed the balance of power and marked the final subjugation of the Ezochi as an appendage to the early modern Japanese state.

Shakushain's War brought the Ezochi into the Tokugawa world order, but it did not immediately bring most Ainu into it. For Ainu communities beyond the southernmost part of Hokkaido, the patterns of everyday life—including both subsistence activities and local trade—continued with few changes for many decades after 1669. The expansion of Matsumae's network of official trading posts restricted their trading activities and thus led to a deterioration of the terms of exchange, but the nature of the exchange itself did not immediately change. That is, Ainu continued to supply the Japanese with commodities like eagle feathers, animal pelts, and salmon they had caught themselves, and in exchange they received Japanese commodities. On the Pacific coast of Hokkaido, and particularly in areas in the far northeast of the island, this pattern of interaction survived intact throughout much of the Tokugawa period. As Brett Walker has shown, Hokkaido Ainu who were able to procure valuable commodities not readily available to the Japanese, such as fur-seal *(ottosei)* and sea-otter *(rakko)* pelts from the Kurils and Chinese brocades acquired via Sakhalin and the Amur River basin, were able to maintain a fair degree of autonomy until the early nineteenth century.

Ainu in the northern Kuril Islands and in much of Sakhalin remained independent traders until the late nineteenth century.[11]

In contrast, Ainu communities in southeastern Hokkaido and all along the Japan Sea coast entered into vastly different relations with the Japanese once merchants began converting the trading posts into contract fisheries in the middle of the eighteenth century. By the end of the century the west coast of Hokkaido was dotted with fisheries that produced salmon, kelp, and above all herring for markets in western Japan. The contractors *(basho ukeoinin)* enjoyed a monopoly over access to Ainu labor, which they employed in combination with seasonal workers from southern Hokkaido and northern Honshu. The fishery expanded steadily in response to the growing demand for the herring-meal fertilizer that was its main product. It grew particularly rapidly after the 1830s, when famine in northeastern Honshu pushed thousands of peasants into the Hokkaido labor market and thereby facilitated the deployment of large nets, known as pound traps, which could be manned by unskilled and semiskilled workers. This prompted independent family fishers from southern Hokkaido to establish operations in the Ezochi. These new operators were denied access to Ainu labor but were free to hire Japanese workers; they were the forerunners of a burgeoning capitalist fishery that became, by the end of the nineteenth century, perhaps the largest fishery in the world.[12]

By focusing on conditions in eastern and northeastern Hokkaido, Sakhalin, and the Kurils before the nineteenth century, as Walker does in his study, it is possible to write a history of the Ainu in the Tokugawa period that makes due note of the development of commercial fishing but does not see it as central to their relationship with the Japanese. Walker's approach is particularly effective in demonstrating, on the one hand, how the Matsumae domain was able to benefit from the Ainu's trade contacts beyond Hokkaido and, on the other, how Matsumae's conquest of the Ainu set into motion a process by which the ecological bases of Ainu subsistence were gradually undermined.

Nevertheless, the Ainu's growing involvement in the commercial fishing economy was critical, for it decisively secured the ability of the Matsumae domain to institutionalize the Ainu's position as barbarians in the geography of civilization. As the herring fishery grew, the domain adapted its relationship with the Ainu to reflect the importance of the Ainu's new role as fishery workers by, for example, privileging the leaders of the seasonal labor camps that grew up around the fisheries in ritual ties. Moreover, the expansion of the fishery drew Ainu from a broadening geographical base into wage labor, which at the very least accelerated the infiltration of Japanese commodities into the everyday lives of Ainu throughout Hokkaido. From the vantage point of the middle of the nineteenth century, the processes Walker examines appear as important contributing factors to the Ainu's loss of independence, but their importance pales in comparison to the development of fishing because it was the commercial fishery that decisively integrated Hokkaido and all its people into the broader Japanese economy. Once the Ainu became integral participants in an economy that tied the Ezochi to the core polity, Matsumae's delineation of a civilizational boundary in Hokkaido became more than a self-serving symbolic gesture. Being marked as barbarians had a determining effect on the terms of the Ainu's participation in the fishing economy and because of the strong pull of the fisheries on Ainu labor, it directly affected the lives and livelihoods of Ainu throughout Hokkaido.

The Ainu needed a variety of commodities—ironware above all, but also weapons, cloth, sake, rice, lacquerware, and tobacco—that were available only through trade with the Japanese.[13] Given their inability to procure other regular sources of needed commodities or to extract them forcibly from the Japanese, they had little choice but to submit to the overlordship of the Tokugawa shogunate and its agent, the Matsumae domain. For their part, the Japanese did not hesitate to make the most of their economic and political advantages over the Ainu, an advantage that the expansion of the fishing economy in the eighteenth and nineteenth centuries only reinforced.[14]

Economic dependence on the Japanese and a loss of political autonomy were fundamental characteristics of Ainu culture from the late seventeenth century onward. But this is not to say that Ainu culture became less vital as a result. A number of important innovations occurred in response to the new relationship with Japan. At the most general level, contact with the Japanese seems to have encouraged the native people of Hokkaido to accentuate the distinctly "Ainu" elements of their culture. Whereas the earliest bearers of Ainu culture (which emerged around the fourteenth century) practiced agriculture widely, their descendants focused more intensively on hunting, fishing, and gathering in inland districts, which not only distanced them from Japanese intrusion into their daily lives but gave them ready access to the commodities most desired by their trading partners, particularly fish and animal pelts.[15] Moreover, according to Emori Susumu, military conflict with the Japanese encouraged the Ainu to close cultural and linguistic ranks, which resulted in greater uniformity within a culture that was an amalgam of elements of the earlier Satsumon and Okhotsk cultures, spread thinly over a broad geographical area. In other words, the threat posed by the intrusion of the Japanese made the Ainu more coherent as a people than they would have been otherwise.[16] Kaiho Mineo has suggested that this homogenization explains why, on the one hand, the early modern Japanese saw the Hokkaido Ainu as a monolithic group, while, on the other hand, their medieval forebears recognized three distinct groups of Ezo: the *hinomoto* Ezo of eastern Hokkaido, the *karako* Ezo of western Hokkaido and Sakhalin, and the *wataritō* Ezo of southern Hokkaido (who were, in fact, the descendants of Japanese immigrants to the island).[17]

Cultural practice sanctified economic necessity. For example, the Ainu valued particularly rare goods as "treasures" *(ikor)* that not only represented a household's wealth but could be offered as indemnities in case of disputes. The Ainu did not regard every Japanese commodity as a treasure, but some, especially lacquer utensils and swords with decorated sheaths, they treated as heirlooms.[18] Moreover, the linguist Okuda Osami notes that wage labor under Japanese supervision is rarely if ever mentioned in the *yukar* and other Ainu oral traditions. Although this may indicate the *yukar* have survived in their pristine forms since sometime before the development of the commercial fishing industry in the eighteenth century, Okuda speculates that in fact their present form is the product of editing by Ainu, who thereby created an autonomous and internally coherent history of their culture.[19]

Perhaps the clearest example of the vitality of Ainu culture during the Tokugawa period is the *iyomante,* or bear ceremony, which was the central—even defining—ritual practice of the culture.[20] The Ainu and their predecessors had long returned animal spirits to the realm of the gods laden with gifts. But according to Utagawa Hiroshi and Sasaki Toshikazu, the *iyomante* in its most elaborate and familiar form, in which its object was a bear cub that had been raised in an Ainu settlement, emerged only at the end of the eighteenth century. Watanabe Hitoshi speculates that the *iyomante* may have developed in this way to secure ready supplies of bear pelts for the Japanese trade, for while the demand for bear pelts and meat within Ainu society was limited, it was quite elastic among the Japanese. In any case, the new version of the *iyomante* gave geographically dispersed lineage groups an opportunity to gather and reaffirm their sense of community. Having lost the ability to form meaningful political units, the Ainu compensated by creating a ritual framework to assert their independence from Japanese domination.[21]

THE RITUAL FRAMEWORK
OF CONSTRUCTIVE MISUNDERSTANDING

Most of the time, it would have been difficult to tell that Iwanosuke, an eighteenth-century Ainu resident of Kennichi village in southwestern Hokkaido, was anything but Japanese: he had a Japanese name, he lived in a Japanese village, and he wore his hair in a style popular among Japanese dandies. Every winter, however, Iwanosuke underwent a curious metamorphosis. He let his hair and beard grow long so that he might look properly Ainu when he went to pay his respects to the lord of the Matsumae domain on the seventh day of the new year. As a representative of the Ainu people, Iwanosuke participated with the daimyo in a relationship known in Ainu as *uimam* (trade) and in Japanese as *omemie* (audience), in which a ritual show of submission on the Ainu's part was rewarded by grants of gifts that had little value to the Japanese, but were often regarded as treasures by the Ainu.

According to the explorer Mogami Tokunai, who visited Kennichi village in 1784, Iwanosuke's annual rediscovery of his roots was a "remnant of the old Ezo [Ainu] customs."[22] In fact, just the opposite was true: Iwanosuke assumed what had become for him a false identity for reasons that had little to do with old Ainu customs and everything to do with the institutions of the Matsumae domain. The practice of *uimam* and the related *umsa*, or traditional "greeting" ceremony, was indeed rooted in Ainu culture, but by the time Iwanosuke appeared on the scene the rituals had long lost their original significance.

An examination of the *uimam* and *umsa* rituals serves as a convenient point of departure for a consideration of the meaning of Ainu identity in the early modern Japanese world order. The *uimam* and *umsa* were the critical ritual manifestations of the relationship between the Ainu people and the Tokugawa state.[23] Traditional Ainu practices were reconstituted to legitimate the mutually dependent, yet profoundly unequal, relationship between the Japanese and Ainu.

The content of the *uimam* and *umsa* rituals changed in response to shifts in the political relationship between the two peoples. *Uimam* originally referred simply to trade conducted between relative equals. Indeed, the word never lost this sense, even after the ceremony assumed a political character, and for the Ainu the trade element always remained paramount. The *umsa*, on the other hand, was originally an elaborate greeting exchanged by Ainu reuniting after a long separation. After the old friends had embraced and exchanged courtesies, the host made an elaborate show of hospitality in the gregarious manner of the Ainu people.

The Matsumae domain co-opted and gradually transformed the two practices after it established hegemony over southern Hokkaido in the late sixteenth century. Attempts to manipulate the rituals could be seen as early as 1633, when domain officials had Ainu residents of Otobe and Kuroiwa, villages at the remote western and eastern extremities of the area of Japanese habitation, perform the *uimam* for the benefit of shogunal inspectors. In general, however, the domain came to stress Ainu submission to Japanese authority over trade in the function of the *uimam* only in the eighteenth century. This change in attitude occurred as commercial fishing began to supplant trade with the Ainu as the basis of the domain economy.[24]

The content of the *uimam* ceremony, too, evolved only gradually into an assertion of Japanese political domination of the Ainu. At the 1633 *uimam* the Otobe Ainu in attendance greeted the inspectors in accordance with their own cultural practices before singing and dancing for the benefit of the visitors. Furukawa Koshōken, writing much later, described it as follows:

> The Ezo [Ainu] came forward, apparently in their native style, the men together in one group and the women in another. They joined hands and stood together like a flock of geese. Then each bowed his head and the group walked steadily sideways into the garden, where the men sat cross-legged on mats, their hands held clasped on their knees and heads unbowed. The women knelt on the sand.[25]

Ainu chieftains visiting Matsumae's Fukuyama castle around 1700 were seated near the domain lord during their audience, an indication that little social distance separated the participants in the ritual. In contrast, their successors a century later were made to kneel on straw mats in the garden, and the domain displayed weapons at the *uimam* site as a way to impress the Ainu with its military power. Moreover, in the early Tokugawa period *uimam* trips to Fukuyama were relatively rare and confined to Ainu living in southern Hokkaido. Conversely, by the late eighteenth century the practice had become highly systematic, with appearances fixed on a regular schedule and predetermined gift lists the rule. Ainu chieftains from throughout the island were expected to appear for an investiture *uimam* on their succession, and others, like Iwanosuke, were called in at regular intervals to commemorate events important to the Japanese, such as New Year's.[26]

In contrast to the *uimam*, which was always performed for the benefit of the lord, the *umsa* greeting was a less formal affair. After being
adopted by Japanese merchants and officials at fisheries and trading
posts as an exchange of greetings between equals, the ritual was eventually transformed into a sort of celebration to commemorate the successful completion of the fishing or trading season. The Japanese merchant
or official hosting the *umsa* made a display of hospitality to his Ainu
workers and clients, who by this time were clearly not perceived as the
social equals of the Japanese.[27] Moreover, by the late eighteenth century
operators of Japanese fishing outposts had assumed important administrative functions from the Matsumae domain, with the result that the
umsa served as an opportunity to read laws and injunctions to the gathered Ainu. As a domain-sanctioned assertion of Japanese power over the
Ainu, the *umsa* thus became a local ancillary to the *uimam* ritual.[28]

A pair of documents at the Hakodate Municipal Library list twenty-
eight *uimam* visits by Ainu between 1823 and 1841.[29] None of the
uimam parties is identified as coming from an inland *kotan*. Rather, Ainu
from one or a group of usually adjacent fisheries presented themselves at
Fukuyama castle to perform the ritual, which was generally performed
between the conclusion of the spring herring fishing and kelp collecting
season and the commencement of the autumn salmon season. The Ainu
received rice, tobacco, cloth, and other commodities in exchange for
their gifts of preserved salmon and other local products. Women are
included in the lists of participants in six of the rituals; they received gifts
of cloth and tobacco along with their male associates, but in lesser quan-
tities. Ainu who presented gifts of especial value, particularly bear gall
bladders (prized for their medicinal value), received a bonus of sixty-four
shō (about 115 liters) of rice. Similarly, those whose houses had rendered
loyal service to the domain—in one case (Shiraoi) assistance during
Shakushain's War, and in another (Nemuro) more recent cooperation
with domain welfare *(buiku)* policies—received extra gifts as well.

Matsumae was not alone in its use of the *uimam* ritual to order its
relations with the Ainu. According to Namikawa Kenji, the Nanbu and
Tsugaru domains conducted *uimam* with the Ainu inhabitants of the
Shimokita and Tsugaru peninsulas, respectively. The earliest known
uimam involving Tōhoku Ainu took place in Tsugaru in 1662 and in
Nanbu in 1665, shortly after the ritual was regularized in Matsumae.
Namikawa suggests that the timing may be related to the fact that the
mid-seventeenth century saw the formalization of the trading-post system in the Ezochi, which linked Ainu trading practices much more

closely to domain institutions on both sides of the Tsugaru Strait than in the past: unable to travel freely to Hokkaido to obtain valuable commodities, local Ainu perforce looked to the domain authorities as trading partners.[30] The *uimam* in Tōhoku ceased after the early eighteenth century as a result of the integration of the Tsugaru and Shimokita Ainu into the status system, a topic to which I shall return below.

Although the 1665 ceremony in Nanbu was the only one portrayed in domain records unambiguously as an *uimam*, the ritual was performed frequently in Tsugaru—which had a much larger Ainu population—in the late seventeenth and early eighteenth centuries; moreover, its form anticipated that of eighteenth-century Matsumae. For example, at the earliest *uimam* the Tsugaru Ainu presented items like live bear cubs that had value to them but were not necessarily useful to the Japanese, but later, in response to domain requests, they presented bear pelts and gall bladders and marine products, such as pearls, abalone, seaweed *(wakame)*, and fur-seal pelts, for which they received rice and copper coins according to a predetermined payment schedule.[31] The 1707 *uimam*, at which the succession of three Ainu headmen was apparently confirmed, was held at Hirosaki castle; the formally dressed Ainu sat on mats in the garden and presented goods to the daimyo in return for gifts of sake. In addition to *uimam* held at Hirosaki castle, the ritual was also performed when the daimyo passed through Ainu villages during tours of his domain. In at least one such instance, in 1694, the *uimam* was conducted along lines closer to a traditional Ainu *umsa*, with music and dance performances and exchanges of sake as its central elements.[32] At the 1655 *uimam* at Morioka castle, the Ainu received swords from the Nanbu daimyo, which is notable because the Ainu particularly prized them as treasures.[33] The Tōhoku domains may have been able to orchestrate *uimam* to emphasize the superiority of the daimyo earlier than the Matsumae domain because the Tsugaru and Nanbu Ainu lacked the formal character of autonomous traders enjoyed by their counterparts in the Ezochi; that is, the *uimam* functioned more authentically as an audience between the lord and his subjects.

Ainu continued to participate in *uimam* and *umsa* ceremonies staged for the benefit of Matsumae officials and merchants until the end of the Tokugawa period. The Meiji state had little use for the rituals, which it saw as impediments to Ainu assimilation into Japanese society. It accordingly abandoned them quickly, although the *umsa* seems to have survived under the auspices of individual merchants as late as 1875.[34]

The assertions of Japanese power and authority conveyed through the *uimam* and *umsa* rituals were not directed primarily toward the Ainu, but rather were designed to reassure the Japanese themselves of their own legitimacy. In that regard, the rituals were similar to the efforts of the Satsuma domain to assert its role as custodian of the boundary with Ryukyu by requiring that Ryukyuan envoys adopt clothing and hairstyles that accentuated their alienness when venturing to Edo.[35] The portrayal of the rituals as Ainu rather than Japanese in origin, despite the fact that by the end of the eighteenth century their form owed more to Japanese bureaucratic protocol than to Ainu tradition, represents an effort by the Japanese to ground their domination of the Ainu in history and the traditions of Ainu culture. In that sense, they were analogous to the invented traditions found in contemporary societies, at least when seen from the Japanese perspective.[36]

Matsumae's declarations of legitimacy became increasingly urgent as the Tokugawa period progressed. By the end of the eighteenth century, a burgeoning fishing industry and its attendant commercial development had rendered simple trade between the Japanese and Ainu unimportant to the Matsumae economy. The legitimacy of the Matsumae house no longer rested on its role as intermediary between Japan and the Ainu, but instead relied increasingly on its symbolic role, exemplified by the *uimam* and *umsa* rituals. Moreover, legitimacy was more than an abstract principle for Matsumae, as the shogunate stepped in twice (1799 to 1821 and 1855 to 1868) to assume control over most of Hokkaido in response to a perceived threat from Russia.

The Ainu almost certainly did not accept at face value the Japanese reading of their role in the rituals. There is ample indirect evidence to suggest that they assigned their own meanings to the ceremonies. For instance, although the Japanese assumed the word *uimam* was derived from the Japanese *omemie*, meaning "audience," the Ainu considered the word to refer exclusively to "trade" and did not assign it the subservient overtones that the Japanese did.[37] Certainly the references to *uimam* in the *yukar*, the Ainu epic oral literature, have no sense of defeat or submission about them.[38] If, as this suggests, the Ainu saw the *uimam* and *umsa* rituals primarily as opportunities to trade, their leaders may have been able to enhance their own standing by distributing the commodities received from the Japanese among their people. Japanese accounts of *umsa* held in the late eighteenth century support this view with descriptions of crowds of Ainu waiting eagerly for the elders to emerge with sake, rice, tobacco, and other goods.[39] Conversely, however favorably the Ainu may have viewed the economic aspects of the ritual relationship, they were rightly suspicious of the Japanese, for they knew that unless they were careful, fishers and petty officials might try to cheat them out of their goods.[40] In any case, the Ainu needed the commodities provided by the Japanese and thus had little choice but to participate in the *uimam* and *umsa* ceremonies. This was particularly true of the Ainu leadership, many of who received privileged treatment in return for providing steady supplies of Ainu workers for Japanese fishing operations.[41] Indeed, the posts occupied by local elders were not native to Ainu society, but rather corresponded to offices in self-governing Japanese agricultural villages.[42] Relations between Ainu elders and Japanese fishery officials were so cozy, complained the explorer Matsuura Takeshirō, a sympathetic observer of the Ainu's plight, that they colluded to exploit the ordinary Ainu workers under their control.[43]

The reliance of Ainu leaders in northeastern Hokkaido on Japanese support was so great that when badly mistreated fishery workers rose in the Kunashiri-Menashi Rebellion of 1789, one Ainu chieftain, Tsukinoe of Kunashiri, not only took the initiative to notify the Matsumae domain authorities of the uprising, but also persuaded his own son, an organizer of the rebellion, to surrender to the Japanese.[44] This is perhaps an extreme example; other leaders apparently co-opted by the Japanese may simply have been trying to make the best of a bad situation by securing goods from the Japanese at terms as favorable as possible. The salient point is that however the Ainu interpreted their role in the *uimam* and *umsa* rituals, as a practical matter they were subject to the political, economic, and military domination of the Japanese.

The *uimam* and *umsa* rituals were effective because they fit both Ainu and Japanese expectations of the proper relationship between the two peoples. For the Ainu, the long and sometimes difficult journey to Fukuyama was literally the stuff of legend, and their oral literature is full of tales of Ainu who overcame hardship with the help of the gods to engage in long-distance trade.[45] The cultural importance of the journey to Fukuyama may account for their willingness to participate in the *uimam* despite the fact that wage labor at fisheries was a more important source of Japanese commodities than the ritual itself. Conversely, the rituals fit into Matsumae's self-image as suzerain over an alien people because they conformed to the Japanese model of proper tributary relations between a civilized center and its barbarian periphery.

Each side may well have realized that the other understood the rituals' significance differently, but they could nonetheless overlook the discrepancy and even make it a cornerstone of their relationship because the dissonance itself contributed to the stability of ties. Hence the relationship between the Ainu and the Japanese was characterized by constructive misunderstanding. The key to maintaining the relationship was the Ainu's externality to the early modern Japanese state. On the one hand, it marked them as barbarians whose proper relationship to Japan centered on the presentation of tribute in exchange for the benevolence of the state; dispensing this benevolence enhanced the Matsumae domain's legitimacy as custodian of the civilizational boundary. On the other hand, however, externality re-created a structure of authority within Ainu communities, which had been stripped of meaningful political autonomy as a consequence of Shakushain's War. Maintaining the internal coherence of Ainu society obviously served the purposes of the native leaders themselves, but it was also vitally important for the domain because of the leaders' role as suppliers of wage labor for the commercial fishing industry.

The *uimam* and *umsa* rituals, in other words, created a ritual framework to mask not only the Ainu's dependence on Japanese commodities, but their integration into the early modern Japanese protoindustrial economy as well. This is why the relationship could continue—and indeed flourish—into the nineteenth century, even as increasing numbers of Japanese from southern Hokkaido and northern Honshu moved into the Ezochi to fish side by side with Ainu laborers. After the Tenpō famine of the 1830s, production in the fishery gradually became dominated by capitalist entrepreneurs. Although the Ainu's employers (contract-fishery operators licensed by the domain, whose access to native labor was not shared by private entrepreneurs) were not, strictly speaking, capitalists, Ainu workers became as dependent on wage labor as the Japanese members of Hokkaido's seasonal proletariat.[46] But so long as the fiction was maintained that relations between the Ainu and Japanese hinged on ritual ties between Ainu communities and the domain leadership rather than on wage contracts between individual laborers and their employers, both the Ainu and their homeland could remain exogenous to the early modern polity, and the Matsumae domain (and, consequently, the contractors dependent on its patronage) could continue to assert the legitimacy of its authority.

For Matsumae, incorporating the Ainu in the Ezochi (as opposed to those remaining within the Wajinchi) into the ranks of commoners was not an option because doing so would have negated the domain's legitimacy. Instead, the Ainu retained a distinctive identity even as their autonomy was undermined by disadvantageous economic relations. The most striking evidence of the Ainu's vulnerability is the brutal treatment they often received at the hands of Japanese fishery workers. Although research by Tajima Yoshiya and Iwasaki Naoko indicates that the Ainu were not consistently subjected to the slave-labor conditions often described in the literature on the contract-fishery system, it is nonetheless true that Japanese managers took advantage of the Ainu's need for imported commodities to appropriate Ainu women as concubines and otherwise disrupt the Ainu's lives.[47] Faced with such abuse, the only practical response was flight. Kikuchi cites a case in which an Ainu elder led about eighty people from Ishikari to the relatively remote Tokachi area, but he notes that such mass escapes appear to have been unusual.[48] Finally, the Japanese inadvertently imported diseases like smallpox and measles into Hokkaido along with the commodities, resulting in a steady decline of the Ainu population throughout the Tokugawa period.[49]

The damaging effects of fishery work on Ainu society is unquestionable. For example, Matsuura Takeshirō noted that the Ainu population in Nemuro, in northeastern Hokkaido, had fallen by more than half between 1808 and 1857, from 1,219 to 581. A number of inland *kotan* in the vicinity of Nemuro and the Shiretoko peninsula disappeared entirely, and those that were left were inhabited by people unfit to work at the fisheries. Kikuchi speculates that overfishing at the mouths of the Shibetsu and other nearby rivers undermined the Ainu's traditional salmon-fishing activities upriver, thereby forcing able-bodied workers to seek employment at Japanese-run fisheries.[50] Once dependent on the Japanese for work, the Ainu had little alternative but to go where they were told.[51] For example, in 1807 the contractor Fujino Kihei closed his fishery on Shikotan, in the southern Kurils, and moved the local Ainu to the Nemuro peninsula, where many died and the rest were subjected to further relocations.[52] Matsuura commented that, "if things are left as they are, this area will no doubt be uninhabited inside of fifty years."[53]

The constructive misunderstanding that characterized the relationship between the Ainu and the Japanese in the Tokugawa period is reminiscent of what Richard White calls the "middle ground" of accommodation and common meaning crafted by Indians and Europeans in North America during the seventeenth and eighteenth centuries. In his *Conquest of Ainu Lands*, Brett Walker makes a case for seeing Hokkaido as a middle ground, and he refers specifically to the ritual relations between Matsumae and the Ainu in support of his argument.[54] However, I believe that early modern Hokkaido did not function as a middle ground, for reasons I shall outline below.

For White, the key process at work in the middle ground is *accommodation,* a concept he differentiates from acculturation, which carries too strong a suggestion of asymmetrical power relations and unidirectional cultural change. As he describes it:

> On the middle ground diverse peoples adjust their differences through what amounts to a process of creative, and often expedient, misunderstandings. People try to persuade others who are different from themselves by appealing to what they perceive to be the values and practices of those others. They often misinterpret and distort both the values and the practices of those they deal with, but from these misunderstandings arise new meanings and through them new practices—the shared meanings and practices of the middle ground.[55]

White limits his analysis to colonial North America, but the concept of the middle ground is clearly applicable in other contexts, particularly in areas remote from centers of political and military power, where accommodation is often the only pragmatic response to the fact of mutual dependence. In any case, because it does not take the existence of rigid cultural and ethnic boundaries for granted, the middle ground offers a way to conceptualize contact and interdependence as the source of new identities.

The French and British trappers, missionaries, and officials who made their way into the *pays d'en haut* (the region surrounding the Great Lakes) in the colonial era were agents of expansive imperial powers. The overwhelming economic, technological, and military power of the European empires—and the undeniable fact of the Indians' eventual subjugation—makes it easy to project outcome on process and see the early European arrivals in the region as bearers of the full and immediate force of the empires they represented. But in reality they were far from home, isolated and vulnerable, and hence in no position to subjugate anyone. At the same time, however, the power of the things they brought to North America—guns, alcohol, and a seemingly insatiable demand for furs—ensured that their impact on Indian society would be profound regardless of their actual numbers. In addition to fostering dependence on imported commodities, the Europeans disrupted relations among Indian nations in the *pays d'en haut* in a way that, ironically, made them a necessary mediating presence. For these and many other reasons, the Europeans and Indians in the North American middle ground needed each other, and so they sought accommodation. But accommodation, with its suggestion of a relatively equal balance of power, did not make the middle ground into an idyllic world of peace and harmony. On the contrary, the mutual misunderstandings that underlay social relations in the middle ground added an ominous element of uncertainty to life. As White demonstrates in bloodcurdling detail, people all too often responded to that uncertainty with violence and brutality.[56]

At first glance, early modern Hokkaido appears to have all the makings of a middle ground. As in the *pays d'en haut,* the relationship between the Ainu and their Japanese neighbors cannot be described in terms of either acculturation or mutual exclusion: both sides engaged in cultural borrowing while retaining discrete identities, and both participated in creating a common world of trade and ritual relations. Moreover, broad similarities link the *pays d'en haut* and Hokkaido in the seventeenth and eighteenth centuries: in both areas, representatives of expanding empires encountered indigenous peoples with whom they built distinctive worlds of trade and conflict; but in both cases creolization was eventually forestalled and the indigenes were marked as Other. In the *pays d'en haut* the middle ground was undermined in part by the sheer force of Anglo-American demographic and economic expansion. In Hokkaido, in contrast, the possibility of a middle ground had vanished by the late seventeenth century, well before substantial numbers of non-Ainu immigrants had entered the island. Considering why a middle ground did not exist in Hokkaido is a way to approach questions about the nature of boundaries of identity and polity in Japanese history, and particularly why "ethnic" difference was not perceived in ethnic terms, despite the existence of clear boundaries separating the Ainu and Japanese realms.

Northernmost Japan in the late medieval period came much closer to the middle ground, as warlords like the Andō moved freely between Japanese and Ezo identities in response to political and economic exigencies.[57] Similarly, the crew of a Dutch ship sailing off the northeastern coast of Hokkaido in 1643 encountered

> a Japanese [named Ori or Orey], being a young smart man, as a master of d° bark, had been aboard with 6 men of his crew, and had said that he came here to trade, like the Dutch came to Japan to trade, and that he came from a place called Matsimay [Matsumae], . . . and there is a Japanese governor in d° place, thus that place is governed by the Japanese, but these people come here to trade skins, whale-oil and blubber. . . . He had also told that he was from a Japanese father, but his mother came from Eso. He spoke the Eso language as well as his Japanese.[58]

Judging from this brief description, Ori seems very similar to many of the characters described by White: the child of a Japanese father and

Ainu mother; bilingual and perhaps equally at home among Japanese and Ainu; based in Matsumae but trading far to the northeast in the Ezochi; and no doubt carrying the Japanese commodities on which the Ainu had become dependent.

After Shakushain's War, however, it becomes impossible to find descriptions of figures like Ori. It would be presumptuous to assert that such people did not exist, however, for in the everyday world of the fisheries at which Ainu and Japanese laborers congregated there were plenty of opportunities for individual identities to become blurred. Nonetheless, in the documentary record everyone is clearly placed as Japanese or Ainu: in contrast to White's middle ground, there is no mention of anything resembling a *métis* identity (much less *métis* society). However specific individuals may have viewed themselves, there were no people in Hokkaido after Shakushain's War whose politically meaningful identities were *essentially* ambivalent—no people, in other words, who were never fully "Ainu" or fully "Japanese." Even Iwanosuke—who took on situationally defined identities as Japanese at home and Ainu when venturing to Fukuyama to perform the *uimam*—was marked unambiguously as one or the other at any given time. Similarly, people of mixed ancestry— of whom there were many by the nineteenth century—were accepted unproblematically by both sides as Ainu; mixed ancestry was neither accompanied by a presumption of insight into Japanese thinking by the Ainu nor did it serve as an entrée into Japanese society.[59] The closest anyone came to an ambivalent identity were the so-called assimilated Ainu (*kizoku Ezo*) of the 1850s and 1860s, whom I shall discuss in the next chapter, but even their ambivalence was seen as a stepping-stone to full integration into Japanese society. By the same token, commentators from the center—but not local Japanese authorities—often saw Matsumae and the Tōhoku domains as an imperfectly civilized border zone between Japan and the Ezochi, but this ambivalence too was portrayed as a trace of the pre-Tokugawa past and not as a distinct category of identity.[60]

The boundary between the Japanese and Ainu realms in Hokkaido transcended the physicality of the spaces it delineated. Whatever an individual's sense of self as Ainu, Japanese, or something in between, the Matsumae domain's internal status order—which functioned only within the Wajinchi—had no category of social identity marked as Ainu, for the Ainu were barbarians who by definition existed (in a socially and politically meaningful manner) only outside the status system. In that sense, transgressions of the physical border did not immediately imperil the integrity of the boundary between civilization and barbarism that the geographical border represented. A special case like Iwanosuke, recruited on occasion to serve the domain's political needs, is the exception that proves the rule, for the need to create an Ainu Iwanosuke highlights the lack of an Ainu social identity in the quotidian world of the Wajinchi.

The Ainu's homeland, the Ezochi, remained securely barbarian until the eve of the Meiji Restoration. After Shakushain's War, the Matsumae domain established physical barriers *(sekisho)* at the borders of the Wajinchi and required all Japanese venturing beyond them to obtain passes. Although the boundary was set more or less arbitrarily (and was even moved a few kilometers north at one point), it was nonetheless critically important, for policies directed at the Ainu applied only to the Ezochi side of the frontier. To be sure, the shogunate moved to integrate Hokkaido more fully into the early modern state by assuming direct administration of much or all of the Ezochi from 1799 to 1821 and again from 1855 to 1868; one aspect of this policy was the decision in 1855 to allow Japanese to establish permanent settlements in the Ezochi. Even so, the administrative distinction between the Ezochi and the Wajinchi was not abolished until the beginning of the Meiji period, when the island of Hokkaido, similar to the rest of Japan, was divided into the provinces *(kuni)* and districts *(gun)* that symbolized imperial suzerainty.[61] Although sovereignty over the Ezochi was intrinsically ambivalent in the sense that the territory was nominally autonomous yet clearly subordinated to the Tokugawa state, this ambivalence itself was articulated through the early modern regime's delineation of civilized and barbarian realms. In other words, the Ezochi appears ambivalent only when viewed in terms of modern Western conceptions of territoriality.[62]

There was no middle ground in early modern Japan because identities were situationally defined according to the rules of the status system. Iwanosuke could switch from being Japanese to Ainu and back to Japanese as necessary, but this switching was "ethnic" only in the sense that the boundary separating the civilized from the barbarian in Hokkaido was an "ethnic" one. Iwanosuke's demeanor was not essentially different from that of Shōsuke, the peasant scribe described in chapter 2 who comported himself as a samurai while on official business, or that of the *gōmune,* who were marked as outcastes while performing but could return to commoner status when they changed their occupation. Insofar as the status system provided a framework to articulate identities, there could not be a social space defined by in-betweenness.

CHAPTER 6

The Geography
of Civilization

Japan's early modern geography of civilization developed out of a Confucian world order of a civilized *(ka)* core surrounded by barbarian *(i)*, or at best imperfectly civilized, peripheries.[1] It largely supplanted—and partially subsumed within itself—an earlier bifurcation of the world into "human" and "demon" realms, replacing it with a tripartite division in which previously demonized aliens on Japan's peripheries were humanized as barbarians and the realm of demons was displaced farther afield.[2] Civilization had a geopolitical character insofar as Japan was by definition civilized in a way its peripheries could not be, but the logic sustaining this tautology required the identification of particular customs to classify people as civilized or barbarian, and the use of customs as classifiers necessarily connected civilization to the status system of the core polity.

In this chapter I will explore the relationship between civilization and barbarism as mediated by customs in the early modern period. After a short introductory discussion of the place of the Ezochi and the Ryukyu kingdom as peripheries of the early modern state I will examine, first, the relationship between customs and status in the core polity and, second, the marking of the Ainu alternately as barbarians and as Japanese through the deployment of customs. My aim is to demonstrate that the geography of civilization was rooted in a spatial understanding of Japan's place in East Asia, yet at the same time was inseparable from the classification of social groups within the core polity.

Surrounding the core polity with buffers of ambivalent sovereignty situated Japan within East Asia and concomitantly lent legitimacy to the regime in an idiom comprehensible to (if not necessarily accepted by) its neighbors in the region. Japan's ostensible national "seclusion" notwithstanding, Tokugawa diplomacy functioned within the greater East Asian international system, which was dominated by China. Indeed, the only two countries with which Japan maintained official diplomatic relations, Korea and Ryukyu, were both leading tributaries of China. Japanese diplomacy was accordingly conducted with an acute awareness of China, despite Japan's lack of official ties, tributary or otherwise, with that country.[3]

However, the Tokugawa world order was not an exact replica of the Chinese model, for unlike China, early modern Japan was not a fully centralized state. The shogunate delegated responsibility for overseeing foreign relations to domains with historical connections to the various "windows" on the outside world: the Matsumae domain conducted trade with the Ainu in the Ezochi; Tsushima mediated relations with Korea; and Satsuma regulated contacts with Ryukyu.[4] The maintenance of these ties was incorporated into the domains' feudal obligations to the Tokugawa house.[5] As a result, the shogunate retained the power to sanctions its proxies' outside contacts and thus set the parameters for their diplomatic and commercial activities. Moreover, the shogunate managed the "window" at Nagasaki itself, although the Dutch and Chinese traders who called there were not recognized as official envoys of their home countries. Nevertheless, the gap between the shogunate's interests and perceptions and those of the domains was wide enough to complicate Tokugawa foreign relations.

One such complication involved the sovereignty of peripheral regions. Participating in a tributary relationship with China did not entail a loss of meaningful sovereignty for the subordinate power; indeed, as in the case of the early Ryukyu kingdom, investiture by the Chinese emperor often lent legitimacy to the rule of a local strongman and thereby hastened state formation.[6] In contrast, in Japan, the hierarchy of sovereignty from shogunate to intermediary domain to periphery worked to maintain the peripheries as exogenous dependencies of the Tokugawa state. At the same time, however, the interests of the shogunate and those of the custodial domains sometimes conflicted. Such was the case in both the Ezochi and the Ryukyu kingdom.

Political ties between the peoples of northern Honshu and southern Hokkaido before the Tokugawa settlement were forged independently of central direction. Accordingly, nothing even resembling a tributary relationship had existed between the Ainu and their Japanese neighbors. The boundary set after Shakushain's War at Kumaishi was, as Hayashi Shihei, put it, "the limit to which Japanese customs extend."[7] It marked the northern limit of Japan and the southern extreme of the Ezochi, but the Ezochi was otherwise left unbounded until the mid-nineteenth century, when an international border was established with Russia in the Kurils and Sakhalin. In practice, the Ezochi as the object of Japanese trade interest and political influence included Hokkaido beyond the Matsumae domain's home territory in the Oshima peninsula, the southern Kuril Islands, and southern Sakhalin—all areas inhabited by the Ainu but not by substantial numbers of other Northeast Asian peoples.[8]

When Russia appeared as a threat in the nineteenth century, the shogunate responded by attempting to absorb the Ezochi within the civilized core of Japan through the assimilation of the Ainu population. This policy undermined the Matsumae domain's raison d'être, for its position as intermediary hinged on the maintenance of a clear distinction between the Ainu and Japanese populations. The shogunate's policy had the further effect of setting a northern boundary for the Ezochi—now unequivocally a part of Japan—in the Kuril Islands and Sakhalin.[9]

After Shō Hashi's establishment of a unified kingdom on the main island of Okinawa in 1429, Ryukyu emerged as a commercial crossroads, where merchants, pirates, and slave traders from China, Japan, Korea, and Southeast Asia came together.[10] Although Ryukyu's economic importance waned after the mid-sixteenth century, its participation in tributary relations with China made it attractive enough to the Satsuma domain of southern Kyushu to prompt an invasion in 1609. Throughout the Tokugawa period, Ryukyu remained in an ambivalent diplomatic position, a tributary of both China and Satsuma (and hence indirectly of the Tokugawa shogunate), while at the same time it retained a measure of autonomy over its internal affairs and a distinct cultural identity. Cumbersome though this arrangement may have been, it served the Japanese, Chinese, and Ryukyuan authorities reasonably well, at least until the intrusion of Britain, France, the United States, and other Western powers into East Asian affairs rendered it untenable in the middle of the nineteenth century.

Unlike the Ezochi, where state formation was prevented by Japanese expansion, Ryukyu before the Satsuma invasion was an autonomous state linked to China (but not to Satsuma or Japan) through tributary relations and the accompanying trade. It was this access to the China trade that made the kingdom attractive to Satsuma. After conquering Ryukyu, Satsuma initially moved to incorporate the kingdom fully within the domain, both politically and civilizationally, according to the rules of the status system: it conducted cadastral surveys to facilitate taxation, carried out sword hunts to disarm the peasantry, and treated the king and his court as enfeoffed vassals of the Satsuma daimyo. At the same time, it ordered the Ryukyuans to adopt Japanese customs *(fūzoku)*. However, once it became clear that Ryukyu was Japan's only remaining reliable point of contact with the faltering Ming empire in China, Satsuma switched from a policy of assimilation informed by the rules of status to one of differentiation based on criteria of civilization, as seen, for example, in a 1617 order forbidding Ryukyuans to wear Japanese-style clothing or hairstyles.[11]

For the shogunate, Ryukyu under Satsuma suzerainty served two purposes. The first was as a source of information on events in the Asian mainland, which was particularly important during the tumultuous decades of the mid-seventeenth century, when the Ming empire fell and the Qing dynasty established control throughout China. Ryukyu's second function was to send embassies to the shogunate and thereby enhance the legitimacy of the Tokugawa regime in the eyes of the community of daimyo.[12] Both functions coincided with Satsuma's own interest in gaining access to the China trade (which became especially important after 1639, by which time the shogunate had closed off most domains' direct access to foreign trade) and in enhancing its own prestige as suzerain over a tributary kingdom. In some ways the demands of legitimacy and prestige were more pressing to Satsuma than to the shogunate itself. According to Kamiya, by the end of the seventeenth century the shogunate had decided that the Ryukyuan embassies to Edo were no longer necessary, but was persuaded to continue them after vigorous lobbying by Satsuma. Shogunal officials were finally moved by the argument that although Ryukyu was one of China's leading vassal nations (by virtue of the fact that it sent more tribute missions than any other country save Korea), it was a mere rear-vassal of the shogunate (owing to Satsuma's intermediary position), thus proving the superior position of the shogun vis-à-vis the Qing emperor.[13] In the 1840s and 1850s, moreover, the shogunate hoped to deflect Western demands for trade by opening Ryukyu but not Japan itself. By the time it became clear that such a strategy would not succeed, Japanese leaders were too preoccupied with troubles at home to worry much about Ryukyu.[14]

CUSTOMS, STATUS, AND CIVILIZATION

Customs *(fūzoku)* marked individuals as civilized or barbarian and, within the core polity, as members of specific status groups. Although the particular package of practices that bore classificatory weight in early modern Japan was unique, a similar emphasis on customs as emblems of political affiliation prevailed elsewhere throughout East Asia, most famously in the Qing dynasty's insistence that Chinese men adopt the Manchu queue.[15] Indeed, hairstyles—men's in particular—were important signifiers of belonging everywhere in the region.[16] By virtue of their significance as markers of politically defined realms of status and civilization, customs made identities subject to unilateral manipulation by the Japanese state. Here identity refers of course not to individuals' sense of self, but rather to the way social groups—both within the core polity and on its peripheries—were situated vis-à-vis feudal authority.

The role of customs as markers of status and civilizational identities raises an intriguing chicken-or-egg problem. Did objective differences in customs naturally come to mark social and political identities? Or were differences in social and political function reified through an essentially arbitrary taxonomy of customs? Not surprisingly, the answer is a bit of each. Real cultural differences—including the outward characteristics accorded significance by the Japanese—set the Ainu and Ryukyuans apart from their Japanese neighbors long before the early modern state and its status system emerged. In that sense, the marking of certain customs simply affirmed preexisting objective differences. But the mere existence of difference—even striking dissimilarity in language, physical appearance, and lifeways—does not require that political significance be attached to it. Accordingly, the need to differentiate social groups prompted a search for practices to serve as boundary markers.

One way the Tokugawa authorities deployed customs in their effort to maintain the integrity of status boundaries was through sumptuary regulations. The shogunate's attack in the seventeenth century on *kabuki-mono*—young men who sported wildly unorthodox clothing and hairstyles—is an early example of this impulse; it can be seen as part of a broader attempt to make topknots, shaved pates, and clean-shaven faces the three pillars of normative appearance for men.[17] Policies such as barring commoners from engaging in practices unbecoming their station (such as wearing silk clothing) and complex guidelines concerning the dress and deportment of men at different levels within the samurai ranks reflected policy makers' fear that luxurious living would distract the populace from honest labor and loyal service. Ogyū Sorai's famous lament that samurai "lived as in an inn" is representative of this attitude.[18] The samurai's detachment from the world of agricultural production had made them dependent on the market for all their needs and as a result had skewed their priorities, turning them away from the selfless rendering of service. But the calls for frugality reflected more than just Confucian moralism; they derived from assumptions about the propriety of specific practices for specific status groups. Although a daimyo might make a show of economy by wearing cotton for everyday activities, if he showed up to a shogunal audience dressed in anything but the proper silk garments, he would disparage his lord's high station and his own ties of vassalage to the shogun. Similarly, commoners who engaged in ostentatious displays of luxury appeared to jeopardize their ability to fulfill their status-based feudal obligations and hence the lord's ability to provide benevolent rule. Moreover, assuming a demeanor inappropriate to one's status threatened the integrity of the status system as a whole by blurring the distinctions that allowed members of different status groups to interact on a basis of proper inequality. The frequent issuance of sumptuary regulations throughout the Tokugawa period no doubt reflects the prevalence of infractions across the status spectrum, but the shogunate's dogged attempts to recalibrate customs with status—despite the evident futility of the enterprise—highlight the centrality of customs to the status order. Likewise, the very ubiquity of transgressors of custom norms demonstrates their recognition of that centrality.

Tokugawa authorities attempted to reserve specific practices for designated status groups or members of certain ranks within them. Without question, the most politically potent practice of this sort was the carrying of two swords (usually paired with the right to use a surname publicly), a privilege that was reserved for the samurai and a select group of non-samurai elites.[19] (Most commoners could own short swords, *wakizashi*, without penalty.) As with sumptuary regulations, infractions against prohibitions on sword bearing by commoners appear to have been frequent, but this, too, reflects a general recognition of the practice's significance. In addition to their monopoly on sword bearing, samurai (or sometimes officers above a certain level in their ranks) enjoyed exclusive rights to engage in activities reflective of their martial status, such as riding on horseback. At the other end of the status spectrum, outcastes were often prohibited from wearing footwear in the presence of commoners and samurai, and they were also sometimes prohibited from binding their hair. Moreover, within the guild of the blind, the *tōdō*, rank was marked by symbols such as robe color; the *tōdō* leadership enforced compliance with its regulations by hiring sighted aides to keep watch for violators.[20]

As these examples suggest, customs most clearly marked the status of groups that occupied a special position in society, such as the samurai, nobles, clergy, and outcastes. This is not surprising considering that commoners constituted the overwhelming majority of the population. Nevertheless, it is important to understand that commoners' customs— their topknots, shaved pates, and clean-shaven faces—were important markers of belonging, too, for they signified normative appearance. That is, men whose occupations placed them outside the mainstream of society adopted customs that deviated from the norm as an external symbol of their extraordinary social position.

Regulations on practices like sword bearing took account of the situational nature of status relations. For example, outcaste leaders in the Kantō sometimes wore swords when visiting the homes of commoner village officials at New Year's.[21] By going to the commoners' homes they recognized the officials' superior social standing, but their sword bearing simultaneously served to assert their standing as leaders of their own communities. The same principle obtained when the headmen of commoner villages wore swords when appearing before samurai on official business. Likewise, a commoner might have permission to wear a formal garment *(kamishimo)* to an official audience, but not in other situations.

In addition to demarcating status differences, customs delineated civilized and barbarian realms within the core polity. The connection between customs and notions of civilization had deep roots in Confucian thought. As Bob Wakabayashi and Tsukamoto Manabu have demonstrated, when early Tokugawa thinkers undertook the project of naturalizing Confucianism, one of the problems they faced was how to situate Japan vis-à-vis China. In particular, they wrestled with the question of whether universal notions of civilization were necessarily tied to the particular geographical space of China, an issue linked to the ways scholars before and after Zhu Xi had read a particular passage in the *Analects*. For example, Itō Jinsai (1627–1705) conceded that the Japanese were barbarians, but through the deployment of some "amazing philological acrobatics" turned that apparent handicap into a virtue and argued that Japan was in fact morally superior to China because "Japan embodied the hierarchical status order of Middle Kingdom Civilization better than China." According to Wakabayashi, "Jinsai emphasized the idea that customs disclosed whether a people were civilized or barbarian. If their customs corresponded to 'ritual and righteousness,' they were civilized, if not, barbarian."[22]

As originally articulated by Jinsai and other early Tokugawa thinkers, civilization was "where Confucian ritual obtain[ed]," the exclusive realm of a mere handful of men well versed in the Chinese classics.[23] Centering above all on mastery of Confucian ritual and classical language, civilization was beyond the reach not only of alien barbarians, but also of the lower orders of society in China as well as in Japan. Yamaga Sokō (1622–85), who regarded barbarism as the realm in which "moral transformation (or suasion) does not extend," argued that commoners and barbarians had a common nature. For Jinsai, Sokō, and like-minded thinkers, the most pressing issue facing the authorities was engagement in jōi, or the sweeping away of barbarian elements through moral edification.[24]

However gratifying such a narrow and explicitly Confucian construction of civilization may have been to individual thinkers, as a geopolitical strategy it made no sense to equate Japanese identity with an impossibly high standard of textual erudition. As a result, the nature of civilization itself changed once Japanese identity became a pressing geopolitical issue in the latter part of the Tokugawa period. Far from requiring ordinary folk to immerse themselves in the Confucian canon, the new standards of civilization focused on easily manipulated customs.

Early-eighteenth-century thinkers like Nishikawa Joken (1648–1724) and Terajima Ryōan (fl. ca. 1712) contributed to this reorientation by pushing the realm of the barbarian outward beyond the boundaries of the core polity and reconceiving Japan as possessing a unique civilization of its own that was different from, but not inherently inferior to, that of China and Korea.[25] One way they did this was by distinguishing between the residents of foreign countries (gaikoku) that, like Japan, accepted the tenets of Confucian civilization, and foreign barbarians (gaii), whose lands lay beyond the realm of civilization. But rather than equating civilization with textual erudition and ritual practice, they saw civilization more as a matter of everyday life. Thus, for Ryōan, barbarians were people "who write using an alphabet and do not know Chinese characters, and who do not use chopsticks, but eat with their hands."[26]

Nevertheless, the ideological purgatives administered to mid-Tokugawa Japan left an unsightly residue of barbarian elements, particularly in the countryside on the peripheries of the archipelago, in such areas as Tōhoku, Sado, Tosa, Iki, and Tsushima.[27] For a time, identifying such barbarian traces was little more than a parlor game for Confucian thinkers because within the political boundaries of the core polity even bearers of barbarian customs—such as married women who lacked the decency and good sense to blacken their teeth—had clearly defined status obligations. So long as deviant customs did not imperil the state's claims to sovereignty over the territories their practitioners occupied, the authorities could turn a blind eye to the cultural diversity reflected in their persistence.

Once the authorities perceived a threat to sovereignty, however, they moved to impose their notions of civilization homogeneously across the land. For example, Kikuchi Isao has described the efforts of Nanbu authorities in the early nineteenth century to eradicate barbarian customs in their domain, particularly the failure of local women to shave their eyebrows as Edo women did. At one point officials took their civilizing mission door to door with razor and whetstone, but peasant women resisted their tonsorial overtures because naked brows offered no protection for the eyes against sweat during farm work. Kikuchi attributes the officials' zeal to their concerns about the frequent appearance of Russian ships in northern Japanese waters.[28] In contrast, a century earlier, officials in the same domain had defended the local dialect and customs as distinctive "provincial customs" (kokufū) and had urged samurai on duty in the shogunal capital to maintain them even in the face of Edoites' laughter.[29]

With the West an increasing concern in the nineteenth century, the concept of barbarism itself began to change. For example, Tsukamoto Manabu argues that Tokugawa Nariaki's enunciation of the principle of sonnō jōi—"revere the monarch [meaning Tokugawa Ieyasu], expel the barbarian"—in 1838 was predicated on the eradication of barbarian elements within the Japanese realm; within about fifteen years, however, the monarch had come to be identified with the emperor and the barbarian with the West, at which point the slogan became a rallying cry for anti-Tokugawa activists.[30] The shogunate implicitly affirmed this identification of the barbarian (i) with the West in documents referring to the Ainu during its second period of direct administration in Hokkaido (1855–68). Beginning in the fifth month of 1856, officials stopped referring to the Ainu as Ezo (a compound that contains the same character as i) and instead began calling them dojin, or "natives." Kikuchi argues that the term dojin, which now carries a pejorative connotation of backwardness, did not take on its negative sense until after the Restoration. At the time of the shift it was a neutral term that referred simply to the local people of a particular area.[31] The new terminology thus symbolically incorporated the Ainu as the (Japanese) local people in Hokkaido and relocated the realm of barbarism outward beyond the Ezochi. Just before this, the shogunate opened the Ezochi to permanent residence by non-Ainu, thus anticipating in geopolitics this shift in nomenclature.

Customs were imperfect markers of status and civilization within the core polity. The authorities attempted, often unsuccessfully, to keep them aligned with the status boundaries they were supposed to delineate, and intellectuals constantly debated the precise significance of civilizational categories. This ambivalence does not, however, weaken customs' overall significance, but merely highlights the fluidity of the feudal order as a whole. So long as institutions functioned more or less effectively, a certain amount of play helped to alleviate the discrepancies between a political order constructed around the regime's expropriative imperatives and a lively and diverse social order, in which social relations and economic interests encompassed much more than individuals' immediate need to pay taxes or perform military duties.

BARBARISM AND STATUS

Despite the imbalance in military and economic power, the relationship between the Japanese and the Ainu after the Tokugawa settlement of 1603 was not simply one of subjugation and submission. The lords of Matsumae needed the Ainu as much as the Ainu needed them. Unlike other Tokugawa period daimyo, the heads of the Matsumae house formally held no land in fief from the Tokugawa shogun; rather, their status was derived from the monopoly they held over trade and other contact with the Ainu.[32] The Japanese in Hokkaido could allow neither the assimilation nor the extermination of the Ainu population because, quite simply, if there were no Ainu, the Matsumae house would have no formal reason to exist. The Ainu's barbarian identity was consequently a cornerstone of the feudal institutional structure of the Matsumae domain.

Matsumae went to considerable lengths to ensure that the Ainu's barbarian identity remained intact. First, it made the division of Hokkaido into areas of exclusive Japanese and Ainu residence a cornerstone of domain law. Officially, the Ainu territory, the Ezochi, which encompassed almost 95 percent of the island's area, was not part of the Tokugawa state, and its Ainu inhabitants were not direct subjects of the shogun. Japanese could make seasonal trading or fishing forays into the Ainu territory, but they could not settle there permanently until 1855, by which time the Ezochi was under the direct administration of the shogunate. Ainu were similarly prohibited from traveling outside their own area except to perform the *uimam* at Fukuyama castle. To be sure, breaches of the boundary were common (at least among Japanese traveling into the Ezochi), but the volume of traffic was less important than the formal demarcation of a border.

The delineation of Japanese and Ainu spheres did not reflect actual residence patterns, but rather was an ad hoc response to Matsumae's incomplete military victory in Shakushain's War.[33] By the time war broke out in 1669, a small number of Japanese gold miners and falconers had established themselves so firmly in the island's interior that they fought as Ainu in the conflict. Indeed, one of them, Shōdayū of Dewa province, was Shakushain's son-in-law.[34] Similarly, Ainu troops fought alongside Matsumae samurai in battle.[35] Ainu left on the Japanese side of the border after the war were cut off from native society and hence ceased to function politically as Ainu, with the result that by the end of the eighteenth century only twelve of them (including Iwanosuke) retained even a vestige of their former identity.[36]

Matsumae's attitude toward visible symbols of Ainu identity similarly reveals the nature of the civilizational boundary in Hokkaido. By the end of the seventeenth century the Ainu's dependence on Japanese commodities was so profound that the culture could not remain intact without them. Consequently, the domain's efforts to keep the two cultures completely distinct were doomed from the beginning. The emergence of the commercial fishing industry in the eighteenth century exacerbated the Ainu's economic dependence, inasmuch as Ainu workers composed the bulk of the labor force. At the same time, Japanese fishery workers from northeastern Honshu took to wearing items of Ainu clothing with such enthusiasm that officials of the Nanbu domain felt compelled to issue repeated prohibitions of their use.[37] Provided that the Ainu's economic dependence on the Japanese remained unaltered, however, the actual degree of cultural difference was not as important as the maintenance of political and institutional distinctions between the two peoples. Civilizational boundaries—like the ethnic ones they resembled—persisted despite occasional or even systematic breaches.[38] More interesting than the success or failure of the particular aspects of Matsumae's segregation policy is an examination of those cultural characteristics that the Japanese considered to be the most significant markers of the Ainu's barbarian identity.

The Matsumae authorities were more concerned with regulating Ainu customs—visible emblems of identity such as hairstyles, language, and

clothing—than matters of diet, religion, or the organization and repro-
duction of households and communities. This policy of abstaining from
direct interference into matters internal to Ainu society paralleled the
internal autonomy granted to status groups within the core polity. But
beyond that, formal intrusion into the deeper levels of culture would
have revealed the fundamental contradiction that lay at the heart of
Matsumae's relationship with the Ainu. On the one hand, the domain's
legitimacy was founded on the Ainu's identity as barbarians living outside the core polity; on the other hand, however, its ability to control the
native people hinged on their continued reliance on Japanese commodities, a reliance that entailed the incorporation of Japanese elements into
Ainu culture. Thus, for example, Matsumae officials encouraged the
Ainu to eat rice, yet never tried to require consumption of the grain: to
do so would have undermined the fiction that the Ainu were exclusively
a hunting, fishing, and gathering people. Similarly, the domain actively
manipulated the Ainu leadership through the *uimam* and *umsa* rituals,
yet refrained from intervening directly into decision-making processes
within the Ainu community for fear of revealing the Ainu's lack of meaningful autonomy. Hairstyles, language, and clothing, on the other hand,
could be regulated without impinging on the economic bases of the relationship between the two peoples.

The preoccupation of the Matsumae authorities with certain cultural
practices reflected the importance of customs as civilizational boundary
markers. Here let us look at men's hairstyles as a case in point.[39] Ainu
men traditionally had long, unbound hair and full, flowing beards. Men
in Tokugawa Japan, in contrast, generally remained clean-shaven and
wore their hair in a topknot, usually with the pate shaved. Although
styles might vary slightly according to fashion and personal taste, most
variations in Japanese men's hairstyles reflected differences in status, so
that samurai were readily distinguishable from commoners, commoners
from outcastes, and so forth.[40] Exceptions to the rules were both systematic and limited to men who were somehow removed from mainstream
society: Confucian scholars sometimes wore beards; court nobles, most
doctors, and masterless samurai did not shave their pates; and Buddhist
priests and some doctors shaved their heads entirely. Only members of
certain outcaste groups did not bind their hair at all.

Given the importance of hairstyle as a symbol of status and participation in Japanese society, the long, unbound hair of the Ainu was necessarily more than a "native custom." In the eyes of Japanese observers the
Ainu's hair was as much a symbol of their status—or rather their lack of

status—as a mark of "ethnic" identity.[41] Matsumae's policy of regulating Ainu hairstyles represented an attempt to preserve the Ainu's barbarian identity while simultaneously (and paradoxically) connecting that identity to the Japanese status order. It follows that the shaved pates of Iwanosuke and other partially assimilated Ainu gave them a new identity not merely as "Japanese," but as "Japanese" of a very specific sort (in this case, commoners [hyakushō]).

The domain tried to prevent most Ainu from using the Japanese language and adopting those items of clothing that threatened their barbarian identity. (Conversely, the use of garments with no civilizational significance, such as the used cotton kimono the Ainu acquired in trade, was not subject to regulation.) Every commercial fishery kept an interpreter (tsūji)—inevitably Japanese or a nominally assimilated Ainu—on its staff as a way to maintain the fiction that the Ainu could not speak Japanese. That this was a fiction is suggested both by the nature of production at the fisheries, which often required mixed boat crews of three or four men who sometimes worked under Ainu supervision, and by ample evidence that Japanese fishers entered into long-term liaisons with Ainu women.[42] Nevertheless, as Mogami Tokunai noted, "If [the Ainu] should happen to speak Japanese, the interpreters rebuke them, saying that they have committed an unforgivable offense, and demand an indemnity in recompense; likewise if they should wear straw raincoats, straw sandals, or leggings. In all matters the policy of not allowing the Ezo [Ainu] to adopt Japanese customs is the law of the Matsumae house."[43] Tokunai attributed this policy to Matsumae's desire to prevent the Ainu from taking up agriculture or other industries that would free them from their economic dependence on the Japanese.[44]

The Ainu's apparent custom of wearing their robes folded to the left (sajin) was a civilizational marker analogous to hairstyle, though scholars have yet to reach a consensus on the question of whether folding one's garment in one direction or the other held any significance in Ainu culture. For the Japanese it clearly did, for only corpses were dressed with their kimono folded to the left. Sasaki Toshikazu and Kikuchi Isao conclude that the Ainu probably did not have strong feelings about the issue, while Shimomura Isao argues less persuasively that they folded to the left except in areas where at least a measure of acculturation had taken place. At the very least, scholars agree that Japanese representations of Ainu customs tended overwhelmingly to portray the Ainu as wearing their clothing folded to the left to conform to Japanese notions about barbarian appearance.[45]

The principal exception to Matsumae's dissimilation policy was the Ainu community on Etorofu, the island in the southern Kurils that marked the border between the Ezochi and Russia. Shogunal officials had promoted the assimilation of the Etorofu Ainu during the first period of direct administration as a means to secure Japanese sovereignty over the southern Kurils and the rest of the Ezochi. Matsumae maintained the fiction that the Etorofu Ainu had assimilated in deference to the shogunate's national-security concerns.[46] Likewise, the small number of Ainu scattered about the Ezochi who had nominally assimilated during the first period of shogunal administration did not return to their earlier barbarian status when the island reverted to Matsumae's control in 1821. But insofar as the Russian threat disappeared for a time after the early nineteenth century, neither Matsumae nor the shogunate felt the need to extend the assimilation effort to the rest of the Ainu population until 1855.[47]

The Ainu's situation as barbarians resembled the position of the outcastes within Tokugawa society. Commentators like Hoashi Banri theorized on the possible Ainu origins of the outcaste community and on occasion even advocated "reuniting" the two groups by forcibly resettling outcastes in Hokkaido as agricultural colonists. This line of thinking was consistent with other attempts to rationalize discrimination against the outcastes by attributing Korean or other non-Japanese origins to them.[48] Of particular interest for our purposes is that this attempt to link the outcastes with the Ainu was based on perceived similarities in the outward physical appearances of the two groups, such as their unbound hair and the barefootedness enforced by Matsumae domain regulations.[49]

Ironically, by defining the Ainu's barbarian identity vis-à-vis the status system, Matsumae paved the way for the shogunate and, later, the Meiji regime to negate the validity of Ainu identity entirely. In 1855 the shogunate assumed direct administration of Hokkaido in response to the threat posed to Japanese sovereignty over the island by Russia. Magistrates dispatched to Hokkaido oversaw an assimilation program designed to win international recognition of the Ainu's Japanese nationality and hence secure Japan's territorial rights to areas inhabited by the Ainu, including the Kuril Islands and southern Sakhalin, as well as Hokkaido.[50] The Meiji state continued this policy after it succeeded to power in 1868.

The shogunate targeted the same visible markers of identity as the Matsumae domain. For instance, Kasahara Gengo, an official posted to the village of Shiraoi in 1856, persuaded local elders to promise to stop wearing earrings and tattooing women's faces and hands. The Ainu also vowed to wear their garments folded to the right, take Japanese names, and learn to speak Japanese.[51] It is unclear whether they followed the precedent set in Etorofu in the early nineteenth century and constructed "whisker mounds" *(higezuka)* out of the shaved-off facial hair of nominally assimilated men.[52] In any case, officials dispatched throughout Hokkaido advocated assimilation to local Ainu. Needless to say, there was nothing intrinsically barbaric about the cultural attributes that Matsumae had focused on when marking the Ainu as barbarians. Nor, for that matter, was there anything intrinsically civilized about the customs the shogunate imposed on them in its attempt at assimilation. What may be less obvious, however, is that there was nothing intrinsically *Ainu* about them, either. Japanese observers inclined to see the Ainu as barbarians could focus on those cultural attributes that happened to resonate with a preexisting roster of barbarian practices that applied equally within the core polity and outside it.

Significantly, the term translated here as "assimilation," *kizoku*, can be more literally rendered as a "return *(ki* or *kaeru)* to the quotidian *(zoku*—the same character as in *fūzoku*, customs)." As this gloss suggests, the word usually refers to a Buddhist priest's return to lay life, but in this case indicates the Ainu's adoption of the normative customs of Japanese civilization. In contrast, when Meiji commentators spoke of Ainu assimilation, they used the word *dōka* ("making the same"), which implies a much more thorough metamorphosis than *kizoku*.

According to Kubota Shizō, a Sakura domain official who visited the Sōya fishery at the northern tip of Hokkaido in 1856, shogunal officials there explicitly justified the assimilation program in terms of the Russian threat. The officials were following the lead of the Council of Elders (Rōjū), the shogunate's effective ruling body, which had mandated assimilation policies with the argument that if the Ainu wore their hair in the Japanese style the differences between them and Japanese would not be apparent to foreigners.[53] Thus Shizō wrote, "Russians sometimes come to the northern Ezochi [southern Sakhalin], and in the past have tried to win over our subjects *[wagakokujin]* there. But if the Russians were to see [the Ainu] with their pates shaved *[hanpatsu]*, we think they would consider them to be our subjects and leave without doing anything to them."[54] Shizō accepted without question the inherent desirability of assimilating the Ainu, but invoked a broader conception of civilization to express his skepticism about the shogunate's policy. He thought it would be better to establish a clear national boundary with Russia first, thereby forestalling Russian overtures toward the Ainu population. Once that was done, a policy of assimilation could be imposed. But he doubted that merely shaving the Ainu's beards and pates would accomplish the state's goals, for it would leave more profound issues of language, diet, ritual, and religion completely unaddressed. The real question, in Shizō's eyes, was how to get the Ainu to abandon their old ways and adopt the "beautiful customs" *(bizoku)* of Japan. "No wonder the Ezo [Ainu] do not believe [officials] who say they have come to help, but then merely encourage them to shave their pates," he complained. In any case, the Japanese workers at the Sōya fishery were hardly apt role models; Shizō dismissed the lot of them as gamblers and rogues, and protested that the various schemes suggested to resettle *eta, hinin,* and masterless samurai in the Ezochi would undermine attempts to expose the Ainu to the benefits of civilization.[55]

The response of the Ainu to the admonishments of the officials was mixed. Local leaders, under pressure to maintain close economic ties to the Japanese, were generally quicker to accommodate the authorities than other members of the Ainu community. During his travels around Hokkaido, Matsuura Takeshirō encountered a certain Shirikanke, who had learned Japanese and even taught himself to read the katakana syllabary several years before the shogunate initiated its assimilation project. As soon as the policy was announced, he shaved his beard and pate and took the name Hachitarō.[56] Not everyone was so enthusiastic, however. According to Shizō, elders in Sōya panicked when shogunal officials admonished them to adopt Japanese customs and thereby set a good example for their underlings:

> Responding through the interpreter, they said, fearfully, "Although it is not our place to refuse [the authorities'] orders, at fisheries in the western Ezochi like Teshio and Tomamai no one has 'assimilated,' or whatever you call it. [In fact, Shizō had noted earlier in his diary that 3 of the 109 Ainu residents of Tomamai had nominally assimilated.] If we in Sōya were the first [in the region] to shave our beards and moustaches, it would make us look bad [to other Ainu], and do grave dishonor to our ancestors. We beseech you to excuse us from this obligation."[57]

At that point the elders attempted to resolve the issue according to Ainu protocol, through the presentation of indemnities, in this case heirloom swords from their stock of treasures. Unmoved, the shogunal officials summoned twenty Ainu workers, whom they attempted to shave forcibly, only to see the alarmed Ainu flee rather than comply. Eventually, however, the officials managed to persuade about forty Ainu to assimilate after providing each with a cotton jacket *(haori)*, sake, tobacco, and rice.[58]

Shogunal officials at other fisheries, anticipating the reluctance of most Ainu to forsake the outward symbols of their cultural identity, also offered material incentives to cooperate. At Shiraoi, for example, Kasahara Gengo distributed about eighteen liters of brown rice to each of the fourteen or fifteen Ainu who volunteered to be registered, the first step toward being incorporated into the local administrative structure as peasants. Those who further agreed to assimilate were given a quantity of cotton cloth in addition to the rice.[59] Although tactics like this resulted in initial success rates of 70 percent or more in a few villages, more commonly the officials encountered men who ran for the hills rather than cut their hair, or others who readily consented to assimilate in return for Japanese commodities, only to return to their customary ways as soon as the officials had moved on.[60]

The reversal of policy from dissimilation to assimilation can also be seen in the shogunate's attitude toward the *uimam* and *umsa* rituals. Ainu continued to perform the *uimam* at Fukuyama castle and the *umsa* at other locations, including the shogunate's Hakodate magistracy, despite the fact that the Matsumae domain had lost its monopoly over trade and other contact with the Ainu. The avowed purpose of the officials in charge in preserving the rituals was to impress the Ainu with the material wealth of the Japanese and to promote assimilation by giving assimilated Ainu markedly better treatment during the ceremonies and more valuable gifts afterward.[61] Indeed, demonstrating Japanese wealth through the presentation of gifts *(kudasaremono)* was one of the cornerstones of the shogunate's policy of "nurturing" *(buiku)* the Ainu.[62]

In addition to attempts to incorporate the Ainu into the Japanese polity through the manipulation of their customs, shogunal officials made a few desultory efforts—all quickly abandoned—to intervene into the deeper structures of Ainu society. Thus, officials occasionally tried to manipulate Ainu communities and thereby transform them into Japanese-style villages; as we have seen, this policy was implemented most thoroughly on the island of Etorofu, where the nearby Russians were a threatening presence. They also tried to transform the Ainu economy through the introduction of money and the encouragement of agriculture and urged the Ainu to use the Japanese language. Officials also tried to intervene in Ainu religious life through prohibitions of the *iyomante* and other rituals, and the construction of Buddhist temples and Shintō shrines. Perhaps the most intriguing of these interventions was an attempt to introduce the Ainu to the legend that the famed medieval warrior, Minamoto no Yoshitsune, had not been driven to suicide by his jealous brother, the founder of the Kamakura shogunate, but rather had escaped north to become the chieftain of the Ainu.[63] (A twentieth-century version of the legend has Yoshitsune moving on again to the continent, where he becomes Genghis Khan.)[64] Presumably the idea behind this last policy was to naturalize the idea of direct Japanese suzerainty over the Ainu.

The shogunate's attempts to assimilate the Hokkaido Ainu in the 1850s resembled earlier efforts by the Nanbu and Tsugaru domains to integrate their own Ainu populations, though the circumstances surrounding each set of policies were very different. First, Nanbu's assimilation policy was essentially symbolic insofar as identifiable Ainu communities had disappeared from the domain well before it began. Namikawa and Kikuchi accordingly view it as part of a broader effort to eliminate perceived barbarian customs among the domain's Japanese population in response to the emergence of Russia as a diplomatic threat in the late eighteenth century. Nanbu authorities had originally defended such distinctive practices as the failure of local women to shave their eyebrows and blacken their teeth as legitimate "provincial customs" (kokufū), but beginning around the end of the eighteenth century they promoted the adoption of customs practiced in Edo. One by-product of this effort was an attempt to prohibit commoners in the Shimokita peninsula from using Ainu vocabulary and wearing attus, an Ainu outer garment made from woven elm bark, which was better suited to work in wet environments than a cotton kimono. The domain thus reinterpreted previously "unorthodox customs" (ifū—kotonaru fū[zoku]) as "barbarian customs" (ifū—Ezo [no] fū[zoku]), regardless of whether their practitioners were Ainu or not, in an attempt to homogenize Japanese cultural practices and thereby affirm the Tokugawa state's sovereignty over northern Japan.[65]

In contrast to Nanbu's largely symbolic policy, Tsugaru's assimilation of the 240 or so Ainu living in a half-dozen villages in the Tsugaru peninsula was a response to economic change within the Ainu community, which in turn was related to the Ainu's function within the domain's status order.[66] Throughout the seventeenth and early eighteenth centuries, the Tsugaru Ainu were treated as a distinct status group. Their feudal obligations to the domain centered on the provision of marine products, particularly shark-liver oil (used in tanning), and the performance of transport services. They paid no land taxes even though many of them owned land and practiced swidden agriculture, and indeed they received material assistance in the form of grain and cash from the domain.

However, in 1756 and again in 1806 the domain undertook the formal assimilation of its Ainu population. That is, it stopped recognizing the Ainu as a separate social group and instead integrated them administratively into the general commoner population. Namikawa argues that this was at root a response to the economic differentiation of the Ainu community, in which a small group of entrepreneurs became wealthy through commercial shipping and trading in lumber, while the bulk of Ainu fell into dire poverty, particularly after Japanese fishers undermined their domain-sanctioned monopoly over the shark-liver-oil trade at the end of the seventeenth century. As a result, many abandoned independent fishing and farming and turned instead to wage labor in commercial fisheries in Tsugaru, Hokkaido, and elsewhere. While economic stratification per se was not a significant concern, it had the effect of rendering the Ainu unable or unwilling to perform their status-based duties to the domain. As one document from the 1710s noted, "Among the Ezojin [Ainu] of Matsumae [i.e., the Wajinchi], and even Tsugaru and Nanbu, there are some who have become Nihonjin [Japanese] and entered into light employment [karuki hōkō]."[67]

The Tsugaru reformer Nyūi Mitsugu is said to have "promoted" (toritate) the domain's Ainu to commoner status (ningen, literally "human," but in this instance meaning "Japanese," reflecting the dubious humanity of barbarians) in 1756. Although some sources portray the Ainu as being "deeply thankful" (makoto ni arigataki), others claim that some Ainu absconded rather than shave their pates or otherwise outwardly assimilate. At the same time, the domain apparently raised its tiny number of outcastes to commoner status as well. In both cases, its aim appears to have been to raise tax revenues by incorporating marginal status groups into the commoner population: in exchange for becoming ordinary peasants, Ainu and outcastes lost their status-based privileges, such as trade monopolies and access to domain welfare, and instead were subjected to the same tax obligations as other commoners. Moreover, political stability in Hokkaido after Shakushain's War eliminated the Tsugaru Ainu's political utility to the domain, so that by the time of the next major Ainu uprising, the Kunashiri-Menashi Rebellion of 1789, the domain included no identifiable Ainu among the forces it readied to support Matsumae. In short, since economic change and political stability had undermined the Ainu's utility to the domain as a status group, the authorities revised the Ainu's status to bring it into line with economic and political reality.[68]

As in the case of the Hokkaido Ainu nominally assimilated by the shogunate in the 1850s, the Tsugaru Ainu's formal status identity was

distinct from actual cultural practice, at least until 1806—a time of anxiety about Russian designs on northern Japan—when the domain began
aggressively to prohibit Ainu cultural practices. Sakakura Genjirō, who
visited Tsugaru in 1739, wrote that the local Ainu maintained a strong
sense of difference from the surrounding Japanese population, despite the
fact that they had partially adopted Japanese customs (for example, the
men shaved the fronts of their pates but otherwise left their hair long and
unbound). By the 1780s and 1790s, however, even travelers eagerly looking for markers of Ainu identity could not discern them: the people all
spoke Japanese, the men shaved their entire pates, and the women's faces
were not tattooed. But Matsuura Takeshirō, who visited Tsugaru in the
early nineteenth century (and was by far more knowledgeable about
Ainu culture than other travelers), observed a few vestiges of Ainu cultural practices—the people's vehement denials of any connection to the
Ainu notwithstanding—particularly their keeping of treasures such as
swords and lacquerware. However, even Takeshirō agreed that in their
outward emblems of identity, such as clothing and hairstyle, the people
were identical to their neighbors.[69]

IDENTITY AND TERRITORIALITY

The establishment of the Tokugawa shogunate and the concomitant
delineation of the political boundaries of the early modern state in the
seventeenth century resulted in the division of the Japanese archipelago
into a clearly demarcated core polity and ambiguously bounded peripheries. The core polity's boundaries had a dual nature: on the one hand,
they separated specific geographical spaces, as symbolized by the barriers
erected in southern Hokkaido to distinguish the Wajinchi from the
Ezochi; and on the other hand, they separated the status order from the
worlds of the Ainu and Ryukyuans, as well as those of other peoples
whose realm lay beyond Japan's peripheries. The porosity of the regime's
physical borders did not undermine the integrity of the boundaries of the
status order, which suggests that participation in the status system, not
residence, was the key marker of the state's sovereignty over its subjects,
though both were important. In any case, it is clear that contemporary
notions of territoriality—in which nations are separated by a single set of
clearly defined physical boundaries—did not apply in early modern
Japan.

The early modern state's boundaries were arbitrary, but they were not
randomly fixed. Rather, they were the products of centuries of trade,

social interaction, and military conflict between the peoples who inhabited the surrounding territories. Thus, the state both affirmed and transformed the peculiar relationship between the Ainu and the Japanese in Hokkaido. It affirmed the relationship by formalizing the de facto division of southern Hokkaido into Japanese and Ainu territories; it transformed it by giving the distinction between Ainu and Japanese a political significance independent of other differences in culture, social organization, and economic activity.

Civilization and barbarism connected core and periphery, and distinguished both from areas with no immediate connection to the Tokugawa state. In some intellectual circles, civilization never broke completely free of its roots in Confucian ideology, in which a thorough grounding in ritual and textual erudition was its true test. Nevertheless, by the early nineteenth century the content of civilization as a politically meaningful construct had been reduced to its core component, customs. This opened the door to a conflation of the realm of civilization with the area incorporated into the status order. As a result, new territory could be brought under the state only after the realm of civilization had been extended there.

Although status and civilization were essentially political constructs, political identity took on the attributes of ethnicity through the deployment of customs as cultural symbols. Everyone living within the territory encompassed by the early modern status system was "Japanese," both institutionally, because status organized obligations to authority, and culturally, because customs were the cultural expression of incorporation within the status order. (I am referring to culture in a very limited sense here, because cultural practice outside the framework of customs was irrelevant to the construction of politically meaningful identity.) Put differently, only territory inhabited by "Japanese" could be part of "Japan." That is why the Ainu had to be nominally assimilated—that is, brought within the status order through the assignment of civilized customs—for the Tokugawa state to assert sovereignty over all of Hokkaido. It is also why, by extension, Japanese territorial claims extended to areas inhabited by Ainu in southern Sakhalin and the southern Kurils, but not beyond. In this manner, boundaries of status and civilization bracketed the identity of the Japanese and held it into place. With the physical and cultural boundaries of "Japan" in place, it became possible to develop a national discourse that applied unequivocally to all those deemed to be "Japanese."

The Japanese constructed Ainu identity through the delineation of both the geography of civilization, which marked the Ainu as barbarians exogenous to the core polity, and the geography of status, which paradoxically brought them within the state's purview through the deployment of status-laden customs. Yet at the root of the relationship with Japan lay the Ainu's dependence on Japanese commodities. For this reason, we cannot attribute the delineation of Ainu and Japanese identities solely to the boundaries constructed by agents of the Tokugawa state: the Ainu's contribution to the drawing of boundaries was as important as that of the agents of the Tokugawa state. The elevation of prized commodities to the status of treasures, the association of participation in *uimam* and *umsa* with high social standing within the Ainu community, and the use of rituals like the bear ceremony to affirm social cohesion in the absence of broad political organization all served to ensure that the Ainu would retain a measure of agency in their dealings with the Japanese. To be sure, their unshaven pates and participation in *uimam* and *umsa* rituals contributed to the demarcation of civilized and barbarian realms in Japan, but at the same time they allowed the Ainu to reproduce their own communities with a minimum of Japanese interference: markers of difference were also emblems of autonomy.

The Ainu's autonomy was undermined by the necessity of intimate contact with Japanese employers, markets, and political institutions to ensure stability in everyday life. The role of economic relations as a solvent of autonomous identities is particularly clear in Tsugaru, where the domain's standing within the early modern polity was not dependent on its ties with the Ainu. The Tsugaru Ainu's formal identity as barbarians was first sublimated into the domain's internal status order, then, once their status identity ceased to serve any economic or political purpose, they were incorporated fully into the commoner population. Similarly, in Nanbu in the late eighteenth century, and again in Hokkaido under shogunal control in the 1850s, even vestigial markers of Ainu identity came under attack once they were perceived to be a diplomatic liability.

Neither essential nor transhistorical, customs were arbitrary attributes, endowed with political significance or not as it suited the needs of the feudal regime. At a certain level of abstraction, therefore, the realms they demarcated were likewise entirely constructs. It is tempting to end the discussion here, for exposing the constructedness of the boundaries of status and civilization complicates our conception of "Japan" in a particularly satisfying way. Revealing the nation (even in its ill-formed early modern guise) as a chimera is the first step toward uncovering the complex social realities hidden by its cloaking mechanism. In the real world, however, to be civilized or barbarian was for the individuals and social groups so labeled less a question of customs than one of distance from the political power of the early modern state.

As we have seen, the Ainu's nominal barbarism informed every aspect of the Tokugawa state's stance toward them, and thereby shaped the political and economic environment in which they lived. To maintain access to Japanese commodities the Ainu participated in ritual and labor on terms largely dictated by the Japanese and in forms that suited the political needs of the Matsumae domain and its merchant proxies and, later, the shogunate. Yet being marked as barbarians by the Japanese had at most an indirect impact on the lives and economic activities of individual Ainu and the communities to which they belonged. To be sure, by the end of the eighteenth century few if any Ainu remained completely aloof of the relationship with Japan, and so in that sense their constructed identity as barbarians was inescapable. At the same time, however, the objective conditions of the Ainu's existence—their dependence on imported commodities and their homeland's subordination to the Tokugawa state—were products of an organic process, an incidental outcome of long-standing economic relations. The Ainu's perception of both ritual and labor as forms of trade reflects the organic quality of the relationship. Of course, the institutional structure of the early modern state deeply affected the actual conditions of ritual, trade, and other contact; constraints on Ainu labor and the loss of direct access to Honshu markets in the wake of Shakushain's War are evidence of that. Nevertheless, being marked as barbarians and thereby being incorporated into the early modern Japanese world order was not immediately relevant to the mundane routines of individual Ainu and their communities, particularly as relations with Japan were naturalized—and thereby taken for granted—over time. Because state power did not intrude directly into Ainu communities, the distance separating the Ainu's world from the Tokugawa regime was both real and important. The Ainu who headed for the hills to escape the barber shears of eager officials understood this principle clearly.

CHAPTER 7

Civilization
and Enlightenment

The creation of a fully centralized regime in the Meiji era undermined the internal autonomies of early modern society, dumping the contents of the nested boxes of the status system into the single container of imperial subjecthood. At the same time, the embrace of Western-style modernity prompted a fundamental reinterpretation of the content of civilization, which led to the delineation of a new roster of normative customs. The independence and security of the nation were linked to economic and industrial development, prompting entrepreneurs to justify their activities in terms of selfless nationalism. Ideologues rushed to the support of each of these projects, celebrating emperor, enlightenment, and enterprise. Although they were hardly the blind servants of the state, their efforts helped to make the attainment of modernity a goal shared broadly by the Japanese people, even as modernity's precise contours were fiercely debated.

In this chapter I will examine the way Tokugawa notions of civilization and barbarism were translated into a new idiom in the years immediately following the Meiji Restoration. A new roster of customs marked subjects as civilized or barbarous, and new technologies of enforcing normative patterns helped to disseminate the new standards quickly around the country. Creating new standards of civilization simultaneously transformed the nature of barbarism and created new forms of differentiation. The era of "civilization and enlightenment" saw the delineation of a realm of discrimination that was in many ways more focused and hence more pernicious than anything found in the Tokugawa era.

THE CUSTOMS OF CIVILIZATION AND ENLIGHTENMENT

The Meiji regime asserted that the Ainu and Ryukyuans and the regions they inhabited were Japanese and thereby subsumed the barbarian realm completely within the boundaries of the modern state. This gave rise to a profound dilemma, for securely situating the realm of civilization within the Japanese archipelago had required the existence of a barbarian sphere around it. Moreover, following the Tokugawa example and simply concluding that shaving the Ainu's pates had completed the process of civilizing Japan and all of its inhabitants was not an option because the early modern concept of civilization had been articulated on the basis of a discredited understanding of Japan's place within East Asia and the broader world order. Abandoning the early modern worldview, in other words, required reinterpreting both civilization and barbarism to make them compatible with the construction of a modern nation-state. Meiji leaders and the thinkers who rushed to their ideological defense responded by proposing a new dichotomy between Western-style civilization (now expressed as *bunmei*) and barbarism *(yaban)*, or, in Oku Takenori's formulation, enlightenment *(kaika)* and darkness *(meimō)*.[1]

Ordinarily, the phrase "civilization and enlightenment" *(bunmei kaika)* brings to mind the intense engagement with Western thought and institutions that characterized intellectual life in the early Meiji period. I should pause here to note that I am following a well-established convention in English-language scholarship in rendering *bunmei kaika* as "civilization and enlightenment," though, as Douglas R. Howland has pointed out, the phrase is misleading: both words mean "civilization." However, in practice "*bunmei* was routinely used as a noun—civilization—and implied the ongoing and total progress of humankind whereas *kaika* was used as an active verb [meaning "civilizing" and "developing"] and, when used as a noun, implied the civilizing process directed toward its projected end," namely, "the public cultivation of civilization through government policy."[2] Thus my discussion below will focus on the *kaika* part of the *bunmei kaika* formulation. However, it is important to note that by the mid-1880s, when the most aggressive attempts to manipulate customs had been completed, commentators dropped the term *kaika* and instead juxtaposed the barbarism they found in the slums of major cities with a universalized conception of civilization, *bunmei*.[3]

In any case, members of the Meiji Six Society (Meirokusha), particularly the educator and journalist Fukuzawa Yukichi, introduced the Japanese public to the ideas and technologies that lay at the heart of Western-style modernity.[4] As politically engaged thinkers, these men and their ideas had a profound impact on both the Meiji leaders and their main political opponents, the participants in the movement for freedom and popular rights in the late 1870s and early 1880s.[5] Civilization and enlightenment as high discourse has received considerable scholarly attention already, so there is no need to discuss the movement beyond making one or two general points.[6]

There is a tendency to see civilization and enlightenment discourse as a stark departure from the ideas and institutions of the Tokugawa period. Fukuzawa himself stressed the idea of shedding the past in his writings, and scholars seeking to explain Meiji Japan's rapid modernization have, reasonably enough, emphasized the progressive elements of early Meiji thought.[7] However, in so doing scholars have obscured the degree to which the language of civilization and enlightenment was used to promote ideas at every point along the ideological spectrum. Indeed, even nativists—usually held up as the reactionary opponents of progressive modernizers like Fukuzawa—justified their ideas in terms of enlightenment, which they equated with a return to the ideas and practices of Japanese antiquity.[8] In short, for a thinker to be taken seriously in the intellectual world of the first decade or so of the Meiji era he had to invoke the language of civilization and enlightenment. In some ways this represented the tremendous influence of Fukuzawa and his cohorts, but it is also true that because the language of civilization and enlightenment was so widely dispersed throughout the intellectual world of early Meiji Japan, any attempt to isolate its particularly Westward-looking and progressive elements is misleading.

Three critical differences distinguished the early modern (ka versus i) and modern (bunmei versus yaban) conceptions of civilization and barbarism. First, under the Meiji regime, the content of civilization—and hence of barbarism—was articulated in relation to the advanced industrial and military powers of the Western world. The westward orientation of Meiji civilization was reflected first in elites' enthusiastic adoption of the outward symbols of Western culture, such as clothing and hairstyles, and later in an institutionalized concern with hygiene, discipline, science, and other technologies of social knowledge. Both impulses had roots in the waning years of Tokugawa rule but gained official sponsorship only after the Restoration. Second, the "ethnic" aspects of the opposition between civilization and barbarism largely disappeared. The Ainu's barbarism during the Tokugawa era was not really an "ethnic" quality at all: although it helped to define them as a people existing outside the core polity, the particular customs that marked them as barbarians applied within the Tokugawa state itself and were therefore not *essentially* Ainu traits. Yet it is also true that by adopting civilized customs one ceased to be Ainu in the eyes of the early modern state. Accordingly, while barbarism was not the exclusive domain of the Ainu, it was not possible simultaneously to be Ainu and anything but a barbarian. After the Meiji Restoration, even those Ainu who had nominally assimilated returned to a barbarian condition, in part because the distinction between the Japanese and Ainu was reconceived as an ethnic one. However, rather than making barbarism a peculiarly ethnic attribute (by linking it to distinctive Ainu cultural practices, for example), Meiji officials and ideologues discovered—to their considerable dismay—large and unruly pockets of barbarism within the core polity itself. This relates to the final point: the internalization of civilization became a pressing issue in the Meiji period, whereas previously it had been (in embryonic form) the nearly exclusive concern of a limited community of Confucian ideologues. It is this politically pertinent concern with internalization that makes the Meiji concept of civilization "modern" in a way that its Tokugawa counterpart had not been. Markers of civilization and barbarism came to include not only superficial customs like dress and hairstyle, but also practices and beliefs at the very core of everyday life, such as religion, personal hygiene, and social interaction. Civilization ceased to be a garment or hairstyle to be worn or discarded at will, but rather became an essential element of individual identity, internalized as a habit of thought, a sense of self and of membership in the national community.

The alacrity with which the Meiji leaders embraced a conception of civilization borrowed from the West is often linked to their realization that achieving diplomatic and economic parity with the imperialist powers required adopting the West's social and political institutions along with its military, industrial, and managerial technologies. Although Western haircuts, beef eating, and the like appear to have little connection to treaty revision or industrial development, ideologues marshaled their newfound knowledge of Western society to justify the change, sometimes in ways that strike the modern reader as ludicrous—by arguing that a shaved pate left a man vulnerable to infectious disease, for instance.[9] As we shall see presently, the state expended scarce administrative and disciplinary resources in its program of instituting Western-style civilization; it persisted despite dogged opposition—some of it violent—from diverse elements throughout society. We could take the ideologues at their word, of course, but that begs the question of why they were willing to go to such considerable lengths to rationalize changes in seemingly incidental customs.

Clearly, something very important was at stake in the rush to adopt the Western trappings of civilization and enlightenment. The imperative to see Japan as civilized was natural enough, particularly considering the concept's importance during the Tokugawa period. However, early modern ideas about civilization lost their geopolitical significance during the process of bringing Japan within the international order. Quite simply, the Western powers did not recognize the validity of Japanese customs as universal markers of civilization, nor did they recognize an organic connection between civilization and territoriality, but they did espouse a relationship between civilization and the right to sovereignty. In other words, only civilized nations (whose borders were more or less self-evident, or at least negotiable) were eligible to govern themselves; uncivilized (and especially uncharted) territories required Western tutelage and stewardship before they could enjoy full independence. Western imperialism in China and India, combined with the assault on Japanese national sovereignty written into the treaties imposed on the shogunate in the 1850s, made the Meiji leadership keenly aware of this connection.

This is not to say, however, that early modern ideas of civilization disappeared along with the Tokugawa regime. The emphasis placed on the regulation of customs in the early Meiji period reflected a Japanese reading of civilization transposed onto the West; that is, officials and ideologues assumed that outward customs lay at the very heart of the Western conception of civilization, just as they had to the Japanese during the Tokugawa period, for they understood the relationship between correct customs and an orderly realm to be a universal truth.[10] Just as the shogunate had tried to assimilate the Ainu by shaving their pates, the early Meiji state thought it could "assimilate" the Japanese population by unbinding the people's hair. And just as it had been obvious to Tokugawa officials that the Ainu needed to wear topknots before they could remake themselves as civilized subjects of the shogun, Meiji Japanese needed to wear top hats to demonstrate to the Western powers their readiness to remake themselves as civilized moderns.[11] The Westerners had to see the top hats, of course, and thereby validate the endeavor. Accordingly, it follows that Tokyo and the treaty ports were the site of the first attempts at the reform of customs.

The Ministry of Justice (Shihōshō) incorporated customs regulations into a series of petty-misdemeanor ordinances *(ishiki kaii jōrei)*, first promulgated in Tokyo in 1872 and later extended throughout the country in slightly different form in each prefecture. Both *ishiki* and *kaii* refer to infringements of the law, but the crimes included under the *ishiki* ordinances were considered more serious and accordingly carried larger fines— 75 to 150 sen (or ten to twenty lashes for those who could not afford to pay) as opposed to the 6.25 to 12.5 sen (or one to two days' detention) that was originally promulgated in Tokyo (corporal punishment was abandoned in 1876). As Oku has noted, the average daily wage of a carpenter in 1874 was 40 sen, so the fines, while hardly ruinous, were nonetheless substantial.[12] In all cases, offenders were not subjected to a legal proceeding; rather, enforcement was entrusted entirely to the new police force.[13]

As a compilation of regulations concerning petty misdemeanors, the ordinances were not exclusively or even primarily concerned with customs; they included prohibitions of threats to public safety (such as riding a horse at night without a light) and public health (selling spoiled fish); petty theft (pilfering fruit from trees); and certain types of economic activity (unlicensed vending). Nonetheless, a number of the ordinances did concern customs, and the prohibition of public nakedness included among the more serious *ishiki* regulations was perhaps the most widely enforced.

The customs regulations incorporated within the petty-misdemeanor ordinances fell into two general categories: a relatively small number governing the body, and a larger group concerning public decorum. In addition to the ban on public nakedness, which was directed mostly toward rickshaw pullers and laborers who stripped down to their loincloths to work, the bodily regulations included prohibitions of tattooing, mixed bathing, public urination, cross-dressing (except by kabuki actors), and the wearing of short hair by women. Those regulating behavior generally covered public nuisances of various sorts, including the careless handling of livestock in city streets, fighting, drunken revelry and singing, and "opening lattices or climbing walls, and wantonly sticking one's face out to peer at or mock passersby from above" (*kaii*, article 56).[14] Others banned public entertainments like dog fighting, snake charming, fireworks in densely populated districts, and unlicensed exhibitions of sumo wrestling by men and women.

Although it is tempting to read into the bodily regulations a desire to inscribe the power of the state directly onto the persons of its subjects, in fact the aim of the regulations seems to have been similar to that of the

ordinances concerned with public decorum more generally. In other
words, the goal of the customs regulations was to contain unruly and outrageous behavior of all sorts. In that sense, there was no essential difference between the assaults on scantily clad rickshaw men and inebriated
crooners. The edict prohibiting women from cutting their hair without
permission is a case in point. It appears that some young women in
Tokyo—particularly students—cut their hair and wore items of men's
clothing in the period preceding the promulgation of the petty-misdemeanor ordinances. At the end of 1871 a newspaper in Chiba praised the
women, saying that the fashion was a commendable sign of economy and
rationality, although in March 1872 another paper, the *Shinbun zasshi,*
excoriated the fad—which it interpreted as either a misguided effort at
civilization and enlightenment, or perhaps an attempt by the women to
desexualize *(iro o saru)* themselves—as both unwomanly and running
counter to the customs of Japan and the West alike. The following month
the newspaper ran a notice saying that the government's recent order
allowing people to cut their hair was directed at men only, and that
women should therefore keep their hair long as before.[15] Sharon Sievers
argues that the prohibition of short hair on women reflected the authorities' desire to mark women as the repositories of tradition, a trail of bread
crumbs to guide Japan back home should it get lost during its romp into
the forest of Western civilization.[16] This reading has a certain appeal, res-
onating as it does with postcolonial discourse on the feminization of the
colonial subject. However, we should keep in mind (as the *Shinbun zasshi*
reporter noted) that Western women in the early 1870s generally did not
wear short hair, and so Japanese women who did so could not have been
imitating their European and American counterparts. So while the students were certainly challenging traditional notions of a woman's proper
appearance, we must nonetheless distinguish the practice from the 1870s
fad for things Western. Indeed, many men also adopted hairstyles that
departed from both traditional and Western patterns during this period,
and although their behavior was not criminalized, officials used the police
to bully these men into wearing their hair more conventionally.[17] In fact,
evidence suggests that the prohibition was directed primarily against
women who cut their hair either as a sign of Buddhist piety on the deaths
of their husbands, or because they preferred not to bother with—or could
not afford—the considerable trouble, expense, and physical hardship of
wearing the elaborate coifs popular at the time, most of which were
adapted from styles pioneered by courtesans and kabuki actors.[18] Indeed,
in 1885 a group of (male) enthusiasts of enlightenment founded the

Women's Upswept Hair Society (Fujin Sokuhatsukai) to promote the adoption of "Western" hairstyles for women (actually a mix of Western and Japanese elements). The group's manifesto marshaled the same arguments in favor of reform—that traditional hairstyles were uncomfortable, unhygienic, and uneconomical—that short-haired women a decade earlier might have made themselves.[19] Thus it is reasonable to conclude that although the daring young women of Tokyo were no doubt a serious concern, the authorities more aggressively attempted to control the far greater number of people who found it easier to be unseemly than decorous, whether they were women who could not cope with the hassle of a Shimada chignon *(wage)* or men who could not contain themselves long enough to find a public urinal.

The concern with decorum is explicit in injunctions issued by local governments. For example, the Chiba prefectural authorities issued a notice to the residents of the communities of Chiba, Samugawa, and Nobuto in August 1874 exhorting them to good behavior. Although the document was not a legal edict, the eleven deplorable practices specifically listed (nakedness, public urination, dumping sewage into the streets, and the like) could all be found in the Tokyo petty-misdemeanor ordinances. Particularly interesting for our purposes is the preface, which stated:

> It goes without saying now that it is everyone's duty to show respect and deference to others, and to improve manners and etiquette. However, it has come to our attention that people have been behaving in an unbearably offensive manner. They act without respect or courtesy, and interfere with the actions of others. Perhaps they do not realize that traditional local practices *[fūshū]* are improper, or perhaps they misinterpret the recent talk of personal freedom and liberty *[jishu jiyū]* to mean that it is acceptable to act selfishly and wantonly. Are these customs not uncouth *[hiya]* and most shameful? Your communities lie near the government offices and must accordingly serve as a model for the entire prefecture. It is therefore imperative that you reform your customs and allow yourselves to be guided by respectfulness. The young must respect the old and the aged cherish the young; commoners must defer to the gentry and the gentry yield to local officials; and local officials must not interfere with the people's rights *[kenri]*. In all respects, from your demeanor to daily interactions, you must be careful to remain faithful, correct your manners and etiquette, and strive toward the attainment of true civilization and enlightenment *[shin no bunmei kaika]*. . . . Each one of you must strive to eliminate the well-nigh barbarous *[yaban]* offenses [listed below].[20]

However strong the Meiji state's desire to get its people to think modern thoughts, it was easier to get them to piss modern piss first. The attack on indecorous behavior was thus a reasonable place to launch the project of introducing Japan to Western-style modernity. Aside from the propaganda value of presenting foreign visitors with orderly streets and a courteous populace, the basic idea of showing deference to superiors and compassion to the lower orders had deep roots in Japanese culture. No one being told to refrain from engaging in drunken street brawls would have been surprised at the admonition, for indeed the annals of Tokugawa jurisprudence were filled with cranky injunctions against disruptions of public order. And although a number of the customs regulations—the prohibitions against public nakedness and mixed bathing in particular—were generally new to the Meiji period, they represented a modest, if significant, incremental step beyond earlier attempts to regulate public morality.

Despite these links to the past, two features clearly differentiated the Meiji customs regulations from Tokugawa practice. The first was the vigor with which they were enforced. For all its teeth gnashing about the unruly masses, the shogunate had never dispatched patrolmen armed with oaken truncheons into the countryside to knock good manners into uncouth people.[21] In 1876, the police arrested 4,495 people for public urination, 2,727 for fighting, and 2,091 for public nakedness in Tokyo prefecture alone. In all, 10,960 people were punished for infractions against the petty-misdemeanor ordinances in the prefecture that year. Enforcement became even stricter in the years immediately following: the Tokyo police arrested 3,179 people for public nakedness in 1877 and 7,545 in 1878.[22] The police's energetic enforcement efforts notwithstanding, rowdy and indecorous behavior hardly disappeared from the streets of Meiji Japan. Years after the promulgation of the petty-misdemeanor ordinances, Western visitors like Edward Sylvester Morse reported seeing (but not being particularly shocked by) many nearly naked rickshaw men and laborers in Yokohama and Tokyo.[23] Even today, a late-night stroll in any urban area will quickly reveal that neither public urination nor drunken merrymaking was eradicated by the good officers of the police force in the 1870s. And although it is debatable whether the salaryman lying in an alcoholic stupor on the Shinjuku Station platform sees himself as an agent of resistance against official meddling into the lifeways of the people, it is nevertheless reassuring that even the contemporary state, with all its technologies for instilling discipline, has never been able fully to attain its vision of an orderly modern society. Still, the die was cast: whereas Edo townsmen had taken pride in their ability to urinate whenever and wherever the urge arose, no taxi driver in his right mind—however pressing his need—would consider relieving himself against the wall of a police box.[24]

The second major departure from Tokugawa practice was the explicit labeling of indecorous behavior as barbarous *(yaban)*. There was an early modern precedent for seeing the unrefined practices of rural people as backward—the countryside was the repository of remnant barbarian customs in the eyes of many Confucian ideologues, after all—but during the Meiji period the locus of barbarism generally shifted from remote country villages to the urban core of Japan, where manual laborers, prostitutes, and other elements at the margins of the developing capitalist economy tended to congregate.[25] In other words, economic activity, rather than preexisting cultural norms, became the key criterion of Meiji barbarism.

This reorientation of barbarism was anticipated by policies like the establishment of the Kyoto workhouse for vagrants in 1868 and similar facilities set up in Tokyo in 1869 and the years thereafter.[26] Japanese travelers' comments about the islands south of Kyushu reflect the changing notions of barbarism as well. The Restoration leader Saigō Takamori, who was exiled to Amami Ōshima in 1859, mocked the local customs, particularly the women's makeup and tattooed hands, and on that basis likened them to the Ainu. (His opinion of Amami improved markedly, however, after he had two children with a local woman.) Sasamori Gisuke, who visited the Sakishima Islands south of Okinawa in 1893, also invoked comparisons to the Ainu, but he applied economic criteria in doing so. Thus he condemned the local residents for their "laziness" and lack of will to "exert themselves through work," characteristics that left them so desperately poor that they were barely better off than "the aborigines of Hokkaido."[27] It is no surprise, then, that the tendency toward economic determinism manifested itself in policy toward the Ainu, as civilizing the Ainu came to be seen mostly as a question of providing them with the means to lead "stable" lives as cultivators, rather than "unsettled" existences as laborers in the fishing, lumber, and construction industries. This shift meshed nicely with not only the reorientation of political identity from status to imperial subjecthood, but also contemporaneous Western notions about the alienness of the urban poor, and as such was a logical outcome of the push to impose Western-style civilization on Japan.

The effort to impose new standards of civilization from above met with all sorts of resistance, of which stubborn noncompliance may have been the most pervasive if the least threatening. The Satsuma Rebellion and other samurai uprisings and peasant movements like the Mimasaka Blood-Tax Rebellion often included demands that the state rescind customs reforms such as the ban on sword bearing for samurai and the encouragement of unbound hair for all men. The 1876 prohibition of sword bearing was part of the state's policy of gradually dismantling samurai status, a program that culminated the same year in the forced commutation of samurai stipends into bonds payable over the course of several years. Just as it had encouraged samurai to accede to the commutation of their stipends voluntarily before forcibly commuting them, the government first issued a call for the voluntary cessation of sword bearing before banning the practice outright. Notably, the Ministry of State's official notice of the eighth month of 1871 called on samurai to adopt unbound hair at the same time they gave up sword bearing. Given that the prohibition on swords was part of a broader package of reforms designed to encourage the samurai population to take up independent livelihoods, it is not surprising that it was frequently listed as a complaint by samurai rebels. In particular, the participants in the Shinpūren Rebellion of 1876, one of the half-dozen or so samurai uprisings to seriously challenge the regime, made sword bearing one of their central issues. The rebels were so earnest in their attachment to the symbols of samurai status that they refused to use firearms, with the result that the uprising amounted to little more than a mass suicide mission.[28]

Strictly speaking, the government's granting of permission to men not to bind their hair was not a direct call for the adoption of Western hairstyles. Although the term used in the Ministry of State's edict, *sanpatsu,* means "haircut" in contemporary Japanese, at the time the term referred to unbound (but not necessarily cut) hair. Accordingly, commentators insisted that the policy was not aimed at imposing Western styles on the populace, but rather represented a return to classical Japanese practice.[29] However, the new hairstyles were commonly known as *zangiri* (or *jangiri*—"cropped" hair), which conjured up images of the loose, roughly cut hair worn by many outcastes.[30] Conversely, a song popular around the time the state ministry issued its edict included a line, "Folks with [long or bound] hair are barbarians—ain't it so? I guess so!"[31] That particular issue was sorted out in March 1873, when the emperor adopted a Western hairstyle, but it took another decade for short hair to spread throughout the male population.

The encouragement of unbound hair (and soon, of Western haircuts) was just that: an exhortation, not a law. In fact, however, local officials frequently took it on themselves to pressure the men under their authority to adopt more or less uniform hairstyles. In such cases the object of their attack was as likely to be new, unconventional styles as the traditional topknot. Oku cites a series of increasingly irate injunctions issued by officials in Aikawa (later part of Niigata) prefecture between 1873 and 1875, including a warning that the police would haul in anyone without an orthodox (short) haircut.[32] As a result of the imperial example and efforts like this, the practice of wearing short hair spread quickly (if unevenly) through the country. In May 1873 a Nagoya newspaper estimated that about 80 percent of men in Tokyo had cut their hair, while the following summer the *Shinbun zasshi* reported wide variation (though a tendency toward short hair) in prefectures in central Japan, with the variation mostly reflecting differences in the ardor of local officials. Thus, about 80 to 90 percent of men in Shiga prefecture had cut their hair rather than pay a monthly tax (the proceeds of which were earmarked for education), while Aichi boasted nearly total compliance, thanks to the fact that the police were empowered to cut the hair of any shaggy-maned prefectural resident they encountered. In contrast, in nearby Mie, only 30 to 40 percent of men had short hair, while further to the east a variety of traditional styles were still common.[33] Although Morse saw many men still wearing traditional styles in Muroran, a port in southern Hokkaido, during his sojourn in Japan in 1877–78, in Tokyo only the aged and rustics failed to sport Western haircuts.[34]

In addition to armed resistance, the government also had to contend with individual attempts to manipulate the new standards in ways that did not jibe with official understandings of civilized behavior. We have already seen that some young women in Tokyo attempted to take advantage of the enlightenment fad to cut their hair. In that case, neither public opinion (at least as given voice by the *Shinbun zasshi*) nor the authorities were on their side. But for men, a haircut could similarly serve as a daring statement of one's aspirations for the new order. Men enjoyed a great deal more leeway than women in making public statements of their individuality. Although this is a complex issue that should not be subsumed completely within the realm of economics, it did have an economic aspect, insofar as it was up to individual men to guide Japan into the modern world order. The following anecdote from an 1874 book by Oka Sankei, although certainly apocryphal, illustrates the relationship between entrepreneurial individualism and the customs of Western civilization quite clearly.

Under the Tokugawa, members of different status groups wore their hair in a style appropriate to their station, but now one can wear his hair however he pleases. Barbers eager for business accordingly go to great pains to accommodate their customers' tastes, sometimes even dividing their shops into two rooms, one for those who prefer traditional styles, the other for enthusiasts of enlightenment *[kaika]*. One day a young man of perhaps twenty-two or twenty-three—from his looks and demeanor, obviously a student—came into a certain barbershop. The barber clicked his scissors and leaned over to ask the customer what sort of haircut he would like. "The French 'Napoleon' style is all the rage right now, but perhaps the gentleman would like something a bit different—say, a 'Victoria' or a 'Washington'?" The student laughed derisively and replied a bit roughly, "Victoria is the queen of England. I am a stalwart fellow *[tenka no daijōfu]*. Why in the world would I want to model myself after a barbarian woman *[ijo]*?" The barber scratched his head and apologized for his error. "Well, then, a 'Columbus' it is." The student grinned and replied, "I am a great man of the world *[tenka no gōketsu]*—those styles are all beneath me. Give me a 'Tamerlane,' or maybe a 'Genghis Khan.'" The proprietor was fed up but did not show it. Instead, he asked the student to wait a moment while he ran over to a nearby photographer's studio [presumably to find a picture to model the haircut after].[35]

The student's (or perhaps the author's—Oka Sankei was a sinologue) ambivalence toward Western civilization is clear from his derisive comment about Queen Victoria and his desire to model his hair after an Asian hero's. But even if Oka intended the anecdote as a critique of the Westernization fad, he nonetheless had to accept the departure from earlier standards, which opens the door to a reading of the story as a call for Asians to beat the West at its own game. In either case, if it were not for the government's encouragement of unbound hair, the student would not have had the opportunity to express his ambitions so forcefully in the first place.

The manipulation of Western standards of civilization for private purposes extended beyond the realm of hairstyle. An attempt to subvert the association between outcaste status and meat eating can be seen in a memorial submitted by a prominent Osaka *eta* on the eve of the Restoration. In the fifth month of 1867, Mataemon, the headman of Watanabe village and hence the most influential outcaste in western Japan, submitted an extraordinary request that the term *eta* be abolished. He began the memorial with an intriguing inversion of the popular understanding of the outcastes' origins. Rather than presenting his people as the descendants of foreign immigrants, he said that they were in fact the progeny of Japanese who had accompanied the Empress Jingū on her (legendary) invasion of the Korean peninsula in the third century. There they adopted the Koreans' custom of eating meat, a practice they took back to Japan with them. This habit rendered them ineligible to serve the court as other Japanese did, giving rise to the distinction between themselves and the rest of the populace. Unfortunate though their situation was, they had served the nation by performing defiling duties and by maintaining the imperial tombs. Now amicable relations have been established with the foreigners. Mataemon noted, however, that "although the foreigners all eat meat and thereby defile our august country [mikuni], they have not been distanced from the 'four estates' [shimin]. Only we have been so distanced, which is a truly lamentable state of affairs. We would be most grateful if, in your boundless compassion, you would remove the two characters eta from [the name of] our status." To add a bit of punch to his rhetoric, Mataemon closed his memorial by assuring the authorities that "we shall bankrupt ourselves to raise the funds [goyōkin] you have requested of us."[36] Here, too, we are presented with an appeal to economic utility over preexisting status, though Mataemon did not go so far as to request outright that the outcastes be made into commoners. At any rate, he got his wish eventually, of course; not only did the Meiji state abolish outcaste status in 1871, but the emperor himself began to eat meat early the following year.[37]

The introduction of Meiji standards of civilization and enlightenment entailed a synchronous process of expanding the notion of civilization so that it gradually penetrated into the core of everyday life, while linking barbarism to the urban poor and others whose livelihoods were marked as unsettled. Although the institutions of the modern state and the technologies at its disposal to order society were fundamentally different from those of the early modern regime, the linking of occupation and civilization as emblems of the individual's place in society were the same. During the Tokugawa period, that link was mediated by the status system, and in modern Japan, the individual was cut loose from the bonds of status and allowed to be as civilized or as barbarous as his ambition and ardor for honest labor dictated. In this way, the transition from Tokugawa to Meiji marked a revolutionary transformation of the relationship between the state and the individual, while at the same time it articulated that transformation in terms of criteria with more than two centuries of institutional history behind them.

THE REALM OF DISCRIMINATION

The transition from Tokugawa to Meiji resulted in the creation of a unitary but not completely uniform order, in which previously valid markers of difference were negated, only to be replaced during the process of negation by a new set of markers. Expanding the boundaries of the polity to include Hokkaido and the Ryukyu Islands made the Ainu and Okinawans Japanese, but in the process rendered their Japanese identities problematic. Abolishing the status system deprived the outcastes of their despised but necessary place in society, leaving them instead despised and extraneous. Internalizing standards of civilization adapted from the West transformed the mundanities of everyday life into hotly contested symbols of the people's aspirations for the future. At the same time, breaking the vessel of the early modern order held out for a time the promise of a liberating nihilism, of a society open enough for commoners to become great men of the world and former outcastes to carry their own portable shrines *(mikoshi)* in festivals. The transformation of the polity thereby created unprecedented opportunities—albeit distributed inequitably— for social mobility and individual expression, while at the same time it left those who could not take advantage of these opportunities exposed to hostility, discrimination, and violence, often tolerated by the state.

This process of joining and separating did not characterize the immediate transition period alone, but rather was incessantly repeated, as changes in the international environment and domestic political and economic conditions—and the intellectual realm that sought to make sense of all of them—prompted attempts to reclassify the Japanese people and the space they occupied. This fluidity gave modern Japan its dynamism, but at the same time it left people uncertain of their proper relationship to the state and to one another. Outcastes who thought they were commoners, Ainu who thought they were Japanese, women who thought they were free to cut their hair: such people were the obvious casualties of modernization, but the same uncertainties and ultimately ephemeral promises affected all Japanese to at least some degree. Indeed, the state itself was a victim of its own policies, for it constantly had to respond to its subjects' attempts to appropriate the symbols of modernity for their own purposes. Even Japanese imperialism was in part an outcome of this uncertainty, for policy makers sometimes found themselves chasing after private adventurers and ideologues who assumed that the acquisition of overseas colonies was as much a part of the modernization process as washing before every meal.[38]

Modernity's unpredictability made it dangerous. Consequently, finding ways to contain modernity and channel its energies was an integral part of the modernization project. During the Meiji period much intellectual energy was expended to rationalize the unitary state and particularly the emperor, who served as its foremost symbol.[39] The state and its formidable team of volunteer ideologues sought to curb heterodoxy in thought and practice by constantly reminding the Japanese that they were a nation united under the sovereign *(ikkun banmin)* and that the emperor's benevolence extended equally to all his subjects *(isshi dōjin)*. Although little about Meiji ideology was either nativist or democratic, it resonated with both the nativism of the late Tokugawa period and the freedom-and-popular-rights thought of the 1870s and 1880s by speaking to the desire to participate in modernization through a connection to the sovereign. It was this promise that helped the regime to secure support among well-educated and influential commoners during its first critical years, just as the regime provoked outraged dissent once it became clear that the state intended to dictate the terms of the people's participation, particularly in the realm of politics.

By forging a direct connection between itself and individual subjects, the Meiji state in effect recruited individuals as active participants in the modernization project; through their adoption of the outward customs, inward discipline, and other accoutrements of civilization, the subjects of the Meiji state signaled their readiness to join. Consequently, although the state decidedly retained the initiative, the people themselves needed an incentive to cooperate—they needed to feel they had a stake in the Meiji reforms. That incentive was the promise of freedom from the bonds of the status order, and the prospect of autonomy in matters of occupation, residence, and demeanor. Not everyone cooperated, of course, but without a broad consensus on the desirability of attaining some sort of "modernity" (as defined vis-à-vis the Western powers), the state could not have bludgeoned the recalcitrant into submission.

Becoming modern was a question of both livelihood and customs. Insofar as occupation and livelihood as previously mediated through the status system were fundamentally reinterpreted after the Restoration, it comes as no surprise that customs as markers of status similarly had to be reinterpreted. Quite simply, people could not maintain their old customs and still be modern because the social and political relations those customs signified had been discredited. This explains why the Kyoto authorities appended to their announcement of the abolition of outcaste status the exhortation that former outcastes abandon "backward customs" (rōshū)—without, however, explicitly stating which customs counted as "backward."[40]

The modernization of customs through the linkage to livelihood was possible only because the political boundaries of the state had been clearly demarcated. The nation's boundaries marked off a uniform field in which some people were civilized and others barbarian, yet all were Japanese nonetheless. In other words, the barbarian (iteki) Ainu of the early modern era were essentially different from the barbarous (yaban) residents of Shiba Shin'amichō, one of Tokyo's most notorious slums, during the Meiji period. Even aside from the differences in the emblems of their distance from civilization—the Ainu's unshaved pates and the slum dwellers' unwashed hands—the people of Shin'amichō never had to justify their Japanese identities. The poor were barbarous because they did not contribute to society, but that did not prevent them from contributing (and hence becoming fully civilized) at some time in the future. In other words, the barbarous peoples at the margins of Meiji society could civilize themselves in a way that the Ainu during the early modern period could not, for the Ainu had been exogenous to the status system and hence to the Tokugawa polity. Moreover, because modern civilization was generated from within, it follows that the state and its ideologues tended to rely on moral suasion rather than on unilateral attempts to impose civilization from above, particularly after the first, tumultuous decade of the Meiji period.[41]

The locus of agency was thus a central feature of the transformation of civilization across the divide of the Meiji Restoration. Whereas the intervention of the shogunate had been necessary to civilize the Ainu in the Tokugawa period, under the modern regime civilization and the full membership in the polity that accompanied it was available to anyone who cared to adopt it. Needless to say, the state and its hordes of freelance ideologues were only too happy to offer guidance in the form of moral suasion and the denunciation of barbarism, but ultimately civilization was a matter of individual agency. The individual bore responsibility for being civilized or not because of the modern emphasis on livelihood. The poor were barbarous because they did not have the ambition or ability to embrace a productive livelihood and the markers of civilization that went along with it.[42]

Yet, barbarism in fact transcended livelihood in ways that the Meiji regime was often unwilling to face head-on. The poor were told that their customs made them barbarous, when in fact it was their poverty that placed them into that category. And although some of the residents of Shin'amichō and other slums no doubt ended up there of their own volition, it is also true that their poverty itself was in part a product of the development of capitalism in the late nineteenth century. Insofar as the ability to earn a livelihood in a burgeoning capitalist economy is inherently uncertain and thereby produces a steady stream of winners and losers, it stands to reason that some of the casual day-laborers, rickshaw men, and unemployed residents of the slums were there out of bad luck as much as an unwillingness to embrace civilization. However, according to the logic of the modern politics of the quotidian, they were marked as losers through their own agency.

This point is clearer when considering the Ainu, Burakumin, and Okinawan and Korean workers in Osaka and Kobe in the early twentieth century. Their impoverishment was the product of a combination of capitalist development, imperialism, and the dismantling of the status system—and of the modernized discrimination that accompanied Japan's transformation in the nineteenth century. The modern state took over the Ainu's homeland, negated their identity and their livelihoods, then labeled them as barbarous not only because of their (negated and hence officially nonexistent) alien ethnicity, but also because they could not support themselves. Similarly, Burakumin who lost their monopoly over leather working and other traditional occupations, and Okinawans and Koreans who sought employment in the Japanese mainland after losing the ability to support themselves at home, became and remained barbarous through an odious combination of capitalist economics and officially tolerated discrimination. All were Japanese because they could not be anything else, but being Japanese left them stranded in a realm of discrimination from which there was no escape.

CHAPTER 8

Ainu Identity
and the Meiji State

After assuming control of Hokkaido in 1868, the newly instituted Meiji regime embarked on an aggressive policy of colonization and development that sought both to exploit the natural resources of the island and to remove any lingering doubts about its sovereignty. At the same time, the state implemented a series of measures designed to "protect" Hokkaido's native Ainu people. "Protection" *(hogo)* was a euphemism for government attempts to turn the Ainu into petty farmers. These policies culminated in 1899 in the enactment of the Hokkaido Former Aborigine Protection Act (Hokkaidō kyūdojin hogohō), which remained on the books in amended form until 1997. More than any other measure, this law, which provided agricultural land to the Ainu under highly restrictive conditions, defined the place of the Ainu people in modern Japanese society. Its symbolic power survived long after it had become a dead letter after World War II.

After the Restoration, common people throughout Japan had to be taught that they were subjects of a modern nation-state, with the emperor at its head. The same was true of the Ainu, though the process was complicated appreciably by the fact that they, along with the Ryukyuans and other peripheral peoples, first had to be persuaded they were indeed Japanese.[1] Because the Meiji paradigm of a family-state was incompatible with what would now be termed multiculturalism, policies designed to hasten the assimilation of the Ainu into Japanese society systematically denied the validity of Ainu culture and indeed Ainu ethnicity itself. Examining the elements of Ainu culture marked for eradication and the new cultural and economic structures the state sought to implant in their place allows us better to understand what it meant to be Japanese in the Meiji period. This understanding, in turn, sheds light on both the issues of participation in the polity that divided the Japanese people during the Meiji period and the state's attitude toward peoples brought under its rule during the course of Japanese imperialist expansion.

Policy toward the Ainu during the Meiji period reflected the state's dual program of bringing peripheral peoples within the polity as Japanese nationals while at the same time attacking those elements of Ainu society and economy deemed incompatible with their eventual participation in the nation as civilized moderns. The promotion of agriculture was a major focus of the "protection" program because neither the Ainu's traditional subsistence economy nor their more recent involvement in seasonal wage labor at fisheries fit official notions of a stable or productive livelihood. In that sense, policy in Hokkaido was merely one manifestation of the broader project of instituting a new politics of the quotidian throughout Japan. It was complicated, however, by the fact that the Ainu bore a twofold burden of nominal barbarity: not only did they have to shed their barbarian *(iteki)* character from the early modern period, they had to abandon the barbarous *(yaban)* practices of their "unsettled" livelihoods as well. The state accordingly directed its earliest assimilation efforts at eradicating visible displays of distinctive Ainu cultural practices, but then turned quickly to the problem of bringing individual Ainu livelihoods into line with the standards of Western-style civilization. Neither set of policies was successful: pressuring the Ainu to abandon their language, religion, and customs did not erase their identity as Ainu (in their own eyes or in the eyes of most Japanese), nor did Ainu who adopted nominally civilized livelihoods as farmers ever fully escape the presumption of barbarity that adhered to them by virtue of their non-Japanese ethnicity.

Nonetheless, the policies did succeed in one critical respect. By making the Ainu legally equivalent to other Japanese, the Meiji state refused to recognize a specifically Ainu category of subjects. For most purposes, Ainu identity was left to be expressed within communities of Ainu and in private transactions between Ainu and Japanese. To be sure, the state developed agricultural-development policies and educational institutions designed to foster the assimilation of the Ainu into Japanese society, but they were directed exclusively at residents of recognized Ainu communities, mostly in eastern and northeastern Hokkaido. The many Ainu who left the *kotan* to work in fisheries, logging camps, and construction crews blended into the body of the Japanese population, at least in a formal, legal sense. In this way, the Meiji state followed a policy of ethnic negation, by which the non-Japanese identity of the Ainu was excluded from the realm of the politically meaningful.

Being Ainu in modern Japan was not recognized as an essential element of one's subjectivity, but rather was reinterpreted as a transitory state occupied by a diminishing number of residents of rural communities, people who could be identified and assimilated in due course. Seeing ethnic negation rather than the enforcement of assimilation policies— particularly the prohibitions of various Ainu cultural practices—as the critical act of the early Meiji state toward the Ainu helps to account for the regime's lackadaisical pursuit of acculturation during the final decades of the nineteenth century. Without a doubt, such policies were critically important, both symbolically and practically, but their true significance lies less in their specific successes or failures than in what they reveal about the model of modern, imperial subjecthood the Meiji state and its agents promoted.

AINU "PROTECTION" POLICIES, 1868–99

By the middle of the nineteenth century, the Hokkaido Ainu had fallen into a state of crisis, as Japanese domination had undermined the social, economic, and demographic foundations of their culture. In particular, the movement of Ainu to the coast to seek employment at fisheries operated by Japanese merchants disrupted indigenous society in a number of ways. In contrast to the very small populations and loose political organization of the inland *kotan*, the dozens or even hundreds of people in the Ainu camps on the coast lived under a hierarchical authority structure designed to supply labor to the fisheries as efficiently as possible. Smallpox, measles, and other contagious diseases periodically decimated local Ainu populations. Japanese fishery workers physically abused Ainu men and appropriated Ainu women as concubines. Even those Ainu who remained in the interior were affected, as the shortage of able-bodied people upset hunting and gathering routines, and the introduction of Japanese commodities by workers returning home after the conclusion of the fishing season disrupted the local economy. In short, by the time Meiji officials arrived on the scene no Ainu community remained untouched by economic relations with Japanese.

The plight of the Ainu was not unusual. Demographic and cultural crisis is a common, though not universal, fate of indigenous peoples who encounter wealthier and more technologically advanced outsiders. Infectious disease, environmental degradation, and outright murder all take their toll on native populations, and the introduction of outside commodities can undermine native social and economic structures. Cultural breakdown is one possible outcome of this contact, but even in such cases collapse is more likely to be the product of an extended cycle of accommodation, adaptation, and readjustment than an immediate consequence of contact with the outside.[2] And so it was for the Ainu during the nineteenth century: although they had been subjected to political, economic, and ecological pressure for hundreds of years, they had always been able to invest ties with Japanese society with their own cultural meanings and thereby retain a certain degree of agency in defining the terms of the relationship. After the Meiji Restoration, however, it became increasingly difficult for the Ainu to accommodate the demands of an insistent state while fashioning new cultural meanings for old practices or new practices to express old meanings. The pressure the state applied to the Ainu was too strong and the pace of change too rapid for the Ainu to adapt readily.

The Ainu became increasingly vulnerable during the Meiji period for two reasons. First, as we have seen, one of the hallmarks of the Meiji state's modernity was its need to integrate itself into the daily lives and beliefs of its subjects. As a result, the regime sought to break down the relatively autonomous sphere of culture and livelihood that the Ainu had occupied in early modern society, and in its place erect a structure in which the key relationship was not between the state and the Ainu people as a whole, but rather between the state and individual Ainu (or their households and local communities). Second, the modern state was able to marshal formidable institutional and technological resources to accomplish its goals. Having swept away the complex institutional structure of the Tokugawa period, and with it the dissonance between the shogunate's and Matsumae domain's respective policies toward the Ainu, the Meiji state was able to implement a more or less uniform set of measures throughout Hokkaido and adjacent areas. The creation of a modern bureaucracy and the eventual emergence of a cadre of technocrats charged with formulating and implementing policies toward the Ainu gave the state immediate access to the Ainu, without, however, endowing the Ainu with a similarly uniform means to respond to state pressure.

This is not to say, however, that Ainu society was immediately subjected to the full force of a modern disciplinary regime. For one thing, the modern state did not rise fully formed out of the wreckage of the Tokugawa order. Even aside from the fact that it took nearly two decades for the Meiji state to settle on an institutional structure for administering Hokkaido, the island's size and remote location meant that the infrastructure necessary to implement policy quickly and efficiently was slow to develop. Furthermore, the early Meiji state had to spread its thin resources across a wide variety of modernizing projects throughout Japan, so funding for Ainu policies was always scarce. Most important, the politically quiescent and militarily impotent Ainu population was small, geographically dispersed, and already partly integrated into the Japanese economy, and so posed no immediate threat to Japanese sovereignty or security. With myriad more pressing problems facing it, the Meiji state had little choice but to move slowly in addressing policy toward the Ainu.

The immediate impact of policies on individual Ainu communities depended on two intimately related conditions: the extent of pre-Meiji economic contact and the authorities' sense of the imperative for immediate change. Although factors like the desire to appropriate specific tracts of Ainu land for the benefit of Japanese colonists could influence their priorities, officials generally saw the greatest need for "protection" policies in the most isolated Ainu communities. This is not at all surprising given the officials' profound disdain for the Ainu's traditional hunting, fishing, and gathering economy, but it is ironic that the Ainu communities with the deepest involvement with their majority Japanese neighbors—and hence presumably the easiest targets for assimilation policies—were ignored while local functionaries set out to "protect" Ainu who lived unaware of their need for succor.

Meiji officials targeted both cultural and economic practices in their efforts to transform the Ainu into imperial subjects. This policy entailed unilateral attempts to eradicate the outward forms of Ainu culture by decree, as in the prohibitions of tattooing issued during the 1870s, as well as less direct measures, such as the distribution of agricultural tools and seed to Ainu communities in the 1880s. In any event, the officials charged with Ainu administration were unwavering in their confidence that their policies served not only the immediate needs of the Japanese state, but the long-term interests of the Ainu people as well. With only a few exceptions, this confidence remained firm in the face of explicit and sometimes even desperate pleas from the Ainu themselves that they be left in peace. The authorities could be so sanguine only because they unquestioningly accepted the superiority of their own culture over that of the Ainu. However, it is only fair to note that the officials' haughtiness and condescension toward the Ainu was in itself nothing extra-ordinary—they were surely haughty and condescending to just about everyone—nor was physical violence the systematic instrument of policy in Hokkaido it was in so many other colonial environments. Rather, most bureaucrats seemed to have perceived their mission as a genuinely humanitarian one, and as such generally preferred moral suasion to physical coercion in their dealings with the native people.

Despite the continuity of the underlying assumptions and goals of the authorities involved, most specific policy decisions before 1899 were reached haphazardly. That is, although it was widely agreed that the Ainu should become farmers, it was usually left to local officials to decide how to go about achieving that goal. The Development Agency (Kaitakushi), established in 1869 and the sole governing authority in Hokkaido between 1872 and 1882, was generally too preoccupied with industrial and agricultural development to devote many resources to Ainu policy. Between 1882 and 1886, when the Ainu finally became a continuing concern of higher officialdom, Hokkaido was divided into three separate prefectures, which maintained independent if similar poli-cies toward the native people. Even after Hokkaido's administrative re-unification in 1886, local bureaucrats generally formulated and imple-mented policy on an ad hoc basis, subject only to general guidance and fiscal constraints at the prefectural and national levels. After 1899, Ainu administration was at last unified under the umbrella of the "protection" law, but by that time the basic task of Ainu assimilation had, in the eyes of the officials concerned, already been completed.

This is not to say that Ainu affairs were unimportant to the Meiji state. Insisting on the Japanese nationality of the Ainu was a critical ele-ment of the state's assertions of sovereignty over Hokkaido, Sakhalin, and the southern Kuril Islands. Although Russia recognized Japanese sovereignty over Hokkaido and the southern Kurils in 1854, the border in Sakhalin remained undetermined until the Treaty of St. Petersburg of 1875, in which Russia received exclusive rights in Sakhalin in exchange for Japanese sovereignty over the entire Kuril chain. The state's most aggressive assimilation policies, including forced relocation, were directed against the Sakhalin and northern Kuril Ainu. In Hokkaido, in contrast, the state could afford to move more slowly in its effort to assim-ilate the Ainu. This was possible because, even aside from the fact that Hokkaido was in no immediate danger of a Russian takeover, indigenous social and economic structures had already been severely compromised through centuries of contact with Japanese. What few traditional Ainu communities remained were found mostly along the Pacific coast and, particularly, inland along rivers feeding into it. These scattered and physically isolated communities could be targeted for assimilation individually as the perceived need arose.

Policy toward the Ainu during the Meiji period evolved through three stages. First, between the Restoration and about 1882 the Development Agency followed a mostly negative policy, attacking both Ainu cultural practices and what remained of the traditional economy without making more than a token effort to replace them (except in the case of the Sakhalin Ainu, as described below). After this initial negative campaign, a belated attempt was made in the mid-1880s to teach farming and animal husbandry to members of some Ainu communities. Although sincere humanitarian concern with the plight of the Ainu did motivate some of the officials involved in the program, their efforts were plagued by chronic underfunding and a lack of institutional support. Finally, with the passage of the Ainu "protection" law in 1899, the legal and institutional basis for assimilation was complete; after that, and throughout the pre–World War II period, government efforts focused on administration of the 1899 legislation. Even after 1899, however, the Ainu remained vulnerable to manipulation and mistreatment at majority Japanese hands. The state did not hesitate to turn the provisions of the "protection" law against the Ainu, particularly to relocate Ainu communities to inferior land. Majority Japanese, moreover, readily took advantage of the Ainu in commercial transactions. And in part reflecting the fact that combating discrimination against the Ainu has never been a significant policy objective, prejudice remains a serious social problem to this day.

Within a few months of the proclamation of imperial rule, the incipient regime sent word of the Restoration to Hokkaido's many commercial fisheries. Instructions directed toward the Ainu called for a maintenance of the status quo: the Ainu were to continue to work as before under the direction of Japanese fishing contractors and their agents and avoid contact with foreigners or unauthorized Japanese traders. At the same time, the new regime assured the Ainu that, as the emperor's subjects, they too would enjoy the benefits of imperial rule.[3] In fact, however, maintaining the status quo soon became impossible. The contract-fishery system— and with it the mechanism for providing Ainu labor to the fishery—was abolished in stages through 1876. This left the Ainu in a position analogous to that of the Burakumin after 1871. Individuals gained the right to enter into wage contracts freely, and evidence suggests that they worked under terms similar to those enjoyed by majority Japanese laborers, which was a clear improvement over the conditions that had prevailed under the Tokugawa regime.[4] At the same time, however, the collapse of early modern institutions undermined the position of the Ainu leaders who had supplied workers to the contract fisheries and may have destabilized Ainu communities as a result. At the very least, the abolition of contracting removed the local Ainu community as a formal mediating institution between individual Ainu and their employers.

Despite the new regime's assertions of authority in 1868, it was not until the following year that the government was in a position actually to implement policy in Hokkaido. As noted above, between 1869 and 1882, when Hokkaido was under the administration of the Development Agency, Ainu policy was confined largely to unilateral attempts to prohibit particular cultural practices. Between 1871 and 1876 the authorities issued edicts banning those Ainu customs that struck them as most different from their own, including the tattooing of women's faces and hands and the wearing of earrings by men (1871 and 1876); the burning of houses after the death of a family member (1871); the practice of the *umsa* greeting ceremony (1870 and 1872); the use of traditional Ainu hunting methods, including poisoned arrows and trip-wired bows (1875, 1876) (in this instance a group of Ainu petitioned unsuccessfully against the prohibitions); and "uncivilized customs" in general (1871). None of these exhortations had much immediate effect, and there is no evidence that officials tried to enforce them. At the same time, the government urged the Ainu to take up agriculture and learn the Japanese language (1871). Administratively, the regime formally incorporated the Ainu into the mass of the Japanese population with the household-registration law of 1871. In 1878, the term "former aborigines" *(kyūdojin)* entered official parlance, ostensibly for use only when there was a need to distinguish the Ainu from others. The term was intended to replace labels in common use, such as "natives" *(dojin)*, "former Ezo" *(kyū-Ezojin)*, "ancient people" *(komin)*, and "former people" *(kyūmin)*, with one that emphasized the Ainu's new status as ordinary commoners; in fact, however, even officials continued to use other terms, particularly *dojin*. In 1879 the Ainu were treated as ordinary commoners under criminal law, though they did not become subject to the draft or taxation until the end of the nineteenth century.[5]

Aside from these unilateral attempts to forbid the practice of Ainu culture and to integrate the Ainu legally into the commoner population, the Development Agency largely limited itself to symbolic efforts to turn the

Ainu into ordinary Japanese subjects. For example, in 1870 an Ainu resident of the vicinity of Sapporo, Kotoni Mataichi, was taken to the imperial palace in Tokyo in an attempt to impress him (and presumably other Ainu who would hear of the visit) with the splendor of imperial rule. A more substantive effort was made in 1872, when officials enrolled twenty-six Ainu men and nine Ainu women, aged thirteen to thirty-eight, in the Development Agency's school in Tokyo, the forerunner of the Sapporo Agricultural College and Hokkaido Imperial University. The students were supposed to learn to read and write Japanese as well as study agriculture and animal husbandry, skills they could later take back to their own communities. In fact, however, the students as a group fell into ill health in Tokyo, and a number even tried to flee the Development Agency's facilities on the grounds of Zōjōji. By 1876 all had returned to Hokkaido. Although a few individuals did end up as low-level Development Agency functionaries, the plan was widely and rightly seen as a failure.[6]

The Meiji state's first systematic effort to remake the Ainu into farmers came after the abolition of the Development Agency and the reorganization of Hokkaido into three prefectures in 1882.[7] Ainu policy in the mid-1880s and after reflected official attitudes toward farming as a way of life and, by extension, highlights an interesting paradox of the Meiji state's industrialization drive: however eager the state may have been to create an industrial economy, it had grave doubts about industrial labor. Officials sent into the field to teach agriculture to Ainu villagers had to contend with the fact that most able-bodied men and many women spent little time at home because they were busy working for wages at fisheries, construction sites, and logging camps. Officials discouraged the Ainu from working for wages in industry and urged them instead to take up farming, however disinclined to do so they might be. This effort was in part motivated by a legitimate concern that Ainu wage laborers were vulnerable to exploitation (conditions at the contract fisheries had been abysmal, after all), but it also reflected a pervasive attitude that farming was the only truly worthwhile occupation available.[8]

The agricultural promotion program developed by Nemuro prefecture, which encompassed the northeastern part of Hokkaido and the Kuril Islands, became the model for that of Sapporo prefecture, which had the most Ainu residents. Accordingly, the following discussion will focus on Nemuro prefecture. The Ainu population of Hakodate prefecture, which comprised the southern third of Hokkaido, was small (663 in 1883), widely dispersed, and already largely assimilated into Japanese society, with the result that the prefecture's Ainu policy was limited to the distribution of token gifts from the imperial family and other allocations from the central government.[9] That is, even at the height of state intrusion into Ainu society, the native people in southern Hokkaido did not become the objects of systematic "protection" measures, in large part because their formal identity as Ainu had already been severely compromised.

The Nemuro policy was implemented under the direction of Yuchi Sadamoto, the prefecture's "potato governor" *(imo kenrei),* so nicknamed for his enthusiastic promotion of that toothsome tuber. Yuchi, the son of a Satsuma samurai, was a skilled technocrat who had studied at the Massachusetts Agricultural College in Amherst and had run the Development Agency's agricultural experimental station at Nanae before being named to head the newly created prefecture in February 1882.[10] He administered a prefectural budget that did not originally include any funds for Ainu welfare. The only allocation, in fact, was a 1,000 yen gift to all Ainu from the imperial household ministry in commemoration of the Meiji emperor's 1881 visit to Hokkaido. As a meticulous bureaucrat in Nemuro duly noted, the imperial beneficence came out to 0.059056 yen for each of Hokkaido's 16,933 Ainu residents.[11] Yuchi, concerned that a paltry six sen per person would not do much to ameliorate the poverty and poor health of his prefecture's 3,408 indigenous residents, ordered an aide to draft a proposal for additional funding for a welfare and education program. The proposal was submitted to the home and finance ministries in December 1883 and approved the following May. The appropriation of 5,000 yen per annum (1.47 yen per person) was inadequate to support Yuchi's ambitious program, but perhaps it was the most he could expect to receive in the midst of the fiscal retrenchment of the 1880s.[12]

The Welfare Policy for Former Aborigines within Nemuro Prefecture (Nemuro-ken kannai kyūdojin kyūsai hōhō) sought to promote family and communal farming among the Ainu, with improving education a secondary objective.[13] It was needed, according to the policy statement, because "the steady influx of immigrants into the prefecture and the concomitant increase in hunting and fishing have as a matter of course deprived the former aborigines of resources, with the result that they have insufficient food and clothing. This policy accordingly aims to put [the Ainu] to work at agriculture and thereby provide them with the means to achieve an independent existence."[14]

Although the plan was to have been implemented over a five-year period, beginning in 1884, it was in fact curtailed on the merger of the three prefectures into the Department of Hokkaido (Hokkaidō-chō) in 1886. According to the proposal, one-fifth of the 825 Ainu households in the prefecture, or 165 households, were to receive assistance in taking up farming each year, with aid going to those in the most remote mountain districts first and to those living in or near urban areas last.

The plan to foster "independence and self-sufficiency" among the Ainu hinged on the establishment of household and communal farms under the close supervision and total economic control of non-Ainu prefectural officials. The program called for the distribution of a meager 0.5 to 1 *chō* (about 1.2 to 2.5 acres) of arable land to each Ainu household in targeted districts; the land was to be rent-free while under development, but once it was cultivated the occupants would be expected to buy it in installments spread over five years. (Yuchi and his colleagues apparently saw no irony in making the Ainu buy land their ancestors had first occupied centuries ago.) To help the novice cultivators get on their feet, the prefecture planned to make grants of agricultural implements and potato, buckwheat, onion, and white-radish *(daikon)* seeds, while at the same time making it clear that all farms were to be economically self-sufficient by the second year. Officials from the prefectural industrial promotion bureau *(kangyōka)* would venture to areas under development and offer guidance on such matters as the use of tools, land-clearing techniques, planting schedules, and the storage and disposition of crops. Although it was assumed that the bulk of the Ainu's agricultural production would be used for their own subsistence, the industrial promotion bureau stood ready to market any surplus on the Ainu's behalf. Meanwhile, the Ainu would be expected to organize themselves into groups of about five households each to provide mutual aid and thereby contribute to the rapid implementation of the development program. Each district, moreover, was to choose a headman to coordinate both agricultural activities and administrative matters.

In addition to promoting family farming, the policy called for the establishment of communal agricultural ventures. Two or three years after development began in a district, 100,000 to 150,000 *tsubo* (about 82 to 123 acres) of undeveloped land would be earmarked as communal farmland to be planted over the course of a decade or longer. True to the governor's proclivities, potatoes were to be the required crop for the first year of cultivation, with other crops permitted only in succeeding seasons. The prefecture would supply Western agricultural implements, including plows, before the first season, but otherwise the communities themselves were to provide seed and other necessities, including labor. A cadre of Ainu adept at Western agricultural practices would be trained at the experimental station at Nanae, then returned to the field to take a leading role in operating the communal farms. Harvests would be marketed by the industrial promotion bureau, with profits assigned as savings against future crop failures and to fund local schools. The schools were conceived as venues to teach Ainu children the Japanese language, although it was assumed that they would provide a rudimentary general education as well.

The policy relegated the Ainu's traditional occupations of hunting, fishing, and gathering, as well as their more recent involvement in wage labor, to the category of by-employments for the winter season. Ainu in mountain villages would be free to hunt during the winter, while those living near the coast or towns could similarly supplement their agricultural incomes with wages from work in commercial fisheries or other jobs. But it was clear that farming was to be the focus of the Ainu's economic lives: officials were empowered to punish anyone who showed disdain for agriculture or proved to be an indifferent worker, and Ainu who were particularly diligent and whose crops were superior to those of others would be rewarded. In this manner the officials who drafted the policy assumed that "sharing joys and setbacks" would encourage the Ainu to "maintain a harmonious and cooperative spirit" and thereby succeed as farmers.[15]

The profound naïveté of the officials involved in the project is plainly revealed in the plan's ambitious goals, strict timetable, and meager funding—not to mention its utter lack of concern for the Ainu's own desires. Predictably, officials sent into the field to implement it encountered resistance from the Ainu as well as a host of practical problems. The experience of Kushima Shigeyoshi, sent in 1883 and 1884 to the district of Ashoro, is representative. The four mountain *kotan* of Ashoro were deemed so isolated and backward that the prefecture began an agricultural promotion project there in 1883, a year before the central government gave its support to the prefecture-wide program.[16] Kushima arrived in Ashoro on June 7 only to discover that virtually all of the district's able-bodied residents were working elsewhere for wages, leaving only the very young and aged behind. Eventually the dispersed workers responded to his call for their return; until his departure on November 2 he concentrated on teaching them to be potato farmers. Rather than divide his time among the four *kotan* in the district, Kushima required the local residents to congregate at one site to farm; before leaving for the winter he ordered the Ainu from outlying *kotan* to relocate permanently.[17]

Kushima spent the following summer and fall in Ashoro and three other districts. By the time he left at the end of November 1884 he had persuaded seventeen of twenty-six Ainu households in Ashoro to start farming, although none had cultivated nearly enough land to subsist on agriculture alone. In two seasons they had cleared 10,697 *tsubo* (about 8.7 acres, or an average of about half an acre per participating household), of which 7,664 *tsubo* (about 6.3 acres) were actually under cultivation. Holdings ranged from a high of 1,169 *tsubo* (almost one acre) to a low of 270 *tsubo* (about a quarter acre) per cultivating household.[18]

In a report filed in December 1884, Kushima complained to Governor Yuchi of the difficulties he had encountered in trying to carry out his mission. First, his attempt to concentrate the Ainu of Ashoro district into one *kotan* was a dismal failure: although the site chosen was well suited to agriculture, the nearby river yielded few salmon and the deer in the surrounding hills had been seriously depleted by a series of harsh winters and by the activities of Japanese hunters, with the result that local residents faced food shortages, at least in the short term. He hoped that sponsoring animal husbandry in the future would permit the Ainu to satisfy their hunger for meat while engaging primarily in agriculture. Second, Kushima noted that the Ainu who had relocated were both homesick and apt to quarrel with those from other communities. He thus concluded that in the future forced relocation should be avoided if possible, and that careful consideration should be given to site selection if relocation proved necessary. Finally, the Ainu were generally unenthusiastic about cultivating food crops. The only crops they had shown any interest in growing were millet, which they brewed into a kind of beer, and tobacco, which nearly all adult Ainu smoked regularly.[19]

The sorts of difficulties faced by Kushima Shigeyoshi in Ashoro were replicated everywhere the authorities tried to turn the Ainu into farmers. The Ainu rightly remained dubious of the advantages of agriculture over the combination of seasonal wage labor and traditional hunting, fishing, and, gathering activities that had sustained them for generations. Moreover, the efforts they did make were hampered by the lack of continuing institutional and material support from the prefecture and by the activities of private Japanese merchants who traveled to Ainu communities to take advantage of the Ainu's relative inexperience in commercial transactions.[20] These difficulties were exacerbated by the fact that, despite Kushima's warnings, Ainu communities were relocated against their will at least twenty times between 1872 and 1902 by the Development Agency, Nemuro and Sapporo prefectures, and the Department of

Hokkaido. Ainu communities were displaced for a variety of reasons: the Sakhalin and Kuril Ainu were moved in an attempt to affirm their Japanese nationality, while many others were forced off lands deemed better suited to majority Japanese settlement.[21] Areas chosen for relocation were often of marginal quality for both agriculture and traditional subsistence activities.[22] This experience no doubt made the Ainu suspicious of all so-called welfare policies ostensibly implemented for their benefit.

By the time Nemuro prefecture was abolished in 1886, 514 Ainu households of an initial target of 825 (in fact, in 1886 there were only 816 Ainu households in Nemuro, exclusive of the northern Kuril Ainu relocated to Shikotan) had received some sort of government assistance under the provisions of the Ainu welfare project. A total of 316,815 tsubo (approximately 259 acres, or half an acre per household) were under cultivation, with potatoes and radishes by far the most important crops.[23]

After the amalgamation of the three prefectures into the Department of Hokkaido in 1886, the government curtailed systematic attempts to transform the Ainu into farmers until the implementation of the Hokkaido Former Aborigine Protection Act of 1899, which made Ainu households eligible to receive grants of up to 15,000 tsubo (12.25 acres) of agricultural land. The law required grantees to cultivate their land within fifteen years or lose it, and it placed numerous restrictions on its alienation. In the long run, the law did help some establish themselves as petty farmers, but in general it did not do much to "protect" the Ainu people. Few households received their full entitlement of land, and in any case the land they did receive tended to be of indifferent quality. Moreover, Ainu cultivators received no practical guidance from the authorities, so that those with no previous farming experience were hard-pressed to make a living off their landholdings.[24]

Regardless of its success or failure, however, the "protection" law represented the culmination of the formal process of integrating the Ainu into the Japanese population. The state continued to direct educational and other policies at the Ainu throughout the prewar period, but Ainu affairs became the backwater concern of a handful of social bureau functionaries in Hokkaido and a scattering of activists, academics, and social commentators. By ostensibly endowing rural Ainu with the ability to pursue independent livelihoods on a par with other subjects, the authorities were satisfied that they had laid the groundwork for the Ainu's complete assimilation.

ASSIMILATION AND AGENCY IN SAKHALIN
AND THE KURILS, 1875–1905

After the signing of the Treaty of St. Petersburg in 1875, in which Japan
ceded to Russia its claims to Sakhalin in exchange for sovereignty over
the entire Kuril Island chain, Japanese authorities removed 841 Ainu
from southern Sakhalin to Hokkaido and ninety-seven from the northern
Kurils to the island of Shikotan in the southern part of the archipelago.
In both cases the authorities sought to assert the Japanese nationality of
the Ainu and shield them from the assimilative influence and possible
political machinations of Russian officials, missionaries, and traders.
Both groups suffered greatly during the years after their relocation, as
they were placed in areas with very different physical environments from
their homelands and subjected to the interference of Japanese officials
who were determined to "protect" them whatever the cost to their culture and society.

The Meiji state conducted an aggressive and extremely disruptive
experiment in social engineering on the Sakhalin and Kuril Ainu.
Although the experiment was by no means successful, the urgency of the
state's efforts contrast sharply with both Nemuro prefecture's haphazard
"protection" efforts in Hokkaido and the shogunate's assimilation project
in the 1850s. A comparison of the state's efforts with those of the late
Tokugawa period is particularly instructive, insofar as both sets of policies
arose out of the need to establish a clear national boundary with Russia.
Whereas shogunal officials had been content to manipulate the Hokkaido
Ainu's customs in their effort to incorporate the island and its native people within the core polity, their counterparts in the Meiji period felt compelled to intervene in the everyday affairs of Ainu households.

The Russo-Japanese frontier in the Okhotsk Sea region has shifted
several times during the past century and a half. In 1854, the shogunate
and Russia established a border in the Kurils that gave Japan the four
southernmost islands but left Sakhalin under joint occupation, a solution
that neither side found palatable. A resolution was reached in 1875 with
the signing of the Treaty of St. Petersburg. As a result of its victory in the
Russo-Japanese War, Japan added the southern half of Sakhalin to its
dominion in 1905. It administered this territory (known as Karafuto)
until the end of World War II, when the Soviet Union brought all of
Sakhalin and the Kurils under its rule, a situation that prevails today.
Japan still claims sovereignty over the southern Kurils (the so-called
Northern Territories: Etorofu, Kunashiri, Shikotan, and the Habomai

Islands), but Russia has shown little inclination to return them to Japanese rule.

The Ainu of Sakhalin and the Kurils suffered dislocation repeatedly as a result of the drawing and redrawing of international boundaries in their homeland. The dispersal and even extinction of their communities testifies to the disruptive effects of international competition in the region. In the middle of the nineteenth century perhaps two thousand Ainu lived in Sakhalin, primarily in coastal areas in the southern half of the island.[25] A few hundred more Ainu inhabited the Kurils, of whom a hundred or so lived in the northern third of the archipelago, while the southernmost Kurils included several communities of Hokkaido Ainu. (The term "Kuril Ainu" refers to those of the northern islands; significant cultural, socioeconomic, and linguistic differences distinguished them from the Hokkaido Ainu.)[26] All of these Sakhalin and Kuril Ainu communities have now disappeared, although a number of people living in Hokkaido continue to identify as Sakhalin Ainu.

The story of the Kuril Ainu's relocation is the more straightforward of the two, in part because Japan maintained sovereignty over the archipelago throughout the pre–World War II period and in part because Japanese policies affected the entire Kuril Ainu population uniformly. Conversely, a number of factors complicate the Sakhalin Ainu's story. First, their original relocation in 1875 was undertaken under false pretences. Contrary to government promises, they were not allowed to remain in their initial relocation site in northernmost Hokkaido, where they expected to maintain their traditional subsistence patterns, but instead they were forced to move to an area better suited to official needs. Second, many Ainu remained in Sakhalin under Russian rule after 1875. Third, nearly all surviving Sakhalin Ainu returned home before or shortly after the Japanese victory in the war with Russia in 1905. Finally, the state treated Ainu brought under Japanese rule for the first time in 1905 differently from those who had relocated to Hokkaido in 1875, most notably by denying them Japanese citizenship until 1933.

Let us begin with the case of the Sakhalin Ainu. Unlike their Kuril Island counterparts, the Ainu of southern Sakhalin had had a great deal of contact with Japanese fishers and officials before the Sakhalin-Kuril exchange of 1875. Japanese entrepreneurs had operated commercial herring and salmon fisheries in Sakhalin since the late eighteenth century, and by the mid-nineteenth century many Ainu in the southern part of the island had experience as wage laborers in those fisheries. At the same time, the Sakhalin Ainu had a history of contact with Russians as well,

and some were able to play one power against the other to secure bene-
ficial treatment. During the period of the Russo-Japanese condominium
in Sakhalin (1854–75), Japanese officials were acutely aware of the competition for Ainu allegiance and even compiled reports on the loyalties of
Ainu communities in various parts of the island.[27]

According to the terms of the exchange treaty, the indigenous peoples
of Sakhalin were given three years to decide whether they wished to
remain at home or relocate to Japan; only those who moved would be
considered Japanese nationals. In fact, however, the Sakhalin Ainu were
pressured to make a decision on very short notice, in many cases just a
few days before Sakhalin was turned over to Russian administration.
Japanese officials apparently made no attempt to recruit emigrants after
1875, even in cases where men who had gone alone with the initial party
later tried to return to the island to get members of their families. Thus
the group of 841 Ainu who crossed to Hokkaido included both entire
communities (mostly from the coast of Aniwa Bay in the south of the
island) and single men (mostly from more remote areas).[28]

Those Ainu who moved to Japan did so thinking that they would be
allowed to settle on the northern coast of Hokkaido, in an area similar
ecologically to the southern part of Sakhalin and whose fisheries were
under the control of the Date house, one of the two major commercial
herring fishers in Sakhalin before 1875. In fact, officials in Sakhalin
made such assurances to the Ainu in good faith, for they were as surprised as the Ainu themselves by the decision of the head of the
Development Agency, Kuroda Kiyotaka, to move the Ainu to Tsuishikari, an inland site on the Ishikari River, not far from Hokkaido's newly
built capital, Sapporo.[29]

The settlement at Tsuishikari, founded in 1876, was the Japanese
state's first systematic attempt to intervene in Ainu culture beyond the
level of outward customs. Despite the failure of the education and agricultural development policies enacted there, similar measures were later
replicated throughout Hokkaido, with similar results. The principal
problems at Tsuishikari were, first, that the inland site was not suited to
the Sakhalin Ainu's needs as a coastal fishing people; and, second, that
the Ainu were not at all interested in the agricultural development that
the authorities assumed would become the focus of their economic lives.
Moreover, in 1886 and 1887, the community was devastated by cholera
and smallpox epidemics that killed nearly 350 people, almost half the
total population at the time.[30]

From the outset, many Sakhalin Ainu spent as much time as possible away from Tsuishikari, mostly working for wages at herring fisheries on the Japan Sea coast. By about 1890, Tsuishikari had been all but abandoned and a new settlement had formed on the coast at Raisatsu. The Ainu community did not remain long at Raisatsu either, however, because beginning in the late 1880s individuals found ways to return home to Sakhalin, usually to work for wages at herring and salmon fisheries leased from the Russian government by Japanese entrepreneurs. Although their trips to Sakhalin were nominally temporary, in fact most who left remained on the island rather than return to Hokkaido. As a result, by the time southern Sakhalin became Japanese territory in the aftermath of the Russo-Japanese War, only about 120 Sakhalin Ainu were still in Hokkaido; of these, all but 27 returned in 1905 or shortly thereafter.

Not surprisingly, Ainu returning to Sakhalin quickly discovered that a reversion to the pre-1875 status quo was impossible, as Russian settlers (mostly convicts and ex-convicts sent to the penal colony on Sakhalin) had appropriated Ainu lands and fishing grounds. Most, therefore, settled into a life as wage laborers in fisheries and other commercial ventures operated by Japanese entrepreneurs. After 1905, Ainu who had participated in the Tsuishikari experiment were treated as Japanese citizens, while those who had remained in Sakhalin during the period of Russian rule, along with the small groups of Nivkhi and Uilta on the island, became stateless. After a protracted legal battle, all Sakhalin Ainu received citizenship rights in 1933, but other native peoples remained stateless during the entire period of Japanese rule.[31] The fate of the Sakhalin Ainu after 1945 is not well known, but Japanese sources suggest that nearly all of them were "repatriated" to Hokkaido, where they were left to fend for themselves in the confusion of the immediate postwar period.[32]

Now let us turn to the case of the Kuril Ainu.[33] Officials involved in Ainu affairs gave two reasons for their decision to remove the Kuril Ainu from their home on Shumushu to the southern Kuril island of Shikotan. On the one hand, it facilitated government efforts to "protect" the Ainu by making them easily accessible to officials who would teach them the Japanese language and skills necessary to pursue an independent livelihood, such as agriculture and animal husbandry. On the other hand, it served Japanese security concerns by distancing the Ainu from contact with Russian subjects (including the indigenous peoples of Kamchatka, with whom the Ainu had traded) and American and European pinniped and sea-otter hunters who frequented the waters surrounding the northern Kurils. No doubt the talk of "protection" served to camouflage the more pressing security concerns, but the officials' humanitarian intentions were probably sincere (if misguided), given their doubts about the viability of hunting and fishing as the basis of a stable livelihood.

The official directly responsible for the decision to uproot the Kuril Ainu was Governor Yuchi of Nemuro prefecture, whose jurisdiction included the Kuril Islands. Between 1875 and 1884, Japanese officials made triennial inspection visits to the northern Kurils, during which they provided food, cloth, and other commodities to the native people. In July 1884, however, Yuchi himself traveled to Shumushu to escort the Kuril Ainu to Shikotan. In his report to Tokyo, the governor wrote that, because Shumushu is so close to Kamchatka, "the islanders travel back and forth constantly, with the result that their language and customs differ in no way from those of the Russians; they still consider Russia to be their home country." Moving the Ainu to Shikotan would not only distance them from Russian influence, he said, but it would also allow Japanese officials to oversee their adoption of new and presumably more stable livelihoods as farmers and pastoralists.[34]

As a welfare policy, the relocation of the Kuril Ainu was an unmitigated disaster. In addition to a precipitous decline in population brought about by exposure to disease and an unfamiliar environment, the group never achieved economic self-sufficiency in Shikotan. Although their difficulties were shared by the Ainu of northern and eastern Hokkaido, the impact on the Kuril Ainu was more severe. Indeed, the Kuril Ainu may have been victims of what James F. Eder calls "deculturation," or the systematic decline of cultural forms in the face of economic and political dependency. Presumably, new forms eventually fill the vacated cultural "space" left by defunct practices and structures during the process of deculturation, but there is a lag time during which culture is, in a sense, "poorer." In his study of the Batak people of the Philippines, Eder cites the demise of the *umbay* ceremony, a rite of initiation that had once been a cornerstone of the culture, as a specific example of deculturation. The decline of any given individual custom is not necessarily evidence of deculturation, but it may be if the meanings expressed by the defunct practice are not somehow transferred to other elements of the culture.[35] Not enough evidence concerning the Kuril Ainu survives to make a convincing case for deculturation, but accounts of their condition in Shikotan in the early twentieth century certainly convey their feelings of impotence and indeed apathy about their situation, leaving little doubt that a cultural crisis had overcome them. At the very least, the steady decline of the Kuril Ainu population after relocation and their disappearance as an identifiable community after World War II reveal the disastrous impact of Japanese policy.

In any case, the Japanese authorities in Shikotan sought to make the Kuril Ainu more like themselves through the creation of an agricultural community, or through the sponsorship of fishing and animal husbandry if farming proved impractical. In fact, officials quickly saw that agriculture was doomed to fail, for even aside from the Ainu's lack of experience and interest in farming, Shikotan's climate was too harsh for the cultivation of any but the hardiest crops. The prospects for fishing were hardly better despite the richness of the Pacific's marine life because of the rough seas and shortage of accessible coastline. Moreover, the Kuril Ainu were sea hunters, not fishers, but the southern Kurils had few of the walruses, seals, sea otters, and other game on which they had once relied. Consequently, officials were forced to focus on animal husbandry, in which the Ainu had engaged on a limited scale on Shumushu, but even that failed because of poor planning, chronic funding problems, and bad luck.

Government welfare, then, necessarily became a significant source of support for the Ainu in Shikotan, but they never became completely dependent on the state, in part because the state was not inclined to let them do so. They accordingly adopted two economic survival strategies: beginning in 1901, the men won government permission to return seasonally to the northern Kurils to hunt (probably as employees of Japanese ship owners, although the sources are not clear), and women formed liaisons with Japanese men who supported them and their children. Intermarriage between Ainu women and Japanese men—occasionally formal, but much more commonly casual—became so prevalent that officials estimated that by 1933 only about ten full-blooded Kuril Ainu remained.[36]

Notwithstanding these attempts at adaptation, the Kuril Ainu declined badly during the years after their relocation. Asano Tadashi, an official who reported on conditions on Shikotan in 1923, said that the strong desire to return home had fostered alcoholism and a general spiritual malaise among the island's Ainu residents.[37] Sten Bergman, a Swedish naturalist who visited Shikotan in 1930, described the Ainu's appearance as "wretched," and said that the older residents remained nostalgic for the northern Kurils.[38]

At the time of Bergman's visit the community was tottering on the verge of extinction as a demographic crisis had left it with a skewed sex ratio and a very high percentage of women beyond childbearing age. This crisis is evident in data from 1933, by which time the community had dwindled to forty-four people, less than half its original size. Of these, nearly three-quarters (thirty-two) were women, and of the women, almost half (fourteen) were at least forty-five years old and three others, ranging in age from thirty-seven to forty-one, were beyond their peak years of fertility. In contrast, the oldest surviving man was thirty-seven years old, and five of the twelve male residents were under the age of fifteen.[39]

Japanese efforts at social engineering included formal education for Ainu children as well as less structured policies designed to instill in the Ainu loyalty to the Japanese state. These policies were often quite crudely conceived, such as the suggestion by one of the first officials on Shikotan that the Ainu be given Japanese flags so that they might "develop a sense of themselves as imperial subjects."[40] Officials were particularly concerned with signs of Russian influence, such as the Ainu's Russian-style names and Orthodox faith, but evidence suggests that the officials did not appreciate the depth of the Ainu's engagement with Russian culture. That is, having distanced them from contact with Russians, the authorities apparently assumed that the Ainu would shed Russian influences of their own accord over time. Consequently, they made no immediate attempts to force the Ainu to conform to Japanese cultural practices and even built a Russian Orthodox church on Shikotan, though priests from Hakodate visited only occasionally. Eventually, however, it became evident that the Ainu would not spontaneously assimilate, and so the state's cultural policies became more aggressive. Thus, beginning in 1899, Buddhist missionaries were allowed to proselytize among the islanders (albeit with little success), and in 1911 the state assigned Japanese-style names to the Ainu on the grounds that their Russian names caused inconvenience for officials and impeded assimilation.[41]

As this brief review of the relocation of the Sakhalin and Kuril Ainu has shown, although the policies implemented in both cases were similar, the response of the Ainu differed in a number of important respects. The differences reflect the gap in the two communities' abilities to exercise agency in their dealings with Japanese officialdom. The Kuril Ainu had far less leeway because of their reliance on government assistance, whether to secure their livelihoods in Shikotan or to reestablish a presence in their homeland in the northern Kurils. As a result, economic dependence and cultural and demographic decline affected them immediately and thoroughly, perhaps to the point that they experienced deculturation. Conversely, the Sakhalin Ainu, thanks to their history of relations with Japanese and Russian officials and entrepreneurs before 1875, were able to take refuge from government assimilation policies by taking up wage labor in Hokkaido and Sakhalin. Thus, although they were affected more directly by Russo-Japanese rivalry, they were more successful at negotiating a path between the two powers than the Kuril Ainu, who were dominated first by one outside force and then by the other.

Neither group of Ainu entered the period of international boundary drawing in a pristine, precontact state, yet the Sakhalin Ainu's economic dependence on Japanese entrepreneurs left them better positioned to function in a modern nation-state than the Kuril Islanders, whose economy in 1884 remained closer to past patterns, yet whose culture had been profoundly affected by contact with Russian missionaries and traders. In short, the Sakhalin Ainu retained a greater measure of agency because they had already become part of an order in which ethnicity was less immediately important than one's relationship to the process of production for an emerging capitalist economy. Of course, they did not live happily ever after beginning in 1875, in large part because the development of capitalist wage-labor in the fishing economy always remained subordinate to the demands of international politics.

ASSIMILATION AND DISCRIMINATION

The Ainu got a hint of the kind of modernity that awaited them in places like Hakodate in the autumn of 1859. A crew member from a Russian vessel calling at the port visited a festival, where he saw

> a family of Ainos, or Hairy Kuriles, as they are sometimes called. They had come with many more from the interior of the island, to witness the festivities. The heads of the males were shaved, and the hair arranged in Japanese fashion; those of the women, so unlike the Japanese, looked as if they had been dragged through a bush. They glided timidly and swiftly through the crowd, which jeered and hooted at them, till they seemed frightened out of their wits, and hurried into a temple which had been set apart for them.[42]

This incident occurred nine years before the Meiji Restoration, of course, but it illustrates the dilemma that faced the Ainu people once the state decided they should embrace Japanese civilization. However readily they answered the call to adopt markers of Japanese identity and thereby become Japanese for political and institutional purposes, they still had to contend with the reality that being Japanese in the eyes of the state was not the same as being Japanese in the eyes of society.

No doubt, for much of the modern period, few Ainu wanted to be Japanese anyway. Until around the end of the nineteenth century, most could avoid the issue entirely by remaining aloof from the state's sporadic efforts at assimilation. The persistence of practices at the core of Ainu culture—such as the bear ceremony and the tattooing of women's faces—despite government efforts at eradication attest to the fact that many Ainu rejected the state's overtures. Within Ainu communities, pressure to maintain Ainu ways *(ainuburi)* helped to preserve their integrity.[43] Sooner or later, however, remaining aloof ceased to be an option. For the elders of strategically located *kotan* like Shiraoi,.that moment came in the 1850s, and for the residents of Ashoro district it arrived in the person of Kushima Shigeyoshi, the functionary from Nemuro who came to teach them potato farming in 1883. Despite differences in timing, however, all Ainu eventually had to face the fact that they were subjects of the Japanese state and hence members of Japanese society, whether they liked it or not.

The Meiji state's attempt to impose Western-style modernity on Japan hinged on its ability, first, to eliminate the intermediary strata of autonomy that had separated state and society during the early modern period and, second, to link a conception of civilization modeled on the West to individual livelihood. For the inhabitants of the core polity, of course, status groups had served as the mediating layers of authority. Consequently, because occupation had been the central criterion of status, imposing modernity was largely a question of dismantling the status system and reforming the customs that had situated individuals within it. For the Ainu, conversely, their position outside the early modern core polity meant that their uncivilized and hence non-Japanese identity served to separate them from the state. In its waning years, the Tokugawa shogunate had tried to incorporate the Ainu within the status order as commoners, but the Meiji state, lacking such an expedient, was forced to insinuate itself into their everyday lives. Making the Ainu modern therefore entailed a two-step process of, first, denying the validity of their non-Japanese ethnicity and, second, endowing them with the ability to pursue independent livelihoods as farmers.

Unlike status groups, the Ainu outside Tsugaru had never enjoyed autonomy within the confines of the early modern state. In that sense, their non-Japanese identity was never politically meaningful in the same way that status identities were. Moreover, since the task of eliminating the status system and the customs that symbolized it had largely been completed by the end of the 1870s, it follows that the state focused its assimilation efforts on livelihood rather than customs. In other words, an Ainu woman's tattooed face did not threaten the foundations of the modern regime in the same way that a samurai's swords did. Instead, Ainu customs fell into the same category of barbarous practices that stood in the way of the full participation of many Japanese people—the poor, the illiterate, the unwashed—within the modern state.

The Ainu were both barbarians and barbarous, but once the physical space in which their culturally articulated barbarity—that is, their distinctive identity as Ainu—might be expressed was safely incorporated into the Japanese state, it became less immediately relevant to their political position than the broader sort of barbarity that adhered to their supposedly unsettled livelihoods. It is no coincidence that throughout the modern period commentators focused their criticism of barriers to assimilation less on distinctive Ainu cultural practices—which they thought would disappear of their own accord anyway—than on the sorts of social ills that reformers found elsewhere in the country, such as alcoholism, unhygienic dwellings, sloth, and ignorance.[44]

Of course, the outcome of the Meiji state's experiment in social engineering depended a great deal on the attitude of the Ainu themselves. Many Ainu resisted the government's intrusions into their lives through individual acts like flight or noncooperation with officials. On several occasions, however, Ainu leaders submitted petitions or took other legal action to block state plans to disrupt their lives; under strong and determined leadership such efforts were sometimes successful.[45] Conversely, many Ainu actively accommodated themselves to the assimilation process. Incongruous as it may seem, this, too, was one strategy adopted by Ainu eager to retain a measure of control over their relations with the state and Japanese society at large.

Ainu who accepted the goal of assimilation did so for a number of reasons. Discrimination against the Ainu was such that many of them felt the only pragmatic means to escape it was through integration into the general population. Informing this pragmatism was a widespread feeling that the Ainu were doomed to extinction anyway, whether through the already common practice of intermarriage or via a social Darwinist struggle for survival of the fittest. Most Ainu activists avoided such fatalism, and those who did accept it generally tried, in the manner of the Ainu teacher and writer Takekuma Tokusaburō, to put a positive spin on it through the notion that Ainu blood would continue to flow in the Japanese body politic even after assimilation.[46]

Flinging oneself into the torrent of the dominant culture seems an unlikely route to ethnic self-preservation. Indeed, it is if one equates ethnic identity with the preservation of language and culture free from outside influence. However, a measure of accommodation to the state's acculturation and assimilation policies, and even active identification as Japanese, by no means precluded a simultaneous identification as Ainu. Ethnic boundaries are fluid, and the ultimate test of ethnicity is group self-awareness.[47] As the continuing presence of thirty thousand Ainu today attests, one can be monolingual in Japanese, cultivate rice for a living, be a practicing Buddhist, and still actively identify as an Ainu.

To be sure, the Japanese government's policies did great violence to Ainu culture and without question weakened Ainu ethnic identity. The point here is simply that when individual Ainu took up farming, the Japanese language, or Japanese religion in the late nineteenth and early twentieth centuries, they did not necessarily do so in a self-conscious rejection of Ainu culture or their own Ainu ethnicity. Rather, if the key to maintaining Ainu ethnicity was the preservation of self-aware communities of Ainu, accommodation to the demands an insistent Japanese state was often the only practical course of action. In any case, by the mid-1880s the disruption of the ecology of traditional fishing and hunting territories had proceeded so far that sustaining the traditional Ainu economy was impossible even in the most isolated parts of Hokkaido. Moreover, busybody officials—armed with the social Darwinist conviction that Ainu culture was doomed, and committed to a policy of cultural euthanasia—could be placated only by at least superficial cooperation with their plans.

The core of the Ainu movement before World War II, and an important element since then, has been concerned with practical issues like raising Ainu living standards, as well as with giving the Ainu people a sense of pride in their heritage while at the same time improving the terms of their participation in Japanese society—as Japanese. For some in this age of ethnic separatism this approach seems indefensible, but when seen in the context of an imperialist Japan that was steamrollering nationalist sentiments in Korea and elsewhere, this was the only realistic course available. It was an attempt to gain recognition of the validity of diversity within Japanese society: one could be both a Japanese subject and an Ainu.

Modernity and Ethnicity

During the early modern period, status ordered social groups within the core polity, and the concept of civilization situated Japan in East Asia. In the modern period, the two combined to constitute the contours of Japanese national identity and, with it, Japanese ethnicity. Japanese national identity did not emerge in its contemporary form during the Tokugawa period, or even during the opening decade or two of the Meiji era, for it goes without saying that Japan's intensive engagement with the rest of the world since the 1850s has had a profound effect on both the state's attitude toward, and the people's notions of, identity. At the same time, however, we cannot understand the impact of that engagement without considering how the Japanese nation was internally defined during the prehistory of the nation-state.

The real story of modern Japanese national identity begins in earnest where I leave off in this book. In contrast to the geographies of identity I have mapped out here, drawn as they were largely by the unilateral power of domestic political institutions, modern national identity requires other modern nations to serve as its foil. As Peter Sahlins has argued, the project of turning "peasants into Frenchmen" cannot be understood solely through a focus on policies implemented from the top down and the center outward because it leaves unanswered the critical question of how the people who were the object of those policies came to think of themselves as French. Sahlins answers the question by examining how otherwise very similar people in the Pyrenees became French and Spanish by adopting the language and ideas of national identity in response to intensely local issues.[1]

Nevertheless, because nations are not organic entities, but rather are the products of particular historical processes, a focus on institutions and the policies implemented through them is a vital prerequisite to understanding the broad contours within which modern national identities would be articulated. In this regard, the early modern geographies of identity contributed to the formation of modern Japanese national identity by bracketing the Japanese in place within the archipelago. Early modern Japan was an imperfectly centralized polity, with political authority dispersed among the shogunate, domains, and a multitude of other autonomous entities. Yet all were joined in a transcendent system of status and civilization, with the result that the network of autonomies never challenged the claims of the Tokugawa house to suzerainty over the polity.

The linking of identity with territoriality was not shared by the states with which nineteenth-century Japan competed, particularly Russia and China. In seventeenth-century Russia, Siberian indigenes who adopted Christianity became Russian in much the same manner as Ainu who took on civilized customs became Japanese in the Tokugawa period. However, by the time Russia and Japan came into contact at the end of the eighteenth century, the Russians had essentialized the Siberian natives' otherness, and Russia was clearly a multiethnic empire.[2] Likewise, the Qing empire, despite sharing with Japan a concern with customs, expanded without being constrained by them; it hardly could be constrained, for the dichotomy between civilized and barbarian realms in China had been thrown into disarray by the establishment of the dynasty by erstwhile barbarians from Manchuria.

Despite an abundance of examples around them, then, it never occurred to shogunal policy makers that Japan could be a multiethnic empire in which non-Japanese (that is, uncivilized) peoples would be subject to the sovereignty of the Japanese state in the same manner as the core population. Such a multiethnic empire could not be imagined because it would have undermined the logic of the status system, which was founded on the premise that the shogun's subjects fulfilled feudal obligations in exchange for benevolent rule. In other words, the shogun could not extend his benevolence systematically to social groups existing outside the status order without implicitly imperiling his other subjects' obligation to perform their own feudal duties. At the same time, the status system was pliable enough to allow the shogunate to achieve its assimilationist goals through the incorporation of a relatively small number of strategically situated Ainu communities. In effect, the shogunate's civilizing intentions sufficed to implicitly bring even unassimilated Ainu into the status order as Japanese. Civilization—and the membership in the status order that came with it—could be imposed unilaterally on the Ainu population as a whole. Those individuals who resisted the shogunate's civilizing overtures could be brought into the order gradually once their normative place was made clear. Their customs, in the meantime, were reduced to the level of remnants of a barbarian past, not unlike the fuzzy brows of Nanbu peasant women.

Likewise, the connection between status and civilization ensured that regional identities in the core polity would not evolve into national ones. To be sure, the inhabitants of large, peripheral domains, and particularly the samurai among them, were often inclined to conceive of the "state" (kokka) in the first instance as the domain, with the shogunate as a remote and in many ways "foreign" entity.[3] Yet even the largest of the domains were tied through economics, vassalage, and ritual to the shogunate, whose authority over the "realm" (tenka) they had to acknowledge.

But the essential unity of the early modern polity was based on much more than the fact of the shogun's place at the pinnacle of the hierarchy of power. Let us briefly consider the linguistic diversity of the archipelago as a case in point. It is a truism that in nineteenth-century Japan common folk spoke so differently that a village official from, say, Kumamoto would not have been able to hold a conversation with one from Tsugaru. Indeed, only with the diffusion of radio and television in the middle of the twentieth century did spoken Japanese become more or less standardized.[4] Yet notwithstanding the mutual unintelligibility of their regional dialects, the village official from Kumamoto would have had no trouble reading a document composed by his counterpart in Tsugaru. In Tokugawa and early Meiji Japan, officials everywhere wrote in sōrōbun, or sinicized literary Japanese,[5] and employed a standard calligraphic style, known as oieryū. The only differences would have involved relatively minor variations in bureaucratic terminology; for example, until the Restoration, village headmen in western Japan were generally called shōya, those in central Japan nanushi, and those in the northeast kimoiri. Likewise, literary and scholarly writing, whether in Japanese or classical Chinese, was standardized throughout the core polity. If a community of readers is a prerequisite for the development of modern nationalism, as Benedict Anderson suggests with his discussion of "print capitalism," early modern Japan already had such a community.[6] In contrast, officials in the Ryukyu kingdom composed documents in any of a number of idioms: depending on the circumstances and particularly on the audience, they wrote in classical Chinese, in *sōrōbun,* or in a Ryukyuan version of the classical literary language of Heian (794–1192) Japan. Moreover, poetry and other literary works were often composed in Ryukyuan.

Of course, one cannot push linguistic arguments based on writing too far, for spoken language is the only language that counts for linguists. And certainly political considerations are important in linguistic taxonomy: the debate over whether Ryukyuan ought to be classified as a distinct language (or even a group of languages) or as a dialect of Japanese is surely informed by contemporary identity politics. In any case, my point is that, outside Okinawa and Hokkaido, officials in the late nineteenth century did not need to contend with Japanese counterparts to Occitan or Provençal and the sorts of regional identities they might have supported because linguistic variation in the core polity had already been contained within the category of regional dialects thanks to the spread of a standard written language down to the village level.

More easily recognized than defined, ethnicity is a vexing phenomenon. Ultimately it can be reduced to a sense of essential difference between self and other as marked by any of a number of arbitrary traits, such as language, customs, and physical characteristics. As Barth has argued, however, "ethnic distinctions do not depend on the absence of social interaction and acceptance, but are quite to the contrary often the very foundation on which embracing social systems are built."[7] In the modern era, ethnicity has often been linked to nationalism, both giving rise to demands for autonomy and forging a sense of community among otherwise disparate individuals.[8] Yet difference, whether bounded by the nation or not, does not necessarily translate group identity into ethnicity. The Irish Travellers and the Sloughters of upstate New York are examples of peoples clearly differentiated from surrounding society who are nonetheless not seen as ethnic minorities.[9] The Travellers come closer to being considered an ethnic minority—their position in Ireland lies somewhere between those of the Japanese Burakumin and the Roma (Gypsies)—while the Sloughters' identity is rooted in the social relations of a small section of New York, with the result that most Americans have never heard of them.

Conversely, the state can effectively create or at least exaggerate difference institutionally. Thus British colonial authorities, expecting to see "tribes" when they assumed administration of Tanganyika from Germany, enlisted the assistance of local leaders in inventing them; the leaders knew they were participating in a sham, but they had their own reasons for cooperating.[10] Similarly, government policy has resulted in the creation of groups of "professional primitives" in India, and the United States Congress, working through the Bureau of Indian Affairs, recognizes some groups as Indians but denies such validation—and the measure of autonomy that goes with it—to others according to haphazardly applied criteria.[11]

The difficulty of isolating ethnicity from other types of identity is evident from an examination of contemporary Japan, where the Ainu are generally seen as an ethnic minority, while the Burakumin are not, despite the fact that few linguistic, cultural, or racial differences now separate either group from their majority neighbors. To be sure, in part this simply reflects the fact that such differences indeed once marked the Ainu as distinct, although they never did in the case of the Burakumin. But this explanation begs the question of why attempts to reify or indeed invent differences between the Burakumin and majority Japanese in ethnic (or racial) terms—by attributing to them Korean or Ainu origins, for example—never took root either among the Burakumin themselves or within Japanese society in general. Rather than attempt to ethnicize former outcastes, the modern Japanese state has consistently tried to Japanize ethnic minorities, including not only the Ainu, but Okinawans and, during the period through 1945, Koreans and Taiwanese as well, through policies of ethnic negation.[12]

To understand why the Ainu were ethnicized while the Burakumin were not we must consider their respective positions within the early modern polity. Ainu and outcastes in early modern Japan shared many characteristics: both existed as objectively identifiable groups prior to the founding of the Tokugawa shogunate—archaeologists date the emergence of Ainu culture to the fourteenth century, while various groups of base people had existed from the earliest days of the Japanese state—yet both acquired their distinctive, unitary identities only as a result of the founding of the Tokugawa state. Trade and ritual relations with the Matsumae domain homogenized Ainu identity to the extent that internal differences within the culture lost political meaning, while medieval base people were similarly homogenized as outcastes only through the imposition of population registration and the delegation of authority to community leaders. Both groups, moreover, enjoyed a measure of internal autonomy throughout the Tokugawa period. The modern Burakumin underwent another process of homogenization after the Meiji Restoration, as former *eta, hinin,* and other marginal peoples were brought under the single Buraku umbrella as a result of the abolition edict of 1871. So, too, did the Ainu, as modernity effaced the considerable differences in language and culture that had distinguished the Hokkaido Ainu from their counterparts in Sakhalin and the Kuril Islands, at least in the eyes of Japanese society, if not the Ainu themselves.[13]

Yet a number of critical differences distinguished the Ainu and outcastes during the Tokugawa period. First, of course, is the fact that the Ainu lived beyond the boundaries of the core polity, while the outcastes' realm lay within them; the first earnest attempt to integrate the Ainu came only in the nineteenth century—about the same time the state imposed its most severe restraints on the outcastes' dress and deportment. As a result, the Ainu were first marked as barbarians and only later incorporated into the status system, but for the outcastes, status came first and their putative barbarian attributes were imposed on them as a function of their position at the margins of society after the Tokugawa settlement. In short, unlike the Ainu, the outcastes were a necessary part of the status system from its inception, and so in that sense they were equivalent to other status groups. Consequently, like other groups whose identities were formalized only with the institutionalization of status, the outcastes were not ethnicized; by the same token, like other groups whose identities were formalized first through the discourse of civilization, the Ainu were.

Not all Ainu, however, were ethnicized: those who lived in the Matsumae domain's home territory in southern Hokkaido, and particularly those in the Nanbu and Tsugaru domains in northern Honshu— that is, those who remained within the core polity—underwent a naturalization process by which their barbarian character as Ainu was sublimated into their status character as a marginal social group (in seventeenth-century Tsugaru) or as ordinary peasants (in Matsumae and Nanbu). These Ainu's presence within the core polity meant that, like the outcastes, their identities were subject from the early Tokugawa period to the rules of the status system.

The same process of selective ethnicization occurred in the Ryukyu Islands. After subduing its rivals on the island of Okinawa in the fourteenth and early fifteenth centuries, the Ryukyu kingdom gradually expanded both northward and southward to encompass the entire Ryukyu archipelago. However, Satsuma annexed the Amami Islands in the north after its invasion of Ryukyu in 1609. Unlike the Ryukyuans who remained under the kingdom's administration, the Amami Islanders were incorporated within the general population of the Satsuma domain, and were thereby subjected to the rules of the status system; they remain residents of Kagoshima prefecture to this day. Since 1879, the inhabitants of the early modern Ryukyu kingdom have been homogeneously ethnicized as Okinawans, despite the fact that considerable linguistic and cultural differences separated the inhabitants of the main island from those of the Miyako and Yaeyama islands far to the southwest. Conversely, like the Ainu of southernmost Hokkaido and northern Honshu, the Amami Islanders have been incorporated within the mass of the Japanese population despite their linguistic and cultural affinities with Okinawans.[14]

Another feature of ethnicity in the Japanese archipelago is the absence of anything like a *métis* identity, despite the fact that people of mixed Ainu-Japanese ancestry have long lived in Hokkaido. People whose identities are somehow problematic—the children of Japanese and resident Koreans or other foreign citizens; mixed-race Japanese (now called *haafu,* "halves," but until recently known as *ainoko,* "half-castes"); Japanese nationals who have spent a lot of time abroad; victims of the atomic bomb and Minamata disease; and so on—are similarly distinguished from the rest of the population but cannot be said to have a distinct ethnic identity. This is no doubt in part a product of the attitude of members of these groups themselves, for it would be difficult to ethnicize them without their active participation in the process.

More importantly, however, the absence of *métis* identity reminds us of the power of the state to shape the formation and articulation of identities, ethnic and otherwise. Contemporary Japan is ethnically "homogeneous" not because there is only one ethnic group within its borders, but because the state, having incorporated Japanese ethnicity into the category of national identity, recognizes only one ethnicity as having political meaning. Competing identities are either subsumed within the homogeneous mass and, through their subsumption, denied immediacy—as the domestication of Ainu and Okinawan cultures as remnants of the Jōmon and early Japanese periods reveals[15]—or excluded entirely, as in the case of resident Koreans. Naturally, the Japanese state is hardly the only one to exert this sort of influence over the way identities are formed and expressed.

The modern Japanese state appropriated Japanese identity by tying modernity to civilization. Building on the early modern linkages among the geographies of polity, status, and civilization, the Meiji regime assumed control over the field in which new identities might be articulated autonomously of the state. A wonderfully circular logic defined the terms by which identities could be expressed politically: to be Japanese was to be civilized, and to be civilized was to contribute to the national project of attaining modernity, and to be modern was to be Japanese because being civilized was a reflection of having adopted the customs of modernity. Turned on its head, the argument demanded that the existence of identities outside the state's control imperiled the project of modernity itself. But perhaps the most exquisite aspect of this argument is that the state had to insist on Japan's homogeneity because, objectively, that homogeneity did not exist. After all, Japanese homogeneity became problematic in the first place only because of the urgency of the need to bring all the people of the archipelago into the fold of the modern nation.

The Meiji state laid the ground rules for the articulation of identities during the critical transition from early modernity to modernity. Having done so, ideologues and minority activists had little choice but to participate in the debate over the nature of the Japanese nation according to terms set by the state. Individuals could reject or ignore the debate, of course, but only at the cost of subjecting themselves to incessant calls—sometimes plaintive, sometimes ominously insistent—to join the modernity team. To be sure, many accommodated themselves to these calls while preserving a private sphere of identity within the household or local community. But to get a hearing on the big questions of the nature of the nation, one had to be modern, to be Japanese.

Status and civilization combined to lay the groundwork for a conception of a unitary ethnicity subsumed within national identity—not in its contemporary guise, of course, but rather in a form that antedated the emergence of the modern nation-state. Once the model of the nation-state was borrowed from the West, modern Japanese ethnicity developed, although it was still informed by its early modern antecedents. After all, if modern ethnicity is a construct, it follows that early modern society provided the raw materials from which it was fashioned. Identities are neither constructed out of thin air, nor imported whole cloth from other societies. Rather, they are the products of specific histories, rooted in distinctive social relations, and backed by political power and the economic relations that support it.

Notes

1. INTRODUCTION

1. Donald Denoon, Mark Hudson, Gavan McCormack, and Tessa Morris-Suzuki, eds., *Multicultural Japan: Palaeolithic to Postmodern* (Cambridge: Cambridge University Press, 1996); Michael Weiner, ed., *Japan's Minorities: The Illusion of Homogeneity* (London: Routledge, 1997); Oguma Eiji, *Tan'itsu minzoku shinwa no kigen: "Nihonjin" no jigazō no keifu* (Tokyo: Shin'yōsha, 1995), translated as Eiji Oguma, *A Genealogy of "Japanese" Self-Images*, trans. David Askew (Melbourne: Trans Pacific Press, 2002); Oguma Eiji, *"Nihonjin" no kyōkai: Okinawa, Ainu, Taiwan, Chōsen, shokuminchi shihai kara fukki undō made* (Tokyo: Shin'yōsha, 1998); John Lie, *Multiethnic Japan* (Cambridge, Mass.: Harvard University Press, 2001). These works build on a large literature critiquing the myth of contemporary Japanese ethnic and cultural homogeneity. See Harumi Befu, *Hegemony of Homogeneity: An Anthropological Analysis of "Nihonjinron"* (Melbourne: Trans Pacific Press, 2001); Peter N. Dale, *The Myth of Japanese Uniqueness* (London: Croom Helm; Oxford: Nissan Institute for Japanese Studies, University of Oxford, 1986); and Kosaku Yoshino, *Cultural Nationalism in Contemporary Japan: A Sociological Inquiry* (London: Routledge, 1992).

2. See Kikuchi Isao, "Kyōkai to etonosu," in *Chiiki to etonosu*, ed. Arano Yasunori, Ishii Masatoshi, and Murai Shōsuke (Tokyo: University of Tokyo Press, 1992), 56–59, for a discussion of early modern Japan's boundaries as reflected in maps compiled by the shogunate in the seventeenth and early eighteenth centuries. See also Marcia Yonemoto, "The 'Spatial Vernacular' in Early Modern Japan: Knowledge, Power, and Pleasure in the Form of a Map," *Journal of Asian Studies* 59, no. 3 (Aug. 2000): 647–66.

3. Kikuchi, "Kyōkai to etonosu," 57; Murai Shōsuke, *Ajia no naka no chūsei Nihon* (Tokyo: Azekura Shobō, 1988).

4. On boundaries in another Asian society, see Thongchai Winichakul, *Siam Mapped: The Geo-body of a Nation* (Honolulu: University of Hawai'i Press, 1994).

5. For a discussion of the boundaries of the city of Edo (modern Tokyo) that illustrates this point, see Katō Takashi, "Governing Edo," in *Edo and Paris: Urban Life and the State in the Early Modern Era*, ed. James L. McClain, John M. Merriman, and Ugawa Kaoru (Ithaca, N.Y.: Cornell University Press, 1994), 41–67.

6. Here I depart from my earlier work on this subject. Compare David L. Howell, "Ainu Ethnicity and the Boundaries of the Early Modern Japanese State," *Past and Present* 142 (Feb. 1994): 69–93. Parts of this article have been incorporated into chapters 5 and 6.

7. Fredrik Barth, "Introduction," in *Ethnic Groups and Boundaries: The Social Organization of Culture Difference,* ed. Fredrik Barth (Boston: Little, Brown, and Co., 1969), 9–38.

8. Ainu Bunka Hozon Kyōkai, ed., *Ainu minzoku shi* (Tokyo: Daiichi Hōki Shuppan, 1970), 6.

9. See Kanazawa Shōsaburō, *Nissen dōsoron* (Tokyo: Tōkō Shobō, 1929); Lie, *Multiethnic Japan,* 122–25; and Kita Sadakichi, "Nissen ryōminzoku dōgenron," in *Kita Sadakichi chosakushū,* ed. Ueda Masaaki (Tokyo: Heibonsha, 1979), 8: 357–415.

10. Numerous writers expressed this view, including Kita Kōyō [Shōmei], *Ainu hatashite horobiru ka* (Sapporo: Hokkaidō Ainu Kyōkai, 1937), 1–7.

11. David L. Howell, "Making 'Useful Citizens' of Ainu Subjects in Early Twentieth-Century Japan," *Journal of Asian Studies* 63, no. 1 (Feb. 2004): 5–29.

12. The usage examples from the Tokugawa period cited under *fūzoku* in the *Nihon kokugo daijiten* (Tokyo: Shōgakukan, 1975), 17: 268, all refer to clothing or appearance, as do the several modern examples from regional dialects, though it is certainly possible to find uses of *fūzoku* in the Tokugawa period that correspond more broadly to *customs*.

2. THE GEOGRAPHY OF STATUS

1. The use of the term *federalism* follows Mary Elizabeth Berry, *Hideyoshi* (Cambridge, Mass.: Council on East Asian Studies, Harvard University, 1982).

2. Ronald Toby, "Rescuing the Nation from History: The State of the State in Early Modern Japan," *Monumenta Nipponica* 56, no. 2 (Summer 2001): 197–238, surveys the debate and argues for a "national" view of the early modern state.

3. Mary Elizabeth Berry, "Public Peace and Private Attachment: The Goals and Conduct of Power in Early Modern Japan," *Journal of Japanese Studies* 12, no. 2 (Summer 1986): 237–71.

4. See Wakita Osamu, "The *Kokudaka* System: A Device for Unification," *Journal of Japanese Studies* 1, no. 2 (Summer 1975): 297–320, on the system's origins.

5. Tsugaru began the Tokugawa period with a relatively modest official yield of 47,000 *koku,* which rose to 70,000 *koku* in 1805 and 100,000 *koku* in 1808. Nanbu's official yield was increased from 100,000 *koku* to 200,000 *koku* in 1808. Both domains had substantially higher actual productivity than their official figures would suggest. Mark Ravina, *Land and Lordship in Early Modern Japan* (Stanford, Calif.: Stanford University Press, 1998), 117; Hosoi Hakaru, "Morioka han," in *Kokushi daijiten,* ed. Kokushi Daijiten Henshū Iinkai (Tokyo: Yoshikawa Kōbunkan, 1992), 13: 862–63. See Luke S. Roberts, *Mercantilism in a Japanese Domain: The Merchant Origins of Economic Nationalism in 18th-Century Tosa* (New York: Cambridge University Press, 1998), 38, for a discussion of the fictive nature of putative yields in many domains.

6. John W. Hall, "Rule by Status in Tokugawa Japan," *Journal of Japanese Studies* 1, no. 1 (Autumn 1974): 39–49; Herman Ooms, *Tokugawa Village Practice: Class, Status, Power, Law* (Berkeley: University of California Press, 1996); Douglas R. Howland, "Samurai Status, Class and Bureaucracy: A Historiographical Essay," *Journal of Asian Studies* 60, no. 2 (May 2001): 353–80; Gerald Groemer, "The Creation of the Edo Outcaste Order," *Journal of Japanese Studies* 27, no. 2 (Summer 2001): 263–94.

7. In addition to works cited elsewhere in this chapter, see Asao Naohiro, "Kinsei no mibunsei to senmin," *Buraku mondai kenkyū* 68 (Oct. 1981): 37–55; Hatanaka Toshiyuki, *"Kawata" to heijin: Kinsei mibun shakairon* (Kyoto: Kamogawa Shuppan, 1997); Tsukada Takashi, *Kinsei mibunsei to shūen shakai* (Tokyo: University of Tokyo Press, 1997); Yokota Fuyuhiko, "Bakuhansei zenki ni okeru shokunin hensei to mibun," *Nihonshi kenkyū* 235 (Mar. 1982): 51–72; and Yoshida Nobuyuki, *Kinsei toshi shakai no mibun kōzō* (Tokyo: University of Tokyo Press, 1998). Despite their common concern with status, these authors are by no mean unanimous in their interpretations of its nature and function.

8. Howland, "Samurai Status, Class and Bureaucracy." In Japanese, see Uematsu Tadahiro, *Shi-nō-kō-shō: Jukyō shisō to kanryō shihai* (Tokyo: Dōbunkan, 1997).

9. Asao Naohiro, "Kinsei no mibun to sono hen'yō," in *Mibun to kakushiki,* ed. Asao Naohiro (Tokyo: Chūō Kōronsha, 1992), 22; Yokota Fuyuhiko, "Kinseiteki mibun seido no seiritsu," in ibid., 41–78.

10. See the laws compiled and translated by John Carey Hall, *Tokugawa Feudal Law,* reprint ed. (Washington, D.C.: University Publications of America, 1979). Some laws applied only to urban areas and accordingly referred to townspeople *(chōnin),* but such measures did not serve to distinguish townspeople from rural commoners in an essential sense, for the key was the geographical limitation of the laws' applicability.

11. The descendants of Christians were known as *ruizoku;* see Yokota, "Kinseiteki mibun seido no seiritsu," 76.

12. For example, see the entries in "Monjin seimeiroku" [n.d.], in *Shinshū Hirata Atsutane zenshū,* ed. Hirata Atsutane Zenshū Kankōkai (Tokyo: Meicho Shuppan, 1981), appendix volume *(bekkan).*

13. A useful introduction to status in early modern society is Asao, "Kinsei no mibun to sono hen'yō"; see also Yamamoto Naotomo, "Kinsei shakai to sono mibun: Jo ni kaete," in *Kinsei no minshū to geinō,* ed. Kyōto Burakushi

Kenkyūjo (Kyoto: Aunsha, 1989), 1–12. The most elaborate theoretical treatment is Tsukada, *Kinsei mibunsei to shūen shakai,* 3–45.

14. Urban commoners without property, and hence without rights in the governance of urban wards *(chō),* were known by a variety of labels, such as "peddlers" *(furiuri)* and "tenants" *(tanagari).* In the countryside, landless peasants
were often called "water-drinking peasants" *(mizunomi-byakushō),* though terminology varied widely around the country.

15. Although the term *samurai* is conventionally used in the Western-language
literature to refer to warriors in general (a practice I follow here), in most domains
the term referred specifically to a relatively small group of high-ranking warriors,
particularly those with the right to appear before the lord in audience *(omemie).*

16. The term "outcaste" is problematic, as Tokugawa Japan was not a caste
society, but I shall follow conventional usage here. Its use has been proposed
most systematically by George DeVos and Hiroshi Wagatsuma, "The Problem:
Caste and Race, a Syncretic View," in *Japan's Invisible Race: Caste in Culture
and Identity,* ed. George DeVos and Hiroshi Wagatsuma (Berkeley: University of
California Press, 1966), xix–xxiii.

17. Aside from Ooms, *Tokugawa Village Practice,* 243–311, and Groemer,
"The Creation of the Edo Outcaste Order," there is relatively little literature in
English on outcastes in the Tokugawa period. John Price, "A History of the Outcaste: Untouchability in Japan," in *Japan's Invisible Race,* ed. DeVos and Wagatsuma, 6–30, is badly dated.

18. Torao Haraguchi, Robert K. Sakai, Mitsugu Sakihara, Kazuko Yamada,
and Masato Mitsui, *The Status System and Social Organization of Satsuma: A
Translation of the* Shūmon Tefuda Aratame Jōmoku (Honolulu: University Press
of Hawaii, 1975), 144–45.

19. Wakita Osamu, "Kinsei ni okeru shokushu sabetsu no kōzō," in *Mibunteki shūen,* ed. Tsukada Takashi, Yoshida Nobuyuki, and Wakita Osamu (Kyoto:
Buraku Mondai Kenkyūjo, 1994), 297–321.

20. Yamamoto, "Kinsei shakai to sono mibun," 4–6.

21. On the *tani-hinin,* see doc. 437 [1869/7–72] in *"Kaihōrei" no seiritsu,* ed.
Harada Tomohiko and Uesugi Satoru (Tokyo: San'ichi Shobō, 1984), 374–75;
on the *ushikubi-kojiki,* Imanishi Hajime, "Bunmei kaika to 'ushikubi kojiki,'" in
Bakumatsu, ishinki no kokumin kokka keisei to bunka hen'yō, ed. Nishikawa
Nagao and Matsumiya Hideharu (Tokyo: Shin'yōsha, 1995), 345–74; and on the
ama, see Robert G. Flershem and Yoshiko Flershem, "Migratory Fishermen on
the Japan Sea Coast in the Tokugawa Period," *Japan Forum* 3, no. 1 (Apr. 1991):
71–90. See also Edward Norbeck, "Little-Known Minority Groups of Japan," in
Japan's Invisible Race, ed. DeVos and Wagatsuma, 184–99.

22. Constantine N. Vaporis, "Post Station and Assisting Villages: Corvée
Labor and Peasant Contention," *Monumenta Nipponica* 41, no. 4 (Winter
1986): 377–414.

23. Haga Noboru, "Nohinin: Daitoshi ni ryūnyū suru furō, mushuku no
hitobito," in *Kinsei no minshū to geinō,* ed. Kyōto Burakushi Kenkyūjo, 126–31;
Tsukada Takashi, *Kinsei Nihon mibunsei no kenkyū* (Kobe: Hyōgo Buraku
Mondai Kenkyūjo, 1987), 287–307.

24. Hall, "Rule by Status," 48.

25. Yamamoto, "Kinsei shakai to sono mibun," 3. *Sabetsu* might also be translated as "differentiation," for social relations between members of different status groups—such as dealings between townspeople and samurai—did not necessarily entail prejudice or intolerance. Herman Ooms, *Tokugawa Ideology: Early Constructs, 1570–1680* (Princeton, N.J.: Princeton University Press, 1985), 139, glosses *sabetsu* as "apartheid."

26. Here I differ from Ooms, *Tokugawa Village Practice,* who characterizes the discrimination against outcastes as "state racism."

27. See Yokota, "Kinseiteki mibun seido no seiritsu," for a discussion of the evolution of ad hoc military and administrative imperatives into the status system.

28. Katō Yasuaki, "Kinsei no shōgaisha to mibun seido," in *Mibun to kakushiki,* ed. Asao, 125–78. The *tōdō* antedated the establishment of the Tokugawa shogunate, but it acquired its centrally recognized administrative authority only in the seventeenth century.

29. Gerald Groemer, "The Guild of the Blind in Tokugawa Japan," *Monumenta Nipponica* 56, no. 3 (Autumn 2001): 349–80.

30. Katō, "Kinsei no shōgaisha to mibun seido," 146–48.

31. Alexander Vesey, "The Buddhist Clergy and Village Society in Early Modern Japan" (Ph.D. diss., Princeton University, 2002).

32. On so-called free cities such as Sakai, see V. Dixon Morris, "The City of Sakai and Urban Autonomy," in *Warlords, Artists, and Commoners: Japan in the Sixteenth Century,* ed. George Elison and Bardwell L. Smith (Honolulu: University of Hawai'i Press, 1981), 23–54; Ōishi Masaaki, "Jiin to chūsei shakai," in *Iwanami kōza Nihon tsūshi* (Tokyo: Iwanami Shoten, 1994): 8: 135–70; on the *Ikkō ikki,* see Nagahara Keiji, "The Medieval Peasant," trans. Suzanne Gay, in *Medieval Japan,* ed. Kozo Yamamura (New York: Cambridge University Press, 1990), 338–40; on the *shōen,* see Ōyama Kyōhei, "Medieval *Shōen,*" trans. Martin Collcutt, in ibid., 89–127, and Nagahara Keiji, "Decline of the *Shōen* System," trans. Michael P. Birt, in ibid., 260–300; and on the imperial institution, see Amino Yoshihiko, *Chūsei minshūzō: Heimin to shokunin* (Tokyo: Iwanami Shoten, 1980).

33. According to Mase Kumiko, as cited by Wakita Osamu, the genealogy was created sometime between 1708 and 1715. See Wakita, "Kinsei ni okeru shokushu sabetsu no kōzō," 298. The Edo *hinin* headman, Kuruma Zenshichi, frequently, though unsuccessfully, challenged Danzaemon's authority. See Groemer, "The Creation of the Edo Outcaste Order," and Anna Beerens, trans., "Interview with a Bakumatsu Official: A Translation from *Kyūji Shimonroku* (2)," *Monumenta Nipponica* 57, no. 2 (Summer 2002): 195–97. In one incident near the end of the Tokugawa period Danzaemon justified his maintenance of authority by asserting the antiquity of his control over the *hinin* and his need to maintain that control to meet the obligations of his own position (Beerens, trans., "Interview with a Bakumatsu Official," 196).

34. See Sasaki Junnosuke, *Yonaoshi to murakata sōdō,* as summarized in Kitajima Masamoto, "Kan'ei ki no rekishiteki ichi," in *Bakuhansei kokka seiritsu katei no kenkyū,* ed. Kitajima Masamoto (Tokyo: Yoshikawa Kōbunkan, 1978), 3–9. Kitajima discusses Sasaki's argument as it applies to the separation of the samurai from the peasantry. See also Sasaki Junnosuke, *Bakuhansei*

kokkaron (Tokyo: University of Tokyo Press, 1984), 1: 109–341. This process can be seen at work in the Kaga domain, as described by Philip C. Brown, *Central Authority and Local Autonomy in the Formation of Early Modern Japan: The Case of Kaga Domain* (Stanford, Calif.: Stanford University Press, 1993). Brown argues, however, that the early modern state in fact had little power over the domain, and that the general institutional convergence seen in seventeenth-century Japan was essentially a fortuitous development.

35. Hatanaka Toshiyuki, "Kinsei 'senmin' mibunron no kadai," in *Sōten Nihon no rekishi: Kinsei hen,* ed. Aoki Michio and Hosaka Satoru (Tokyo: Shinjinbutsu Ōraisha, 1991), 176–78. Involvement with outcaste duties as by-employments had important demographic implications, as Dana Morris and Thomas C. Smith, "Fertility and Mortality in an Outcaste Village in Japan, 1750–1869," in *Family and Population in East Asian History,* ed. Susan B. Hanley and Arthur P. Wolf (Stanford, Calif.: Stanford University Press, 1985), 229–46, have demonstrated.

36. There were some exceptions to this general rule. See Hatanaka Toshiyuki, *Kinsei sonraku shakai no mibun kōzō* (Kyoto: Buraku Mondai Kenkyūjo, 1990), 11–41.

37. See the panel discussion in Kyōto Burakushi Kenkyūjo, ed., *Kinsei no minshū to geinō,* 196–97.

38. See Hatanaka, "Kinsei 'senmin' mibunron no kadai," 176–83. However, the village examined by Morris and Smith, "Fertility and Mortality in an Outcaste Village," was marked by extreme poverty despite a heavy reliance on outcaste occupations.

39. "Kaidai," in *Suzuki-ke monjo,* ed. Saitama-ken Dōwa Kyōiku Kenkyū Kyōgikai (Urawa: Saitama-ken Dōwa Kyōiku Kenkyū Kyōgikai, 1977–79), 1: 28. Data on *kokudaka* and overlords reflect conditions that prevailed between about 1844 and 1868 (official *kokudaka* changed little during the Tokugawa period, but *hatamoto* fiefs were shuffled frequently), and were compiled from Kadokawa Nihon Chimei Daijiten Hensan Iinkai, ed., *Saitama-ken* (Tokyo: Kadokawa Shoten, 1980). The Sakura domain (100,000 *koku*) was based in Sakura, Shimōsa province (Chiba); the villages in Musashi were part of its detached territory *(tobichi).*

40. The exact geography of the territories is unclear, but a 1789 list of fifty villages to which directives from Edo were routed probably corresponds to the local *kogashira*'s bases. For the list, see Saitama-ken Dōwa Kyōiku Kenkyū Kyōgikai, ed., *Suzuki-ke monjo,* doc. 6, 1: 6–7.

41. Kanda Yutsuki, "Saikoku no kyokaku to chiiki shakai: Bungo Kitsuki no 'suihō' o chūshin to shite," in *Kinsei no shakaiteki kenryoku: Ken'i to hegemonii,* ed. Yoshida Nobuyuki and Kurushima Hiroshi (Tokyo: Yamakawa Shuppan, 1996), 239–72.

42. On groups bound to the Tsuchimikado house, see Yamamoto Naotomo, "Innai: Koyomi o uri, uranai ya kitō o suru," in *Kinsei no minshū to geinō,* ed. Kyōto Burakushi Kenkyūjo, 30–34, and Yamaji Kōzō, "Manzai: Danna o tayori, teritorii o kakuritsu," in ibid., 65–71; on the *ebune,* see Kawaoka Takeharu, *Umi no tami: Gyoson no rekishi to minzoku* (Tokyo: Heibonsha, 1987).

43. Donald H. Shively, "Sumptuary Regulation and Status in Early Toku-

gawa Japan," *Harvard Journal of Asiatic Studies* 25 (1964–65): 123–64. The decrees' notorious inefficacy does not diminish their significance.

44. This practice was quite common. For one example, see the case of Kane, adopted in 1860 by her employer, Yanagioka Heinai, preparatory to marriage to Kawai Eikichi, in "Hayashi-ke monjo: Ban nikki" [1860–66], in *Matsumae-chō shi: Shiryōhen,* ed. Matsumae-chō Shi Henshūshitsu (Matsumae: Matsumae-chō, 1977), 2: 691.

45. Hatanaka Toshiyuki, "Mibun o koeru toki," in *Mibunteki shūen,* ed. Tsukada, Yoshida, and Wakita, 403–60.

46. Tsukada Takashi, *Mibunsei shakai to shimin shakai: Kinsei Nihon no shakai to hō* (Tokyo: Kashiwa Shobō, 1992), 196–201.

47. Kikuchi Shunsuke, ed., *Tokugawa kinreikō,* 6 vols. (Tokyo: Yoshikawa Kōbunkan, 1931–32), 5: 539–40.

48. "Oboe" [1809/5], "Miyazu zaikata gohattosho," in *Kyōto no burakushi,* ed. Kyōto Burakushi Kenkyūjo, 10 vols. (Kyoto: Aunsha, 1988), 5: 23.

49. Yokokawa Ryōsuke, *Naishiryaku* [ca. 1854], ed. Iwate Kenritsu Toshokan (Morioka: Iwate-ken Bunkazai Aigo Kyōkai, 1974), 3: 209–33.

50. See the panel discussion in Kyōto Burakushi Kenkyūjo, ed., *Kinsei no minshū to geinō,* 226–28, and Takayanagi Kaneyoshi, *Edo no daidōgei* (Tokyo: Kashiwa Shobō, 1982), 29–30.

51. See Tsukada Takashi, Teraki Nobuaki, Hatanaka Toshiyuki, Yamamoto Naotomo, and Wakita Osamu, *Senmin mibun ron: Chūsei kara kinsei e* (Tokyo: Akashi Shoten, 1994).

52. Amino Yoshihiko, *Muen, kugai, raku: Nihon chūsei no jiyū to heiwa* (Tokyo: Heibonsha, 1978); Amino, *Chūsei minshūzō.*

53. See, for example, the case of the *eta* doctor who was denied elevation to commoner status by Danzaemon, cited in Asao, "Kinsei no mibun to sono hen'yō," 7–10.

54. Tsukada, *Kinsei Nihon mibunsei no kenkyū,* 175–78. The documents pertaining to this dispute do not discuss the villagers' motives, but Tsukada argues that the performance of duties was an important way for villages to assert higher standing within the outcaste community, in both a political and an economic sense. Elsewhere (*Mibunsei shakai to shimin shakai,* 203–4) Tsukada offers evidence from analogous cases in Edo, in which outcaste communities that participated in executions received monopolies over the local leather-soled sandal *(setta)* trade, a major source of livelihood for outcastes throughout Japan. Because dealings with commoners were an integral part of the trade, it was subject to samurai authority.

55. Ooms, *Tokugawa Village Practice,* 125–37.

56. Ibid., 12–70.

3. STATUS AND THE POLITICS OF THE QUOTIDIAN

1. The original *gōmune* is said to have been a masterless samurai *(rōnin)* who was driven to perform arts he had studied as a form of self-cultivation during better times. Yamamoto Nidayū, "Gōmunegashira kaden" [n.d.], in *Buraku,* ed. Harada Tomohiko (Tokyo: San'ichi Shobō, 1971), 487.

2. See Yamamuro Shin'ichi, "Meiji kokka no seido to rinen," in *Iwanami kōza Nihon tsūshi*, 17: 113–48.

3. See Amino Yoshihiko, "Emperor, Rice, and Commoners," in *Multicultural Japan*, ed. Denoon, Hudson, McCormack, and Morris-Suzuki, 235–44, for a discussion of the range of meanings encompassed by the term *hyakushō* through Japanese history.

4. See Osamu Saitō, "The Rural Economy: Commercial Agriculture, By-employment, and Wage Work," in *Japan in Transition: From Tokugawa to Meiji* ed. Marius B. Jansen and Gilbert Rozman (Princeton, N.J.: Princeton University Press, 1986), 400–420; Kären Wigen, *The Making of a Japanese Periphery, 1750–1920* (Berkeley: University of California Press, 1995); William B. Hauser, *Economic Institutional Change in Tokugawa Japan: Ōsaka and the Kinai Cotton Trade* (New York: Cambridge University Press, 1974).

5. Thomas C. Smith, *Native Sources of Japanese Industrialization, 1750–1920* (Berkeley: University of California Press, 1988), 82–83.

6. See David L. Howell, "Hard Times in the Kantō: Economic Change and Village Life in Late Tokugawa Japan," *Modern Asian Studies* 23, no. 2 (May 1989): 349–71, for some examples. The fulfillment of status obligations was mediated by the peasant village as a corporate unit of administration. The land-tax bill was divided among village landowners, with the result that landless peasants technically paid no taxes themselves. Tenants paid indirectly through rents (including rents on homestead land). Villages typically barred landless peasants from participating in community governance. Such disfranchised residents were considered peasants nonetheless because they were registered as members of the village community. Hence, the village community as a whole fulfilled the status-based obligations for all residents in exchange for jurisdiction over them. Villages could levy their own duties on members of the community, and there was considerable variation in practice in the treatment of landless residents.

7. The development of financial institutions, including what Ronald Toby calls genuine banking, was important in fostering economic development. Ronald P. Toby, "Both a Borrower and a Lender Be: From Village Moneylender to Rural Banker in the Tempō Era," *Monumenta Nipponica* 46, no. 4 (Winter 1991): 483–512.

8. Edward Pratt, *Japan's Protoindustrial Elite* (Cambridge, Mass.: Harvard University Asia Center, 1999).

9. Arai Eiji, *Kinsei no gyoson* (Tokyo: Yoshikawa Kōbunkan, 1970); Arne Kalland, *Fishing Villages in Tokugawa Japan* (Honolulu: University of Hawai'i Press, 1995).

10. Anne Walthall, *Social Protest and Popular Culture in Eighteenth-Century Japan* (Tucson: University of Arizona Press, 1986).

11. Miura Meisuke, "Gokuchūki" [1859–61], annot. Mori Kahei, in *Minshū undō no shisō*, ed. Shōji Kichinosuke, Hayashi Motoi, and Yasumaru Yoshio (Tokyo: Iwanami Shoten, 1970), 15–86. See also Herbert P. Bix, "Leader of Peasant Rebellions: Miura Meisuke," in *Great Historical Figures of Japan*, ed. Murakami Hyoe and Thomas J. Harper (Tokyo: Japan Culture Institute, 1978), 243–60. The title, "Gokuchūki," was given to Miura's letters by later scholars.

12. Hayashi Hachiemon, "Kannō kyōkunroku" [1826/5], in *Gunma-ken shi*:

Shiryōhen 14 (*Kinsei* 6), ed. Gunma-ken Shi Hensan Iinkai (Maebashi: Gunma-ken, 1986), 784–810.

13. On jails in Tokugawa Japan, see Daniel V. Botsman, "Crime, Punishment and the Making of Modern Japan, 1790–1895" (Ph.D. diss., Princeton University, 1999).

14. Hayashi, "Kannō kyōkunroku," 805.

15. Ibid., 807–8.

16. Tsukada Takashi, "Mibun shakai no kaitai: Ōsaka Watanabe mura-Nishihama no jirei kara," *Rekishi hyōron* 527 (Mar. 1994): 73–99.

17. Thomas C. Smith, *The Agrarian Origins of Modern Japan* (Stanford, Calif.: Stanford University Press, 1959); Ooms, *Tokugawa Village Practice*, is an insightful examination of social conflict within villages beyond the immediate context of economic relations.

18. For a fuller treatment of this point, see David L. Howell, "Proto-Industrial Origins of Japanese Capitalism," *Journal of Asian Studies* 52, no. 2 (May 1992): 269–86.

19. Hatanaka, "Mibun o koeru toki."

20. Tsukada, *Mibunsei shakai to shimin shakai*, 19–21. It is impossible to know how much or how rapidly the *mushuku* population grew during the final decades of the Tokugawa period, but without question there was a widely shared perception of such growth.

21. I am grateful to Daniel Botsman for pointing this out to me.

22. The case is the topic of Takahashi Satoshi, *Edo no soshō: Mishuku mura ikken tenmatsu* (Tokyo: Iwanami Shoten, 1996).

23. Shimazaki Tōson's epic novel *Before the Dawn (Yoakemae)* conveys the onerous weight of feudal duty on the post stations on Kiso Road in southern Shinano province. Shimazaki Tōson, *Before the Dawn*, trans. William E. Naff (Honolulu: University of Hawai'i Press, 1987).

24. Howell, "Hard Times in the Kantō"; Patricia Sippel, "Abandoned Fields: Negotiating Taxes in the Bakufu Domain," *Monumenta Nipponica* 53, no. 2 (Summer 1998): 197–224; Michiko Tanaka, "Village Youth Organizations *(Wakamono Nakama)* in Late Tokugawa Politics and Society (Japan)" (Ph.D. diss., Princeton University, 1983).

25. Imanishi Hajime, *Kindai Nihon no sabetsu to sei bunka: Bunmei kaika to minshū sekai* (Tokyo: Yūzankaku, 1998), 55–60.

26. Ravina, *Land and Lordship in Early Modern Japan.*

27. Kasaya Kazuhiko, "Bushi no mibun to kakushiki," in *Mibun to kakushiki*, ed. Asao, 179–224.

28. Kozo Yamamura, *A Study of Samurai Income and Entrepreneurship: Quantitative Analyses of Economic and Social Aspects of the Samurai in Tokugawa and Meiji, Japan* (Cambridge, Mass.: Harvard University Press, 1974).

29. Marius B. Jansen, "Japan in the Early Nineteenth Century," in *The Nineteenth Century*, ed. Marius B. Jansen (New York: Cambridge University Press, 1989), 69–70.

30. Mori Kahei, *Nanbu han hyakushō ikki no kenkyū* (Tokyo: Hōsei University Press, 1974), 345–570.

31. Saitama-ken Dōwa Kyōiku Kenkyū Kyōgikai, ed., *Suzuki-ke monjo.*

32. For an example of an approved project, see Hiraku Shimoda, "Bad Sushi or Bad Merchant? The 'Dead Fish Poisoning Incident' of 1852," *Modern Asian Studies* 35, no. 3 (July 2001): 513–31. For an unapproved one, see Nakai Nobuhiko, *Ōhara Yūgaku* (Tokyo: Yoshikawa Kōbunkan, 1963), 158–68.

33. I am thankful to Anne Walthall for encouraging me to think about this issue and its implications for the nineteenth-century economy. On the exceptional nature of the financial bureaucracy, see Kasaya Kazuhiko, *Bushidō to gendai* (Tokyo: Sankei Shinbunsha, 2002), 83–84.

34. Other domains had rural samurai, but they were often remnants of sixteenth-century warrior bands that were displaced when new daimyo were brought in from the outside through the hegemonic power of Toyotomi Hideyoshi or Tokugawa Ieyasu. The groups in Tosa (Roberts, *Mercantilism in a Japanese Domain*) and Kaga (Brown, *Central Authority and Local Autonomy in the Formation of Early Modern Japan*) are examples.

35. Hidemura Senzō, "Josetsu: Shiron teki ni," in *Satsuma han no kiso kōzō*, ed. Hidemura Senzō (Tokyo: Ochanomizu Shobō, 1970), 13–14.

36. Ibid., 7–10, 15–16.

37. Ibid., 12–13.

38. Yoshida, *Kinsei toshi shakai no mibun kōzō*, 259–83.

39. Ibid., 282.

40. William H. Sewell, Jr., *Work and Revolution in France: The Language of Labor from the Old Regime to 1848* (New York: Cambridge University Press, 1980), 115–17; quotations from p. 116.

41. Ibid., 117.

42. "Goyōdome sono ni" [1869/8/24], doc. *i*–51–2, Asō-ke monjo, Chiba Prefectural Archives.

43. Herbert Plutschow, *Japan's Name Culture: The Significance of Names in a Religious, Political, and Social Context* (Sandgate, Folkestone: Japan Library, 1995), surveys naming practices and regulations through the beginning of the Meiji period.

44. Ōtaka Eiichi, "Ōtaka Zenbei," *Chiba-ken no rekishi* 4 (Aug. 1972): 36.

45. Tsukada, *Mibunsei shakai to shimin shakai*, 226–37. Tsukada, following Minegishi Kentarō, argues that the use of the name Shirōbei suggests that the relationship between commoners and *hinin* in Otojirō's ward had taken on a "personal" *(jinkakuteki)* character, while among the *hinin* relations were governed by principles of communal life *(seikatsu kyōdō)*.

46. Doc. 466 [1870/110/24], in Harada Tomohiko and Uesugi Satoru, eds., *"Kaihōrei" no seiritsu* (Tokyo: San'ichi Shobō, 1984), 395–96.

47. See Yamamuro, "Meiji kokka no seido to rinen," 140–45.

48. According to Iwai Tadakuma, "Shoki Meiji kokka to buraku mondai: Senshō haishirei o megutte," in *Burakushi no kenkyū: Kindai hen,* ed. Buraku Mondai Kenkyūjo (Kyoto: Buraku Mondai Kenkyūjo, 1984), 32, officials in only a few districts added notations like "former *eta*" and "new commoner" to entries in the 1872 registry.

49. Ibid., 33.

50. Hirota Masaki, "Nihon kindai shakai no sabetsu kōzō," in *Sabetsu no shosō,* ed. Hirota Masaki (Tokyo: Iwanami Shoten, 1990), 458–70.

51. Yamamuro, "Meiji kokka no seido to rinen," 142.

52. Imanishi, *Kindai Nihon no sabetsu to sei bunka,* 51–55; Chiba-ken Shi Hensan Shingikai, ed., *Chiba-ken shiryō: Kindai hen: Meiji shoki 3* (Chiba: Chiba-ken, 1970), 245.

53. Makihara Norio, *Kyakubun to kokumin no aida: Kindai minshū no seiji ishiki* (Tokyo: Yoshikawa Kōbunkan, 1998).

54. Pratt, *Japan's Protoindustrial Elite,* describes many *gōnō* brought down by forced loans and extraordinary levies.

55. Imanishi Hajime, *Kindai Nihon no sabetsu to sonraku* (Tokyo: Yūzankaku, 1993), 93–118.

56. Ibid., 102–3.

57. Doc. 255 [1871/9–1872/5], in Harada and Uesugi, eds., *"Kaihōrei" no seiritsu,* 217–18.

58. Obinata Sumio, *Nihon kindai kokka no seiritsu to keisatsu* (Tokyo: Azekura Shobō, 1992), 53–54.

59. Okayama-ken Buraku Kaihō Undō Rokujūnenshi Hensan Iinkai, ed., *Okayama-ken buraku mondai shiryōshū* (Okayama: Okayama-ken Buraku Kaihō Undō Rengōkai, 1987), 64–65.

60. Ooms, *Tokugawa Village Practice,* 11–70, relates an incident in which this disinterest is evident.

61. Kozo Yamamura, "The Meiji Land Tax Reform and Its Effects," in *Japan in Transition: Tokugawa to Meiji,* ed. Marius B. Jansen and Gilbert Rozman (Princeton, N.J.: Princeton University Press, 1986), 382–99.

62. Ōshima Mitsuko, *Meiji no mura* (Tokyo: Kyōikusha, 1977), 35–50.

63. "Kaika no hanashi" [1872], in *Meiji bunka zenshū: Bunmei kaika hen,* ed. Yoshino Sakuzō (Tokyo: Nihon Hyōronsha, 1929), 75. In his introduction to the piece ("Kaika no hanashi kaidai," in ibid., 3), Ishii Kendō writes that the work was originally published in 1872 by Hakubundō in Gyōda, a town in present-day Saitama prefecture, and reissued by Hakubundō under the name of Tsuji Kōsō in Takasaki Tamachi, in Gunma prefecture, in 1880. It is the reissued version that is reprinted in the *Meiji bunka zenshū.*

64. Ibid., 76.

65. Ogawa Tameji, "Kaika mondō" [1874], in ibid., 152–56. For an analysis of this work, see Michael Cusumano, "An Enlightenment Dialogue with Fukuzawa Yukichi: Ogawa Tameji's *Kaika Mondo, 1874–1875," Monumenta Nipponica* 37, no. 3 (Autumn 1982): 375–401.

66. Ogawa, "Kaika mondō," 155.

67. Imanishi, *Kindai Nihon no sabetsu to sei bunka,* 66–69.

68. See Ann Waswo, *Japanese Landlords: The Decline of a Rural Elite* (Berkeley: University of California Press, 1977).

69. See Ochiai Hiroki, *Chitsuroku shobun: Meiji ishin to bushi no risutora* (Tokyo: Chūō Kōron Shinsha, 1999), and Thomas Richard Schalow, "The Role of the Financial Panic of 1927 and Failure of the 15th Bank in the Economic Decline of the Japanese Aristocracy" (Ph.D. diss., Princeton University, 1989).

70. See David L. Howell, "Early *Shizoku* Colonization of Hokkaidō," *Journal of Asian History* 17 (1983): 40–67.

71. See Stephen Vlastos, "Opposition Movements in Early Meiji, 1868–1885,"

in *The Nineteenth Century,* ed. Jansen, 367–431, and Charles L. Yates, *Saigō Takamori: The Man Behind the Myth* (London: Kegan Paul International, 1995).

72. I borrow the phrase from Neil Waters, *Japan's Local Pragmatists: The Transition from Bakumatsu to Meiji in the Kawasaki Region* (Cambridge, Mass.: Council on East Asian Studies, Harvard University, 1983), 3.

73. Smith, *Native Sources of Japanese Industrialization,* 133–47.

74. Makihara, *Kyakubun to kokumin no aida.*

75. Andrew Gordon, *Labor and Imperial Democracy in Prewar Japan* (Berkeley: University of California Press, 1991).

76. Nicholas B. Dirks, *Castes of Mind: Colonialism and the Making of Modern India* (Princeton, N.J.: Princeton University Press, 2001).

4. VIOLENCE AND THE ABOLITION OF OUTCASTE STATUS

1. Even the few works in English on the Burakumin dwell only briefly on the abolition policy. See, for example, George O. Totten and Hiroshi Wagatsuma, "Emancipation: Growth and Transformation of a Political Movement," in *Japan's Invisible Race,* ed. DeVos and Wagatsuma, 33–67, which discusses the abolition edict in less than a page (p. 34); and Ian Neary, *Political Protest and Social Control in Pre-War Japan: The Origins of* Buraku *Liberation* (Atlantic Highlands, N.J.: Academic Press, 1989), which devotes about two pages (pp. 30–32) to the issue.

2. Kaiho Seiryō, "Zenchūdan" [1817], in *Kyōto no burakushi,* ed. Kyōto Burakushi Kenkyūjo 5: 505–7. On Kaiho's thought in general, see Tetsuo Najita, "Method and Analysis in the Conceptual Portrayal of Tokugawa Intellectual History," in *Japanese Thought in the Tokugawa Period, 1600–1868: Methods and Metaphors,* ed. Tetsuo Najita and Irwin Scheiner (Chicago: University of Chicago Press, 1978), 23–36.

3. See Buyō Inshi, *Seji kenmonroku* [ca. 1816], vol. 1 of *Kinsei shakai keizai sōsho,* ed. Honjō Eijirō, Tsuchiya Takao, Nakamura Naokatsu, and Kokushō Iwao (Tokyo: Kaizōsha, 1926), 271–74.

4. Hatanaka, "Kinsei 'senmin' mibunron no kadai," 181–83.

5. "Sonobe mura shōya nikki" [1858/10], in *Kyōto no burakushi,* ed. Kyōto Burakushi Kenkyūjo, 5: 63.

6. Senshū Tōtoku, "Eta o osamuru no gi" [1864], in *Buraku,* ed. Harada, 563–67.

7. "Kita machibugyō Koide Yamato-no-kami dono oyakusho ni oite kore o mōshiwatasu" [1868/1/13], in *Sabetsu no shosō,* ed. Hirota, 69–71. See also the documents collected as "Dan Naiki mibun hikiage ikken" [1868], in *Buraku,* ed. Harada, 459–84.

8. See the statements by Dan Naiki of 1869/5/12 and 1869/5/13, incorporated into the report by prison officials to Tokyo prefecture (1869/5), in Harada and Uesugi, eds., *"Kaihōrei" no seiritsu,* 139.

9. Dan Naoki to Tokyo Prefecture [1870/12], in *Buraku,* ed. Harada, 504–7.

10. See Takahashi Bonsen, "Buraku kaihō to Dan Naoki no kōgyō," in *Kinsei Kantō no hisabetsu buraku,* ed. Ishii Ryōsuke (Tokyo: Akashi Shoten, 1978), 143–74.

11. Katō Kōzō, "Hinin eta gohaishi no gi" [1869/4], in *"Kaihōrei" no seiritsu*, ed. Harada and Uesugi, 12. See also Okamoto Wataru's reminiscences of his contact with Katō, excerpted from Okamoto Wataru, *Tokushu buraku no kaihō* (Tokyo: Keiseisha Shoten, 1921), in ibid., 12–14.

12. Uchiyama Sōsuke, "Eta hinin no mibun gokaisei no gi" [1869/5], in *"Kaihōrei" no seiritsu*, ed. Harada and Uesugi, 18.

13. Ōe Takuzō to Ministry of Civil Affairs [1871/1 and 1871/3], in *Buraku*, ed. Harada, 507–10; the petitions are also reprinted in Harada and Uesugi, eds., *"Kaihōrei" no seiritsu*, 32–33, 39. Compare Ministry of Civil Affairs to Ministry of State [1869/3/15], in ibid., 37. See also Ōe's reminiscences, "Eta hinin shōgō haishi no tenmatsu o nobete eta no kigen ni oyobu," *Minzoku to rekishi* 2, no. 1 (July 10, 1919), reprinted in ibid., 34–36, in which he stresses the importance of the Charter Oath's fourth article (which called for the repudiation of the evil customs of the past) in guiding his thought about outcaste liberation. These reminiscences are reproduced in large part in Saiga Hiroyoshi, *Ōe Ten'ya denki* (Tokyo: Ōzorasha, 1987 [1926]), 129–46.

14. The order is reprinted in Kyōto Burakushi Kenkyūjo, ed., *Kyōto no burakushi*, 6: 47.

15. Ibid., 2–4.

16. Ibid., 48–50; see also the discussion in Imanishi, *Kindai Nihon no sabetsu to sei bunka*, 59.

17. Kyōto Burakushi Kenkyūjo, ed., *Kyōto no burakushi*, 6: 48–49.

18. "Hōjō-ken kanka shinheiminkan no kōsai ni kan shi, sa no tōri yutatsu su" [Mar. 5, 1876], in *Sabetsu no shosō*, ed. Hirota, 113.

19. Chiba-ken Shi Hensan Shingikai, ed., *Chiba-ken shiryō: Kindai hen: Meiji shoki 3*, 247.

20. Suzuki Ryō, "Jiyū minken undō to buraku mondai," in *Burakushi no kenkyū: Kindai hen*, ed. Buraku Mondai Kenkyūjo, 91–124.

21. See the examples in ibid., 93–104, and Imanishi, *Kindai Nihon no sabetsu to sei bunka*, 47–51. According to Iwai, "Shoki Meiji kokka to buraku mondai," 37–38, there were at least four hundred cases of disputes between commoners and Burakumin relating to shrines, including more than eighty related to the carrying of portable shrines in festivals, during the early Meiji period.

22. Imanishi, *Kindai Nihon no sabetsu to sei bunka*, 183, 186.

23. All important materials relating to the incident have been published in Nagamitsu Norikazu, ed., *Bizen, Bitchū, Mimasaka hyakushō ikki shiryō* (Tokyo: Kokusho Kankōkai, 1978), 5: 1973–2159. My account of the rebellion is based mostly on *Hōjō-ken shi*, reprinted in ibid., 1977–2012. See also a nearly contemporary account of the rebellion, "Meiji rokunen natsu Mimasaka zenkoku sōjō gaishi" [n.d.], in *Sabetsu no shosō*, ed. Hirota, 100–112.

24. Regarding *hinin-goshirae*: Kurachi Katsunao, "Mimasaka 'hinin sōdō' no dentō no hitokoma," *Okayama chihōshi kenkyū* 54 (July 1987), 28–29. In the sixth month of 1871, the Tsuyama domain, which controlled most of Mimasaka, did not mention *hinin* (as a status group) in a population report submitted to the central government, but it did refer to them in an order issued concerning the promulgation of the household-registration system in the third month of the

same year: see docs. 469 [1871/6/20] and 467 [1871/3/25] in Harada and Uesugi, eds., *"Kaihōrei" no seiritsu*, 397, 396. On local oral traditions, see Tsuyama no Ayumi Henshū Iinkai, ed., *Buraku kaihō undō: Tsuyama no ayumi* (Tsuyama: Zenkoku Buraku Kaihō Undō Rengōkai Tsuyama-shi Kyōgikai, 1986), 16. These traditions are corroborated in an account of a protest in the Tsuruta domain in 1868: doc. 462 [ca. 1870] in Harada and Uesugi, eds., *"Kaihōrei" no seiritsu*, 390–94. For accounts of the 1866 protest, see Anne Walthall, *Peasant Uprisings in Japan: A Critical Anthology of Peasant Histories* (Chicago: University of Chicago Press, 1991), 193–217; and Herbert Bix, *Peasant Protest in Japan, 1590–1884* (New Haven, Conn.: Yale University Press, 1986), 174–93.

25. See docs. 479 [1871/10], 480 [1871/10], and 478 [1871/8/17–1872/2/5], in Harada and Uesugi, eds., *"Kaihōrei" no seiritsu*, 406–7, 407, 399–406.

26. Doc. 482 [1871/11/12], in ibid., 408.

27. Tsuyama-shi Shi Hensan Iinkai, ed., *Tsuyama-shi shi* (Tsuyama: Tsuyama-shi, 1980), 6: 49–51.

28. Doc. 478 [1871/10/23], in Harada and Uesugi, eds., *"Kaihōrei" no seiritsu*, 399.

29. Tsuyama-shi Shi Hensan Iinkai, ed., *Tsuyama-shi shi*, 6: 51; doc. 486 [n.d.], in Harada and Uesugi, eds., *"Kaihōrei" no seiritsu*, 409.

30. Docs. 468 [1871/3] and 483 [1871/11], in Harada and Uesugi, eds., *"Kaihōrei" no seiritsu*, 396, 408.

31. Nakano Michiko and Zushi Tomonori, "Mimasaka Tsuyama han hisabetsu buraku kankei shiryō (2)," *Okayama buraku kaihō kenkyūjo kiyō* 3 (1985), 163.

32. Doc. 484 [1871/11], in Harada and Uesugi, eds., *"Kaihōrei" no seiritsu*, 408–9; on the Kaiami house, see Nakano and Zushi, "Mimasaka Tsuyama han hisabetsu buraku kankei shiryō (2)," 81–123.

33. Recall the order from Hōjō prefecture (March 5, 1876) decrying wealth-based discrimination within the Buraku community discussed in the previous chapter: Okayama-ken Buraku Kaihō Undō Rokujūnenshi Hensan Iinkai, ed., *Okayama-ken buraku mondai shiryōshū*, 64–65.

34. On charcoal production, see Iwama Kazuo, *Shibuzome ikki, Mimasaka ketsuzei ikki no shūhen: Aru bohimei e no chū* (Okayama: Okayama Buraku Mondai Kenkyūjo, 1996), 318.

35. See Imanishi, *Kindai Nihon no sabetsu to sei bunka*, 186–90.

36. Satake Akihiro, *Shuten dōji ibun* (Tokyo: Heibonsha, 1977), 197–252; Gerald Figal, *Civilization and Monsters: Spirits of Modernity in Meiji Japan* (Durham, N.C.: Duke University Press, 1999), 21–37. Interestingly, similar rumors circulated in colonial Korea. According to George Hicks, *The Comfort Women: Japan's Brutal Regime of Enforced Prostitution in the Second World War* (New York: Norton, 1995), 54, it was said of one Korean woman recruited as a so-called comfort woman in 1939 that, "her body oil was allegedly to be extracted for use in aircraft. Another [Korean] was sentenced to seven days in gaol for charging that a girl had been bought for ¥17 from her parents, for blood and oil extraction for use in Manchuria."

37. Hirota Masaki, *Bunmei kaika to minshū ishiki* (Tokyo: Aoki Shoten, 1980); Yoshinami Takashi, "Meiji rokunen Mimasaka ikki to sono eikyō," in

Meiji shonen kaihōrei hantai ikki no kenkyū, ed. Yoshinami Takashi (Tokyo: Akashi Shoten, 1987), 3–36; Iwama, *Shibuzome ikki, Mimasaka ketsuzei ikki no shūhen;* and Imanishi, *Kindai Nihon no sabetsu to sonraku.*

38. Nagamitsu, *Bizen, Bitchū, Mimasaka hyakushō ikki shiryō,* 5: 1989–2009.

39. Ibid., 1990.

40. Ishitaki Toyomi, " 'Kaihōrei' kara Chikuzen takeyari ikki e: Buraku yaki-uchi ni itaru hitsuzenteki katei no kentō," in *Meiji shonen kaihōrei hantai ikki no kenkyū,* ed. Yoshinami, 37–75; Imanishi, *Kindai Nihon no sabetsu to sei bunka;* Suzuki, "Jiyūminken undō to buraku mondai."

41. Yabuta Yutaka, *Kokuso to hyakushō ikki no kenkyū* (Tokyo: Azekura Shobō, 1992); Uchida Mitsuru, "Emono kara takeyari e," in *Ikki to shūen,* ed. Hosaka Satoru (Tokyo: Aoki Shoten, 2000), 117–42.

42. Hosaka Satoru, "Hyakushō ikki no sahō: Sono seiritsu to henshitsu," in *Ikki to shūen,* ed. Hosaka, 5–45.

43. Yabuta, *Kokuso to hyakushō ikki no kenkyū,* 190.

44. Ibid., 190–202.

45. Ibid., 202–11; Uchida, "Emono kara takeyari e," 132–36; Hosaka, "Hyakushō ikki no sahō."

46. Tsukamoto Manabu, *Shōrui o meguru seiji: Genroku no fōkuroaa* (Tokyo: Heibonsha, 1983), 7–81. See also Mizutani Mitsuhiro, *Edo wa yume ka* (Tokyo: Chikuma Shobō, 1992), 160–66, 231–34. As the following discussion reveals, Noel Perrin, *Giving Up the Gun: Japan's Reversion to the Sword* (Boulder, Colo.: Shambhala, 1980), seriously overstates the Tokugawa shogunate's success in disarming the countryside.

47. Yabuta, *Kokuso to hyakushō ikki no kenkyū,* 191.

48. Mori Yasuhiko, *Bakuhansei kokka no kiso kōzō: Sonraku kōzō no tenkai to nōmin tōsō* (Tokyo: Yoshikawa Kōbunkan, 1981); Yasumaru Yoshio, " 'Kangoku' no tanjō," in *Bakumatsu, ishinki no kokumin kokka keisei to bunka hen'yō,* ed. Nishikawa Nagao and Matsumiya Hideharu (Tokyo: Shin'yōsha, 1995), 279–312.

49. See for example, "Ofuregaki no hikae" [1860/i3], Hishinuma-kuyū monjo o-38, Chiba Prefectural Archives; Kamifukuoka-shi Kyōiku Iinkai and Kamifukuoka-shi Shi Hensan Iinkai, eds., *Kamifukuoka-shi shi: Shiryōhen,* vol. 2: *Kodai, chūsei, kinsei* (Kamifukuoka: Kamifukuoka-shi 1997), 604.

50. "Kantō otorishimari goshutsuyakusama gokaijō utsushi" [1861/2], Maejima-ke monjo *shi*-85, Chiba Prefectural Archives. Similar orders can be found among the documents of numerous Kantō villages; for example, see "Toridoshi rōnin toriosaekata gosatagaki" [1861/4], Asō-ke monjo *ku*-36, Chiba Prefectural Archives. The original order is reprinted in Ishii Ryōsuke and Harafuji Hiroshi, eds., *Bakumatsu ofuregaki shūsei,* doc. 5028 [1861/2] (Tokyo: Iwanami Shoten, 1994), 5: 538–39.

51. Yabuta, *Kokuso to hyakushō ikki no kenkyū,* 174–78; Nagamitsu, ed., *Bizen, Bitchū, Mimasaka hyakushō ikki shiryō* 5: 1981–82.

52. James W. White, "State Growth and Popular Protest in Tokugawa Japan," *Journal of Japanese Studies* 14, no. 1 (Winter 1988): 1–25, characterizes the shogunate's monopoly over violence as the cornerstone of its legitimacy.

53. "Kantō otorishimari goshutsuyakusama yori ofuregaki utsushi" [1867/4], Maejima-ke monjo so-22, Chiba Prefectural Archives; Kamifukuoka-shi Kyōiku Iinkai and Kamifukuoka-shi Shi Hensan Iinkai, ed., *Kamifukuoka-shi shi: Shiryōhen*, 2: 606.

54. See, for example, "Totō rōzekisha uttaegaki" [1864/1], Takagi-ke monjo *a*-22, and "Ofuregaki utsushi" [1861/6], Takagi-ke monjo *a*-33, Chiba Prefectural Archives.

55. Sugi Hitoshi, *Kinsei no chiiki to zaison bunka* (Tokyo: Yoshikawa Kōbunkan, 2001), 259–73. The Tama region was by no means the only area to see this sort of phenomenon. See, for example, Kurachi Katsunao, "Bakumatsu no minshū to bugei," *Okayama chihōshi kenkyū* 56 (1988): 1–8, regarding a number of groups active in the Okayama domain.

56. Patricia Sippel, "Popular Protest in Early Modern Japan: The Bushū Outburst," *Harvard Journal of Asiatic Studies* 37, no. 2 (Dec. 1977): 273–322.

57. M. William Steele, "The Rise and Fall of the Shōgitai: A Social Drama," in *Conflict in Modern Japanese History,* ed. Tetsuo Najita and J. Victor Koschmann (Princeton, N.J.: Princeton University Press, 1982), 128–44.

58. Sugi, *Kinsei no chiiki to zaison bunka,* 267–71. Sugi notes that the use of the term *kigasa* is unusual in legal documents. He compares it with *furachi,* which is extremely common in documents concerning commoners' behavior. *Furachi* suggests a failing committed by one who is not intelligent or knowledgeable enough to follow the rules necessary to maintain order: one guilty of *furachi* has done wrong, but without questioning the legitimacy of the underlying order. *Kigasa,* conversely, is the attitude of an underdog who behaves as if could actually win, and thus suggests an active flaunting of status-based rules of social interaction.

59. See the extremely complex networks described by Kanda, "Saikoku no kyokaku to chiiki shakai," including a description of local authorities' attempts to limit the violence of traveling sumo wrestlers, who had a tendency to trash inns, taverns, and other public establishments and to get into fights with locals.

60. Nagamitsu, ed., *Bizen, Bitchū, Mimasaka hyakushō ikki shiryō* 5: 2000–2001.

61. The order was issued on June 5, 1873. See Okayama-ken Buraku Kaihō Undō Rokujūnenshi Hensan Iinkai, ed., *Okayama-ken buraku mondai shiryōshū,* 104–5.

62. Nagamitsu, ed., *Bizen, Bitchū, Mimasaka hyakushō ikki shiryō* 5: 2000.

63. Ibid.

64. Ibid., 1977–78, 2002–3.

65. Ibid., 2001.

66. Ibid.

67. Ibid.

68. Ibid.

69. Ibid., 1981.

70. Ibid., 1990, 2003.

71. White, "State Growth and Popular Protest in Tokugawa Japan."

72. Niigata-ken, ed., *Niigata-ken shi: Shiryōhen* (Niigata: Niigata-ken, 1982), 15: 572–76.

73. Irwin Scheiner, "Benevolent Lords and Honorable Peasants: Rebellion and Peasant Consciousness in Tokugawa Japan," in *Japanese Thought in the Tokugawa Period*, ed. Najita and Scheiner, 39–62.

74. Quoted in Imanishi, *Kindai Nihon no sabetsu to sei bunka*, 187.

75. Imanishi, *Kindai Nihon no sabetsu to sonraku*, 104–5.

76. See Vlastos, "Opposition Movements in Early Meiji, 1868–1885."

77. In addition to ibid., see David L. Howell, "Visions of the Future in Meiji Japan," in *Historical Perspectives on Contemporary East Asia*, ed. Merle Goldman and Andrew Gordon (Cambridge, Mass.: Harvard University Press, 2000), 85–118.

5. AINU IDENTITY AND THE EARLY MODERN STATE

1. I will use Ezochi in the sense it was used by Japanese during the Tokugawa period, to refer to those areas of Hokkaido, southern Sakhalin, and the southern Kuril Islands inhabited by the Ainu. The Ezochi is therefore distinct from Ezo, the premodern term for the island of Hokkaido, insofar as it both comprised areas beyond Hokkaido and excluded that part of southern Hokkaido that constituted the Matsumae domain's home territory (conventionally known as the Wajinchi).

2. Brett L. Walker, *The Conquest of Ainu Lands: Ecology and Culture in Japanese Expansion, 1590–1800* (Berkeley: University of California Press, 2001).

3. Kamiya Nobuyuki, "Nihon kinsei no tōitsu to Dattan," in *Nihon zenkindai no kokka to taigai kankei*, ed. Tanaka Takeo (Tokyo: Yoshikawa Kōbunkan, 1987), 145–76.

4. Emori Susumu, *Hokkaidō kinseishi no kenkyū* (Sapporo: Hokkaidō Shuppan Kikaku Sentaa, 1982), 159–61; Kaiho Mineo, *Kinsei Ezochi seiritsushi no kenkyū* (Tokyo: San'ichi Shobō, 1984), 177–206.

5. Walker, *The Conquest of Ainu Lands*, 48–72, gives a detailed account of Shakushain's War. Other discussions of the conflict and its significance include Emori, *Hokkaidō kinseishi no kenkyū*, 183–89, and particularly Ōi Haruo, "'Shakushain no ran (Kanbun 9-nen Ezo no ran)' no saikentō," *Hoppō bunka kenkyū* 21 (1992): 1–66.

6. Kikuchi Isao, *Bakuhan taisei to Ezochi* (Tokyo: Yūzankaku, 1984), 50–52.

7. "Ezo hōki" [n.d.], in *Tanken, kikō, chishi (Hokuhen hen)*, ed. Takakura Shin'ichirō (Tokyo: San'ichi Shobō, 1969), 643–45.

8. Kikuchi Isao, *Hoppōshi no naka no kinsei Nihon* (Tokyo: Azekura Shobō, 1991), 124–25.

9. "Ezo hōki," 646–47.

10. On the demarcation of the Ezochi and Wajinchi as areas of Ainu and Japanese residence and its political and economic significance, see David L. Howell, *Capitalism from Within: Economy, Society, and the State in a Japanese Fishery* (Berkeley: University of California Press, 1995), 24–49.

11. Walker, *The Conquest of Ainu Lands*.

12. I examine the development of the fishery in detail in Howell, *Capitalism from Within*.

13. Yuriko Fukasawa, *Ainu Archaeology as Ethnohistory: Iron Technology*

among the Saru Ainu of Hokkaido, Japan, in the 17th Century (Oxford: British Archaeological Reports, 1998), 51–67, has found archaeological evidence to suggest that the Ainu engaged in metalworking, including the forging and smelting of iron, on a small scale until at least 1669, when the Matsumae domain prohibited smithing in the wake of Shakushain's War, and perhaps secretly thereafter. The center of ironworking in Hokkaido was in the Hidaka region of eastern Hokkaido, where Japanese influence was relatively weak. Nonetheless, the Ainu were not able to fulfill their need for iron implements indigenously because they depended on scrap iron from Honshu as the raw material for their own activities.

14. For a similar instance of outside manufactures taking on an increasingly important cultural role, see Richard White, *The Roots of Dependency: Subsistence, Environment, and Social Change among the Choctaws, Pawnees, and Navajos* (Lincoln: University of Nebraska Press, 1983).

15. Ōi Haruo, "Satsumon bunka to iwayuru 'Ainu bunka' to no kankei ni tsuite," *Hoppō bunka kenkyū* 15 (1984), 171. A similar situation can be seen among the Choctaws of Mississippi in the eighteenth century, though they did not embrace market relations with the English and French until the Europeans introduced rum into trade. White, *The Roots of Dependency*, chaps. 1–4. Sake may have played a similar role in Japanese-Ainu relations.

16. Emori, *Hokkaidō kinseishi no kenkyū*, 157–59.

17. Kaiho Mineo, *Chūsei no Ezochi* (Tokyo: Yoshikawa Kōbunkan, 1987), 150–72.

18. Donald L. Philippi, *Songs of Gods, Songs of Humans: The Epic Tradition of the Ainu* (Princeton, N.J.: Princeton University Press; Tokyo: University of Tokyo Press, 1979), 178; Iwasaki Naoko, "Zenkindai Ainu no 'takara' to sono shakaiteki kinō," *Shirin* 78 (Sept. 1995): 107–28. See also Iwasaki Naoko, *Nihon kinsei no Ainu shakai* (Tokyo: Azekura Shobō, 1998).

19. Okuda Osami, personal communication, 1996. Interpretation of the *yukar* has long been a subject of debate among historians. See Emori Susumu, "Omoro to yūkar," in *Chiiki to etonosu*, ed. Arano, Ishii, and Murai, 251–85. For translations of selections of *yukar* into English, see Philippi, *Songs of Gods, Songs of Humans*.

20. Watanabe Hitoshi has called the *iyomante* the defining element of Ainu culture. See his "Ainu bunka no seiritsu: Minzoku, rekishi, kōko shogaku no gōryūten," in *Hoppō bunka to nantō bunka*, ed. Saitō Tadashi (Tokyo: Yoshikawa Kōbunkan, 1987), 220–43. See also Inukai Tetsuo and Natori Takemitsu, "Iomante (Ainu no kuma matsuri) no bunkateki igi to sono keishiki," *Hoppō bunka kenkyū hōkoku* 2 (Oct. 1939): 1–34 and 3 (May 1940): 1–57, which is based on fieldwork conducted in the late 1930s.

21. Sasaki Toshikazu, "Iomante kō: Shamo ni yoru Ainu bunka rikai no kōsatsu," *Rekishigaku kenkyū* 613 (Nov. 1990): 111–20; Utagawa Hiroshi, *Iomante no kōkogaku* (Tokyo: University of Tokyo Press, 1989), 34, 101. Sasaki bases his argument on documentary sources, while Utagawa relies on archaeological evidence. See also Watanabe, "Ainu bunka no seiritsu," 225–26.

22. Mogami Tokunai, "Ezo no kuni fūzoku ninjō no sata" [1790], in *Tanken, kikō, chishi*, ed. Takakura, 445.

23. On these ceremonies, see Walker, *The Conquest of Ainu Lands*, 204–26; Inagaki Reiko, "Kinsei Ezochi ni okeru girei shihai no tokushitsu: Uimamu, omusha no hensen o tōshite," in *Minshū seikatsu to shinkō, shisō*, ed. Minshūshi Kenkyūkai (Tokyo: Yūzankaku, 1985), 111–30; Inagaki Reiko, "Ainu minzoku ni taisuru girei shihai: 'Uimamu,' 'omusha' ni tsuite," in *Kita kara no Nihonshi*, ed. Hokkaidō-Tōhoku Shi Kenkyūkai (Tokyo: Sanseidō, 1988), 1: 315–21; and Takakura Shin'ichirō, *Ainu seisakushi* (Tokyo: Nihon Hyōronsha, 1942), 77–85. A lengthy synopsis of this last work has been published in English as Takakura Shin'ichirō, "The Ainu of Northern Japan: A Study in Conquest and Acculturation," trans. and annot. John A. Harrison, *Transactions of the American Philosophical Society*, new series, vol. 50, part 4 (Apr. 1960).

24. On the 1633 performance of the *uimam*, see Inagaki, "Kinsei Ezochi ni okeru girei shihai no tokushitsu," 114; for a general discussion of changes in the significance of the ceremony over time, see Takakura, *Ainu seisakushi*, 77–85, 172; Takakura, "The Ainu of Northern Japan," 67–69.

25. Furukawa Koshōken, "Tōyū zakki" [1789], as quoted in Kaiho, *Kinsei Ezochi seiritsushi no kenkyū*, 213.

26. Inagaki, "Kinsei Ezochi ni okeru girei shihai no tokushitsu," 115. See Takakura, *Ainu seisakushi*, 223–26, for the *uimam* schedule for 1851–55 and sample gift lists. On investiture *uimam*, see Mogami Tokunai, "Watarishima hikki" [1808], in *Tanken, kikō, chishi*, ed. Takakura, 525.

27. The dominance of the Japanese was acknowledged even in cultural practices still under the control of the Ainu, such as the *iyomante*. Japanese in attendance—typically fishing contractors and their agents—were given the place of honor among the guests. Sasaki, "Iomante kō."

28. See Takakura, *Ainu seisakushi*, 219–23, for samples of injunctions read at various *umsa*. See also the discussion of official gatherings of Ainu and Japanese at the Nemuro fishery in 1858 in Kikuchi, *Bakuhan taisei to Ezochi*, 108–12.

29. Twenty-three between 1823 and 1833 are listed in "Bunsei roku hitsujidoshi irai Ezojin omemie kenjōhin narabi ni kudasaremono shirabegaki" [n.d.], Hakodate Municipal Library; another five between 1839 and 1841 are listed in "Tenpō jū tsuchinotoidoshi gogatsu yori omemie Ezojin kenjōbutsu narabi ni kudasare shina" [n.d.], Hakodate Municipal Library.

30. Namikawa Kenji, *Kinsei Nihon to hoppō shakai* (Tokyo: Sanseidō, 1992), 54.

31. Ibid., 55–58. After 1662, there are references to *uimam* in Tsugaru records in 1677, 1688, 1690, 1691, 1701, and 1707.

32. Ibid., 59.

33. Ibid., 59–63.

34. Inagaki, "Kinsei Ezochi ni okeru girei shihai no tokushitsu," 123–24.

35. Kamiya Nobuyuki, *Bakuhansei kokka no Ryūkyū shihai* (Tokyo: Azekura Shobō, 1990), 255.

36. Eric Hobsbawm, "Introduction: Inventing Traditions," in *The Invention of Tradition*, ed. Eric Hobsbawm and Terence Ranger (Cambridge: Cambridge University Press, 1983), 1–14.

37. Takakura, *Ainu seisakushi*, 77; Inagaki, "Kinsei Ezochi ni okeru girei shihai no tokushitsu," 112–14. On "trade" as the only meaning of *uimam* in Ainu,

see John Batchelor, *An Ainu-English-Japanese Dictionary,* 4th ed. (Tokyo: Iwanami Shoten, 1938), 522; compare the entries for *umusa* (that is, *umsa*), 532. Ainu and Japanese, incidentally, are not related languages: Masayoshi Shibatani, *The Languages of Japan* (Cambridge: Cambridge University Press, 1990), 5–8.

38. Philippi, *Songs of Gods, Songs of Humans,* for example, 175–84, 315–16.

39. Mogami, "Ezo no kuni fūzoku ninjō no sata," 450–51; Kushihara Masamine, "Igen zokuwa" [1793], in *Tanken, kikō, chishi,* ed. Takakura, 516–17. Mogami, "Watarishima hikki," 525, makes a similar point about the function of *uimam.*

40. For example, Mogami, "Ezo no kuni fūzoku ninjō no sata," 451, relates how Ainu participants at an *umsa* in 1785 carefully checked the contents of the sake barrels given to them. See also Philippi, *Songs of Gods, Songs of Humans,* 247–53, for a *yukar* about a treacherous Japanese interpreter. Walker, *The Conquest of Ainu Lands,* 208–12, analyzes this *yukar* in detail.

41. Kaiho Mineo, *Bakuhansei kokka to Hokkaidō* (Tokyo: San'ichi Shobō, 1978), 228–29.

42. See ibid., 242–43, for a description of the exact correspondence between the posts held by Ainu and Japanese peasant officials. See also Iwasaki Naoko, "Ainu 'otona' kō," in *Nihon shakai no shiteki kōzō: Kinsei, kindai,* ed. Asao Naohiro Kyōju Taikan Kinenkai (Kyoto: Shibunkaku Shuppan, 1995), 251–74.

43. Matsuura Takeshirō, "Kinsei Ezo jinbutsushi" [mid-1850s], in *Tanken, kikō, chishi,* ed. Takakura, 752. For a translation into contemporary Japanese, see Matsuura Takeshirō, *Ainu jinbutsushi,* trans. Sarashina Genzō and Yoshida Yutaka (Tokyo: Nōsangyoson Bunka Kyōkai, 1981).

44. The uprising was the most serious instance of Ainu resistance to Japanese control after 1672. For a brief summary, see Kikuchi, *Hoppōshi no naka no kinsei Nihon,* 303–13. The most comprehensive account is Iwasaki Naoko, "Kinsei kōki ni okeru tashazō no sōshutsu: 'Kunashiri-Menashi no tatakai' no kaishaku to Ainu-zō," *Nihonshi kenkyū* 403 (Mar. 1996): 65–96.

45. Philippi, *Songs of Gods, Songs of Humans,* 175–84, 315–16.

46. See Howell, *Capitalism from Within,* 24–92.

47. Tajima Yoshiya, "Basho ukeoisei kōki no Ainu no gyogyō to sono tokushitsu: Nishi Ezochi Yoichi basho no baai," in *Zenkindai no Nihon to higashi Ajia,* ed. Tanaka, 271–95; Iwasaki, "Kinsei kōki ni okeru tashazō no sōshutsu." For a typical portrayal of the mistreatment of Ainu workers, see Howell, *Capitalism from Within,* 40. On the disruption of Ainu society by the predations of Japanese fishers, see the numerous examples cited in Matsuura, "Kinsei Ezo jinbutsushi," passim.

48. Kikuchi, *Hoppōshi no naka no kinsei Nihon,* 325.

49. See, for example, the nineteenth-century population statistics in Kaiho Yōko, *Kindai hoppōshi: Ainu minzoku to josei to* (Tokyo: San'ichi Shobō, 1992), 47. On the devastating impact of smallpox on the Ainu population and shogunal attempts to demonstrate official benevolence through the provision of Jennerian vaccinations, see Brett L. Walker, "The Early Modern Japanese State and Ainu Vaccinations: Redefining the Body Politic, 1799–1868," *Past and Present* 163 (May 1999): 121–60.

50. Kikuchi, *Hoppōshi no naka no kinsei Nihon*, 313–15.

51. Sasaki Toshikazu, "Kyōsei kotan no hensen to kōzō ni tsuite: Toku ni Abuta-kotan o chūshin ni," in *Hokkaidō no kenkyū: Kōkohen II*, ed. Ishizuki Kisao (Osaka: Seibundō, 1984), 275–95.

52. Kikuchi, *Hoppōshi no naka no kinsei Nihon*, 315.

53. Matsuura Takeshirō, "Bochū nisshi," cited in ibid.

54. Walker, *The Conquest of Ainu Lands*, 8–12, 206.

55. Richard White, *The Middle Ground: Indians, Empires, and Republics in the Great Lakes Region, 1650–1815* (New York: Cambridge University Press, 1991), x.

56. White makes his point about brutality and violence quickly and forcefully: ibid., 1–10.

57. See Howell, "Ainu Ethnicity and the Boundaries of the Early Modern Japanese State."

58. Cornelius Coen, *Voyage to Cathay, Tartary, and the Gold- and Silver-Rich Islands East of Japan, 1643: The Journal of Cornelius Jansz. Coen Relating to the Voyage of Marten Gerritsz. Fries to the North and East of Japan*, trans. and ed. Willem C. H. Robert (Amsterdam: Philo Press, 1975), 187.

59. See, for example, Matsuura, "Kinsei Ezo jinbutsushi."

60. Namikawa, *Kinsei Nihon to hoppō shakai*, 171–75, 260, 290–92.

61. See Suzue Eiichi, *Hokkaidō chōson seidoshi no kenkyū* (Sapporo: Hokkaido University Press, 1985).

62. Compare Thongchai, *Siam Mapped*.

6. THE GEOGRAPHY OF CIVILIZATION

1. Ronald P. Toby, *State and Diplomacy in Early Modern Japan: Asia in the Development of the Tokugawa Bakufu* (Princeton, N.J.: Princeton University Press, 1984); Arano Yasunori, *Kinsei Nihon to higashi Ajia* (Tokyo: University of Tokyo Press, 1988); Tessa Morris-Suzuki, "A Descent into the Past: The Frontier in the Construction of Japanese Identity," in *Multicultural Japan*, ed. Denoon, Hudson, McCormack, and Morris-Suzuki, 81–94.

2. See Ronald Toby, "The 'Indianness' of Iberia and Changing Japanese Iconographies of Other," in *Implicit Understandings: Observing, Reporting, and Reflecting on the Encounters between Europeans and Other Peoples in the Early Modern Era*, ed. Stuart Schwartz (New York: Cambridge University Press, 1994), 324–51; Murai, *Ajia no naka no chūsei Nihon*, 32–59; and Hino Tatsuo, "Kinsei bungaku ni arawareta ikokuzō," in *Sekaishi no naka no kinsei*, ed. Asao Naohiro (Tokyo: Chūō Kōronsha, 1991), 265–304.

3. Private Chinese ships (sometimes, in fact, from Southeast Asia) were allowed to trade at the port of Nagasaki, but this trade was not accompanied by any official diplomatic contact. On the origins and functioning of the Tokugawa regime's official foreign relations, including an account of the failure of attempts to establish official ties with China, see Toby, *State and Diplomacy in Early Modern Japan*. On the similarities between the Tokugawa "national seclusion" *(sakoku)* and Chinese prohibitions on unofficial foreign contact *(haijin; J. kaikin)*, see Arano, *Kinsei Nihon to higashi Ajia*. On the place of China in gen-

eral in early modern Japan, see Marius B. Jansen, *China in the Tokugawa World* (Cambridge, Mass.: Harvard University Press, 1992).

4. On relations with Korea, see Tashiro Kazui, "Foreign Relations during the Edo Period: *Sakoku* Reexamined," *Journal of Japanese Studies* 8, no. 2 (Summer 1982): 283–306.

5. Arano, *Kinsei Nihon to higashi Ajia,* 43–44.

6. Asato Susumu, "Ryūkyū ōkoku no keisei," in *Chiiki to etonosu,* ed. Arano, Ishii, and Murai, 128–29.

7. Hayashi Shihei, *Sankoku tsūran zusetsu* [1786], as cited in Bob Tadashi Wakabayashi, *Anti-Foreignism and Western Learning in Early-Modern Japan* (Cambridge, Mass.: Council on East Asian Studies, Harvard University, 1986), 73.

8. There were small populations of Nivkhi and Uilta in southern Sakhalin, and by the time of the Sakhalin-Kuril exchange of 1875 a group of Aleuts had been brought to the central Kurils by Russia.

9. Kikuchi, "Kyōkai to etonosu," 64–65.

10. The standard (if dated) English-language survey of Ryukyuan and Okinawan history is George Kerr, *Okinawa: The History of an Island People* (Rutland, Vt.: Tuttle, 1958). Gregory Smits, *Visions of Ryūkyū: Identity and Ideology in Early-Modern Thought and Politics* (Honolulu: University of Hawai'i Press, 1999), and Mitsugu Sakihara, *A Brief History of Okinawa Based on the Omoro Sōshi* (Tokyo: Honpo Shoseki Press, 1987), treat the history of the early modern Ryukyu kingdom in detail.

11. Kamiya Nobuyuki, "Tai-Min seisaku to Ryūkyū shihai: Ikoku kara 'ikoku' e," in *Bakuhansei kokka to iiki, ikoku,* ed. Katō Eiichi, Kitajima Manji, and Fukaya Katsumi (Tokyo: Azekura Shobō, 1989), 270–71.

12. See Toby, *State and Diplomacy in Early Modern Japan,* and Ronald P. Toby, "Carnival of the Aliens: Korean Embassies in Edo-period Art and Popular Culture," *Monumenta Nipponica* 41, no. 4 (Winter 1986): 415–56.

13. Kamiya, *Bakuhansei kokka no Ryūkyū shihai,* 242–68.

14. Taminato Tomoaki and Kaiho Mineo, "Bakuhanseika no Ryūkyū to Ezochi," in *Iwanami kōza Nihon no rekishi* (Tokyo: Iwanami Shoten, 1976), 11: 266.

15. See Philip A. Kuhn, *Soulstealers: The Chinese Sorcery Scare of 1768* (Cambridge, Mass.: Harvard University Press, 1990).

16. Kikuchi Isao, "Kinsei ni okeru Ezo-kan to 'Nihon fūzoku,' " in *Kita kara no Nihonshi,* ed. Hokkaidō-Tōhoku Shi Kenkyūkai, 1: 216–21, notes that in China, Korea, Ryukyu, and Japan men wore their hair in distinctive ways, with the hair piled on top of the head in some way, divided into two bunches left and right, or covered with some kind of hat. See also Alf Hiltebeitel and Barbara D. Miller, eds., *Hair: Its Power and Meaning in Asian Cultures* (Albany: State University of New York Press, 1998).

17. Kikuchi, *Hoppōshi no naka no kinsei Nihon,* 71.

18. J. R. McEwan, *The Political Writings of Ogyū Sorai* (Cambridge: Cambridge University Press, 1969), 37–38.

19. The Edict in 100 Articles (Osadamegaki hyakkajō), the compendium of penal laws first collected in 1742, explicitly prohibited commoners from bearing two swords without official leave. See Article 94 in Hall, *Japanese Feudal Law,*

249. John Michael Rogers, "The Development of the Military Profession in Tokugawa Japan" (Ph.D. diss., Harvard University, 1998), 16–26, traces the evolution of sword bearing as the prerogative of the samurai.

20. Katō, "Kinsei no shōgaisha to mibun seido."

21. Tsukada, *Mibunsei shakai to shimin shakai*, 201–2.

22. Wakabayashi, *Anti-Foreignism and Western Learning in Early-Modern Japan*, 26, 27. Tsukamoto Manabu, *Kinsei saikō: Chihō no shiten kara* (Tokyo: Nihon Editaa Sukūru Shuppanbu, 1986), 76–83, makes essentially the same point.

23. Wakabayashi, *Anti-Foreignism and Western Learning in Early-Modern Japan*, 18, 28.

24. Ibid., 28–29.

25. Tsukamoto, *Kinsei saikō*, 75–105, esp. 83–89.

26. Ibid., 87, citing Terajima Ryōan, *Wakan sansai zue* [1712].

27. In Tsukamoto's phrase, *inaka wa 'i'-naka* (the countryside *[inaka]* is in the midst *[naka]* of barbarism *[i]*): ibid., 90–97.

28. Kikuchi, *Bakuhan taisei to Ezochi*, 216–20.

29. Kikuchi, *Hoppōshi no naka no kinsei Nihon*, 75–76.

30. Tsukamoto, *Kinsei saikō*, 83–89.

31. Kikuchi, *Bakuhan taisei to Ezochi*, 158–60.

32. Kaiho, *Bakuhansei kokka to Hokkaidō*, 9–34.

33. Kaiho Mineo, *Kinsei no Hokkaidō* (Tokyo: Kyōikusha, 1979), 72–73, 75.

34. Matsumiya Kanzan, "Ezo dan hikki" [1710], in *Tanken, kikō, chishi*, ed. Takakura, 398.

35. "Ezo hōki," 647–49.

36. Emori, *Hokkaidō kinseishi no kenkyū*, 74–139. See also the discussion of the Ainu of Satsukari village in Kaiho, *Bakuhansei kokka to Hokkaidō*, 225–31.

37. Murabayashi Gensuke, *Genshi manpitsu fudo nenpyō* [1804–18], in *Michinoku sōsho*, ed. Aomori Ken Bunkazai Hogo Kyōkai, reprint ed. (Tokyo: Kokusho Kankōkai, 1982 [1960]), 6: 138, 150, 246.

38. Barth, "Introduction," 9.

39. The following discussion is based on Kikuchi, *Bakuhan taisei to Ezochi*, 153–76; Kikuchi, "Kinsei ni okeru Ezo-kan to 'Nihon fūzoku,'" 206–29.

40. See the examples presented in Kitagawa Morisada, *Morisada mankō*, ed. Asakura Haruhiko and Kashikawa Shūichi (Tokyo: Tōkyōdō Shoten, 1992 [1853]), 2: 15–28.

41. Kikuchi, "Kinsei ni okeru Ezo-kan to 'Nihon fūzoku,'" 226.

42. On the Ainu role as supervisors at fisheries, see Tajima, "Basho ukeoisei kōki no Ainu no gyogyō to sono tokushitsu"; on liaisons between fishers and Ainu women, see Matsuura, "Kinsei Ezo jinbutsushi," 732, 757.

43. Mogami, "Ezo no kuni ninjō fūzoku no sata," 460.

44. Mogami, "Watarishima hikki," 523.

45. Kikuchi, "Kinsei ni okeru Ezo-kan to 'Nihon fūzoku,'" 208–16; Kikuchi, *Bakuhan taisei to Ezochi*, 166–68; Shimomura Isao, "Ainu no sajin," *Nihon rekishi* 566 (July 1995): 1–20; Sasaki Toshikazu, "Ainu-e ga egaita sekai," in *Ainu bunka ni manabu* (1990), as cited in ibid., 2.

46. See Kikuchi Isao, *Etorofu-tō: Tsukurareta kokkyō* (Tokyo: Yoshikawa Kōbunkan, 1999).

47. Kaiho Mineo, *Rettō hoppōshi kenkyū nōto: Kinsei no Hokkaidō o chūshin to shite* (Sapporo: Hokkaidō Shuppan Kikaku Sentaa, 1986), 180–85.

48. Kikuchi, "Kinsei ni okeru Ezo-kan to 'Nihon fūzoku,'" 224–26.

49. Ibid., 208–16; Kikuchi, *Bakuhan taisei to Ezochi,* 166–68.

50. For the magistrates' basic statement of policy, see "Shihaimuki ichidō kokoroekata narabi ni basho basho ukeoinin mōshiwatashi an" [1855] and "Ijin satoshigaki an" [1855], as cited in Takakura, *Ainu seisakushi,* 343–46.

51. Kasahara Gengo, "Ezojin fūzoku no gi mōshiokuri sho" [1856], Resource Collection for Northern Studies (hereafter RCNS), MS 107, Hokkaido University Library (Sapporo). See also similar programs at the Akkeshi fishing station: Rihei, "Ezo jinmin e osatoshi mōshiwatashi tsūben kakitsuke" [1856], MS 109, RCNS.

52. Kikuchi, *Hoppōshi no naka no kinsei Nihon,* 11, 352, referring to incidents in 1807.

53. Kikuchi, *Bakuhan taisei to Ezochi,* 164–65.

54. Kubota Shizō, "Kyōwa shieki" [1857], in *Tanken, kikō, chishi,* ed. Takakura, 239.

55. Ibid.

56. Matsuura, "Kinsei Ezo jinbutsushi," 748.

57. Kubota, "Kyōwa shieki," 235, 239.

58. Ibid., 239.

59. Kasahara, "Ezojin fūzoku no gi mōshiokuri sho."

60. Takakura, *Ainu seisakushi,* 382–83.

61. Ibid., 375–76. For a contemporary account of an *uimam* held during the period of shogunal control, see "Dojin omemie ni tsuki nikki" [1859], in *Saisenkai shiryō,* ed. Takakura Shin'ichirō (Sapporo: Hokkaidō Shuppan Kikaku Sentaa, 1982), 99–125.

62. Kikuchi, *Hoppōshi no naka no kinsei Nihon,* 20–23, 110–11.

63. Kikuchi, *Bakuhan taisei to Ezochi,* 107.

64. See ibid., 69–88, for a thorough and fascinating analysis of the origins and development of the Yoshitsune legend.

65. Namikawa, *Kinsei Nihon to hoppō shakai,* 252–63; Kikuchi, *Bakuhan taisei to Ezochi,* 216–22. Honda Yūko, "Kinsei Hokkaidō ni okeru attus no sanbutsuka to ryūtsū," *Hokkaidō-ritsu Ainu minzoku bunka kenkyū sentaa kenkyū kiyō* 8 (2002): 1–40, describes the commodification of *attus* beginning in the late eighteenth century.

66. The following discussion is based on Namikawa, *Kinsei Nihon to hoppō shakai,* 264–302.

67. The document, "Etorofu-tō hyōryūki," is cited in ibid., 271.

68. Ibid., 279–82.

69. Ibid., 278–79, 290–96.

7. CIVILIZATION AND ENLIGHTENMENT

1. Oku Takenori, *Bunmei kaika to minshū: Kindai Nihon seishinshi no danshō* (Tokyo: Shinhyōron, 1993), 5–44, 159–90.

2. Douglas R. Howland, *Translating the West: Language and Political Rea-*

son in Nineteenth-Century Japan (Honolulu: University of Hawai'i Press, 2002), 38–45; quote from p. 43.

3. See Narita Ryūichi, "Teito Tōkyō," in *Iwanami kōza Nihon tsūshi* 16: 175–214.

4. Two of Fukuzawa's representative works have been translated into English: Fukuzawa Yukichi, *An Encouragement of Learning*, trans. David A. Dilworth and Umeyo Hirano (Tokyo: Sophia University Press, 1969), and Fukuzawa Yukichi, *Outline of a Theory of Civilization*, trans. David A. Dilworth and G. Cameron Hurst (Tokyo: Sophia University Press, 1973). Studies of Fukuzawa's thought in English include Carmen Blacker, *The Japanese Enlightenment: A Study of the Writings of Fukuzawa Yukichi* (Cambridge: Cambridge University Press, 1964), and Albert M. Craig, "Fukuzawa Yukichi: The Philosophical Foundations of Meiji Nationalism," in *Political Development in Modern Japan*, ed. Robert E. Ward (Princeton, N.J.: Princeton University Press, 1968), 99–148. For selections from the journal of the Meiji Six Society, see William R. Braisted, trans., *Meiroku Zasshi: Journal of the Japanese Enlightenment* (Cambridge, Mass.: Harvard University Press, 1976). Howland, *Translating the West*, 15–18, briefly surveys the literature on the intellectual movement for civilization and enlightenment.

5. On Western thought and its popularity among rural elites, see Irokawa Daikichi, *The Culture of the Meiji Period*, trans. ed. Marius B. Jansen (Princeton, N.J.: Princeton University Press, 1985), and Roger Bowen, *Rebellion and Democracy in Meiji Japan* (Berkeley: University of California Press, 1980). See also Shimazaki, *Before the Dawn*.

6. Howland, *Translating the West*, is the most recent and most intellectually sophisticated contribution to this literature.

7. Throughout his autobiography, Fukuzawa emphasizes how innovative his ideas and outlook were. See Fukuzawa Yukichi, *The Autobiography of Fukuzawa Yukichi*, trans. Eiichi Kiyooka (Tokyo: Hokuseido, 1948).

8. See, for example, Katō Sukekazu, "Bunmei kaika" [1873–74], in *Meiji bunka zenshū: Bunmei kaika hen*, ed. Yoshino, 5.

9. Oku, *Bunmei kaika to minshū*, 171.

10. For an explicit statement of this sentiment, see Hagiwara Otohiko, "Tōkyō kaika hanjōshi" [1874], in *Meiji bunka zenshū: Fūzoku hen*, ed. Meiji Bunka Kenkyūkai (Tokyo: Nihon Hyōron Shinsha, 1955 [1928]), 236.

11. An analogous concern with hair and clothing can be seen in China in the early twentieth century. See Karl Gerth, *China Made: Consumer Culture and the Creation of the Nation* (Cambridge, Mass.: Harvard University Asia Center, 2003), 68–121.

12. Oku, *Bunmei kaika to minshū*, 164.

13. The ordinances and explanatory notes can be found in Ogi Shinzō, Kumakura Isao, and Ueno Chizuko, eds., *Fūzoku/sei* (Tokyo: Iwanami Shoten, 1990), 3–29; see also the illustrations relating to customs culled from pictorial guides to the ordinances in ibid., 30–39. Albert G. Hess and Shigeyo Murayama, *Everyday Law in Japanese Folk Art: Daily Life in Meiji Japan as Seen Through Petty Law Violations* (Aalen: Scientia Verlag, 1980), reprint various pictorial materials related to the ordinances, but the quality of the reproductions is poor.

14. Ogi, Kumakura, and Ueno, eds., *Fūzoku/sei*, 20.

15. "Joshi no danpatsu sanbi," *Chiba shinbun shūroku* (1871/11); "Joshi no danpatsu wa miru ni shinobizu," *Shinbun zasshi* [Mar. 1872]; "Fujoshi no kami wa jūrai dōri," ibid. [Apr. 1872]. All are reprinted in Meiji Nyūsu Jiten Hensan Iinkai, ed., *Meiji nyūsu jiten* (Tokyo: Mainichi Komyunikeishonsu Shuppanbu, 1983), 1: 273.

16. Sharon L. Sievers, *Flowers in Salt: The Beginnings of Feminist Consciousness in Modern Japan* (Stanford, Calif.: Stanford University Press, 1983), 14–15.

17. Oku, *Bunmei kaika to minshū*, 16–17.

18. Ibid., 18–20.

19. Murano Tokusaburō, "Yōshiki fujin sokuhatsuhō" [1885], in Meiji Bunka Kenkyūkai, ed., *Meiji bunka zenshū: Fūzoku hen*, 425–34. See also Watanabe Kanae, "Sokuhatsu annai" [1887], excerpted in Ogi, Kumakura, and Ueno, eds., *Fūzoku/sei*, 306–19; Watanabe was central to the founding of the association.

20. "Chiba machi narabi ni Samugawa Nobuto ryōson e futatsu" [1874/8/12], in Chiba-ken Shi Hensan Shingikai, ed., *Chiba-ken shiryō: Kindai hen: Meiji shoki 3*, 249–50.

21. Oku, *Bunmei kaika to minshū*, 12–13.

22. Ibid., 11 (1876 statistics); Ogi, Kumakura, and Ueno, eds., *Fūzoku/sei*, 27 (1877 and 1878).

23. Edward S. Morse, *Japan Day by Day* (Tokyo: Kobunsha, 1936), 1: 89, 97–100.

24. Oka Sankei, "Kinseki kurabe" [1874], in *Meiji bunka zenshū: Fūzoku hen*, ed. Meiji Bunka Kenkyūkai, 157.

25. See Narita, "Teito Tōkyō."

26. The first poorhouse in post-Restoration Tokyo was established in Takanawa in 1869 and was designed to accommodate unregistered transients, *nohinin*, and *gōmune*—all commoners who nonetheless came under the authority of the *hinin* headmen Kuruma Zenshichi and Matsuemon. Facilities set up in 1872 and after—by which time the outcaste authority structure had been abolished—took in vagrants of all sorts. See "Takanawa kyūikusho kyūmindomo tōbun toriatsukai an" [1869/9/27], in Hirota, ed., *Sabetsu no shosō*, 289–91, and the discussion in Hirota, "Nihon kindai shakai no sabetsu kōzō," 485.

27. These comments are cited in Matsushita Shirō, *Kinsei Amami no shihai to shakai* (Tokyo: Daiichi Shobō, 1983), 6 (Sasamori) and 9–12 (Saigō).

28. Vlastos, "Opposition Movements in Early Meiji," 391–93.

29. Hirota, "Nihon kindai shakai no sabetsu kōzō," 490–91; Oka, "Kinseki kurabe," 167.

30. See Imanishi, *Kindai Nihon no sabetsu to sei bunka*, 185.

31. "Kaika dondonbushi" [1871], in *Yomeru nenpyō: Nihonshi*, rev. ed. (Tokyo: Jiyū Kokuminsha, 1995), 827.

32. Oku, *Bunmei kaika to minshū*, 16–17.

33. "Tōkyō no jūmin daibubun wa danpatsu," *Nagoya shinbun* [Mar. 1873], and "Chikuhatsusha ni wa zeikin no ken mo," *Shinbun zasshi* [Aug. 1873], both in Meiji Nyūsu Jiten Hensan Iinkai, ed., *Meiji nyūsu jiten*, 273–74.

34. Morse, *Japan Day by Day*, 2: 36.

35. Oka, "Kinseki kurabe," 167–68.

36. "Sesshū Watanabe mura etadomo shorui" [1867/5], in Hirota, ed., *Sabetsu no shosō*, 71–72.

37. *Shinbun zasshi* [Jan. 1872], in Meiji Nyūsu Jiten Hensan Iinkai, ed., *Meiji nyūsu jiten*, 540.

38. See, for example, Peter Duus, *The Abacus and the Sword: The Japanese Penetration of Korea, 1895–1910* (Berkeley: University of California Press, 1995).

39. On Meiji ideology, see Tetsuo Najita, *Japan: The Intellectual Foundations of Modern Japanese Politics* (Chicago: University of Chicago Press, 1974); Carol Gluck, *Japan's Modern Myths* (Princeton, N.J.: Princeton University Press, 1985); and T. Fujitani, *Splendid Monarchy: Power and Pageantry in Modern Japan* (Berkeley: University of California Press, 1996).

40. Kyōto Burakushi Kenkyūjo, ed., *Kyōto no burakushi*, 6: 48–50.

41. On the centrality of moral suasion *(kyōka)* to the project of creating modernity in Japan, see Sheldon Garon, *Molding Japanese Minds: The State in Everyday Life* (Princeton, N.J.: Princeton University Press, 1997).

42. For a sampling of the extensive early Meiji literature on the poor's responsibility for their own situation, see Hirota, "Nihon kindai shakai no sabetsu kōzō," 481–89, and Yamamuro, "Meiji kokka no seido to rinen," 126–27.

8. AINU IDENTITY AND THE MEIJI STATE

1. In addition to the Ainu and Ryukyuans, non-Japanese peoples brought into the modern polity included the descendants of Korean potters brought to the Naeshirogawa district of the former Satsuma domain after Hideyoshi's invasions of the continent in the 1590s, and European and Polynesian settlers in the Ogasawara Islands. These peoples were made Japanese citizens through incorporation into the household-registry system in 1871 and 1886, respectively. Yamamuro, "Meiji kokka no seido to rinen," 142.

2. See White, *The Roots of Dependency*, and White, *The Middle Ground*, for treatments of this process in North America.

3. "Mōshiwatashi" [1868], RCNS.

4. Howell, *Capitalism from Within*, 96.

5. Kaiho, *Bakuhansei kokka to Hokkaidō*, 245; Kaiho, *Kindai hoppōshi*, 24–26. The Development Agency's order of November 4, 1878, is reprinted in Hirota, ed., *Sabetsu no shosō*, 15–16. According to Kōno Tsunekichi, *Hokkaidō kyūdojin* (Sapporo: Hokkaidō-chō, 1911), 33, the Ainu were officially subjected to the draft in 1898, though some were called up as early as 1896.

6. Kaiho, *Bakuhansei kokka to Hokkaidō*, 251.

7. For discussions of agricultural promotion policies, see Takakura Shin'ichirō, "Sanken jidai ni okeru Ainu no kannōsaku," *Hōkeikai ronsō* 2 (1932): 1–38; Katō Noriko, "Hokkaidō sanken ikkyoku jidai ni okeru tai-Ainu seisaku to sono jitsujō," *Hokudai shigaku* 20 (1980): 14–26; and Ogawa Masahito, "'Ainu gakkō' no setchi to 'Hokkaidō kyūdojin hogohō,' 'kyūdojin jidō kyōiku kitei' no seiritsu," *Hokkaidō Daigaku Kyōikugakubu kiyō* 55 (1991): 257–325. Many of Ogawa's writings on the Ainu in modern Japan have

been collected as Ogawa Masahito, *Kindai Ainu kyōiku seidoshi kenkyū* (Sapporo: Hokkaido University Press, 1997).

8. See Amino Yoshihiko's intriguing deconstruction of the term *hyakushō* (commonly understood in Japan to mean "farmer") and the notion that Japan has always been an agricultural society: Amino, "Emperor, Rice, and Commoners."

9. "Hakodate-ken kyūdojin" [1883], RCNS.

10. "Yuchi Sadamoto," in *Hokkaidō kaitaku kōrōsha kankei shiryō shūroku*, ed. Hokkaidō Sōmubu Gyōsei Shiryōshitsu (Sapporo: Hokkaidō, 1972), 2: 197; Toyoda Nobuo, "Yuchi Sadamoto," in *Hokkaidō daihyakka jiten*, ed. Hokkaidō Shinbunsha (Sapporo: Hokkaidō Shinbunsha, 1981), 2: 858.

11. In 1882 Sapporo prefecture had 12,862 Ainu residents; Nemuro prefecture 3,408; and Hakodate prefecture 663. Sapporo governor Zusho Hirotake, Nemuro governor Yuchi Sadamoto, and Hakodate governor Tokitō Tamemoto to imperial household minister [Mar. 13, 1883], "Kenrei shukkyōchū shorui" [Dec. 1882–Mar. 1883], in "Nemuro-ken kyūdojin," RCNS. On the Meiji emperor's 1876 and 1881 visits to Hokkaido, see Hokkaidō-chō, *Meiji tennō gojunkōki* (Sapporo: Hokkaidō-chō, 1930).

12. Hirota Chiaki to Yuchi Sadamoto [Dec. 1883], in "Nemuro-ken kyūdojin."

13. The following summary of the policy is based on Hirota Chiaki, on behalf of Yuchi Sadamoto, to home and finance ministers [Dec. 23, 1883], "Kyūdojin kyūsai jisshi hōhō narabi ni yosan torishirabe ukagai," and response from both ministers [May 23, 1884], in "Nemuro-ken kyūdojin." A number of documents related to the policy are reprinted in Ogawa Masahito and Yamada Shin'ichi, eds., *Ainu minzoku kindai no kiroku* (Tokyo: Sōfūkan, 1998), 433–37. A slightly different version is reproduced without citation of the original source in Kōno Motomichi, ed., *Tai-Ainu seisaku hōki ruijū* (Sapporo: Hokkaidō Shuppan Kikaku Sentaa, 1981), 91–99, under the title "Nemuro ken kyūdojin kyūsai hōhō (Meiji 16-nen)."

14. Hirota, "Kyūdojin kyūsai jisshi hōhō narabi ni yosan torishirabe ukagai," chapter 1, article 1.

15. Ibid., chapter 4, article 28.

16. "Nemuro-ken kyūdojin buiku kaikon no gaikyō" [June 7, 1884], in "Nemuro-ken kyūdojin."

17. Report from Kushima Shigeyoshi to Yuchi Sadamoto, "Fukumeisho" [November 20, 1883], in "Nemuro-ken kyūdojin."

18. "Tanbetsuhyō" [Nov. 18, 1884], in "Nemuro-ken kyūdojin."

19. Report from Kushima Shigeyoshi to Yuchi Sadamoto, "Fukumeisho" [Dec. 10, 1884], in "Nemuro-ken kyūdojin."

20. Miyamoto Chimaki, "Bunai Kawakami, Akan, Ashoro sangun kakuson ni atsukaisho setchi no gi jōshin" [Jan. 26, 1885], in "Nemuro-ken kyūdojin." See also the account of Gō Masatoshi's apparently fraudulent mismanagement of a salmon fishery belonging to Ainu in the Tokachi district: "Tokachi hoka yongun dojin kankei shorui" [1885–92], RCNS.

21. Ogawa, "'Ainu gakkō' no setchi to 'Hokkaidō kyūdojin hogohō,' 'kyūdojin jidō kyōiku kitei' no seiritsu," 277.

22. The relocation of a twenty-seven-household community of Ainu from

the outskirts of Kushiro city to a site far up the Setsuri River in 1885 is but one example of this phenomenon. See Kushiro district head Miyamoto Chimaki to Yuchi Sadamoto, "Kaikon jugyō no tame Kushiro dojin o iten seshimuru gi ukagai" [May 11, 1884], in "Nemuro-ken kyūdojin," and the discussion by Katō, "Hokkaidō sanken ikkyoku jidai ni okeru tai-Ainu seisaku to sono jit-sujō," 18–19.

23. All statistics are from "Kyūdojin kyūsai" [n.d.], in "Nemuro-ken kyūdojin."

24. Howell, "Making 'Useful Citizens' of Ainu Subjects in Early Twentieth-Century Japan."

25. For a map of Sakhalin Ainu communities in 1935, see Karafuto Ainushi Kenkyūkai, ed., *Tsuishikari no ishibumi: Karafuto Ainu no kyōsei ijū no rekishi* (Sapporo: Hokkaidō Shuppan Kikaku Sentaa, 1992), frontispiece.

26. Torii Ryūzō, *Chishima Ainu* (Tokyo: Yoshikawa Kōbunkan, 1903).

27. On Ainu attempts to manipulate Japanese and Russian officials, see the account of Tokonbe, an Ainu who fled from a Japanese fishery to Russian protection in 1862, in Kikuchi, *Hoppōshi no naka no kinsei Nihon*, 279–301. On Japanese concern with Ainu loyalties, see Karafuto Ainushi Kenkyūkai, ed., *Tsuishikari no ishibumi*, 48–50.

28. Except where otherwise noted, the following account of the relocation of the Sakhalin Ainu is based on Karafuto Ainushi Kenkyūkai, ed., *Tsuishikari no ishibumi*. See also John J. Stephan, *Sakhalin: A History* (Oxford: Clarendon Press, 1971), and the autobiography of a Sakhalin Ainu, Yamabe Yasunosuke, *Ainu monogatari*, ed. Kindaichi Kyōsuke (Tokyo: Hakubunkan, 1912).

29. One of the officials, Matsumoto Jūrō, resigned his post in protest. See the discussion in Karafuto Ainushi Kenkyūkai, ed., *Tsuishikari no ishibumi*, 118–24.

30. The Ainu expressed a fear of contagious disease in a letter of protest against the government's bait-and-switch tactic, reprinted in Ogawa and Yamada, eds., *Ainu minzoku kindai no kiroku*, 15–16.

31. In 1916, the Ainu population of Sakhalin was approximately 1,700 persons, of whom slightly more than 200 were returnees from Hokkaido. Aoyama Tōen, *Kyokuhoku no bettenchi* (Tokyo: Hōbunsha, 1918), 2; Kaiho, *Kindai hoppōshi*, 104–5. A leader of the movement to gain citizenship rights was Kawamura Saburō, head of the Karafuto Indigenous People's Alliance Youth Group (Karafuto Senjūmin Rengōkai Seinendan). See Kakekawa Gen'ichirō, *Bachiraa Yaeko no shōgai* (Sapporo: Hokkaidō Shuppan Kikaku Sentaa, 1988), 220–21. The most complete account of the citizenship battle is Tessa Morris-Suzuki, "Becoming Japanese: Imperial Expansion and Identity Crises in the Early Twentieth Century," in *Japan's Competing Modernities: Issues in Culture and Democracy, 1900–1930*, ed. Sharon A. Minichiello (Honolulu: University of Hawai'i Press, 1998), 157–80.

32. Since the late 1980s a group of descendants of Sakhalin Ainu and concerned non-Ainu Japanese have been engaged in an effort to trace the whereabouts of survivors and their offspring. Karafuto Ainushi Kenkyūkai, ed., *Tsuishikari no ishibumi*, a history of the Sakhalin Ainu, is one product of their work.

33. See John J. Stephan, *The Kuril Islands* (Oxford: Clarendon Press, 1974), 104–10, and Hokkaidō-chō, ed., *Hokkaidō kyūdojin hogo enkakushi* (Sapporo:

Hokkaidō-chō, 1934), 137–74, for overviews of the forced relocation of the Shikotan Ainu. In 1992 there were press reports that descendants of the Kuril Ainu were found in Poland, but Akizuki Toshiyuki (personal communication, 1992) speculates that the "Kuril Ainu" in Poland are actually descendants of the ninety Aleuts who lived in the Kurils at the time of the Sakhalin-Kuril exchange of 1875, and whose whereabouts are otherwise unknown.

34. Yuchi Sadamoto to Yamagata Aritomo, "Uruppu-tō itō keibi no gi ni tsuki jōshin" [July 15, 1884], in "Nemuro ken kyūdojin."

35. James F. Eder, *On the Road to Tribal Extinction: Depopulation, Deculturation, and Adaptive Well-Being Among the Batak of the Philippines* (Berkeley: University of California Press, 1987); see especially 189–91.

36. On hunting in the northern Kurils, see Asano Tadashi, "Shikotan dojin chōsa" [1923], RCNS. (Kaiho, *Kindai hoppōshi*, 107–8, says that hunting trips began in 1898.) On matches between Ainu women and Japanese men, see Takahashi Fusaji, *Chishima Ainu ron* (Shiraoi: Takahashi Fusaji, 1933), 37–38. On the population of full-blooded Kuril Ainu, see Hokkaido-chō, *Hokkaidō kyūdojin hogo enkakushi*, 169–70.

37. Asano, "Shikotan dojin chōsa."

38. Sten Bergman, *Sport and Exploration in the Far East: A Naturalist's Experiences in and around the Kurile Islands*, trans. Frederic Whyte (London: Methuen, 1933), 211–17.

39. Calculated from data in Takahashi, *Chishima Ainu ron*, 37.

40. Matsushita Kanekiyo to Yuchi Sadamoto, "Fukumeisho" [Aug. 7, 1884], in "Nemuro ken kyūdojin."

41. Hokkaidō-chō, *Hokkaidō kyūdojin hogo enkakushi*, 155–56; Asano, "Shikotan dojin chōsa"; Kaiho, *Kindai hoppōshi*, 108–9.

42. Henry Arthur Tilley, *Japan, the Amoor, and the Pacific: With Notices of Other Places, Comprised in a Voyage of Circumnavigation in the Imperial Russian Corvette "Rynda," in 1858–1860* (London: Smith, Elder & Co., 1861), 198.

43. See the anecdote about a young Ainu woman chastised for wearing Japanese wooden clogs *(geta)* in Shiraoi sometime around 1897 in Mitsuoka Shin'ichi, *Ainu no ashiato*, 6th rev. ed. (Shiraoi: Miyoshi Chikuyū, 1941), 4–6.

44. Kita Shōmei, *Tokachi Ainu no ashiato to konogo no michi* (Obihiro: Tokachi Kyokumeisha, 1927), 4–8; Yoshida Iwao, "Kyūdojin hogo shisetsu kaizen gaian," *Hokkaidō shakai jigyō* 52 (Aug. 1936): 17–20; "Horobitsutsu aru Shikotan dojin no konjaku," *Hokkai taimusu* (Mar. 18, 1930), reprinted in Hokkaidō Utari Kyōkai Ainu Shi Hensan Iinkai, ed., *Ainu shi: Shiryō hen* (Sapporo: Hokkaidō Utari Kyōkai, 1989), 4: 880–81; Sekiba Fujihiko, *Ainu iji dan* (Sapporo: Sekiba Fujihiko, 1896).

45. For example, see the petitions submitted by an Ainu representative, Ōtsu Kuranosuke, to local officials to end the custodianship held by a Hakodate businessman, Gō Masatoshi, over a group of Ainu fisheries collected in "Tokachi hoka yongun dojin kankei shorui."

46. Takekuma Tokusaburō, *Ainu monogatari* (Sapporo: Fukidō Shobō, 1918). Chiri Yukie, *Ainu shin'yōshū* (Tokyo: Iwanami Shoten, 1978), 3–4, expressed regret at the apparent inevitability of the Ainu's passing, but even she

maintained the hope that someday a strong leader would appear to guide the Ainu through the tumult of modernity. For an account of her short life, see Fujimoto Hideo, *Gin no shizuku furu furu mawari ni: Chiri Yukie no shōgai* (Tokyo: Sōfūkan, 1991).

47. Barth, "Introduction."

EPILOGUE: MODERNITY AND ETHNICITY

1. Peter Sahlins, "State Formation and National Identity in the Catalan Borderlands During the Eighteenth and Nineteenth Centuries," in *Border Identities: Nation and State at International Frontiers,* ed. Thomas M. Wilson and Hastings Donnan (Cambridge: Cambridge University Press, 1998), 31–33; Peter Sahlins, *Boundaries: The Making of France and Spain in the Pyrenees* (Berkeley: University of California Press, 1989). The reference to "peasants into Frenchmen" is an allusion to Eugen Weber, *Peasants into Frenchmen: The Modernization of Rural France, 1870–1914* (Stanford, Calif.: Stanford University Press, 1976).

2. Yuri Slezkine, *Arctic Mirrors: Russia and the Small Peoples of the North* (Ithaca, N.Y.: Cornell University Press, 1994).

3. See Roberts, *Mercantilism in a Japanese Domain,* for an elaboration of this point.

4. See the discussion in Lie, *Multiethnic Japan,* 186–88.

5. The grammar of *sōrōbun* is basically the same as that of literary Japanese with a few variations, most notably the use of the verb ending *–sōrō* (hence *mairisōrō* rather than *mairu* for "to come" or "to go"); it is a "sinicization" of literary Japanese because of its conventional use of Chinese (rather than Japanese) character syntax in certain constructions: *sōrōbun* is read in Japanese, with the result that some characters are read out of the order in which they are written.

6. Benedict Anderson, *Imagined Communities: Reflections on the Origin and Spread of Nationalism* (London: Verso Editions, 1983).

7. Barth, "Introduction," 10.

8. Anderson, *Imagined Communities;* Eric Hobsbawm, *Nations and Nationalism Since 1789* (Cambridge: Cambridge University Press, 1990).

9. The Sloughters of New York are a group of perhaps a dozen families who live in an isolated community. Their origins are unclear, but they appear to be the descendants of mixed-race people who settled in the area in the eighteenth century. Similar communities are scattered along the Atlantic seaboard of the United States. Chris Hedges, "A Small, Despised Band Stays in Its Remote Polly Hollow," *New York Times* (July 18, 1991).

10. John Illife, *A Modern History of Tanganyika* (Cambridge: Cambridge University Press, 1979), 418–41.

11. Richard Fox, "'Professional Primitives': Hunters and Gatherers of Nuclear South Asia," *Man in India* 49, no. 2 (1969): 139–60; Alexandra Harmon, *Indians in the Making: Ethnic Relations and Indian Identities around Puget Sound* (Berkeley: University of California Press, 1998); "Means of Recognition Splits Indians," *New York Times* (Aug. 4, 1991).

12. For arguments in favor of the importance of racialized discourse in mod-

ern Japan, see Richard Siddle, *Race, Resistance and the Ainu of Japan* (London: Routledge, 1996), and Michael Weiner, *Race and Migration in Imperial Japan* (London: Routledge, 1994).

13. To some extent, the Hokkaido Ainu continued to recognize regional differences among themselves as well. See, for example, Fushine Kōzō, "Ainu seikatsu no hensen," in *Keimeisha daijūhachikai kōenshū*, ed. Kasamori Denpan (Tokyo: Keimeisha Jimusho, 1926), 62.

14. On the Amami Islands during the early modern period, see Matsushita, *Kinsei Amami no shihai to shakai.*

15. See Mark Hudson, *Ruins of Identity: Ethnogenesis in the Japanese Islands* (Honolulu: University of Hawai'i Press, 1999).

Works Cited

ARCHIVES

Chiba Prefectural Archives, Chiba (Asō-ke monjo, Hishinuma-kuyū monjo, Maejima-ke monjo, Takagi-ke monjo).
Hakodate Municipal Library, Hakodate (documents cited individually below).
Resource Collection for Northern Studies, Hokkaido University Library, Sapporo (documents cited individually below).

PUBLISHED WORKS

Ainu Bunka Hozon Kyōkai, ed. *Ainu minzoku shi.* Tokyo: Daiichi Hōki Shuppan, 1970.
Amino Yoshihiko. *Chūsei minshūzō: Heimin to shokunin.* Tokyo: Iwanami Shoten, 1980.
———. "Emperor, Rice, and Commoners." In *Multicultural Japan: Palaeolithic to Postmodern,* edited by Donald Denoon, Mark Hudson, Gavan McCormack, and Tessa Morris-Suzuki, 235–244. Cambridge: Cambridge University Press, 1996.
———. *Muen, kugai, raku: Nihon chūsei no jiyū to heiwa.* Tokyo: Heibonsha, 1978.
Anderson, Benedict. *Imagined Communities: Reflections on the Origin and Spread of Nationalism.* London: Verso Editions, 1983.
Aoyama Tōen. *Kyokuhoku no bettenchi.* Tokyo: Hōbunsha, 1918.
Arai Eiji. *Kinsei no gyoson.* Tokyo: Yoshikawa Kōbunkan, 1970.
Arano Yasunori. *Kinsei Nihon to higashi Ajia.* Tokyo: University of Tokyo Press, 1988.

Asano Tadashi. "Shikotan dojin chōsa" [1923]. Resource Collection for North-
    ern Studies, Hokkaido University Library.
Asao Naohiro. "Kinsei no mibun to sono hen'yō." In *Mibun to kakushiki
    (Nihon no kinsei, vol. 7)*, edited by Asao Naohiro, 7–40. Tokyo: Chūō
    Kōronsha, 1992.
———. "Kinsei no mibunsei to senmin." *Buraku mondai kenkyū* 68 (Oct.
    1981): 37–55.
Asato Susumu. "Ryūkyū ōkoku no keisei." In *Chiiki to etonosu (Ajia no naka no
    Nihonshi, vol. 4)*, edited by Arano Yasunori, Ishii Masatoshi, and Murai
    Shōsuke, 111–36. Tokyo: University of Tokyo Press, 1992.
Barth, Fredrik. "Introduction." In *Ethnic Groups and Boundaries: The Social
    Organization of Culture Difference*, edited by Fredrik Barth, 9–38. Boston:
    Little, Brown, and Co., 1969.
Batchelor, John. *An Ainu-English-Japanese Dictionary*. Fourth edition. Tokyo:
    Iwanami Shoten, 1938.
Beerens, Anna, trans. "Interview with a Bakumatsu Official: A Translation from
    Kyūji Shimonroku (2)." *Monumenta Nipponica* 57, no. 2 (Summer 2002):
    173–202.
Befu, Harumi. *Hegemony of Homogeneity: An Anthropological Analysis of
    "Nihonjinron."* Melbourne: Trans Pacific Press, 2001.
Bergman, Sten. *Sport and Exploration in the Far East: A Naturalist's Experiences
    in and around the Kurile Islands*, translated by Frederic Whyte. London:
    Methuen, 1933.
Berry, Mary Elizabeth. *Hideyoshi*. Cambridge, Mass.: Council on East Asian
    Studies, Harvard University, 1982.
———. "Public Peace and Private Attachment: The Goals and Conduct of Power
    in Early Modern Japan." *Journal of Japanese Studies* 12, no. 2 (Summer
    1986): 237–71.
Bix, Herbert P. "Leader of Peasant Rebellions: Miura Meisuke." In *Great His-
    torical Figures of Japan*, edited by Murakami Hyoe and Thomas J. Harper,
    243–60. Tokyo: Japan Culture Institute, 1978.
———. *Peasant Protest in Japan, 1590–1884*. New Haven, Conn.: Yale Univer-
    sity Press, 1986.
Blacker, Carmen. *The Japanese Enlightenment: A Study of the Writings of
    Fukuzawa Yukichi*. Cambridge: Cambridge University Press, 1964.
Botsman, Daniel V. "Crime, Punishment and the Making of Modern Japan,
    1790–1895." Ph.D. diss., Princeton University, 1999.
Bowen, Roger. *Rebellion and Democracy in Meiji Japan*. Berkeley: University of
    California Press, 1980.
Braisted, William R., trans. *Meiroku Zasshi: Journal of the Japanese Enlighten-
    ment*. Cambridge, Mass.: Harvard University Press, 1976.
Brown, Philip C. *Central Authority and Local Autonomy in the Formation of
    Early Modern Japan: The Case of Kaga Domain*. Stanford, Calif.: Stanford
    University Press, 1993.
"Bunsei roku hitsujidoshi irai Ezojin omemie kenjōhin narabi ni kudasaremono
    shirabegaki" [n.d.]. Hakodate Municipal Library.
Buyō Inshi. *Seji kenmonroku* [ca. 1816] (*Kinsei shakai keizai sōsho*, vol. 1),

edited by Honjō Eijirō, Tsuchiya Takao, Nakamura Naokatsu, and Kokushō Iwao. 12 vols. Tokyo: Kaizōsha, 1926.

Chiba-ken Shi Hensan Shingikai, ed. *Chiba-ken shiryō: Kindai hen: Meiji shoki 3*. Chiba: Chiba-ken, 1970.

Chiri Yukie. *Ainu shin'yōshū*. Tokyo: Iwanami Shoten, 1978.

Coen, Cornelius. *Voyage to Cathay, Tartary, and the Gold- and Silver-Rich Islands East of Japan, 1643: The Journal of Cornelius Jansz. Coen Relating to the Voyage of Marten Gerritsz. Fries to the North and East of Japan (Contributions to a Bibliography of Australia and the Pacific, supplement 4)*, translated and edited by Willem C. H. Robert. Amsterdam: Philo Press, 1975.

Craig, Albert M. "Fukuzawa Yukichi: The Philosophical Foundations of Meiji Nationalism." In *Political Development in Modern Japan*, edited by Robert E. Ward, 99–148. Princeton, N.J.: Princeton University Press, 1968.

Cusumano, Michael. "An Enlightenment Dialogue with Fukuzawa Yukichi: Ogawa Tameji's *Kaika Mondo*, 1874–1875." *Monumenta Nipponica* 37, no. 3 (Autumn 1982): 375–401.

Dale, Peter N. *The Myth of Japanese Uniqueness*. London: Croom Helm; Oxford: Nissan Institute for Japanese Studies, University of Oxford, 1986.

"Dan Naiki mibun hikiage ikken" [1868]. In *Buraku (Nihon shomin seikatsu shiryō shūsei*, vol. 14), edited by Harada Tomohiko, 459–84. Tokyo: San'ichi Shobō, 1971.

Denoon, Donald, Mark Hudson, Gavan McCormack, and Tessa Morris-Suzuki, eds. *Multicultural Japan: Palaeolithic to Postmodern*. Cambridge: Cambridge University Press, 1996.

DeVos, George, and Hiroshi Wagatsuma. "The Problem: Caste and Race, a Syncretic View." In *Japan's Invisible Race: Caste in Culture and Identity*, edited by George DeVos and Hiroshi Wagatsuma, xix–xxiii. Berkeley: University of California Press, 1966.

Dirks, Nicholas B. *Castes of Mind: Colonialism and the Making of Modern India*. Princeton, N.J.: Princeton University Press, 2001.

"Dojin omemie ni tsuki nikki" [1859]. In *Saisenkai shiryō*, edited by Takakura Shin'ichirō, 99–125. Sapporo: Hokkaidō Shuppan Kikaku Sentaa, 1982.

Duus, Peter. *The Abacus and the Sword: The Japanese Penetration of Korea, 1895–1910*. Berkeley: University of California Press, 1995.

Eder, James F. *On the Road to Tribal Extinction: Depopulation, Deculturation, and Adaptive Well-Being Among the Batak of the Philippines*. Berkeley: University of California Press, 1987.

Emori Susumu. *Hokkaidō kinseishi no kenkyū*. Sapporo: Hokkaidō Shuppan Kikaku Sentaa, 1982.

———. "Omoro to yūkar." In *Chiiki to etonosu (Ajia no naka no Nihonshi*, vol. 4), edited by Arano Yasunori, Ishii Masatoshi, and Murai Shōsuke, 251–85. Tokyo: University of Tokyo Press, 1992.

"Ezo hōki" [n.d.]. In *Tanken, kikō, chishi (Hokuhen hen) (Nihon shomin seikatsu shiryō shūsei*, vol. 4), edited by Takakura Shin'ichirō, 639–50. Tokyo: San'ichi Shobō, 1969.

Figal, Gerald. *Civilization and Monsters: Spirits of Modernity in Meiji Japan*. Durham, N.C.: Duke University Press, 1999.

Flershem, Robert G., and Yoshiko Flershem. "Migratory Fishermen on the Japan Sea Coast in the Tokugawa Period." *Japan Forum* 3, no. 1 (Apr. 1991): 71–90.

Fox, Richard G. "'Professional Primitives': Hunters and Gatherers of Nuclear South Asia." *Man in India* 49, no. 2 (1969): 139–60.

Fujimoto Hideo. *Gin no shizuku furu furu mawari ni: Chiri Yukie no shōgai.* Tokyo: Sōfūkan, 1991.

Fujitani, T. *Splendid Monarchy: Power and Pageantry in Modern Japan.* Berkeley: University of California Press, 1996.

Fukasawa, Yuriko. *Ainu Archaeology as Ethnohistory: Iron Technology among the Saru Ainu of Hokkaido, Japan, in the 17th Century.* BAR International Series 744. Oxford: British Archaeological Reports, 1998.

Fukuzawa Yukichi. *The Autobiography of Fukuzawa Yukichi,* translated by Eiichi Kiyooka. Tokyo: Hokuseido, 1948.

———. *An Encouragement of Learning,* translated by David A. Dilworth and Umeyo Hirano. Tokyo: Sophia University Press, 1969.

———. *Outline of a Theory of Civilization,* translated by David A. Dilworth and G. Cameron Hurst. Tokyo: Sophia University Press, 1973.

Fushine Kōzō. "Ainu seikatsu no hensen." In *Keimeisha daijūhachikai kōenshū,* edited by Kasamori Denpan, 52–72. Tokyo: Keimeisha Jimusho, 1926.

Garon, Sheldon. *Molding Japanese Minds: The State in Everyday Life.* Princeton, N.J.: Princeton University Press, 1997.

Gerth, Karl. *China Made: Consumer Culture and the Creation of the Nation.* Cambridge, Mass.: Harvard University Asia Center, 2003.

Gluck, Carol. *Japan's Modern Myths.* Princeton, N.J.: Princeton University Press, 1985.

Gordon, Andrew. *Labor and Imperial Democracy in Prewar Japan.* Berkeley: University of California Press, 1991.

Groemer, Gerald. "The Creation of the Edo Outcaste Order." *Journal of Japanese Studies* 27, no. 2 (Summer 2001): 263–94.

———. "The Guild of the Blind in Tokugawa Japan." *Monumenta Nipponica* 56, no. 3 (Autumn 2001): 349–80.

Haga Noboru. "Nohinin: Daitoshi ni ryūnyū suru furō, mushuku no hitobito." In *Kinsei no minshū to geinō,* edited by Kyōto Burakushi Kenkyūjo, 126–31. Kyoto: Aunsha, 1989.

Hagiwara Otohiko. "Tōkyō kaika hanjōshi" [1874]. In *Meiji bunka zenshū: Fūzoku hen,* edited by Meiji Bunka Kenkyūkai, 179–238. Tokyo: Nihon Hyōron Shinsha, 1955 [1928].

"Hakodate-ken kyūdojin" [1883]. Resource Collection for Northern Studies, Hokkaido University Library.

Hall, John Carey. *Tokugawa Feudal Law.* Reprint edition. Washington, D.C.: University Publications of America, 1979.

Hall, John W. "Rule by Status in Tokugawa Japan." *Journal of Japanese Studies* 1, no. 1 (Autumn 1974): 39–49.

Harada Tomohiko, ed. *Buraku (Nihon shomin seikatsu shiryō shūsei,* vol. 14). Tokyo: San'ichi Shobō, 1971.

Harada Tomohiko and Uesugi Satoru, eds. *"Kaihōrei" no seiritsu (Kindai burakushi shiryō shūsei,* vol. 1). Tokyo: San'ichi Shobō, 1984.

Haraguchi, Torao, Robert K. Sakai, Mitsugu Sakihara, Kazuko Yamada, and Masato Mitsui. *The Status System and Social Organization of Satsuma: A Translation of the* Shūmon Tefuda Aratame Jōmoku. Honolulu: University Press of Hawai'i, 1975.

Harmon, Alexandra. *Indians in the Making: Ethnic Relations and Indian Identities around Puget Sound.* Berkeley: University of California Press, 1998.

Hatanaka Toshiyuki. *"Kawata" to heijin: Kinsei mibun shakairon.* Kyoto: Kamogawa Shuppan, 1997.

———. "Kinsei 'senmin' mibunron no kadai." In *Sōten Nihon no rekishi: Kinsei hen,* edited by Aoki Michio and Hosaka Satoru, 169–86. Tokyo: Shinjinbutsu Ōraisha, 1991.

———. *Kinsei sonraku shakai no mibun kōzō.* Kyoto: Buraku Mondai Kenkyūjo, 1990.

———. "Mibun o koeru toki." In *Mibunteki shūen,* edited by Tsukada Takashi, Yoshida Nobuyuki, and Wakita Osamu, 403–60. Kyoto: Buraku Mondai Kenkyūjo, 1994.

Hauser, William B. *Economic Institutional Change in Tokugawa Japan: Ōsaka and the Kinai Cotton Trade.* New York: Cambridge University Press, 1974.

"Hayashi-ke monjo: Ban nikki" [1860–66]. In *Matsumae-chō shi: Shiryōhen,* edited by Matsumae-chō Shi Henshūshitsu, vol. 2, pp. 655–1040. 6 vols. Matsumae: Matsumae-chō, 1977.

Hayashi Hachiemon. "Kannō kyōkunroku" [1826/5]. In *Gunma-ken shi: Shiryōhen* vol. 14 (*Kinsei 6*), edited by Gunma-ken Shi Hensan Iinkai. Maebashi: Gunma-ken, 1986.

Hess, Albert G., and Shigeyo Murayama. *Everyday Law in Japanese Folk Art: Daily Life in Meiji Japan as Seen Through Petty Law Violations.* Aalen: Scientia Verlag, 1980.

Hicks, George. *The Comfort Women: Japan's Brutal Regime of Enforced Prostitution in the Second World War.* New York: Norton, 1995.

Hidemura Senzō. "Josetsu: Shiron teki ni." In *Satsuma han no kiso kōzō,* edited by Hidemura Senzō, 3–26. Tokyo: Ochanomizu Shobō, 1970.

Hiltebeitel, Alf, and Barbara D. Miller, eds. *Hair: Its Power and Meaning in Asian Cultures.* Albany: State University of New York Press, 1998.

Hino Tatsuo. "Kinsei bungaku ni arawareta ikokuzō." In *Sekaishi no naka no kinsei (Nihon no kinsei,* vol. 1), edited by Asao Naohiro, 265–304. Tokyo: Chūō Kōronsha, 1991.

Hirota Masaki. *Bunmei kaika to minshū ishiki.* Tokyo: Aoki Shoten, 1980.

———. "Nihon kindai shakai no sabetsu kōzō." In *Sabetsu no shosō (Nihon kindai shisō taikei,* vol. 22), edited by Hirota Masaki, 463–509. Tokyo: Iwanami Shoten, 1990.

———, ed. *Sabetsu no shosō (Nihon kindai shisō taikei,* vol. 22). Tokyo: Iwanami Shoten, 1990.

Hobsbawm, Eric. "Introduction: Inventing Traditions." In *The Invention of Tradition,* edited by Eric Hobsbawm and Terence Ranger, 1–14. Cambridge: Cambridge University Press, 1983.

————. *Nations and Nationalism Since 1789*. Cambridge: Cambridge University Press, 1990.

Hokkaidō-chō, ed. *Hokkaidō kyūdojin hogo enkakushi*. Sapporo: Hokkaidō-chō, 1934.

————. *Meiji tennō gojunkōki*. Sapporo: Hokkaidō-chō, 1930.

Hokkaidō Utari Kyōkai Ainu Shi Hensan Iinkai, ed. *Ainu shi: Shiryō hen*. 4 vols. Sapporo: Hokkaidō Utari Kyōkai, 1988–90.

Honda Yūko. "Kinsei Hokkaidō ni okeru attus no sanbutsuka to ryūtsū." *Hokkaidō-ritsu Ainu minzoku bunka kenkyū sentaa kenkyū kiyō* 8 (2002): 1–40.

Hosaka Satoru. "Hyakushō ikki no sahō: Sono seiritsu to henshitsu." In *Ikki to shūen*, edited by Hosaka Satoru, 5–45. Tokyo: Aoki Shoten, 2000.

Hosoi Hakaru. "Morioka han." In *Kokushi daijiten*, ed. Kokushi Daijiten Henshū Iinkai, vol. 13, pp. 862–63. 15 vols. Tokyo: Yoshikawa Kōbunkan, 1992.

Howell, David L. "Ainu Ethnicity and the Boundaries of the Early Modern Japanese State." *Past and Present* 142 (Feb. 1994): 69–93.

————. *Capitalism from Within: Economy, Society, and the State in a Japanese Fishery*. Berkeley: University of California Press, 1995.

————. "Early *Shizoku* Colonization of Hokkaidō." *Journal of Asian History* 17 (1983): 40–67.

————. "Hard Times in the Kantō: Economic Change and Village Life in Late Tokugawa Japan." *Modern Asian Studies* 23, no. 2 (May 1989): 349–71.

————. "Making 'Useful Citizens' of Ainu Subjects in Early Twentieth-Century Japan." *Journal of Asian Studies* 63, no. 1 (Feb. 2004): 5–29.

————. "Proto-Industrial Origins of Japanese Capitalism." *Journal of Asian Studies* 52, no. 2 (May 1992): 269–86.

————. "Visions of the Future in Meiji Japan." In *Historical Perspectives on Contemporary East Asia,* edited by Merle Goldman and Andrew Gordon, 85–118. Cambridge, Mass.: Harvard University Press, 2000.

Howland, Douglas R. "Samurai Status, Class and Bureaucracy: A Historiographical Essay." *Journal of Asian Studies* 60, no. 2 (May 2001): 353–80.

————. *Translating the West: Language and Political Reason in Nineteenth-Century Japan*. Honolulu: University of Hawai'i Press, 2002.

Hudson, Mark J. *Ruins of Identity: Ethnogenesis in the Japanese Islands*. Honolulu: University of Hawai'i Press, 1999.

Illife, John. *A Modern History of Tanganyika*. Cambridge: Cambridge University Press, 1979.

Imanishi Hajime. "Bunmei kaika to 'ushikubi kojiki.'" In *Bakumatsu, ishinki no kokumin kokka keisei to bunka hen'yō,* edited by Nishikawa Nagao and Matsumiya Hideharu, 345–74. Tokyo: Shin'yōsha, 1995.

————. *Kindai Nihon no sabetsu to sei bunka: Bunmei kaika to minshū sekai*. Tokyo: Yūzankaku, 1998.

————. *Kindai Nihon no sabetsu to sonraku*. Tokyo: Yūzankaku, 1993.

Inagaki Reiko. "Ainu minzoku ni taisuru girei shihai: 'Uimamu,' 'omusha' ni tsuite." In *Kita kara no Nihonshi,* edited by Hokkaidō-Tōhoku Shi Kenkyūkai, vol. 1, pp. 315–21. 2 vols. Tokyo: Sanseidō, 1988.

————. "Kinsei Ezochi ni okeru girei shihai no tokushitsu: Uimamu, omusha no hensen o tōshite." In *Minshū seikatsu to shinkō, shisō,* edited by Minshūshi Kenkyūkai, 111–30. Tokyo: Yūzankaku, 1985.

Inukai Tetsuo and Natori Takemitsu. "Iomante (Ainu no kuma matsuri) no bunkateki igi to sono keishiki." *Hoppō bunka kenkyū hōkoku* 2 (Oct. 1939): 1–34 and 3 (May 1940): 1–57.

Irokawa Daikichi. *The Culture of the Meiji Period,* translation edited by Marius B. Jansen. Princeton, N.J.: Princeton University Press, 1985.

Ishii Kendō. "Kaika no hanashi kaidai." In *Meiji bunka zenshū: Bunmei kaika hen,* edited by Yoshino Sakuzō, 3. Tokyo: Nihon Hyōronsha, 1929.

Ishii Ryōsuke and Harafuji Hiroshi, eds. *Bakumatsu ofuregaki shūsei.* 7 vols. Tokyo: Iwanami Shoten, 1994.

Ishitaki Toyomi. "'Kaihōrei' kara Chikuzen takeyari ikki e: Buraku yakiuchi ni itaru hitsuzenteki katei no kentō." In *Meiji shonen kaihōrei hantai ikki no kenkyū,* edited by Yoshinami Takashi, 37–75. Tokyo: Akashi Shoten, 1987.

Iwai Tadakuma. "Shoki Meiji kokka to buraku mondai: Senshō haishirei o megutte." In *Burakushi no kenkyū: Kindai hen,* edited by Buraku Mondai Kenkyūjo, 19–52. Kyoto: Buraku Mondai Kenkyūjo, 1984.

Iwama Kazuo. *Shibuzome ikki, Mimasaka ketsuzei ikki no shūhen: Aru bohimei e no chū.* Okayama: Okayama Buraku Mondai Kenkyūjo, 1996.

Iwasaki Naoko. "Ainu 'otona' kō." In *Nihon shakai no shiteki kōzō: Kinsei, kindai,* edited by Asao Naohiro Kyōju Taikan Kinenkai, 251–74. Kyoto: Shibunkaku Shuppan, 1995.

———. "Kinsei kōki ni okeru tashazō no sōshutsu: 'Kunashiri-Menashi no tatakai' no kaishaku to Ainu-zō." *Nihonshi kenkyū* 403 (Mar. 1996): 65–96.

———. *Nihon kinsei no Ainu shakai.* Tokyo: Azekura Shobō, 1998.

———. "Zenkindai Ainu no 'takara' to sono shakaiteki kinō." *Shirin* 78 (Sept. 1995): 107–28.

Jansen, Marius B. *China in the Tokugawa World.* Cambridge, Mass.: Harvard University Press, 1992.

———. "Japan in the Early Nineteenth Century." In *The Nineteenth Century (The Cambridge History of Japan,* vol. 5), edited by Marius B. Jansen, 87–111. New York: Cambridge University Press, 1989.

Kadokawa Nihon Chimei Daijiten Hensan Iinkai, ed. *Saitama ken (Kadokawa Nihon chimei daijiten,* vol. 11). Tokyo: Kadokawa Shoten, 1980.

Kaiho Mineo. *Bakuhansei kokka to Hokkaidō.* Tokyo: San'ichi Shobō, 1978.

———. *Chūsei no Ezochi.* Tokyo: Yoshikawa Kōbunkan, 1987.

———. *Kinsei Ezochi seiritsushi no kenkyū.* Tokyo: San'ichi Shobō, 1984.

———. *Kinsei no Hokkaidō.* Tokyo: Kyōikusha, 1979.

———. *Rettō hoppōshi kenkyū nōto: Kinsei no Hokkaidō o chūshin to shite.* Sapporo: Hokkaidō Shuppan Kikaku Sentaa, 1986.

Kaiho Seiryō. "Zenchūdan" [1817]. In *Kyōto no burakushi,* edited by Kyōto Burakushi Kenkyūjo, vol. 5, pp. 505–7. 10 vols. Kyoto: Aunsha, 1984–95.

Kaiho Yōko. *Kindai hoppōshi: Ainu minzoku to josei to.* Tokyo: San'ichi Shobō, 1992.

"Kaika dondonbushi" [1871]. In *Yomeru nenpyō: Nihonshi,* 827. Revised edition. Tokyo: Jiyū Kokuminsha, 1995.

"Kaika no hanashi" [1872]. In *Meiji bunka zenshū: Bunmei kaika hen,* edited by Yoshino Sakuzō, 69–88. Tokyo: Nihon Hyōronsha, 1929.

Kakekawa Gen'ichirō. *Bachiraa Yaeko no shōgai.* Sapporo: Hokkaidō Shuppan Kikaku Sentaa, 1988.

Kalland, Arne. *Fishing Villages in Tokugawa Japan.* Honolulu: University of Hawai'i Press, 1995.

Kamifukuoka-shi Kyōiku Iinkai and Kamifukuoka-shi Shi Hensan Iinkai, eds. *Kamifukuoka-shi shi: Shiryōhen,* vol. 2: *Kodai, chūsei, kinsei.* Kamifukuoka: Kamifukuoka-shi, 1997.

Kamiya Nobuyuki. *Bakuhansei kokka no Ryūkyū shihai.* Tokyo: Azekura Shobō, 1990.

———. "Nihon kinsei no tōitsu to Dattan." In *Nihon zenkindai no kokka to taigai kankei,* edited by Tanaka Takeo, 145–76. Tokyo: Yoshikawa Kōbunkan, 1987.

———. "Tai-Min seisaku to Ryūkyū shihai: Ikoku kara 'ikoku' e." In *Bakuhansei kokka to iiki, ikoku,* edited by Katō Eiichi, Kitajima Manji, and Fukaya Katsumi, 247–89. Tokyo: Azekura Shobō, 1989.

Kanazawa Shōsaburō. *Nissen dōsoron.* Tokyo: Tōkō Shobō, 1929.

Kanda Yutsuki. "Saikoku no kyokaku to chiiki shakai: Bungo Kitsuki no 'suihō' o chūshin to shite." In *Kinsei no shakaiteki kenryoku: Ken'i to hegemonii,* edited by Yoshida Nobuyuki and Kurushima Hiroshi, 239–72. Tokyo: Yamakawa Shuppan, 1996.

Karafuto Ainushi Kenkyūkai, ed. *Tsuishikari no ishibumi: Karafuto Ainu no kyōsei ijū no rekishi.* Sapporo: Hokkaidō Shuppan Kikaku Sentaa, 1992.

Kasahara Gengo. "Ezojin fūzoku no gi mōshiokuri sho" [1856]. MS. 107, Resource Collection for Northern Studies, Hokkaido University Library.

Kasaya Kazuhiko. "Bushi no mibun to kakushiki." In *Mibun to kakushiki* (*Nihon no kinsei,* vol. 7), edited by Asao Naohiro, 179–224. Tokyo: Chūō Kōronsha, 1992.

———. *Bushidō to gendai.* Tokyo: Sankei Shinbunsha, 2002.

Katō Kōzō. "Hinin eta gohaishi no gi" [1869/4]. In *"Kaihōrei" no seiritsu* (*Kindai burakushi shiryō shūsei,* vol. 1), edited by Harada Tomohiko and Uesugi Satoru, 12. Tokyo: San'ichi Shobō, 1984.

Katō Noriko. "Hokkaidō sanken ikkyoku jidai ni okeru tai-Ainu seisaku to sono jitsujō." *Hokudai shigaku* 20 (1980): 14–26.

Katō Sukekazu. "Bunmei kaika" [1873–74]. In *Meiji bunka zenshū: Bunmei kaika hen,* edited by Yoshino Sakuzō, 1–47. Tokyo: Nihon Hyōronsha, 1929.

Katō Takashi. "Governing Edo." In *Edo and Paris: Urban Life and the State in the Early Modern Era,* edited by James L. McClain, John M. Merriman, and Ugawa Kaoru, 41–67. Ithaca, N.Y.: Cornell University Press, 1994.

Katō Yasuaki. "Kinsei no shōgaisha to mibun seido." In *Mibun to kakushiki* (*Nihon no kinsei,* vol. 7), edited by Asao Naohiro, 125–78. Tokyo: Chūō Kōronsha, 1992.

Kawaoka Takeharu. *Umi no tami: Gyoson no rekishi to minzoku.* Tokyo: Heibonsha, 1987.

Kerr, George. *Okinawa: The History of an Island People.* Rutland, Vt.: Tuttle, 1958.

Kikuchi Isao. *Bakuhan taisei to Ezochi.* Tokyo: Yūzankaku, 1984.

———. *Etorofu-tō: Tsukurareta kokkyō.* Tokyo: Yoshikawa Kōbunkan, 1999.

———. *Hoppōshi no naka no kinsei Nihon.* Tokyo: Azekura Shobō, 1991.

———. "Kinsei ni okeru Ezo-kan to 'Nihon fūzoku.'" In *Kita kara no Nihonshi,* edited by Hokkaidō-Tōhoku Shi Kenkyūkai, vol. 1, pp. 206–29. 2 vols. Tokyo: Sanseidō, 1988.

———. "Kyōkai to etonosu." In *Chiiki to etonosu (Ajia no naka no Nihonshi,* vol. 4), edited by Arano Yasunori, Ishii Masatoshi, and Murai Shōsuke, 55–80. Tokyo: University of Tokyo Press, 1992.

Kikuchi Shunsuke, ed. *Tokugawa kinreikō.* 6 vols. Tokyo: Yoshikawa Kōbunkan, 1931–32.

Kita Kōyō [Shōmei]. *Ainu hatashite horobiru ka.* Sapporo: Hokkaidō Ainu Kyōkai, 1937.

"Kita machibugyō Koide Yamato-no-kami dono oyakusho ni oite kore o mōshi-watasu" [1868/1/13]. In *Sabetsu no shosō (Nihon kindai shisō taikei,* vol. 22), edited by Hirota Masaki, 69–71. Tokyo: Iwanami Shoten, 1990.

Kita Sadakichi. "Nissen ryōminzoku dōgenron." In *Kita Sadakichi chosakushū,* edited by Ueda Masaaki, vol. 8, pp. 357–415. 10 vols. Tokyo: Heibonsha, 1979.

Kita Shōmei. *Tokachi Ainu no ashiato to konogo no michi.* Obihiro: Tokachi Kyokumeisha, 1927.

Kitagawa Morisada. *Morisada mankō* [1853], edited by Asakura Haruhiko and Kashikawa Shūichi. 5 vols. Tokyo: Tōkyōdō Shoten, 1992.

Kitajima Masamoto. "Kan'ei ki no rekishiteki ichi." In *Bakuhansei kokka sei-ritsu katei no kenkyū,* edited by Kitajima Masamoto, 1–20. Tokyo: Yoshi-kawa Kōbunkan, 1978.

Kōno Motomichi, ed. *Tai-Ainu seisaku hōki ruijū.* Sapporo: Hokkaidō Shuppan Kikaku Sentaa, 1981.

Kōno Tsunekichi. *Hokkaidō kyūdojin.* Sapporo: Hokkaidō-chō, 1911.

Kubota Shizo. "Kyōwa shieki" [1857]. In *Tanken, kikō, chishi (Hokuhen hen) (Nihon shomin seikatsu shiryō shūsei,* vol. 4), edited by Takakura Shin'ichirō, 223–70. Tokyo: San'ichi Shobō, 1969.

Kuhn, Philip A. *Soulstealers: The Chinese Sorcery Scare of 1768.* Cambridge, Mass.: Harvard University Press, 1990.

Kurachi Katsunao. "Bakumatsu no minshū to bugei." *Okayama chihōshi kenkyū* 56 (1988): 1–8.

———. "Mimasaka 'hinin sōdō' no dentō no hitokoma." *Okayama chihōshi kenkyū* 54 (July 1987): 28–29.

Kushihara Masamine. "Igen zokuwa" [1793]. In *Tanken, kikō, chishi (Hokuhen hen) (Nihon shomin seikatsu shiryō shūsei,* vol. 4), edited by Takakura Shin'ichirō, 485–520. Tokyo: San'ichi Shobō, 1969.

Kyōto Burakushi Kenkyūjo, ed. *Kinsei no minshū to geinō.* Kyoto: Aunsha, 1989.

———. *Kyōto no burakushi.* 10 vols. Kyoto: Aunsha, 1984–95.

Lie, John. *Multiethnic Japan.* Cambridge, Mass.: Harvard University Press, 2001.

McEwan, J. R. *The Political Writings of Ogyū Sorai.* Cambridge: Cambridge University Press, 1969.

Makihara Norio. *Kyakubun to kokumin no aida: Kindai minshū no seiji ishiki.* Tokyo: Yoshikawa Kōbunkan, 1998.

Matsumiya Kanzan. "Ezo dan hikki " [1710]. In *Tanken, kikō, chishi (Hokuhen hen) (Nihon shomin seikatsu shiryō shūsei,* vol. 4), edited by Takakura Shin'ichirō, 387–400. Tokyo: San'ichi Shobō, 1969.

Matsushita Shirō. *Kinsei Amami no shihai to shakai.* Tokyo: Daiichi Shobō, 1983.

Matsuura Takeshirō. *Ainu jinbutsushi,* translated by Sarashina Genzō and Yoshida Yutaka. Tokyo: Nōsangyoson Bunka Kyōkai, 1981.

———. "Kinsei Ezo jinbutsushi" [mid-1850s]. In *Tanken, kikō, chishi (Hokuhen hen) (Nihon shomin seikatsu shiryō shūsei,* vol. 4), edited by Takakura Shin'ichirō, 731–813. Tokyo: San'ichi Shobō, 1969.

Meiji Nyūsu Jiten Hensan Iinkai, ed. *Meiji nyūsu jiten.* Tokyo: Mainichi Komyunikeishonsu Shuppanbu, 1983.

"Meiji rokunen natsu Mimasaka zenkoku sōjō gaishi" [n.d.]. In *Sabetsu no shosō (Nihon kindai shisō taikei,* vol. 22), edited by Hirota Masaki, 100–112. Tokyo: Iwanami Shoten, 1990.

Mitsuoka Shin'ichi. *Ainu no ashiato.* Sixth revised edition. Shiraoi: Miyoshi Chikuyū, 1941.

Miura Meisuke. "Gokuchūki" [1859–61], annotated by Mori Kahei. In *Minshū undō no shisō (Nihon shisō taikei,* vol. 58), edited by Shōji Kichinosuke, Hayashi Motoi, and Yasumaru Yoshio, 15–86. Tokyo: Iwanami Shoten, 1970.

Mizutani Mitsuhiro. *Edo wa yume ka.* Tokyo: Chikuma Shobō, 1992.

Mogami Tokunai. "Ezo no kuni fūzoku ninjō no sata" [1790]. In *Tanken, kikō, chishi (Hokuhen hen) (Nihon shomin seikatsu shiryō shūsei,* vol. 4), edited by Takakura Shin'ichirō, 439–84. Tokyo: San'ichi Shobō, 1969.

———. "Watarishima hikki" [1808]. In *Tanken, kikō, chishi (Hokuhen hen) (Nihon shomin seikatsu shiryō shūsei,* vol. 4), edited by Takakura Shin'ichirō, 521–43. Tokyo: San'ichi Shobō, 1969.

"Monjin seimeiroku" [n.d.]. In *Shinshū Hirata Atsutane zenshū,* edited by Hirata Atsutane Zenshū Kankōkai, appendix volume. 20 vols. Tokyo: Meicho Shuppan, 1977–81.

Mori Kahei. *Nanbu han hyakushō ikki no kenkyū (Mori Kahei chosakushū,* vol. 7). Tokyo: Hōsei University Press, 1974.

Mori Yasuhiko. *Bakuhansei kokka no kiso kōzō: Sonraku kōzō no tenkai to nōmin tōsō.* Tokyo: Yoshikawa Kōbunkan, 1981.

Morris, Dana, and Thomas C. Smith. "Fertility and Mortality in an Outcaste Village in Japan, 1750–1869." In *Family and Population in East Asian History,* edited by Susan B. Hanley and Arthur P. Wolf, 229–46. Stanford, Calif.: Stanford University Press, 1985.

Morris, V. Dixon. "The City of Sakai and Urban Autonomy." In *Warlords, Artists, and Commoners: Japan in the Sixteenth Century,* edited by George Elison and Bardwell L. Smith, 23–54. Honolulu: University of Hawai'i Press, 1981.

Morris-Suzuki, Tessa. "Becoming Japanese: Imperial Expansion and Identity Crises in the Early Twentieth Century." In *Japan's Competing Modernities:*

Issues in Culture and Democracy, 1900–1930, edited by Sharon A. Minichiello, 157–80. Honolulu: University of Hawai'i Press, 1998.

———. "A Descent into the Past: The Frontier in the Construction of Japanese Identity." In *Multicultural Japan: Palaeolithic to Postmodern,* edited by Donald Denoon, Mark Hudson, Gavan McCormack, and Tessa Morris-Suzuki, 81–94. Cambridge: Cambridge University Press, 1996.

Morse, Edward S. *Japan Day by Day.* 2 vols. Tokyo: Kobunsha, 1936.

"Mōshiwatashi" [1868]. Resource Collection for Northern Studies, Hokkaido University Library.

Murabayashi Gensuke. *Genshi manpitsu fudo nenpyō* [1804–18]. (*Michinoku sōsho,* vols. 6–7), edited by Aomori Ken Bunkazai Hogo Kyōkai. Tokyo: Kokusho Kankōkai, 1982 [1960].

Murai Shōsuke. *Ajia no naka no chūsei Nihon.* Tokyo: Azekura Shobō, 1988.

Murano Tokusaburō. "Yōshiki fujin sokuhatsuhō" [1885]. In *Meiji bunka zenshū: Fūzoku hen,* edited by Meiji Bunka Kenkyūkai, 425–34. Tokyo: Nihon Hyōron Shinsha, 1955 [1928].

Nagahara Keiji. "Decline of the Shōen System," translated by Michael P. Birt. In *Medieval Japan (The Cambridge History of Japan,* vol. 3), edited by Kozo Yamamura, 260–300. New York: Cambridge University Press, 1990.

———. "The Medieval Peasant," translated by Suzanne Gay. In *Medieval Japan (The Cambridge History of Japan,* vol. 3), edited by Kozo Yamamura, 301–43. New York: Cambridge University Press, 1990.

Nagamitsu Norikazu, ed. *Bizen, Bitchū, Mimasaka hyakushō ikki shiryō.* 5 vols. Tokyo: Kokusho Kankōkai, 1978.

Najita, Tetsuo. *Japan: The Intellectual Foundations of Modern Japanese Politics.* Chicago: University of Chicago Press, 1974.

———. "Method and Analysis in the Conceptual Portrayal of Tokugawa Intellectual History." In *Japanese Thought in the Tokugawa Period, 1600–1868: Methods and Metaphors,* edited by Tetsuo Najita and Irwin Scheiner, 3–38. Chicago: University of Chicago Press, 1978.

Nakai Nobuhiko. *Ōhara Yūgaku.* Tokyo: Yoshikawa Kōbunkan, 1963.

Nakano Michiko and Zushi Tomonori. "Mimasaka Tsuyama han hisabetsu buraku kankei shiryō (2)." *Okayama buraku kaihō kenkyūjo kiyō* 3 (1985), entire issue.

Namikawa Kenji. *Kinsei Nihon to hoppō shakai.* Tokyo: Sanseidō, 1992.

Narita Ryūichi. "Teito Tōkyō." In *Iwanami kōza Nihon tsūshi,* vol. 16, pp. 175–214. Tokyo: Iwanami Shoten, 1994.

Neary, Ian. *Political Protest and Social Control in Pre-war Japan: The Origins of Buraku Liberation.* Atlantic Highlands, N.J.: Academic Press, 1989.

"Nemuro-ken kyūdojin" [1882–86]. Resource Collection for Northern Studies, Hokkaido University Library.

Nihon kokugo daijiten. 20 vols. Tokyo: Shōgakukan, 1975.

Niigata-ken, ed. *Niigata-ken shi: Shiryōhen.* 24 vols. Niigata: Niigata-ken, 1982.

Norbeck, Edward. "Little-Known Minority Groups of Japan." In *Japan's Invisible Race: Caste in Culture and Identity,* edited by George DeVos and Hiroshi Wagatsuma, 184–99. Berkeley: University of California Press, 1966.

Obinata Sumio. *Nihon kindai kokka no seiritsu to keisatsu*. Tokyo: Azekura Shobō, 1992.

Ochiai Hiroki. *Chitsuroku shobun: Meiji ishin to bushi no risutora*. Tokyo: Chūō Kōron Shinsha, 1999.

Ogawa Masahito. "'Ainu gakkō' no setchi to 'Hokkaidō kyūdojin hogohō,' 'kyūdojin jidō kyōiku kitei' no seiritsu." *Hokkaidō Daigaku Kyōikugakubu kiyō* 55 (1991): 257–325.

———. *Kindai Ainu kyōiku seidoshi kenkyū*. Sapporo: Hokkaido University Press, 1997.

Ogawa Masahito and Yamada Shin'ichi, eds. *Ainu minzoku kindai no kiroku*. Tokyo: Sōfūkan, 1998.

Ogawa Tameji. "Kaika mondō" [1874]. In *Meiji bunka zenshū: Bunmei kaika hen*, edited by Yoshino Sakuzō, 105–68. Tokyo: Nihon Hyōronsha, 1929.

Ogi Shinzō, Kumakura Isao, and Ueno Chizuko, eds. *Fūzoku/sei (Kindai Nihon shisō taikei*, vol. 23). Tokyo: Iwanami Shoten, 1990.

Oguma, Eiji. *A Genealogy of "Japanese" Self-Images*, translated by David Askew. Melbourne: Trans Pacific Press, 2002.

Oguma Eiji. *"Nihonjin" no kyōkai: Okinawa, Ainu, Taiwan, Chōsen, shoku-minchi shihai kara fukki undō made*. Tokyo: Shin'yōsha, 1998.

———. *Tan'itsu minzoku shinwa no kigen: "Nihonjin" no jigazō no keifu*. Tokyo: Shin'yōsha, 1995.

Ōi Haruo. "Satsumon bunka to iwayuru 'Ainu bunka' to no kankei ni tsuite." *Hoppō bunka kenkyū* 15 (1984): 1–201.

———. "'Shakushain no ran (Kanbun 9-nen Ezo no ran)' no saikentō." *Hoppō bunka kenkyū* 21 (1992): 1–66.

Ōishi Masaaki. "Jiin to chūsei shakai." In *Iwanami kōza Nihon tsūshi*, vol. 8, pp. 135–70. Tokyo: Iwanami Shoten, 1994.

Oka Sankei. "Kinseki kurabe" [1874]. In *Meiji bunka zenshū: Fūzoku hen*, edited by Meiji Bunka Kenkyūkai, 151–78. Tokyo: Nihon Hyōron Shinsha, 1955 [1928].

Okayama-ken Buraku Kaihō Undō Rokujūnenshi Hensan Iinkai, ed. *Okayama-ken buraku mondai shiryōshū*. Okayama: Okayama-ken Buraku Kaihō Undō Rengōkai, 1987.

Oku Takenori. *Bunmei kaika to minshū: Kindai Nihon seishinshi no danshō*. Tokyo: Shinhyōron, 1993.

Ooms, Herman. *Tokugawa Ideology: Early Constructs, 1570–1680*. Princeton, N.J.: Princeton University Press, 1985.

———. *Tokugawa Village Practice: Class, Status, Power, Law*. Berkeley: University of California Press, 1996.

Ōshima Mitsuko. *Meiji no mura*. Tokyo: Kyōikusha, 1977.

Ōtaka Eiichi. "Ōtaka Zenbei." *Chiba-ken no rekishi* 4 (Aug. 1972): 36–39.

Ōyama Kyōhei. "Medieval *Shōen*," translated by Martin Collcutt. In *Medieval Japan (The Cambridge History of Japan*, vol. 3), edited by Kozo Yamamura, 89–127. New York: Cambridge University Press, 1990.

Perrin, Noel. *Giving Up the Gun: Japan's Reversion to the Sword*. Boulder, Colo.: Shambhala, 1980.

Philippi, Donald L. *Songs of Gods, Songs of Humans: The Epic Tradition of the*

Ainu. Princeton, N.J.: Princeton University Press; Tokyo: University of Tokyo Press, 1979.

Plutschow, Herbert. *Japan's Name Culture: The Significance of Names in a Religious, Political, and Social Context.* Sandgate, Folkestone: Japan Library, 1995.

Pratt, Edward. *Japan's Protoindustrial Elite.* Cambridge, Mass.: Harvard University Asia Center, 1999.

Price, John. "A History of the Outcaste: Untouchability in Japan." In *Japan's Invisible Race: Caste in Culture and Identity,* edited by George DeVos and Hiroshi Wagatsuma, 6–30. Berkeley: University of California Press, 1966.

Ravina, Mark. *Land and Lordship in Early Modern Japan.* Stanford, Calif.: Stanford University Press, 1998.

Rihei. "Ezo jinmin e osatoshi mōshiwatashi tsūben kakitsuke" [1856]. MS. 109, Resource Collection for Northern Studies, Hokkaido University Library.

Roberts, Luke S. *Mercantilism in a Japanese Domain: The Merchant Origins of Economic Nationalism in 18th-Century Tosa.* New York: Cambridge University Press, 1998.

Rogers, John Michael. "The Development of the Military Profession in Tokugawa Japan." Ph.D. diss., Harvard University, 1998.

Sahlins, Peter. *Boundaries: The Making of France and Spain in the Pyrenees.* Berkeley: University of California Press, 1989.

———. "State Formation and National Identity in the Catalan Borderlands During the Eighteenth and Nineteenth Centuries." In *Border Identities: Nation and State at International Frontiers,* edited by Thomas M. Wilson and Hastings Donnan, 31–61. Cambridge: Cambridge University Press, 1998.

Saiga Hiroyoshi. *Ōe Ten'ya denki.* Tokyo: Ōzorasha, 1987 [1926].

Saitama-ken Dōwa Kyōiku Kenkyū Kyōgikai, ed. *Suzuki-ke monjo.* 5 vols. Urawa: Saitama-ken Dōwa Kyōiku Kenkyū Kyōgikai, 1977–79.

Saitō, Osamu. "The Rural Economy: Commercial Agriculture, By-employment, and Wage Work." In *Japan in Transition: From Tokugawa to Meiji,* edited by Marius B. Jansen and Gilbert Rozman, 400–420. Princeton, N.J.: Princeton University Press, 1986.

Sakihara, Mitsugu. *A Brief History of Okinawa Based on the Omoro Sōshi.* Tokyo: Honpo Shoseki Press, 1987.

Sasaki Junnosuke. *Bakuhansei kokkaron.* 2 vols. Tokyo: University of Tokyo Press, 1984.

Sasaki Toshikazu. "Iomante kō: Shamo ni yoru Ainu bunka rikai no kōsatsu." *Rekishigaku kenkyū* 613 (Nov. 1990): 111–20.

———. "Kyōsei kotan no hensen to kōzō ni tsuite: Toku ni Abuta-kotan o chūshin ni." In *Hokkaidō no kenkyū: Kōkohen II,* edited by Ishizuki Kisao, 275–95. Osaka: Seibundō, 1984.

Satake Akihiro. *Shuten dōji ibun.* Tokyo: Heibonsha, 1977.

Schalow, Thomas Richard. "The Role of the Financial Panic of 1927 and Failure of the 15th Bank in the Economic Decline of the Japanese Aristocracy." Ph.D. diss., Princeton University, 1989.

Scheiner, Irwin. "Honorable Peasants and Benevolent Lords: Rebellion and Peasant Consciousness in Tokugawa Japan." In *Japanese Thought in the Toku-*

gawa Period, 1600–1868: Methods and Metaphors, edited by Tetsuo Najita and Irwin Scheiner, 39–62. Chicago: University of Chicago Press, 1978.

Sekiba Fujihiko. *Ainu iji dan.* Sapporo: Sekiba Fujihiko, 1896.

Sewell, William H., Jr. *Work and Revolution in France: The Language of Labor from the Old Regime to 1848.* New York: Cambridge University Press, 1980.

Senshū Tōtoku. "Eta o osamuru no gi" [1864]. In *Buraku (Nihon shomin seikatsu shiryō shūsei,* vol. 14), edited by Harada Tomohiko, 563–67. Tokyo: San'ichi Shobō, 1971.

Shibatani, Masayoshi. *The Languages of Japan.* Cambridge: Cambridge University Press, 1990.

Shimazaki Tōson. *Before the Dawn,* translated by William E. Naff. Honolulu: University of Hawai'i Press, 1987.

Shimoda, Hiraku. "Bad Sushi or Bad Merchant? The 'Dead Fish Poisoning Incident' of 1852." *Modern Asian Studies* 35, no. 3 (July 2001): 513–31.

Shimomura Isao. "Ainu no sajin." *Nihon rekishi* 566 (July 1995): 1–20.

Shively, Donald H. "Sumptuary Regulation and Status in Early Tokugawa Japan." *Harvard Journal of Asiatic Studies* 25 (1964–65): 123–64.

Siddle, Richard. *Race, Resistance and the Ainu of Japan.* London: Routledge, 1996.

Sievers, Sharon L. *Flowers in Salt: The Beginnings of Feminist Consciousness in Modern Japan.* Stanford, Calif.: Stanford University Press, 1983.

Sippel, Patricia. "Abandoned Fields: Negotiating Taxes in the Bakufu Domain." *Monumenta Nipponica* 53, no. 2 (Summer 1998): 197–224.

———. "Popular Protest in Early Modern Japan: The Bushū Outburst." *Harvard Journal of Asiatic Studies* 37, no. 2 (Dec. 1977): 273–322.

Slezkine, Yuri. *Arctic Mirrors: Russia and the Small Peoples of the North.* Ithaca, N.Y.: Cornell University Press, 1994.

Smith, Thomas C. *The Agrarian Origins of Modern Japan.* Stanford, Calif.: Stanford University Press, 1959.

———. *Native Sources of Japanese Industrialization, 1750–1920.* Berkeley: University of California Press, 1988.

Smits, Gregory. *Visions of Ryukyu: Identity and Ideology in Early-Modern Thought and Politics.* Honolulu: University of Hawai'i Press, 1999.

"Sonobe mura shōya nikki" [1858/10]. In *Kyōto no burakushi,* edited by Kyōto Burakushi Kenkyūjo, vol. 5, p. 63. 10 vols. Kyoto: Aunsha, 1984–95.

Steele, M. William. "The Rise and Fall of the Shōgitai: A Social Drama." In *Conflict in Modern Japanese History,* edited by Tetsuo Najita and J. Victor Koschmann, 128–44. Princeton, N.J.: Princeton University Press, 1982.

Stephan, John J. *The Kuril Islands.* Oxford: Clarendon Press, 1974.

———. *Sakhalin: A History.* Oxford: Clarendon Press, 1971.

Sugi Hitoshi. *Kinsei no chiiki to zaison bunka.* Tokyo: Yoshikawa Kōbunkan, 2001.

Suzue Eiichi. *Hokkaidō chōson seidoshi no kenkyū.* Sapporo: Hokkaido University Press, 1985.

Suzuki Ryō. "Jiyū minken undō to buraku mondai." In *Burakushi no kenkyū: Kindai hen,* edited by Buraku Mondai Kenkyūjo, 94–124. Kyoto: Buraku Mondai Kenkyūjo, 1984.

Tajima Yoshiya. "Basho ukeoisei kōki no Ainu no gyogyō to sono tokushitsu: Nishi Ezochi Yoichi basho no baai." In *Zenkindai no Nihon to higashi Ajia*, edited by Tanaka Takeo, 271–95. Tokyo: Yoshikawa Kōbunkan, 1995.

Takahashi Bonsen. "Buraku kaihō to Dan Naoki no kōgyō." In *Kinsei Kantō no hisabetsu buraku*, edited by Ishii Ryōsuke, 143–74. Tokyo: Akashi Shoten, 1978.

Takahashi Fusaji. *Chishima Ainu ron*. Shiraoi: Takahashi Fusaji, 1933.

Takahashi Satoshi. *Edo no soshō: Mishuku mura ikken tenmatsu*. Tokyo: Iwanami Shoten, 1996.

Takakura Shin'ichirō. "The Ainu of Northern Japan: A Study in Conquest and Acculturation," translated and annotated by John A. Harrison. *Transactions of the American Philosophical Society*, new series, vol. 50, part 4 (Apr. 1960).

———. *Ainu seisakushi*. Tokyo: Nihon Hyōronsha, 1942.

———. "Sanken jidai ni okeru Ainu no kannōsaku." *Hōkeikai ronsō* 2 (1932): 1–38.

———, ed. *Tanken, kikō, chishi (Hokuhen hen)* (*Nihon shomin seikatsu shiryō shūsei*, vol. 4). Tokyo: San'ichi Shobō, 1969.

Takayanagi Kaneyoshi. *Edo no daidōgei*. Tokyo: Kashiwa Shobō, 1982.

Takekuma Tokusaburō. *Ainu monogatari*. Sapporo: Fukidō Shobō, 1918.

Taminato Nobuaki and Kaiho Mineo. "Bakuhanseika no Ryūkyū to Ezochi." In *Iwanami kōza Nihon no rekishi*, vol. 11, pp. 249–98. Tokyo: Iwanami Shoten, 1976.

Tanaka, Michiko. "Village Youth Organizations *(Wakamono Nakama)* in Late Tokugawa Politics and Society (Japan)." Ph.D. diss., Princeton University, 1983.

Tashiro Kazui. "Foreign Relations during the Edo Period: Sakoku Reexamined." *Journal of Japanese Studies* 8, no. 2 (Summer 1982): 283–306.

"Tenpō jū tsuchinotoidoshi gogatsu yori omemie Ezojin kenjōbutsu narabi ni kudasare shina" [n.d.]. Hakodate Municipal Library.

Thongchai Winichakul. *Siam Mapped: The Geo-body of a Nation*. Honolulu: University of Hawai'i Press, 1994.

Tilley, Henry Arthur. *Japan, the Amoor, and the Pacific: With Notices of Other Places, Comprised in a Voyage of Circumnavigation in the Imperial Russian Corvette "Rynda," in 1858–1860*. London: Smith, Elder & Co., 1861.

Toby, Ronald P. "Both a Borrower and a Lender Be: From Village Moneylender to Rural Banker in the Tempō Era." *Monumenta Nipponica* 46, no. 4 (Winter 1991): 483–512.

———. "Carnival of the Aliens: Korean Embassies in Edo-period Art and Popular Culture." *Monumenta Nipponica* 41, no. 4 (Winter 1986): 415–56.

———. "The 'Indianness' of Iberia and Changing Japanese Iconographies of Other." In *Implicit Understandings: Observing, Reporting, and Reflecting on the Encounters between Europeans and Other Peoples in the Early Modern Era*, edited by Stuart Schwartz, 324–51. New York: Cambridge University Press, 1994.

———. "Rescuing the Nation from History: The State of the State in Early Modern Japan." *Monumental Nipponica* 56, no. 2 (Summer 2001): 197–238.

————. *State and Diplomacy in Early Modern Japan: Asia in the Development of the Tokugawa Bakufu.* Princeton, N.J.: Princeton University Press, 1984.

"Tokachi hoka yongun dojin kankei shorui" [1885–92]. Resource Collection for Northern Studies, Hokkaido University Library.

Torii Ryūzō. *Chishima Ainu.* Tokyo: Yoshikawa Kōbunkan, 1903.

Totten, George O., and Hiroshi Wagatsuma. "Emancipation: Growth and Transformation of a Political Movement." In *Japan's Invisible Race: Caste in Culture and Personality,* edited by George DeVos and Hiroshi Wagatsuma, 33–67. Berkeley: University of California Press, 1966.

Toyoda Nobuo. "Yuchi Sadamoto." In *Hokkaidō daihyakka jiten,* edited by Hokkaidō Shinbunsha, vol. 2, p. 858. Sapporo: Hokkaidō Shinbunsha, 1981.

Tsukada Takashi. *Kinsei mibunsei to shūen shakai.* Tokyo: University of Tokyo Press, 1997.

————. *Kinsei Nihon mibunsei no kenkyū.* Kobe: Hyōgo Buraku Mondai Kenkyūjo, 1987.

————. *Mibunsei shakai to shimin shakai: Kinsei Nihon no shakai to hō.* Tokyo: Kashiwa Shobō, 1992.

————. "Mibun shakai no kaitai: Ōsaka Watanabe mura-Nishihama no jirei kara." *Rekishi hyōron* 527 (Mar. 1994): 73–99.

Tsukada Takashi, Teraki Nobuaki, Hatanaka Toshiyuki, Yamamoto Naotomo, and Wakita Osamu. *Senmin mibun ron: Chūsei kara kinsei e.* Tokyo: Akashi Shoten, 1994.

Tsukamoto Manabu. *Kinsei saikō: Chihō no shiten kara.* Tokyo: Nihon Editaa Sukūru Shuppanbu, 1986.

————. *Shōrui o meguru seiji: Genroku no fōkuroaa.* Tokyo: Heibonsha, 1983.

Tsuyama no Ayumi Henshū Iinkai, ed. *Buraku kaihō undō: Tsuyama no ayumi.* Tsuyama: Zenkoku Buraku Kaihō Undō Rengōkai Tsuyama-shi Kyōgikai, 1986.

Tsuyama-shi Shi Hensan Iinkai, ed. *Tsuyama-shi shi.* 7 vols. Tsuyama: Tsuyama-shi, 1980.

Uchida Mitsuru. "Emono kara takeyari e." In *Ikki to shūen,* edited by Hosaka Satoru, 117–42. Tokyo: Aoki Shoten, 2000.

Uchiyama Sōsuke. "Eta hinin no mibun gokaisei no gi" [1869/5]. In *"Kaihōrei" no seiritsu (Kindai burakushi shiryō shūsei,* vol. 1), edited by Harada Tomohiko and Uesugi Satoru, 18. Tokyo: San'ichi Shobō, 1984.

Uematsu Tadahiro. *Shi-nō-kō-shō: Jukyō shisō to kanryō shihai.* Tokyo: Dōbunkan, 1997.

Utagawa Hiroshi. *Iomante no kōkogaku.* Tokyo: University of Tokyo Press, 1989.

Vaporis, Constantine N. "Post Station and Assisting Villages: Corvée Labor and Peasant Contention." *Monumenta Nipponica* 41, no. 4 (Winter 1986): 377–414.

Vesey, Alexander M. "The Buddhist Clergy and Village Society in Early Modern Japan." Ph.D. diss., Princeton University, 2002.

Vlastos, Stephen. "Opposition Movements in Early Meiji, 1868–1885." In *The Nineteenth Century (The Cambridge History of Japan,* vol. 5), edited by Marius B. Jansen, 367–431. New York: Cambridge University Press, 1989.

Wakabayashi, Bob Tadashi. *Anti-Foreignism and Western Learning in Early-Modern Japan: The* New Theses *of 1825.* Cambridge, Mass.: Council on East Asian Studies, Harvard University, 1986.

Wakita Osamu. "Kinsei ni okeru shokushu sabetsu no kōzō." In *Mibunteki shūen,* edited by Tsukada Takashi, Yoshida Nobuyuki, and Wakita Osamu, 297–321. Kyoto: Buraku Mondai Kenkyūjo, 1994.

———. "The *Kokudaka* System: A Device for Unification." *Journal of Japanese Studies* 1, no. 2 (Summer 1975): 297–320.

Walker, Brett L. *The Conquest of Ainu Lands: Ecology and Culture in Japanese Expansion, 1590–1800.* Berkeley: University of California Press, 2001.

———. "The Early Modern Japanese State and Ainu Vaccinations: Redefining the Body Politic, 1799–1868." *Past and Present* 163 (May 1999): 121–60.

Walthall, Anne. *Peasant Uprisings in Japan: A Critical Anthology of Peasant Histories.* Chicago: University of Chicago Press, 1991.

———. *Social Protest and Popular Culture in Eighteenth-Century Japan.* Tucson: University of Arizona Press, 1986.

Waswo, Ann. *Japanese Landlords: The Decline of a Rural Elite.* Berkeley: University of California Press, 1977.

Watanabe Hitoshi. "Ainu bunka no seiritsu: Minzoku, rekishi, kōko shogaku no gōryūten." In *Hoppō bunka to nantō bunka* (*Nihon kōkogaku ronshū,* vol. 9), edited by Saitō Tadashi, 220–43. Tokyo: Yoshikawa Kōbunkan, 1987.

Waters, Neil. *Japan's Local Pragmatists: The Transition from Bakumatsu to Meiji in the Kawasaki Region.* Cambridge, Mass.: Council on East Asian Studies, Harvard University, 1983.

Weber, Eugen. *Peasants into Frenchmen: The Modernization of Rural France, 1870–1914.* Stanford, Calif.: Stanford University Press, 1976.

Weiner, Michael, ed. *Japan's Minorities: The Illusion of Homogeneity.* London: Routledge, 1997.

———. *Race and Migration in Imperial Japan.* London: Routledge, 1994.

White, James W. "State Growth and Popular Protest in Tokugawa Japan." *Journal of Japanese Studies* 14, no. 1 (Winter 1988): 1–25.

White, Richard. *The Middle Ground: Indians, Empires, and Republics in the Great Lakes Region, 1650–1815.* New York: Cambridge University Press, 1991.

———. *The Roots of Dependency: Subsistence, Environment, and Social Change among the Choctaws, Pawnees, and Navajos.* Lincoln: University of Nebraska Press, 1983.

Wigen, Kären. *The Making of a Japanese Periphery, 1750–1920.* Berkeley: University of California Press, 1995.

Yabuta Yutaka. *Kokuso to hyakushō ikki no kenkyū.* Tokyo: Azekura Shobō, 1992.

Yamabe Yasunosuke. *Ainu monogatari,* edited by Kindaichi Kyōsuke. Tokyo: Hakubunkan, 1912.

Yamaji Kōzō. "Manzai: Danna o tayori, teritorii o kakuritsu." In *Kinsei no minshū to geinō,* edited by Kyōto Burakushi Kenkyūjo, 65–71. Kyoto: Aunsha, 1989.

Yamamoto Naotomo. "Innai: Koyomi o uri, uranai ya kitō o suru." In *Kinsei no minshū to geinō,* edited by Kyōto Burakushi Kenkyūjo, 30–34. Kyoto: Aunsha, 1989.

———. "Kinsei shakai to sono mibun: Jo ni kaete." In *Kinsei no minshū to geinō,* edited by Kyōto Burakushi Kenkyūjo, 1–12. Kyoto: Aunsha, 1989.

Yamamoto Nidayū. "Gōmunegashira kaden" [n.d.]. In *Buraku (Nihon shomin seikatsu shiryō shūsei,* vol. 14), edited by Harada Tomohiko, 485–88. Tokyo: San'ichi Shobō, 1971.

Yamamura, Kozo. "The Meiji Land Tax Reform and Its Effects." In *Japan in Transition: Tokugawa to Meiji,* edited by Marius B. Jansen and Gilbert Rozman, 382–99. Princeton, N.J.: Princeton University Press, 1986.

———. *A Study of Samurai Income and Entrepreneurship: Quantitative Analyses of Economic and Social Aspects of the Samurai in Tokugawa and Meiji, Japan.* Cambridge, Mass.: Harvard University Press, 1974.

Yamamuro Shin'ichi. "Meiji kokka no seido to rinen." In *Iwanami kōza Nihon tsūshi,* vol. 17, pp. 113–48. Tokyo: Iwanami Shoten, 1994.

Yasumaru Yoshio. " 'Kangoku' no tanjō." In *Bakumatsu, ishinki no kokumin kokka keisei to bunka hen'yō,* edited by Nishikawa Nagao and Matsumiya Hideharu, 279–312. Tokyo: Shin'yōsha, 1995.

Yates, Charles L. *Saigō Takamori: The Man Behind the Myth.* London: Kegan Paul International, 1995.

Yokokawa Ryōsuke. *Naishiryaku* [ca. 1854] (*Iwate shisō,* vols. 1–5), edited by Iwate Kenritsu Toshokan. Morioka: Iwate-ken Bunkazai Aigo Kyōkai, 1974.

Yokota Fuyuhiko. "Bakuhansei zenki ni okeru shokunin hensei to mibun." *Nihonshi kenkyū* 235 (Mar. 1982): 51–72.

———. "Kinseiteki mibun seido no seiritsu." In *Mibun to kakushiki (Nihon no kinsei,* vol. 7), edited by Asao Naohiro, 41–78. Tokyo: Chūō Kōronsha, 1992.

Yonemoto, Marcia. "The 'Spatial Vernacular' in Early Modern Japan: Knowledge, Power, and Pleasure in the Form of a Map." *Journal of Asian Studies* 59, no. 3 (Aug. 2000): 647–66.

Yoshida Iwao. "Kyūdojin hogo shisetsu kaizen gaian." *Hokkaidō shakai jigyō* 52 (Aug. 1936): 14–25.

Yoshida Nobuyuki. *Kinsei toshi shakai no mibun kōzō.* Tokyo: University of Tokyo Press, 1998.

Yoshinami Takashi. "Meiji rokunen Mimasaka ikki to sono eikyō." In *Meiji shonen kaihōrei hantai ikki no kenkyū,* edited by Yoshinami Takashi, 3–36. Tokyo: Akashi Shoten, 1987.

Yoshino, Kosaku. *Cultural Nationalism in Contemporary Japan: A Sociological Inquiry.* London: Routledge, 1992.

"Yuchi Sadamoto." In *Hokkaidō kaitaku kōrōsha kankei shiryō shūroku,* edited by Hokkaidō Sōmubu Gyōsei Shiryōshitsu, vol. 2, p. 197. Sapporo: Hokkaidō, 1972.

Index

Compositor: Bookmatters, Berkeley
Text: 10/13 Sabon
Display: Sabon
Printer and binder: Thomson-Shore, Inc.